Revised
Edition

# THE MOVIES

By
**Richard Griffith**
and
**Arthur Mayer**
with the assistance of
**Eileen Bowser**

**SPRING BOOKS**

LONDON · NEW YORK · SYDNEY · TORONTO

*An acknowledgment to*

# THE MUSEUM OF MODERN ART DEPARTMENT OF FILM

When, in 1935, the trustees of The Museum of Modern Art founded the Museum's Department of Film, they opened to the student and to the film public a new field of study and enjoyment. Through the Department of Film it became possible, for the first time, to examine and to analyze the record of achievement of this newest of the modern arts.

Certainly the present book could not have been written and compiled without access to the Department's collections of motion pictures, stills, books, magazines, and memorabilia. The authors wish to thank the members of the Museum staff for much intelligent help. Former staff members who gave us particular assistance on the original edition include: John Adams, who secured many rare stills for it; the late Rene d'Harnoncourt, Director of the Museum; Monroe Wheeler, former Director of Exhibition and Publications, who gave useful advice; and Eileen Bowser, now the Associate Curator of the Department of Film, who at that time contributed research. For the revised edition, we also wish to acknowledge the help of Marilyn Goldin and Mary Corliss, who helped us obtain stills, and that of Richard Corliss, who assisted with research.

We also wish to extend our thanks to Sidney Deneau, Cinema V; Irving Ludwig, Buena Vista; Ruth Pologe, American International; John Sutherland, Warner-Seven Arts; Jonas Rosenfeld, Twentieth Century-Fox; and Sheila Whitaker, British Film Institute.

RG AND AM

Published in the U.S.A. by Simon and Schuster, Inc., New York

This edition published 1971 by

The Hamlym Publishing Group Limited
London . New York . Sydney . Toronto
Hamlyn House, The Centre, Feltham, Middlesex, England

Second Impression 1972

Printed in Spain by Mateu Cromo Artes Gráficas, S. A., Madrid

ISBN 0 600 36044 X

*To*

**ANNIE and LILLIE,**

*our best critics and severest friends.*

# CONTENTS

# PREFACE

A MORE UNLIKELY pair of collaborators for a book about the movies than the authors of this volume could scarcely be found. One of them is, or thinks he is, a thoroughly commercial character who drifted into the picture industry purely by chance and remained in it because he found it pleasurable and profitable. The other is, or at least is frequently so regarded, an unworldly purist who, as a small boy thirty-five years ago, fell in love with the flickers and grew up to become the chronicler of their lightning development. One thing, however, we two had in common: the conviction that of the machines which have changed our lives in the twentieth century, only the internal-combustion engine rivals the movie camera in the scope of its influence. The movie was born at the beginning of what Frederick Lewis Allen called "the big change," the biggest change in human history, the industrialization of much of mankind in less than half a century. The movie has been the mirror of that change, and in mirroring it became the agent of change as well. Other mass media have played their parts in constructing the image of mechanized civilization, but the movie did it first and did it most vividly. Future historians, when they search the ruins of our vanished life, will look not only for manuscripts but for motion pictures—if we have the sense to preserve them.

This conception we sold to our simple-minded publishers as the basis for a book, along with the idea that such a book must necessarily be profusely illustrated with stills of our favorite films and performers. The project, however, had a substantial flaw. It would have taken a book twice as long as this to correlate what was happening on the American screen with what was happening on the American scene, and one even longer than that to include a tithe of the stills which we thought it close to criminal to discard. The mayhem involved in selection has been considerable. Reluctantly we had to abandon any idea of discussing most of the great foreign pictures which at critical moments fertilized and reinvigorated domestic production. Sadly, and only after long discussion, we excluded cartoons, even the most delectable of Disney and the craftsmen of the UPA; these masters have created a cinematic world of their own and deserve a book of their own. The vast field of documentary films, except when they reached mass audiences, as in wartime, was also obviously beyond our scope. And we have dealt with post-World War II picture developments in briefer compass than their importance justifies, suspecting that time must elapse before we or anybody can have sufficient perspective to appraise them.

Whatever preconceptions we brought to it, we found ourselves dominated in the making of this book by one overriding feeling—the fun we've had in more than three decades of moviegoing—and it is this that we have tried to render here. Reliving that fun was also fun, but fun of a different and rather special kind, one we hope the reader is now about to experience. The quality of it is indicated by an observation by Iris Barry, founder of the Museum of Modern Art Film Library, who earlier and better than anyone else understood what makes people of all kinds love the movies. "To the average adult today, his own past can be most quickly recaptured or recalled through the medium of old phonograph discs and old films. But to hear the discs and see the films again is not to recall one's past; that is achieved better by pure recollection of past music and past movies. Actually to hear and see again what pleased one so much in music or in photographic imagery is, rather, to get a sharp critical slant on one's own past. That was what one enjoyed ten years ago; this is what seemed the most exciting or beautiful thing in one's adolescence. *Cabiria* and *Male and Female* and "I Must Have That Man" have not changed: it is we who have changed and the world we live in."

RICHARD GRIFFITH
ARTHUR MAYER

*New York*
*March 1957*

# ANOTHER PREFACE: 1969

"IT IS WE WHO HAVE CHANGED, and the world we live in." With these words of Iris Barry's we ended the preface to the first edition of this book. We were thinking, then, of how far we had all come since the movie age of innocence, and of how at once enchanting and confounding it was to confront in these pages the visible evidence of all that we had once loved and believed in. Little did we dream, however, of the extent to which the world in which we lived, and we ourselves (or maybe our children) were about to be transformed. The sixty-year growth of an art and an industry which we had pictured between The Nickelodeon Days and The Post-War Decade is no greater than—maybe not as great as—the metamorphosis which has taken place between *The Ten Commandments* of 1957 and *Midnight Cowboy* of 1969.

The new movie audience which now constitutes 65 percent of our theater patrons is the best-educated in history. It was nurtured on images long before it was educated in words. Hollywood is no longer the film capital of the world. Pictures have become international in cast, content, location and financing, and today it is no longer possible, as it still was when the first edition of *The Movies* appeared, to confine any book about films to American productions. Who is to say whether the Bond pictures, the Beatles films, *The Bible* (de Laurentiis version), Antonioni's *Blow-Up*, or Truffaut's *Fahrenheit 451* are American, British, Italian, or French?

As the chapters we have added will indicate, no generalizations about the movies of the Sixties can be securely cemented. All over the world *The Sound of Music* was the joyful crash of broken boxoffice records. But *The Graduate*, which dared to deal with the abrasive subject of the generation gap, is a close second, with *Midnight Cowboy* and *Easy Rider* in hot pursuit. Nor can the popularity of Europe's great directors with young American film-makers and film-goers, or the emergence of the underground, be discarded as insignificant or as a passing fad. The brightest stars are fading, along with their million-dollar salaries and a share in the gross receipts. Their presence in a film cannot salvage it if its other elements fail to arouse public approval. Independent film production, varying from studio-controlled to genuine independent-independent, has largely replaced the old assembly-line system. Television, which was to have buried the movies, has proved, next to theaters, their most reliable customer. Meanwhile at least half-a-dozen mini-majors are destroying the old oligarchy which for forty years dominated American picture production, distribution, and exhibition.

"Everybody knows that the movies are *in*," said Pauline Kael a few years ago, "but nobody knows what to do about it." Not knowing in this sense can be a fertilizing thing. Studios are abandoned; new performers, writers and directors are in demand; old executives are replaced by men as young as those who originally made Hollywood famous. Since nobody knows what to do, everybody tries just about everything. The spirit of inquiry and experiment at last dominates a medium so long given over to repetition and routine. The varieties of that spirit are now so many as to leave the future wholly an open question. As Rene Clair said, as far back as 1927, "If it does not die in its youth, the cinema will be— well, what will it be? It is not what it was yesterday, it will not be what it is today, it will be what the children of the cinema century make it. Our task is merely to prepare the tool that they will use."

Eileen Bowser's work in the making of this book was greater than our original acknowledgment indicated. In preparing the new edition, she has been our full partner. We are more grateful than we can put into words for her devotion, her toil, and her sense of the period through which we now vertiginously hurtle.

ARTHUR MAYER
*1969*                                                        RICHARD GRIFFITH

The new edition of *The Movies* was all but completed, indeed a draft for its last words was in his typewriter, when Richard Griffith met sudden and unexpected death. His stunned colleagues were forced to gather up, without him, the final loose ends. We've wanted to respect his ideas and to make no changes that he would not agree with, but it is our loss that we can no longer test our thoughts against his.

# THE BIRTH OF THE MOVIES

Thomas Alva Edison

## WHITE MAGIC

The nineteenth century was rushing toward its close, propelled by steam and electricity. The railroad, the steamship, the telegraph, the telephone, the phonograph, and the internal combustion engine took their places in human life in bewildering succession, but the American people never tired of exclaiming, "What hath God wrought?" even though they were more inclined to attribute most of these marvels to Thomas A. Edison. The barbarous human past was dead, and with it all superstitious beliefs and forebodings. "White Magic," the miracle of science was called in the 1890s, and it was to be the successor to those dark, abandoned superstitions. It led straight to Utopia, everybody agreed, and no one mentioned Pandora and her box.

Edison himself, the high priest of the new gospel, had invented the phonograph in 1876 and shortly thereafter began to try to contrive its visual equivalent. Thanks to the inventive genius of William Kennedy Laurie Dickson, Edison's assistant, the rudiments of the motion picture were developed. Having solved the basic problems, Edison had little interest in going further. He regarded the invention as a toy and did not respond to the urging of his associates that he try to find a way of projecting these one-inch film images from the confines of a small box onto a screen large enough to be looked at by a theater audience. But, always the practical man, he made his invention available to the first outlet which appeared. By 1892, "moving pictures" could be seen in places originally called Penny Arcades or Peep Shows, which soon became known as Kinetoscope Parlors.

The Kinetoscope Arcade, San Francisco, c. 1899. Penny arcades for a while also featured "Kinetophones" which enabled the spectator to hear music or "sound effects."

# THE KINETOSCOPE

Penny arcades were for the poor and the young. They were storerooms with wide entrances decked with circus posters and lurid stills, forerunners of the garish movie advertising of later years. Phonographs had been installed in them early, and now sound and picture were crudely harnessed together to provide such naïvely comic or pornographic bits of life as "What the Bootblack Saw" or "How Bridget Served the Salad Undressed." (A trend manifested itself from the beginning: the risqué and slapstick were immediately popular, while "Surf at Dover" or "Beavers at Play" brought in meager returns.) To see these scraps of film, you dropped a penny in a slot, looked into an aperture like that of a stereoscope, and ground a crank. A light flashed on, and for a minute you watched Fatima wiggle her torso or a small boy squirt the garden hose on a well-dressed gentleman. You can see them today, in the flea circuses of the world,

and now they are disarmingly redolent of an age of innocence. Then, they were glimpses of a far *less* innocent world than the poor and the young knew from their own experience.

The Kinetoscope was as far as Edison considered it expedient to take his new invention. Pleased with the flood of pennies that flowed in from the peep-show parlors, he feared that if he were to project his images so that more than one person could see them at a time, the audience would soon be exhausted. But the pull of "living pictures" magnetized a host of would-be Edisons here and abroad. By 1895, the Kinetoscope had a lively imitative competitor in the Mutoscope, and strenuous efforts were being made by a score of mechanically minded men to combine the Kinetoscope principle with that of the magic lantern, so as to throw a larger-than-life-size picture on a sheet or on some other white surface.

# THE MOVIES ACHIEVE THE SCREEN

Prodded by the many imitators who threatened to reap the rewards of his ingenuity, Edison finally sanctioned the projection of his tiny film images on the rudimentary equivalent of today's theater screen. The first public performance under his aegis was held on April 23, 1896, in the famed Koster and Bials' Music Hall in New York. Next morning, the *Times* reported: ". . . an unusually bright light fell upon the screen. Then came into view two precious blond persons of the variety stage, in pink and blue dresses, doing the umbrella dance with commendable celerity. Their motions were all clearly defined."

These "wonderfully real and singularly exhilarating" scenes were mostly moving photographs of standard vaudeville acts, and vaudeville houses, then in their heyday, became the first home of the movies. For a time the new invention took the place of the star turn. There was something marvelous and magical about even routine acts when they were blown up by the camera to ten times life size—and when they involved the onlooker in a new physical experience. The distance between the movie viewer and what happens on the screen is in a state of perpetual flux. He is either drawn into the midst of the action or the action comes toward or recedes away from him. In 1896, this was a new and godlike experience.

The turning of a historic page: Koster and Bials' letter inviting the managers of the Kinetoscope Company to put on the first public showing of motion pictures.

Fatima, the sensation of the 1896 Chicago World's Fair, was filmed in her famous *danse du ventre*, to general shock. The compassionate censors of those early days, not wanting to deprive audiences of the lady altogether, simply blotted out the offending portions of her Egyptian shimmy.

# SCIENTIFIC AMERICAN

[Entered at the Post Office of New York, N. Y. as Second Class matter.]

A WEEKLY JOURNAL OF PRACTICAL INFORMATION, ART, SCIENCE, MECHANICS, CHEMISTRY, AND MANUFACTURES.

Vol. LXXVI.—No. 16.
Established 1845.

NEW YORK, APRIL 17, 1897.

[$3.00 A YEAR,
WEEKLY.

Fig. 1.—THE DARK ROOM AND REEL FOR DEVELOPING FILMS.

Fig. 2.—THE BIOGRAPH AT WORK IN A NEW YORK THEATER.

Fig. 3.—INTERIOR OF THE "MUTOSCOPE."

A year after the first projection of movies, the *Scientific American* was satisfying the curiosity of mechanically minded Americans about the workings of the movie marvel.

*Cripple Creek Barroom*, 1898. This authentic-looking vignette of the Old West was actually produced in Edison's "Black Maria" studio in Menlo Park, New Jersey.

# THE FIRST MOVIES

The American Mutoscope and Biograph Company was Edison's first important rival, the Mutoscope being a peep-show machine similar to the Kinetoscope, while the Biograph was a projector operating on principles nearly identical with Edison's but artfully varied to circumvent his patents. On the page opposite, the cumbrous Biograph camera photographs the Pennsylvania Limited running "at sixty miles an hour," while the equally ponderous Biograph projector throws it on the screen. Audiences of 1896 shrieked in fear when they saw the train speeding upon them. It was an experience not repeated until the advent of Cinerama and 3-D in 1953.

Audiences soon grew used to snippets of faked "news" and faked adventure, wonderful as they seemed at first. By 1900, moving pictures were relegated to the closing act on the bill in the vaudeville houses where they were shown. A scientific toy in the eyes of its own inventor, a "chaser" to the variety tycoons, the film seemed headed for the limbo of outworn novelties.

# GEORGES MÉLIÈS

The movies received their next impetus from a man as typical of the era of White Magic as Edison himself. Georges Méliès, proprietor of the Théâtre Robert-Houdin in Paris, was a popular magician and specialist in legerdemain and electromagnetic marvels. He saw the movie as a mechanical extension of magical illusion, with which he could achieve effects never before conceived. Buying a camera from the father of the French movie, Louis Lumière, Méliès set about filming anything that moved, for the sheer miracle of animation. He soon discovered something still more miraculous. As he filmed a truck passing down a street, his camera jammed. By the time he had set it in motion again, the truck had passed on and a hearse succeeded it. When projected on a screen, this bit of film showed the truck turn into a hearse. Movie magic had been born.

Within a few years Méliès invented or stumbled upon double exposure, stop motion, fast and slow motion, animation, fades, dissolves, almost the entire repertory of the trick film as it exists now. In 1900 he did something of even greater significance. He filmed the old fairy tale *Cinderella.* Though the film, less than 1000 feet long, was little more than picture-book illustration, it had a beginning, middle, and end. It told a story.

Méliès' imaginative films astonished and delighted movie-goers the world over. He flung himself into the work of writing scenarios, designing and painting scenery, drilling his little corps of artists and helpers, and appearing himself in the rich succession of "transformations, tricks, fairy tales, apotheoses, artistic and fantastic scenes, comic subjects, war pictures, fantasies and illusions" which his letterhead offered. But this versatile and ingenious pioneer was no businessman. He sold prints of his films instead of renting them, and he became a victim of the illegal duping prevalent in the early movie days. In 1914 the war ended his career as a producer; in 1925 he lost his theater, destroyed all the films in his possession and vanished.

Four years later, he was recognized hawking newspapers in the Paris streets, and for a brief moment he was photographed and feted as the founding father of the French movie industry. Then friends bought him a little toy and candy stand at the Gare Montparnasse. When he became too old to sell toys, he was made a Chevalier of the Legion of Honor and was admitted to the old actors' home at Orly. Here he spent the last years of his life, receiving such visitors as called to pay their respects to a pioneer of the world's most lucrative art, and hoping to be again actively employed in film-making. He died, still hoping, on January 22, 1938.

Innumerable science-fiction films were made by Méliès. *An Impossible Voyage*, 1904 (left), and *A Trip to the Moon*, 1902, were the most notable. His pictures both satirized and celebrated scientific progress. Caption of this scene is: "Tableau 17: To the summit of the Jungfrau at full speed."

← A French family group at the height of the era of "white magic." Georges Méliès, right, *en famille* at Garches, France, 1892.

*Le Rêve de Shakespeare*, 1907, known in English as *Shakespeare Writing Julius Caesar*, with Méliès as the dramatist envisioning Caesar's assassination. In Méliès' films the sets were backdrops painted by the director himself. He seems here to have Rome as already in ruins. →

*Long - Distance Wireless Photography*, 1907. Hardly had Marconi invented the "wireless" when Méliès produced this burlesque in which a whiskered inventor displays his radioed photo of three damsels, who symbolically float above. The girls are from the Folies Bergère, which Méliès used in some capacity in nearly all his films.

In imitation of Méliès, Edwin S. Porter made many films for the Edison Co., such as *Dream of a Rarebit Fiend*, a trick movie of 1906.

Thomas L. Tally's Los Angeles "Electric Theatre" was speedily imitated throughout the world. This one was probably in Robert Dooner's fairground in South Wales, Britain.

The definitive edition of the movie showplace finally became known by the generic name of Nickelodeon. Here are the Warner brothers standing in front of one.

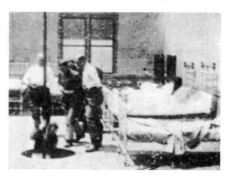

*Life of an American Fireman,* 1903, by Edwin S. Porter.

# THE NICKELODEON AGE

## THE STORE SHOWS

Before 1900, screen-projected movies were practically a monopoly of the vaudeville theaters and even in them had lost favor. But in the first year of the century, the nation's vaudeville actors formed a union and struck for higher wages. The managers, refusing to recognize the union, either closed their theaters or ingeniously kept their houses open by presenting programs consisting solely of motion pictures. Projection manufacturers found themselves swamped with orders as vaudeville managers clamored for equipment. With the end of the strike, however, the cumbersome machines abruptly became a drug on the market. Manufacturers were overstocked, and the eager buyers of yesterday were prepared to sell their machines secondhand at any price.

At bargain prices, though, a new market appeared. Penny arcade owners of the Nineties had seen their peep-show movies eclipse cooch dancers and flea circuses as the most popular attractions of their motley emporia. When films projected on the large screen outdistanced peep shows, they longed to compete, but equipment had been as scarce as it was costly. Now, with projectors going begging, came the opportunity of the penny-ante boys.

In Los Angeles, Thomas L. Tally set up a movie show in the rear of the amusement parlor he owned. He converted skeptics by cutting a hole in the partition which separated the darkened projection room from the rest of the arcade, so that doubting Thomases could see for themselves that life-sized pictures were being shown in the rear. So successful was this device that he soon jettisoned his other ventures, turned his arcade into an auditorium, and advertised "The Electric Theater. For Up-to-Date High-Class Motion Picture Entertainment Especially for Ladies and Children."

Tally's success—and it was sensational—attracted a horde of followers from the fringes of show business—ex-barkers, hawkers, pitchmen, and medicine-show men, as well as the owners of the peep shows where the infant movie had first found a home. They shared two things in common: a hunch that an untapped, unsophisticated public was avid for low-priced entertainment, and a lack of cash with which to capitalize on that hunch. They knew that the theater and vaudeville magnates were convinced that movies had already exhausted their brief popularity, but they hoped that they could exploit the vestiges of the movies' fame among the lowly by renting unused stores and equipping them with projection machines, a screen, and some chairs. The "store shows" were usually family enterprises, managed, staffed, and cleaned up by papa, mama, and the boys. They were dank, noisome places, repulsive to the elect. But there were plenty of the unelected, and they kept coming.

## THE MOVIES LEARN TO TELL STORIES

Till Edwin S. Porter's *Life of an American Fireman*, U. S. movies still consisted of "topical views"— tidbits of nature study, brief comic interludes, and nearly as brief scenes from stage successes (Joseph Jefferson as Rip Van Winkle, Sarah Bernhardt enacting the duel scene from *Hamlet*). But, taking his cue from Méliès, Porter captured the popular imagination by introducing narrative and thus gave the movies a fresh lease on life. Georges Méliès had told stories on the screen in the manner of the theater, but an Edison film by Edwin S. Porter was the first to arrive at a cinematic form of narration. It shows a fire chief sitting in his office dreaming (in what was then called a "dream balloon") of his wife at home. We cut to a close shot (the first known) of a street-corner fire alarm and to another of a hand setting off the alarm. We cut again to another distant scene, that of the firemen jumping from bed, sliding down the firehouse pole, and starting toward the fire. The remaining frames of this short film detail the rescue of a woman and child from a burning home. Today, film scholars dispute the order and the meaning of these frames, the argument turning on whether Porter merely anticipated or actually invented the principal device of screen narrative, cross-cutting, which enables the director to annihilate space and time.

Porter had begun his career as an itinerant cameraman for the Edison Company. *The Life of an American Fireman* and *The Great Train Robbery* made him the foremost director of the Nickelodeon Age, and even after the advent of D. W. Griffith he remained a leading figure in the industry. In 1915, his fortune made, he retired, but the crash of 1929 wiped out his wealth, and Porter spent his old age as a minor employee of an appliance corporation, a modest spectator of the growth of an industry to which he had given the initial creative push.

# The Great Train Robbery

**1** The telegraph operator's daughter prays for her father, bound and sandbagged by the train robbers.

**2** The robbers force the engineer to uncouple the locomotive.

**3** They make their escape into the woods.

**4** The sheriff's posse is found in a saloon, forcing a tenderfoot to dance.

**5** At the end of the film, for no reason connected with the story, one of the characters draws his pistol and fires at the audience.

## THE FIRST

More famous than any American picture except *The Birth of a Nation* and possibly *Gone with the Wind, The Great Train Robbery* has lingered in the national consciousness as the first real movie. In it, Edwin S. Porter merely extended and refined the storytelling principles he had used in *Life of an American Fireman*. But this was a story of crime and the Far West (it was actually filmed in New Jersey), and these favorite themes of American popular entertainment acquired a new potency in the new and flexible medium of the screen. *The Great Train Robbery* became a classic overnight. For

# Uncle Tom's Cabin

**1** A super-production of 1903: the background is painted, the steamboats are toys, the water is real.

**2** Eliza shakes a defiant fist at Simon Legree.

**3** Death of Little Eva. Aunt Sally bows her head, Uncle Tom his knee, while the angel gathers up the departed.

**4** Death of Uncle Tom, with Little Eva beckoning him to heaven.

## REAL MOVIES

years newly opened nickelodeons invariably billed it as their initial attraction, just as years later, with the coming of the talkies, theaters which had closed to be wired for sound always reopened with Al Jolson's *The Singing Fool*.

As soon as the movies learned to tell stories, they began to film the classics. Porter himself brought *Uncle Tom's Cabin* to the screen in what, for the nickelodeon era, had all the earmarks of a modern super-production. The tableaux, backdrops, and painted light of this delicious film breathe forth the odor of the nineteenth-century popular theater.

**5** After the death of Uncle Tom, a symbolic tableau of Lincoln promises the freeing of the slaves.

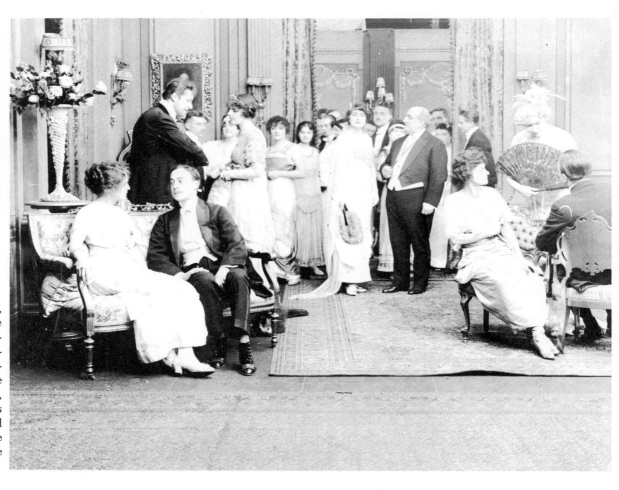

*The Reception,* Edison, *c.* 1911. Though the close-up had been invented by 1902, most directors insisted on arranging action in the manner of the stage, with all the characters shown full length and considerable floor space between them and the camera.

# FILMS OF THE NICKELODEON AGE

With a lively partisanship unknown today, films of the nickelodeon era tore into current issues as they came along. Labor vs. capital, votes for women, graft, political chicanery, race discrimination—all found reflection on the screen. Production was con-

*The Suffragette,* Edison, *c.* 1912. Films of the period ridiculed the "unwomanly woman" who wanted to vote. Here one of them tells the dog to keep watch on her husband and see that he minds the baby and gets dinner while she is out speech-making.

*Romeo and Juliet*, Vitagraph, 1908. Early filmmakers made municipal architecture do duty for classical or medieval settings, as amateurs do today. Here the death of Mercutio is staged against the background of the Central Park Mall in New York.

trolled by wealthy men, but they were not as yet aware of the power of the films to influence human thought and conduct, while directors and writers were ready and willing to supply situations and solutions satisfactory to their humble audiences.

The murder of Stanford White by Harry K. Thaw on the Madison Square Garden roof re-enacted for the Biograph Mutoscope and rushed to the nickelodeons a few hours after the shooting occurred.

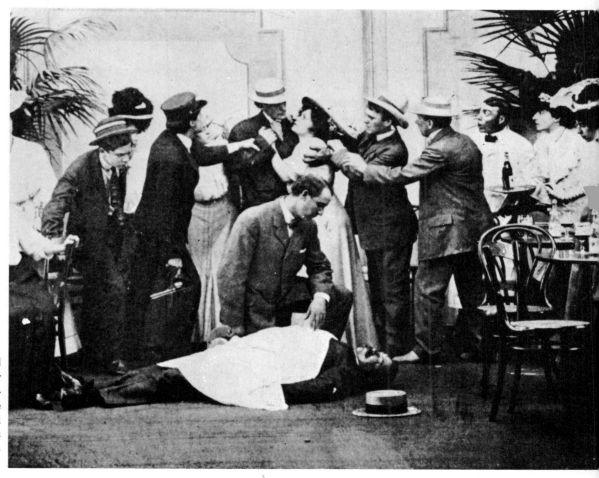

PERSONAL—"Young French Nobleman, recently arrived, desires to meet wealthy American girl, object, matrimony; will be at Grant's Tomb at 10 this morning, wearing boutonniere of violets."

A subtitle from the 1904 film, *How the French nobleman got a wife through the New York* Herald *Personal columns.*

# FILMS OF THE NICKELODEON AGE

Magic remained a mainstay of the movies' appeal in the Nickelodeon Age. Descendants of Méliès, forerunners of Disney and Clair, the merrymakers of these deliberately mad films took their audiences on flights of fancy which today's producers think themselves too sophisticated to attempt.

*The Disintegrated Convict,* 1907. A convict, hiding from police

*Roosevelt in Africa,* 1910. Theodore Roosevelt was a "natural" for the movies. An enterprising producer, Col. William N. Selig, hired a vaudeville actor bearing a slight resemblance to "T.R.," and while the ex-President was on safari in Africa, made a movie of a lion hunt in his Chicago studio. The public accepted it as genuine.

*The Fighting Roosevelts,* 1919. A year after his death, Roosevelt was the hero of a film which perpetuated the legend of the

in a barrel, escapes them by changing into a striped hose.

*Gertie the Dinosaur,* 1909. One of the first animated films, drawn by Winsor McCay, famous cartoonist of the period.

weakling bespectacled Easterner who, hardened by the Wild West, became the nation's leading exponent of the strenuous life.

LADIES AND CHILDREN
ARE CORDIALLY INVITED
TO THIS THEATRE
NO OFFENSIVE PICTURES
ARE EVER SHOWN HERE

Ladies Ki...
you...

The Bijou Dream (Rochester, New York, c. 1909) usurped the entire ground floor of a commercial building, but its proudest boast remained "Admission 5c."

## THE NICKELODEON AND ITS PATRONS

Nickelodeons like the Bijou Dream in Rochester sprang up in storerooms, hotel ballrooms, disused lecture halls, any place that could be improvised into the semblance of a theater. Carrying on the tradition of the visiting Lyceum lecturer or touring stock company, managed as often as not by local people, they gradually developed into community centers which met an entertainment need that could be filled in no other way. Concert singers, Wild West shows, and stock companies reached small American towns only once or twice a year, and even then only the comfortably off could afford to attend them. But the nickelodeon was a local fixture whose price was within reach of all. Its cheapness and ready access were something new under the sun. "The telegraph, the telephone, the electric light," says Benjamin B. Hampton, pioneer movie financier and producer, ". . . had created a sensation but they had not entered into the lives of millions of people. The common man and his family still used kerosene lamps; none but the well-to-do had telephones; and the telegram was a form

of communication seldom known in the average household except to announce serious illness or death. But this new thing—this 'living picture' affair—was not a prosaic tool to reduce labor or to save time; it was not an instrument to create more comfort and luxury for the well-to-do. It was a romantic device to bring entertainment to the common people."[*]

Soon the nickelodeons became a home away from home for the whole family. Local advertisers found the screen a profitable billboard. Slides familiarly instructed patrons in the elementary courtesies and neatnesses. Baritones and tenors led the audience in song, while scenes illustrating the lyrics were thrown on the screen. And always there were the movies themselves—still "flickers," "galloping tintypes" yet, but bringing new sights and new thoughts to people whose imaginative world had been bounded by the village, slum, or farm.

[*] *A History of the Movies,* by Benjamin B. Hampton, Covici-Friede, 1931.

"*Hello, Central, Give Me Heaven,*" says the little girl whose mother lives there. A nickelodeon song slide.

"*Trust Him Not, the Gypsy Fortune Teller Said.*" J. D. Cress was the author of this, the above, and many other songs popular in the nickelodeons.

All persons arriving late may remain for the next show. ....

Change of Song to-morrow

Our Patrons are Our friends.

WATCH FOR OUR NEXT SENSATION!

## ST. LOUIS'S HIGH-CLASS MOVING-PICTURE THEATRES

**GEM**

ONE PRICE TO EVERY THING
**10c**

### Read What They Say

about this week's big special feature at THE GEM. Without doubt, one of the most thrilling and interesting acts extant.

### You Can't Afford to Miss This!

Besides this high-priced novelty, we offer a variety of new moving picture films, just received and shown for the first time

PRETTIEST!
BEST VENTILATED!
HIGHEST CLASS!
UP-TO-DATE!

**6th st.**

East side, between Walnut and Market Streets.

### The Moving Picture Theater Now a Permanent Factor in Public Amusement

WE LIVE in an age when the genius of invention is abroad in the land—an age of mechanical ingenuity, mystery of revolving wheels and might of electrical power applied alike to the serious business of life and its amusements and recreations.

Meanwhile that much-abused mechanical mirth-provoker, the moving picture show, has come to stay, for it has evolved as the climax to a popular demand for cheap amusement, and its rapid growth, perfection of construction and ease of operation entitle it to a definite place among important factors in our modern life.

The history of the moving picture show is interesting. It is an outgrowth of scientific improvements and deeper investigations into the arts of photography.

Time was when the twomen photographer was regarded almost as a miracle by the uninitiated. Amateurs and professionals vied with each other in producing pictures of greater and more superior excellence. Finally came delvers into the laws of vibration, who were also practical photographers, and who made this important discovery, viz: that apparently continuous motion is but a series of repeated vibrations, and that a series of photographs can be taken of a moving object, which, in their rapid review, constitute what has been called a moving picture. The application of this discovery at once widened the horizon so far as photography was concerned.

That this has been abused and made to subserve evil ends and pander to the depraved tastes of a large section of the public there is no doubt, but this is not the rule. It is emphatically the exception. In earlier days, when the moving picture was in its infancy, it was natural that those who saw its possibilities in a commercial sense should wear as little time as possible and should endeavor to apply the discovery to whatever most conveniently lent itself to the purpose best and at least expense.

But the interest in the moving picture and its wonderful possibilities grew apace. The genuine, scientific and mechanical side of the invention awoke much inquiry and the moving picture began to assert itself and once its way into public recognition as a great exemplar of educational and scientific wonders.

To-day the great moving panoramas that show magnificent scenes and transport us suddenly, as if we were carried by spell, to distant parts of the earth have risen to a place and plane as a civilizing factor, and in our quest for hourly amusement and recreation we cannot do better than witness some of the wonderful exhibitions furnished us by the splendidly managed amusement halls that now cater for the best, in place of pandering to the worst, side of human nature.

Added to the moving panorama is the accompaniment of wondrously sweet music. Electricity, that mysterious force about which we still now so little, has been harnessed by man, and now drives the motors that connect with the machinery, and for the consideration of 5 and 10 cents the visitor may now enter a luxuriously-upholstered hall, brilliantly illuminated, and while sitting spellbound by the rapidly shifting scenes that transport him in imagination to tropical climes, he may ravish his soul with the fine orchestral effects from deep-toned instruments whose wonderful voices pour forth upon the air the melodies of New York's famous songsters or St. Louis' leading musicians.

St. Louis has nearly two hundred moving picture theaters, many of them housed in expensive and ornate buildings. Considerably more than $1,000,000 is invested in these enterprises and about 1,500 persons find direct employment in them. The moving picture business in this city has been placed upon a systematic and businesslike basis, enabling the public to get the utmost value at a minimum of cost.

### THE PINNACLE of Motion PICTURE PERFECTION

#### GRAND CENTRAL THEATER
SIXTH AND MARKET STREETS

#### The McKinley Theater
2218 South Jefferson Avenue,

Is one of the finest Moving-Picture Theaters and is under the able management of Mr. C. Young, whose business experience ably fits him for the management. The house is packed to the doors each evening and many good words are said of the show. The best special acts that money can obtain are put on each week. A few words to the public from Mr. Young: At the outset there were some people dissatisfied with the location, through the general known prejudice against the moving-picture theater. These same people are now much pleased with the show given and may be found in the audience each week. A visit to The McKinley and you will be convinced that Mr. Young is giving much for the money.

C. YOUNG, Prop. and Manager.

### FROM NOWHERE TO THE FRONT RANK IN FOUR DAYS

**O. T. Crawford's NOVELTY THEATER**

BIG SUCCESS
Opened Wednesday, Feb. 2, 1910
THRONGED NIGHTLY
Investment $78,000, Yet All Seats
**10 Cents 10**
Fireproof. Open on All Sides.
EVERY NIGHT,
Saturday, Sunday and Holidays
AFTERNOONS.
EASTON AVENUE,
Just East of Grand Avenue.

ROOF GARDEN
OPEN NOW Only One in St. Louis.
2 BIG SHOWS UNDER 1 ROOF
VAUDEVILLE
On Perfect Stages
MOTION PICTURES,
ORCHESTRAS,
SINGING.
Wellston, Grand and Page Cars.

**NEWEST, MOST MODERN, MOST UNIQUE SHOW PLACE IN ST. LOUIS.**

### CASINO THEATER
Olive and 6th Sts.
(Opposite Barr's)
=WHERE=
THE REFINED PEOPLE OF ALL ST. LOUIS GO.
The place for ladies to rest while downtown shopping.

### The VICTOR
Gravois and Victor
Highest-Class Moving-Picture Theater on the South Side.

Some time ago several men conceived the idea to amuse the public at large. One must fool 'em," Barnum, the circus man, once said. This may or may not be true. However, we are not going to try out Mr. Barnum's adage. It is and always will be our aim to amuse you in a wholesome and educational way. The title instruction—the business man that seeks recreation does not care to have his or her nerves stung to death by hilarious, cheap vaudeville. So when we put on any feature, the first question that arises is—Is it instructive? Will it offend? Is it going to amuse?" And we are quite confident that we will keep our house standard where we have placed it. We show pictures that are works of art and are classed under the head of Feature Reels. We have a four-piece orchestra and splendid vocal talent. Our Theater Programme changes Sunday, Tuesday, Wednesday and Friday.

### THE ASTOR
5 N. Broadway
Where you see the new and latest pictures first
ILLUSTRATED SONGS
Everything First-class and Up-to-date
5 N. BROADWAY

### THE WHITE HOUSE
BLACKSTONE AND PAGE AVS.
HIGH-CLASS MOTION PICTURES AND MUSIC.
COMING SOON!
RICE'S TRAVELOGUES
SHOWING EVERY COUNTRY IN THE WORLD.
VIEWS OF ONE COUNTRY EACH NIGHT, DESCRIBED BY ONE OF THE BEST LECTURERS OBTAINABLE.
First Time in Any Motion-Picture Theater in St. Louis.

### THE NIGHTINGALE
2309 South Broadway
Illustrated Songs and Moving-Picture Parlor.
CHANGE OF PROGRAM
Sunday, Tuesday, Thursday, Saturday
PICTURES TO PLEASE EVERYONE.
Admission 5c.    Established 7 Years
Handsome prize given away the first Tuesday in each month
RENTAL FOR RENT and MONDAY.
ALBERT LYNN, Prop. and Mgr.

### The best Child's Shoe Made Anywhere—There's Double Wear In Every Pair.

**BUSTER BROWN BLUE RIBBON SHOES**
FOR BOYS—FOR GIRLS
All styles — all leathers — all sizes — and every pair built for service
THE BROWN SHOE CO.,
Makers—St. Louis, Mo.
ASK YOUR SHOE DEALER FOR THEM

### THE SAVOY
VANDEVENTER AND MORGAN.
THE HOUSE OF QUALITY
Commencing Sunday, February 13,
**The Savoy Players**
in Comedy and Dramatic
**Playlets**
Novelty Vaudeville Features, Vocal Selections, High-Class Motion Pictures. Savoy Feature Orchestra.
COMPLETE CHANGE OF PROGRAMME
SUNDAY, WEDNESDAY AND FRIDAY.

### The Dewey
M. KAISER, Prop.
2302 S. Broadway
High-Class Motion Pictures.
Program Changed Four Times A Week.
Tuesday, Wednesday, Friday and Sunday.
ADMISSION 5c.

### St. Louis Calcium Light Co.
OXYGEN HYDROGEN GAS FURNISHED IN TANKS FOR STEREOPTICON AND MOVING-PICTURE MACHINES.
STEREOPTICON VIEWS
OUR ILLUSTRATED SONG SLIDE SERVICE

### THE HIPPODROME
13 N. BROADWAY
Programme Changes
Sunday, Wednesday, and Friday
The Moving-Picture Show for Ladies and Children.
Illustrated Songs.
Admission 5 Cts.

### FAMILY THEATER
Broadway and Bremen.
Change of program Mondays, Wednesdays, Fridays and Sundays.
Music by Professors Gieselmann, J. Donovan and Hartman.
**J. MOGLER,** Proprietor.

### ONE OF THE PIONEERS OF BROADWAY
—IN THE—
MOTION-PICTURE BUSINESS
**DEWEEZ BROS.** Proprietors of the
**Broadway Theater**
South Broadway at Victor St.
It is always our policy to procure the LATEST and BEST Motion Pictures Obtainable.
Entire Change of Program Every
SUNDAY, TUESDAY, WEDNESDAY AND FRIDAY.
MUSIC BY THE BROADWAY ORCHESTRA.
Latest Illustrated Songs by our Eminent Artist, MR. BURNS.
ONE CALL AND YOU WILL BE A STEADY PATRON OF OUR SHOW.

### The Alice
SIXTEENTH AND CASS AVENUE
"The House of Quality"
Life Motion Pictures and Illustrated Songs
JNO. J. POWERS, Proprietor.
THEO. T. HAMILTON, Manager.

---

Newspapers ignored the nickelodeons until they began to take advertising space. Then they suddenly discovered—as in the above story from the St. Louis *Republic*—that: "Electricity, that mysterious force about which we still know so little, has been harnessed by man and now drives the motors that connect with the machinery, and for a consideration of 5 or 10 cents a visitor may now enter a luxuriously upholstered hall, brilliantly illuminated, and while sitting spellbound by the rapidly shifting scenes that transport him in imagination to tropical climes, he may ravish his soul with fine orchestral effects from deep-toned instruments whose wonderful voices pour forth upon the air the melodies of New York's famous songsters or St. Louis' leading musicians." What press agent ever went further?

Had any of the owners of the motion picture trust walked past the Crystal Hall on Fourteenth Street one day in 1914, they would have been confirmed in their contempt for the commodity they produced. The theater's poster artist had transformed—probably in all innocence—the Italian import *Tigris* to *Tigress, The Mysterious Criminal.*

## THE NICKELODEON AND ITS PATRONS

In contrast to the small-town store shows, nickelodeons in New York and other big cities grew out of penny arcades in many cases, and they looked as dark, dirty, and smelly as penny arcades and flea circuses look to us today. Their first patrons were often tramps and drunks; the respectable shuddered away from them and murmured against them. It began to be said that something ought to be done about policing them or maybe banning them altogether. But the city nickelodeons thrived. Even more than in rural America, they were the only entertainment available to the poor.

Especially were they the chief entertainment of the hordes of immigrants from southern and eastern Europe who poured into the metropolis in the early 1900s. Barred from the theater by their ignorance of English, they could follow the one-reel picture dramas of the nickelodeons, learning much

about American life and values in the process, and piecing out their English as they gradually related the subtitles to the action. Observing this, some of the more farsighted social workers of the period began to think that the despised "poor man's show" might become his university as well.

By the end of the Nickelodeon Age, even the city nickelodeons were safe and comfortable places which the most fastidious might (and some surreptitiously did) attend without offense. Exhibitors began to clamor for longer films with better stories and acting, knowing that audiences would pay more if they got more, but their clamor went unheeded. The real powers of the new industry, the producers, refused to believe that anybody would ever shell out more than a nickel to see a movie. They didn't think the pictures they made were worth even a plugged one.

# THE MEN WHO OWNED THE BUSINESS

High above the "mob" which attended nickelodeons and the "gypsies and bunco artists" who ran them sat the mighty Thomas Alva Edison and his eight associates in the Motion Picture Patents and the General Film companies. They were not offended when the movies were called a "plaything for children of all ages" or a "cheap show for cheap people." They fully agreed and they did not care, so long as the nickels of the cheap people continued to flow into their coffers.

Edison's initial indifference to the possible profits of his invention had opened the way for numerous small operators to enter production. By 1907, the gross income from film production exceeded that of the legitimate theater and vaudeville combined, and the Wizard belatedly thought of the profits he was losing. At first he tried to sue his competitors for violation of his basic patents, but all claimed patents of their own, and the Edison Company seemed in danger of spending a decade in the courts with no certainty of the outcome. His advisers then suggested that he invite his more "substantial" competitors to join with him in forming a company in which each would acknowledge the validity of the others' claims. Accordingly, the leading American companies of the day, Vitagraph, Selig, Essanay, Kalem, Biograph, Lubin, and Kleine, together with two important French concerns, Pathé and Méliès, joined Edison in forming the Motion Picture Patents Company. In January 1909, the ten partners announced that they alone owned the right to photograph, develop, and print motion pictures, that they alone could do so under the patent laws of the U.S., Great Britain, France, Germany, and Italy, and that no license to do so would ever be issued to anyone else.

Having declared a monopoly on production, the combine speedily sought to extend its stranglehold to distribution and exhibition. It formed the General Film Company, which was to be its instrument of control over the wholesaling and retailing of pictures. The leading film exchanges were acquired and the exhibitors were informed that they could continue to operate only at the pleasure of General Film. Since the manufacturers controlled production, exhibitors could book only films made by the members of Motion Picture Patents; since they controlled the manufacture of projectors, exhibitors needed a license from General Film in order even to show the motion pictures of General Film itself. And that license cost each of them two dollars a week fifty-two weeks a year. This license fee was to net the General Film Company an income of $1,250,000 per year.

The nine producers whom Edison had so generously taken to his bosom could not believe their good luck. Their lawyers advised them that Motion Picture Patents and General Film constituted between them an "airtight trust," but that the beauty of it was that they could not be prosecuted under the Sherman Act because their monopoly was firmly based on patent protection. Their competitors were eliminated, their business standardized, and, best of all, the "riff-raff" of exhibitors far below them in the industry structure would have to pay them to continue to exist. The license fee was the hallmark of their impregnable position, or so they thought.

It proved, however, the rock on which the trust broke. The nickelodeon operators reacted to it much as the colonists of 1760 reacted to the Stamp Act. Legal it might or might not be, but it was taxation without representation, and they needed only leadership to declare their independence.

Making movies for ten cents a foot was lots of fun. A jovial meeting of the Motion Picture Patents Company—Thomas A. Edison surrounded by (left to right) Albert Smith, Vitagraph; George Scull, Edison; George Kleine, Edison; Siegmund Lubin, Lubin; H. N. Marvin, Biograph; J. Stuart Blackton, Vitagraph; Frank Marion, Kalem.

# THE FIGHTING INDEPENDENTS

The nickelodeon operators found leadership in William Fox and Carl Laemmle, two exhibitors who had climbed into the distributing end of the business by operating "exchanges." Exchanges were at first literally just that: offices where exhibitors met to barter prints of films they had already used for others their patrons had not yet seen. When renting instead of buying films became the rule, the exchanges developed into wholesaling outlets, buying films in job lots from producers and renting them individually to nickelodeons. They were the middlemen between manufacturers and consumers, and as such had to be brought into the closed system General Film was creating. But when General Film announced that it was buying the leading independent exchanges and that those it did not condescend to buy out must get out, Laemmle and Fox refused either to sell or to quit. They proclaimed the right to run their businesses as they pleased, and to hell with the patent laws.

Their position seemed hopeless. Lately risen from obscurity, they lacked the capital which General Film with its vast resources could array against them in the form of lawsuits, injunctions, and boycotts. All they had on their side was the resentment of exhibitors against the trust and their willingness to flout its requirements whenever they could get away with it. But that turned out to be all they needed.

Fox at first contented himself with ignoring the Patents Company, although eventually he fought and won a lawsuit against the trust. But Laemmle declared open war. He created the character of "General Flimco," and in a series of cartoons contrasted the trust's wealth and greed with the plight of the small exhibitor. When the trust threatened to boycott exhibitors who dealt with him, Laemmle

printed the threatening letters as evidence that General Film was a coercive monopoly. When the trust, as a precaution against exhibitors' "going independent," added to its exhibition contract a "3rd Condition" requiring the payment of the hated weekly license fee in advance and on a yearly basis, Laemmle declaimed, "Read that '3rd Condition' again. Take it home and play it on your pianola. Play it upside down, sidewise, before and behind. Tell, when you're all through, tell me what you think of it!!!" When the trust cut off his exchanges' supply of films, he began to make them himself, significantly calling his producing firm The Independent Motion-Picture Company. And all the time he harped on the frustration of exhibitors, horse-traders all, at the trust's rule that all films, good and bad, should be paid for at ten cents a foot.

"Ten cents a foot" was indeed as good a war cry for Laemmle as "two dollars a week," and this the moguls completely failed to understand. The corporation lawyers, big-business executives, and financiers who controlled the trust believed that their films as well as everybody else's were shoddy stuff fit only for illiterates, and what was the use of trying to improve them? They were too far removed from their audiences to sense what exhibitors and exchange men knew at first hand—that this motley rabble of "immigrants, children, chambermaids, and streetcar conductors" wanted better films. As more and better independent films came on the market, more and more exhibitors were willing to pay high for them and unwilling to abide by the trust's ten cents a foot and two dollars a week. Long before General Film was abolished by judicial decision in 1915, it had become a hollow shell.

William Fox parlayed a small nickelodeon into a $20,000,000 producing and distributing corporation by working even while he ate.

Carl Laemmle smilingly returning from his annual visit to his German birthplace many years after his defeat of the General Film Company.

21

## THE FIGHTING INDEPENDENTS

Carl Laemmle encouraged exhibitors to defy the trust by ridiculing it. His weekly full-page advertisements in the *Moving Picture World* impressed the humbler nickelodeon operators with the heights to which one of their number had risen, at the same time that they rubbed salt in the wound of the humiliating license fee. Laemmle's ads usually began, "Good Morrow! Have you paid $2 for a license to pick your teeth this week?" and ended, "By the way, have you paid $2 for a license to kiss your wife?" When the trust brought two hundred and forty court actions against him, he entered a countersuit claiming "Relief from Multiplicity of Suits."

# THE DEVELOP-MENT OF NARRATIVE

## The Wild Duck.

LOOK—how beautiful he is !
Swift his flight as a bullet
As he comes in from the sea in the morning.
For the wind is from the sea in the morning.
See ! He is bound for the hilltops,
The gold hilltops, the gold hilltops.
There he will rest 'neath the flowers,
The red flowers—the white and red,
The poppy—the flower of dreams,
The crimson flower of dreams.
There must he rest in the morning.
Happy wild duck ! Happy wild duck !
For the wind is from the sea in the morning.

So will he rest 'neath the roses,
The red roses, the love roses,
And their petals will fall around him,
Sweet and warm around him,
Closer and closer around him,
Warmer and warmer around him,
Till even in the day-time the stars shall be shining.
Happy wild duck ! Happy wild duck !
For the wind is from the sea in the morning.
There by the roses bloom the lilies, the flowers of peace,
The white flowers of peace,
Red and white together, red and white and red,
Waving and blowing together,
Blooming and waving together
On the gold hilltops in the morning,
For the wind is from the sea in the morning.

Ah me ! but the wind soon changes in these parts,
Ah me ! Ah me !
It was not so in the old days.
Look, look, ah, look, see, even now it is changing out, out
    to the sea !
Look, look, above the hilltops,
With eyes turned back to the mainland,
And tired wings wearily beating, but vainly,
For the wind blows out to the sea in the evening.
Poor little wild duck ! Poor little wild duck !
Look, there is crimson, warm on his breast !
Look, red drops fall from his breast !
Poor little wild duck ! Poor little wild duck !
In the evening,
For the wind is out to the sea in the evening.

Look ! He is falling, falling out to the sea.
Ah, there is mist on the sea !
There is always mist on the sea in the evening.
Perhaps his nest is beyond, I know not ;
Perhaps it is built of the mist, I know not.
Only with tired wings wearily beating,
And eyes turned back to the mainland,
To the red and white and red,
Waving and blowing together,
Blooming and blowing together,
He is falling out, out to the sea.
Poor little wild duck ! Poor little wild duck !
In the evening when the wind blows out to the sea !
Ah me ! Ah me ! Ah me !
In the evening when the wind blows out to the sea.

DAVID WARK GRIFFITH.

This early poem by D. W. Griffith, published in
*Leslie's Weekly* in 1907, foreshadows the literary
style of his later subtitles.

## D. W. GRIFFITH

In 1907 most films were still produced as though
they were plays. Each scene began with the entrance of the actors and lasted unbroken until their
exit. The players were always shown full size and
at a fixed distance from the camera. The action
consisted of their movements and gesticulations,
greatly exaggerated to compensate for the absence
of dialogue. By now, crude subtitles attempted to
do duty for speech, but the motion picture still
looked to most people like a shadowy carbon of
the living theater. No one knew how to break its
umbilical cord to the older medium.

The man who did break it, and so brought to
birth a new art, was an unlikely choice for his
historic role. Like all stage people of the time,
David Wark Griffith regarded the movies with
contempt—nor was he particularly proud of his
career as journeyman actor in touring stock companies, interrupted of necessity by work as a sub-
scription salesman, ore shoveler, hop picker; and
day laborer. When, as a youth of twenty-two, he
had joined the Meffert Stock Company in Louisville, Kentucky, he had assumed the name of Lawrence Griffith. He thought he owed it to his heritage
to reserve his right name for more respectable
enterprises.

His heritage was one familiar enough—of high
traditions, past glories, and present straits. His
family had held property and position in Maryland
and Kentucky for a hundred years, and his father,
Col. Jacob Wark Griffith was a member of the
Kentucky legislature and a hero of the Confederacy; but after the Civil War the Griffith fortunes had declined. The family home, at the time
of David Wark Griffith's birth on January 23, 1875,
was heavily mortgaged. At his father's death ten
years later, there was less than nothing left. The
family moved into Louisville and young David
helped out by working as cashboy in a dry-goods
store, where he was embarrassed to be seen by his
father's more prosperous friends.

Col. Griffith was unquestionably visionary and
improvident, but his son idolized him and absorbed
from him, along with a militant "Southron" tradition, a love of literature and an ambition to write.
When in 1897 he embarked on an acting career he
looked upon it only as a stopgap until he should
establish himself as a novelist and playwright. But
ten years later the sum of his writing achievements
was a few published stories and poems and an
unsuccessful play, and when marriage to a young
actress pushed him into seeking steady employment outside the theater, his future seemed bleak
indeed.

G. W. Bitzer and D. W. Griffith.

## "AMERICAN BIOGRAPH"

"Duping" made the piracy of films an easy practice in the business chaos of the early Nickelodeon Age. To prevent rivals from removing the main title from a film, making a duplicate negative, and releasing prints of it as their own work, the leading companies formed the practice of inserting a symbol or trade name into every possible scene, tacked up on the wall or otherwise conspicuously displayed. One such trade symbol, the famous "AB" of the American Mutoscope and Biograph Company, came to have actual cash value. Joseph Wood Krutch recalls that, as a boy in Tennessee, he and his companions wandered from one nickelodeon to another looking for a display of the "AB" symbol, signifying that it was "Biograph night" at the theater. No one knew who made films or who played in them, but the nickelodeon public came to realize that Biograph films were somehow superior to other productions.

It was D. W. Griffith's contribution to motion-picture narrative that gave Biograph its lead. As a stage actor and proud Southerner, he was ashamed at being reduced to this low form of occupation, and even when Biograph offered him a chance to direct, he said to his wife, "In a way it's very nice,

but, you know, we can't go on forever and not tell our friends and relatives how we are earning our living." He was also far from sure that he could master this new knack of "canning" drama on film. Before he would undertake the direction of his first film, *The Adventures of Dollie* (1908), H. N. Marvin, vice-president of Biograph, had to reassure him that if he failed as a director he could continue with the company as writer and actor.

Before work began on *The Adventures of Dollie*, it was thought advisable that the new director should be given some advice by the most experienced hand at the studio. G. W. "Billy" Bitzer had joined the firm in 1896 as an electrician and had risen to be head cameraman and trouble shooter. "The cameraman was the whole works at that time," Bitzer wrote in 1940, "responsible for everything except the immediate handling of the actors. It was his say not only as to whether the light was bright enough but make-up, angles, rapidity of gestures, etc., besides having enough camera troubles of his own. I agreed to help Griffith in every way. He needed a canvas covering for a gypsy wagon. I would get that—in fact, all the props. I also offered to condense the script and lay out the opportunities it had so that he would be able to understand it. I had divided off half a dozen columns on the back of a laundry-shirt cardboard and headed the columns with titles—Drama, Comedy, Pathos, Pretty Scenes—and wrote in what I thought he should stress. Judging the little I had caught from seeing his acting, I didn't think he was going to be so hot."

Bitzer could not know that theirs was to be the most famous creative partnership in film history, but he soon found that this apparently unpromising novice was a "human short-circuit type" whose energy and initiative earned him the grudging respect and then the admiration of the studio hacks. "He was very grateful for the tips I gave him. All through the following sixteen years that I was at his side he always was not above taking advice, yes, even asking for suggestions and ideas. He always said to me, 'Four eyes are better than two.'"

Before Griffith was given the direction of *The Adventures of Dollie*, Biograph had fallen upon evil days. The company was selling fewer than twenty prints of each subject and the management was worried. By the end of the next year, during which Griffith had directed every Biograph production—more than a hundred one-reel films—the quality of the Biographs had improved so noticeably that exhibitors were clamoring for them. The studio, and gradually the entire industry, realized that a man had arrived in their midst who knew how to make these cheap, unconvincing pictures express ideas and arouse emotion.

# CLOSE-UPS
# AND LONG SHOTS

D. W. Griffith began to experiment with radical innovations, sometimes discarding what he had done, only to return to it later. He departed from the "one scene–one shot" method by demanding a change of camera position in the middle of a scene. He moved the camera closer to the actors instead of maintaining stage distance. Biograph officials were shocked; people would think that the camera work was amateurish and the actors' legs had been cut off by mistake when Griffith had Bitzer move in closer. But audiences, pleased at being able to read the actors' thoughts in their expressions, unmistakably endorsed the new method. Despite studio opposition, in the next four years Griffith moved his camera nearer and nearer to the players. In this close approach to the action, the stereotyped gestures and "artistical attitudes" inherited from the theater were unnecessary. Moreover, for this new kind of acting, stage training was not important and could even prove a handicap. The intense light needed for close-ups grew harder and harder on the human face, and Griffith began to gather round him young boys and girls on whose round cheeks time had not yet marked a single line. Only a few of them, such as Blanche Sweet and the sixteen-year-old veteran, Mary Pickford, had had stage experience. Robert Harron had been a studio errand boy, Mabel Normand a model, and Mae Marsh a movie-struck fan.

Under Griffith's intense rehearsal, these malleable young people registered exactly the expressions he wanted from them, often without knowing the plot of the film or even the content of the scene of which they were a part. Clearly it was he, not they, who was responsible for the effect of their work. And it was equally clear, as the results of these methods became apparent, that the movie was not a speechless copy of the stage but a new and uncharted medium of expression.

When Griffith began to take close-ups not only of his actors' faces but also of objects and other details of the scene, he demonstrated that it was the "shot" and not the actor which was the basic unit of expression of the motion picture. When to the full shot and the close-up he added the extreme long shots of *Ramona,* 1910, he had completed the "long shot–mid shot–close shot" combination which remains today the classic approach to the material in any motion-picture scene. When to these discoveries he added that of a method of assembly and composition of these lengths of film taken at varying distances from the action, the basis of modern technique had been established.

*Lines of White on a Sullen Sea,* 1909, directed by Griffith for Biograph, with Linda Arvidson (Mrs. D. W. Griffith).

*The Lonedale Operator,* 1911, directed by Griffith for Biograph, with Blanche Sweet, Frank Grandon.

*Fighting Blood,* 1911, directed by Griffith for Biograph, with Blanche Sweet.

# BIOGRAPH MASTERPIECES

Long after the rise of the feature film, people remembered the "Griffith Biographs" with affection (for years they were regularly revived and became the staff of Biograph's declining days). Elderly people today, who were young enough then not to mind the social stigma that attached to attending nickelodeons, remember how exciting it was to go to the movies in those days. As, almost from week to week, Griffith introduced technical novelties and expanded and refined his narrative style, as he turned the camera on social problems, far lands, and distant epochs, seeing each successive film was a new and thrilling adventure, and to thoughtful people a thought-provoking one. When Vachel Lindsay published his *Art of the Moving Picture* in 1915, the respectable press was astonished that a poet should take the movies seriously, but the audiences of the despised nickelodeons had known for years that they were witnesses at the birth of a new experience.

By now Griffith also knew that the movie was a new form of storytelling radically unlike the traditional ones, and that few people besides himself sensed its possibilities. He began to take pride in his work and to intensify his experimentation. The type copy of his third contract with Biograph was made out to Lawrence Griffith, but "Lawrence" is altered to David in pen, and the fourth contract, signed the next year, 1911, is made out directly to David Wark Griffith. The degree of success and self-expression he had attained not only recon-

ciled him to working in motion pictures but also to admitting it.

All that now restricted the fluid narrative technique he had developed was the brevity of films. In 1911, Biograph had reluctantly permitted him to advance from the one- to the two-reel length, but beyond two reels—twenty minutes of screen time —the company refused to go. Longer films would cause eyestrain, they would weary audiences, said the lords of Biograph; what they really meant was that nickelodeon patrons could not appreciate and therefore did not deserve an improved product. But Griffith could not attain in the two-reel length the humanity and impressiveness which were now his goals, and his bitterness increased as imported

*Man's Genesis*, 1912, with Robert Harron, Mae Marsh. This "psychological study founded upon the Darwinian Theory" portrayed a Stone Age battle between "Weak-hands" and "Brute-force" which "Weak-hands" wins by inventing the ax.

*The Musketeers of Pig Alley*, 1912, with Lillian Gish. Social problems had always interested Griffith, and he turned his attention to the East Side slums in this little masterpiece, an ancestor of the gangster films of later decades.

European films of three, four, and even five reels began to appear in the United States and steal the spotlight from him. Finally he could bear his frustration no longer. He took his company to the town of Chatsworth, California, far from other movie units operating out of Los Angeles, and farther still from the Biograph home office in New York, and there in great secrecy made the four-reel spectacle film *Judith of Bethulia* in 1913. *Judith* was an early example of movie gigantism, but when Griffith returned to New York with it in triumph, he found himself not only in disgrace with the Biograph executives but also outclassed by the new flood of foreign spectacles and the sudden craze for "Famous Players in Famous Plays."

## The Fade-Out

To basic film grammar Griffith and Bitzer contributed many punctuation devices, notably the fade-out, which they hit upon by accident. Bitzer mounted a large iris diaphragm on the front of his camera, to which he had added a handle. While he was photographing, the weight of the handle gradually closed the iris, and when the shot was projected a ring of shadow blotted out the action. "This was just what we needed," Bitzer wrote. "The climax of all these films was the kiss. We couldn't linger over the embrace, for then the yokels in the audience would make catcalls. We couldn't cut abruptly—that would be crude. The fade-out gave a really dignified touch; we didn't have a five-cent movie any more."

27

The chariot race from *Quo Vadis?*, 1913.

# THE FEATURE FILM ARRIVES

The trust refused to let Griffith and other directors move toward quality and length, but nothing restrained the independents. The man who became their leader and soon a veritable trust in himself was a deceptively inconspicuous little exhibitor named Adolph Zukor, who had waited for his chance at the big time for years and took it by importing the French feature film *Queen Elizabeth,* so obviously an august and respectable production that the trust was forced to license him to show it in America. Its success was immediately followed by the even greater vogue of a colossal Italian version of *Quo Vadis?*. Actually these elaborate productions, theatrical and even operatic in technique, were technically and aesthetically far behind the one-reel American movies of the preceding five years. They were, however, initially shown in legitimate theaters on Broadway to upper-income groups who, knowing nothing of the progress of the movies in America, were impressed by their exotic air of tradition and prestige. And they abruptly awakened the magnates of the legitimate theater from their scornful indifference to the "nickel show." If imported films like these could be shown in legitimate theaters at stage prices, then the Broadway producers' own backlogs of old plays could be filmed at great profit with little trouble. For the first time the independents found a ready hearing in Broadway offices. Zukor again led the way by announcing that he was forming a corporation to produce "Famous Players in Famous Plays," beginning with James O'Neill in 1913 in his greatest success, *The Count of Monte Cristo.*

Even now, the old-line trust companies held back. They were sure the "feature fad" would be only temporary, just as they had been sure that the "movie craze" itself would not last. They would continue to make two-reelers as long as there was a demand. The dwindling market lasted about four more years—till the last of the nickelodeons ex-

28

*Quo Vadis?*, 1913. George Kleine, one of the more progressive members of the trust, imported this twelve-reel Italian spectacle which opened at the Astor Theatre on April 21, 1913. This first version of the Sienkiewicz perennial was as wooden as it was gigantic, but its "uncommon elegance" kept it running at the Astor for 22 weeks at the record admission charge of $1.50, and the following summer "road companies" were showing it throughout the United States in theaters usually devoted to stage attractions. *Quo Vadis?* proved that the movies had arrived at respectability—as long as they came from Europe and dealt with traditional subjects. Don't ask us to explain the hammer and sickle.

*Queen Elizabeth*, 1912. "This is my one chance of immortality," said Sarah Bernhardt when she made this four-reel version of one of her stage successes. The camera was hard on the aging favorite, who by now had to hobble through her scenes on a wooden leg. But she could do no wrong, and if she was willing to make pictures, then pictures must at last have become respectable. The fashionable crowd which turned out for the première of *Queen Elizabeth* at the Lyceum Theatre in July 1912 would not have been caught dead at a "five-cent movie."

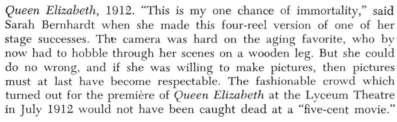

pired. By then the heads of the trust had retired, many of them millionaires in spite of themselves.

Biograph made one attempt to maintain its leadership. While continuing to produce one- and two-reelers, it also contracted with the famous theatrical firm of Klaw and Erlanger to photograph its stage successes in five reels, for summer showings in legitimate theaters across the country. D. W. Griffith naturally expected to be given the direction of this ambitious new project, but he was ordered to continue to produce two-reel films. The big Klaw and Erlanger specials would be filmed by "stage experts." "If you stay with Biograph," he was told, "it will be to make the same kind of short pictures you have in the past. You will not do that. You've got the hundred-thousand-dollar idea in the back of your head."

No, Griffith would not do that—not continue what both he and his employers had always considered hack work when at last the vision of a new art and a new public was before him. Harry Aitken, president of the Mutual Film Corporation, lured him with a contract for a thousand dollars a week, supervision of the entire product of the company, and the privilege of making two independent pictures a year. On October 1, 1913, Griffith left Biograph for Mutual.

The fate of the Biograph–Klaw and Erlanger photographed plays illustrated the results of the trust's attempt to compromise with the new era. The legitimate theaters to which they were offered for off-season showing refused to play speechless copies of dramas which they had played in past seasons in the flesh. The nickelodeons refused to pay high rentals for plays and players known only to legitimate audiences. Eventually the K. and E. productions were cut down from five reels to three and sold for what they could get in competition with the regular fare of the nickelodeons. They got little or nothing.

Lillian Gish, heroine of *The Birth of a Nation*.

Tantalizing glimpses such as this from the production location of *The Clansman* made all Hollywood wonder what

## THE FEATURE CRAZE

The picture business seethed with excitement after the success of *Quo Vadis?*. Now every ambitious young man wanted to make features. The bonds of the old trust system were burst beyond repair and the young hopefuls had their way. With little or no capital, often against the direct orders of their superiors, they somehow put together five- and six-reel pictures to which their audiences responded enthusiastically. The diehards were bewildered. The safe, sane "manufacturing" business was being transformed before their eyes into a nonesuch somewhere between art and speculation—and transformed by the public itself. No one could deny the reality of the feature craze when the stream of nickels and dimes from the store shows was joined by the torrent of quarters and dollars from Broadway.

Griffith was stung anew at being outclassed not only by the European imports but also by the bright youngsters who were making their *Traffic in Souls* and *Spoilers* and *Sea Wolves* and taking them to market. He was the prisoner of his partial success: Mutual could pay him his high salary only if he turned out pictures fast. But while he super-

vised potboilers he was marshaling his forces. Most of the Biograph stock company had followed him to Mutual, and he now made special efforts to persuade his reluctant cameraman, Billy Bitzer, to join him in his bid for fame and independence. Said Bitzer, "Among the inducements Mr. Griffith pictured to me was one in which he said, 'We will bury ourselves in hard work out at the Coast for five years and make the greatest pictures ever made, make a million dollars and retire, and then you can have all the time you want to fool around with your camera gadgets, and I shall settle down to write.' Now I thought, How can he be so sure of that when even now in the pictures we had, we never did know whether we had a bestseller until it went out?"

But Griffith in the end proved persuasive. He was on fire with an idea for the "greatest picture ever made," which, Bitzer said, "changed D. W. Griffith's personality entirely. Where heretofore he was wont to refer in starting on a new picture to 'grinding out another sausage' and go at it lightly, his attitude in beginning on this one was all eagerness. He acted like here we have something worth

Griffith was up to. Here he directs Sherman's march on Atlanta helped by G.A.R. veterans as "technical experts."

Mae Marsh, the "little pet sister" of *The Birth of a Nation*.

while. Personally I did not share his enthusiasm. I had read the book and figured that a Negro chasing a white girl was just another sausage after all and how would you show it in the South?"

The "something worth while" was the Rev. Thomas E. Dixon's *The Clansman*, which, as novel and barnstorming play, had enjoyed success for years. Griffith remembered that in 1907 he had been hired and then fired as leading man in another of the Rev. Dixon's melodramas, *The One Woman*, but the clergyman had been watching his ex-actor's career ever since *The One Woman*, and showed his confidence in him by selling the screen rights to *The Clansman* for $2,500 and 25 per cent of the profits. The two men had much in common; Southerners both, they worked harmoniously throughout the production of the film. When it was finished and shown to Dixon, he exclaimed, "It's too big to be called *The Clansman*. Let's call it *The Birth of a Nation*."

Griffith combined the plot of *The Clansman* with that of another Dixon novel, *The Leopard's Spots*, for his scenario—only there was never a scenario for this or Griffith's other important films. "He car-

ried the ideas in his head," says Lillian Gish, "or I should say in his heart. As the son of 'Roaring Jake' Griffith he firmly believed that the truth of the Civil War and Reconstruction had never been told, and he was quite ready to tell, through this new medium of the silent screen, the story he believed in above all else in the world. I am sure it seemed more real to him than the World War which was then taking place."

*The Clansman* was to be one of the two independent productions which Griffith's contract with Mutual permitted him to make. While nominally supervising Mutual productions, he was secretly arranging to hire thousands of extras, horses, costumes. As the picture grew, its size horrified his backers. Harry Aitken invested $25,000 of Mutual's money in it, but his board of directors insisted that he personally underwrite the investment. The cast and technicians chipped in, often going without salary. "Griffith reached everywhere for money," says Terry Ramsaye. "His struggles are reminiscent of Bernard Palissy, the sixteenth-century ceramic artist, burning his very home to keep the fires of his furnace going."

The Battle of Antietam, Billy Bitzer at the camera, lower left corner. Bitzer modeled his photography on the work of Matthew Brady, wheedling the Brady prints from a librarian, who parted with her precious collection for a box of chocolates. The orthochromatic film of those days aided the illusion of nineteenth-century photography.

As Lillian Gish leaves the hospital in *The Birth of a Nation*, Griffith inserted a bit in which a sentry sighs wistfully over Miss Gish's beauty as she passes. Audiences of 1915 demanded to know who the man was who played the sentry. He had been picked out of the extra ranks, and by the time Griffith sent for him he had disappeared. The sentry was identified in *Photoplay*, October 1916, as W. F. Freeman.

# THE BIRTH OF A NATION

No doubt Griffith wanted to make his battle scenes surpass in scope and spectacle all that had been shown on the screen before, but even greater was his urge to show the Civil War as his father had described it and as the whole South had cherished it in legend for three generations. The war is sketched in this film, but sketched with the sensitive selectivity, almost, of a nostalgic remembering.

The battle scenes, and the whole of *The Birth of a Nation*, were shot by only one camera and one cameraman, G. W. Bitzer. It was necessary for Bitzer to stick to his camera while lying flat on the ground when Griffith thought a shot of horses leaping directly over the camera would be a great effect. World War I had put a premium on blue-blooded horseflesh, and Griffith had to content himself with nags of lower pedigree. In his old age Bitzer wrote, "Well, nothing to do but put the camera on the ground and if they come too close maybe it would be easy to roll out of the way off to one side. Mr. Griffith, who always stood near the camera, would shoo them off somehow. After the

## The Little Colonel Returns

The returning Little Colonel (right) sees his fire-ravaged home for the first time. Women of the South tried to hide their poverty from returning menfolk by wearing "Southern ermine," made by dotting cotton with coal dust and sewing it on their old dresses. Here Henry B. Walthal detects Mae Marsh's innocent deception. The highest point of emotion in *The Birth of a Nation* "was made profound and universal," wrote Gilbert Seldes, "because the face of the principal player was not shown. . . . From behind the door, as the soldier enters, comes the arm of his mother drawing in her son with an immemorial gesture, taking to her heart his sorrows and the sorrows still to come."

leaders passed, the dust became thick, and, sensing the cameraman's danger, Mr. Griffith rushed wildly in, waving his arms and yelling madly, thus preventing all but one of the horses from smashing into the camera on the ground, not, however, before he had kicked in the side of the wooden camera. It was soon repaired with some tape and we were taking another run.

"Just the same, there were times when I wished that Mr. Griffith didn't depend on me so much, especially in battle scenes. The fireworks men shooting smoke bombs over the camera—most of them exploding outside camera range—and D. W. shouting, 'Lower, lower, can't you shoot those damn bombs lower?' 'We'll hit the cameraman if we do,' answered the fireworks brigade, and bang! one of them whizzed past my ear. The next one may have gone between my legs for all I knew. But the bombs were coming into the camera field so it was okay. As I write this, looking at my hand, it still shows the blue powder specks from the battlefield of *The Birth of a Nation*."

A rather jocose Lincoln (Joseph Henabery) tells club-footed Austin Stoneman (Ralph Lewis) that he will not treat the Confederacy as a conquered province. Though he appears in relatively few scenes, Lincoln is an important figure in *The Birth of a Nation,* especially important to the fabric of Southern belief which it expresses. When the news of his assassination reaches Cameron Hall, Col. Cameron sadly exclaims: "The South has lost its best friend!" the implication being that had he lived the Confederate states would have been allowed to resume their former position in the Union. The blame for the evils of Reconstruction Griffith placed on Senator Charles Sumner of Massachusetts and the leader of the Republican radicals, Thaddeus Stevens. Both men were powerfully concerned lest the Republican party lose power if the white South was at once allowed to send representatives to Congress. But neither profited from Reconstruction or personally participated in its administration. Stevens died before the full force of the Reconstruction Acts could be felt. But the Hon. Austin Stoneman who is Stevens in *The Birth of a Nation* visits South Carolina to enjoy to the full the triumph of his policies and lives to witness their consequences.

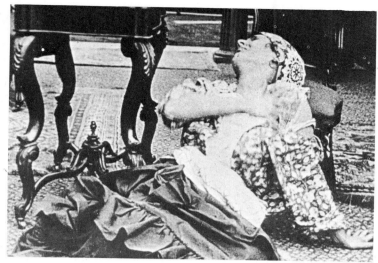

The real Thaddeus Stevens lived for years with a Negro woman, but in spite of his equalitarian ideas never married her because this would have excluded him from Washington society. Austin Stoneman in *The Birth of a Nation* has a mulatto housekeeper who is, by implication, his mistress. Stevens' personal relationship with Negroes obviously seemed more important to Dixon and Griffith than his political affiliations. To Southerners like these two, sex, not economics, lay at the core of the race question. Their horror of miscegenation made it impossible for them to believe that Sumner and Stevens acted from moral motives, and they therefore believed them to be monsters of hypocrisy. Early in the film, Senator Sumner (who is given his real name in the picture) calls on Stoneman. The mulatto housekeeper, who opens the door, hopes that the Senator will treat her as an equal, but he snubs her roundly and passes to the next room where Stoneman is announcing his plans to make his protégé, Silas Lynch, governor of South Carolina, and says he will "crush the white South under the heel of the black South." When Sumner comes out and asks for his hat, the housekeeper haughtily drops it on the floor (above), forcing Sumner to stoop for it. After he leaves, the housekeeper tears her bodice to ribbons and disarranges her hair. The following scene (right) is without subtitles but seems to mean that the disheveled housekeeper convinces Stoneman that Sumner tried to rape her.

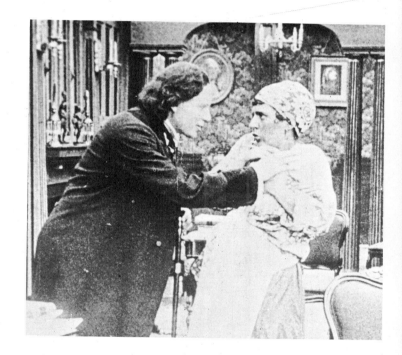

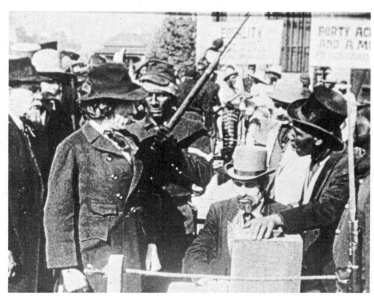

Col. Cameron is turned from the polls by Negro soldiers and white carpetbaggers. The Negroes—except the few who remain loyal to their recent owners—are shown as apelike morons, both foolish and vicious.

The Little Colonel (Henry B. Walthal) refuses the handshake of the mulatto Silas Lynch (George Siegmann), while Austin Stoneman and his daughter (Lillian Gish) look on enraged.

The Rise and Fall of Free Speech in America
by David Wark Griffith

*This copy is for*

# THE IMPACT OF THE BIRTH OF A NATION

*The Birth of a Nation* opened at the Liberty Theatre in New York on March 3, 1915, at $2 admission. The sensation it created was without precedent and has never been duplicated. People had not known that they could be so moved, so roused, by what is, after all, only a succession of pictures passing across a screen. Everything depends, they discovered, on the order and the manner of that passing. All that Griffith had been striving for in the six years since he had begun directing at Biograph was now actual achievement; almost single-handed he had created a new art form, independent of the spoken word. His picture went on to a success whose dimensions can never be accurately calculated, since Griffith and his backers sold distribution rights to small companies here and abroad for a flat fee rather than a rental or royalty. Even on this unbusiness-like basis, it had by 1939 grossed for its owners $18,000,000 and netted $5,000,000, and it has continued to be shown intermittently ever since. Its initial earnings rocked Wall Street, evoked a press

## A PLEA FOR THE ART OF THE MOTION PICTURE

We do not fear censorship, for we have no wish to offend with improprieties or obscenities, but we do demand, as a right, the liberty to show the dark side of wrong, that we may illuminate the bright side of virtue—the same liberty that is conceded to the art of the written word—that art to which we owe the Bible and the works of Shakespeare.

In an effort to stem the rising tide of protest, Griffith inserted this plea as a foreword to the film and published a pamphlet (top), a quaint but not ineffective defense of the screen's right to deal with controversial subjects.

The Ku Klux Klan threatens death to the would-be rapist of Flora, sister of the Little Colonel (right). Triumph of the Klan (far right). Lillian Gish and Miriam Cooper lead the procession after their rescue from Silas Lynch and his Negroes. Griffith portrayed the Little Colonel as the inventor of the Ku Klux Klan, in a scene which emphasized the power of white sheets over the imagination of Negroes. *The Birth of a Nation* movingly revealed the extent of the white South's allegiance to the Klan, which at its height had more than 700,000 members. As a result, the revived Ku Klux Klan of 1915-27 continually claimed Griffith's approval and sought his active support.

interest which the movies had never before been able to attract, and brought comment even from governmental figures. After it was shown at the White House, the first movie ever to be screened there, President Wilson was said to have commented, "It is like writing history with lightning, and my one regret is that it is all so terribly true."

This quote was important to Griffith. He had poured into *The Birth of a Nation* all that he believed and had been taught about the South's degradation and humiliation in the Reconstruction period—a period which had seen the collapse of his own family's fortunes. He felt impelled to bear witness, to tell the North and the world of the sorrows that had been brought upon his land and his people in a period which coincided with his own childhood. Yet he wished to be fair. He would document his charges. He culled from Woodrow Wilson's American histories and those of others actual incidents of Reconstruction days which supported the dark story he told. That there was another side to that story he would not or could not admit. He expressed bewilderment at the storms of protest it evoked when Negroes and the friends of Negroes realized what this much-discussed film was saying about them.

A storm it was. The mildest comment was George Foster Peabody's "It distressed me to see such exceptional ability of organization directed into the wrong channels," and the shrewdest, A. E. Pillsbury's "It gambles on the public ignorance of our own history." Judge Braithwaite charged, "It is not only the hate of the South against the Negro but against the North. It is shown in the figure of Sumner." The elderly Moorfield Storey, who had been Sumner's secretary in his youth, calmly pointed to the chronological inaccuracies of the film: "The Ku Klux Klan had really run its course before the colored voters exercised any substantial power," and continued more cholerically, "Unless the only immorality is sexual immorality, this play tends to corrupt public morals and should be suppressed, as it certainly would be if instead of libeling the weakest among our fellow citizens, it were in like manner to attack a body of great political strength." In view of all this, the White House hastened to disavow its accolade.

It remained for President Charles W. Eliot of Harvard to express the ultimate in remote-control judgment: "I have not seen this play, [but] I want to say that it presents an extraordinary misrepresentation of the birth of this nation."

# Demand Walsh Stop 'Birth of

## AFTER CONFERENCE WITH THE GOVERNOR IT IS ANNOUNCED PRODUCERS WILL BE PROSECUTED.

As a result of a protest made at the State House today by a crowd of more than 1,000 negroes, Governor Walsh and a ...ittee of the protesting peo-

The colored delegations began to ar-ive singly and in groups from all points of the compass an hour ...arlier. It was hot in the sun, but they stood close. Women and chil-ren squatted on the stone steps. They were good-natured, but terribly n earnest. They talked about Satur-ay night's trouble and the ringing ...entiments expounded by th...
...ht in the...

**BIG MEETING IN HUB**

**Protest Of Negroes**

ACCOUNT OF THE E

DELIBERATE PLOT

Negroes Deny It—Mini... Was Struck When F Speak to Crowd.

As a racial demonstration

For weeks before *The Birth of a Nation* opened in Boston, mysterious rumors spread about the film, and after it was first shown crowds stormed the theater and the Boston State House to get the performances stopped. The Rev. Thomas Dixon

*The Mother and the Law*, 1914. Before *The Birth of a Nation* was released Griffith had begun a new film attacking factory owners who pose as philanthropists but who subtract their benefactions from the wages of the workers.

## GRIFFITH'S ANSWER

Observing from afar the tumult over *The Birth of a Nation*, Booker T. Washington remarked, "The managers of this play encourage and even skillfully initiate opposition on account of the advertising the play receives when attempts are made to stop it." That was the dilemma of the liberal leaders who deplored the film. Most of them were against any attempt to censor it. They were content to attack it —but their attacks only brought it greater notoriety and patronage. Moreover, they were aware that the South *had* suffered wrongs in Reconstruction, that there was wrong and right on both sides, and that for the good of the nation the best comment on the whole episode was a healing silence. Jane Addams and Lillian Wald in a joint statement said that the picture was made at a time "too near the period it depicts to be given without danger of inciting hate, hostility, prejudice, and sectionalism." Albert Bigelow Paine, the biographer of Wilson and

Nation'

the crowd that filled steps of the State House today in protest to Governor Walsh against photoplay "The Birth of a Nation."

## PICTURE FILM CAUSES RI[

Negroes Storm Boston P[
house In Effort to Gain
mission to See Pictures.

Big Protest Meeting Held L[
er and Matter Is To
Taken to the Governor,

BOSTON, APRIL 19—The Tre[
theatre was stormed by hundreds o[
groes Saturday night in an effort to[
admission to the performance of the[
toplay, "The Birth of a Nation[
on "The Clansman," by Thomas [
over which there had been much pr[
because of the alleged unfavorable r[
sentations of the negroes in the S[
immediately after the war. Admi[
was refused all negroes and there en[
a melee during which 60 plain cl[
men, assisted the 200 officers in uni[
in keeping control of the situation.[
negroes were arrested, among them,[
liam Munroe Trotter, secretary of th[
tional equal rights league and edit[
The Guardian.

As the result of this near riot, a[
meeting of more than 2000 negroe[
Greater Boston, together with 250 [
persons, was held in Faneuil hall y[
day afternoon as a demonstration of[
test against the continued exhibiti[
the film. Good order prevailed d[
the meeting and the police officers[
ent as a precautionary measure had[
...d... ...ointed to [
...and [

**Pastor Tells Story.**

Rev Aaron W. Puller, pasto[
People's Baptist church, South [
seen at his home Saturday night[

"I regret the whole situation v[
After visiting Mayor Curley at [
yesterday I concluded not to [
...s-meeting on the[
...that it might s[

tion was sufficient to keep order as far as
we know.

"The management regrets that this incident has occurred, but feels that the men
and women engaged in this attempt
to destroy property and disturb the
performance are not representative of
the colored people of Boston. That there
was no serious damage to property and
perhaps injury to patrons we lay entirely
...th the efficient [

**Orators on the Common.**

Crowds numbering several hundred,
among whom were many colored people,
collected several times during the evening
on the common opposite the theater and
listened to orations from various colored
leaders. Here is a sample speech by W.
H. Whaley, ...lored lawyer.
of N...

was on hand for the occasion and observed, "The silly legal opposition they are giving will make me a millionaire if they keep it up. . . . [We knew] that if we could get it by in Boston we would be able to go anywhere else in the country."

Taft, and, incidentally, of Lillian Gish, remarked, with an historian's faint distaste, "It is within the facts, but it is not within the proprieties."

Griffith himself remained bewildered, if perhaps secretly delighted, at the vituperation poured on the head of a man previously unknown to the national leaders who now pronounced him the devil's advocate. He protested that he loved the Negro. The Negroes replied that they did not want his love if they had to take *The Birth of a Nation* with it. Unskilled in controversy, Griffith was easily worsted in the newspaper battles. Perhaps he sensed that he was in danger of making himself ridiculous as well as of making enemies in high places. But his sense of injury remained. If he could not successfully answer his critics through the press and pamphleteering, he would turn to the medium of which even his critics acknowledged him the master.

Griffith barred all visitors from the sets of *The Mother and the Law*. As the walls of Babylon began to tower over Sunset Boulevard, Hollywood marveled: what could they have to do with a modern story about industrial unrest?

39

# INTOLERANCE

What had loomed over the bungalows of Sunset Boulevard was the
palace of Belshazzar, King of Babylon, setting for the Feast of Belshazzar on the eve of Cyrus of
Persia's conquest of the city. Griffith's opulent and untutored imagination festooned this vast set with
Egyptian bas-reliefs and Hindu elephant gods as well as Babylonian
bearded bulls. To take it all in, he
sent Bitzer and his camera aloft in
a captive balloon, slowly drawn
back to earth in the first equivalent
of the modern crane shot. Until
Douglas Fairbanks' castle set for
*Robin Hood* in 1922, it remained
the largest backdrop for a movie
scene, and neither has ever been
topped.

The attacks on *The Birth of a
Nation* had resolved Griffith to turn
*The Mother and the Law* into an
epic sermon, a mighty purge for
hypocrisy through the ages, called
*Intolerance*. The slums of today,
Renaissance France, Belshazzar's
Babylon, and the Crucifixion itself
should all speak of man's inhuman-
ity to man in the name of virtue.
Hollywood was awed as Griffith
flung up halls in which men looked
like flies, walls on which an army
could march. Extras were hired in
regiments. When Griffith's backers
faltered, he bought them out with
long-term notes which he did not
finish paying off until the early
Twenties. The picture reached a
length of 400 reels, with no end in
sight, but Griffith went grimly on.
"If I approach success in what I
am trying to do in my coming picture," he said, "I expect an even
greater persecution than that which
met *The Birth of a Nation*."

The Modern story. Robert Harron gives the eye to Miriam Cooper, moll of gangster Walter Long.

The Babylonian story. Seena Owen as the Princess Beloved; Alfred Paget as Belshazzar.

The French story. Margery Wilson, today's teacher of charm by mail, and Eugene Pallette.

The Nazarene story. Howard Gaye as Jesus, Erich von Stroheim as the shorter of the two Pharisees.

# "THE ONLY FILM FUGUE"

In adding three more stories to that of *The Mother and the Law* to make up the film *Intolerance*, Griffith, as *Variety* said, departed "from all previous forms of legitimate or film construction. . . ." In *Pippa Passes*, *Judith of Bethulia*, and *Home Sweet Home* he had made four-part films. Now the attraction he felt for this form led him to attempt something entirely new. He told all four stories simultaneously, uniting them by the constantly repeated shot of Lillian Gish rocking a cradle, an image derived from Walt Whitman's "Out of the cradle, endlessly rocking." In Griffith's own words: "The stories begin like four currents looked at from a hilltop. At first the four currents flow apart, slowly and quietly. But as they flow, they grow nearer and nearer together, and faster and faster, until in the end, in the last act, they mingle in one mighty river of expressed emotion."

As such, *Intolerance* is, in Terry Ramsaye's words, "the only film fugue," and as such it entirely failed to win public favor. In spite of the splendor of its spectacle, in spite of its incredible cast—among those who played minor roles were Constance Talmadge, Monte Blue, Bessie Love, Alma Rubens, Carmel Myers, Colleen Moore, Carol Dempster, and Douglas Fairbanks—audiences were cold to it. Two years after its release, Griffith, realizing the inevitable, released the modern and Babylonian episodes as two separate films, but even their receipts did relatively little to relieve him of the burden of debt with which *Intolerance* had saddled him.

Many reasons have been advanced for the failure of this great and unique film. The commonest and most probable is that audiences found it simply too overwhelming, that they could not follow, or become emotionally involved in, these stories which wove in and out of one another with such awesome speed. It has also been suggested that the pacifism which was a leading motif of *Intolerance* was hardly the note to strike in a year when America was preparing to enter World War I.

No one has ever imitated the formal idea on which *Intolerance* was based, but its spectacle has been in Cecil B. De Mille's mind ever since, and but for it Eisenstein might never have made *Potemkin*, Chaplin *The Gold Rush*, or Von Stroheim *Greed*. Equivocal, inconclusive, naïve, *Intolerance* yet marks the furthest advance of screen art.

". . . Out of the cradle, endlessly rocking, uniter of here and hereafter . . ." Lillian Gish as the Woman Who Rocks the Cradle.

Babylon's war engines make a sally through the great gate of Bel.

The Princess Beloved sends a love-message to Belshazzar, all of two feet away, in a little cart drawn by doves.

# THE MASTER

Between 1909 and 1916, David Wark Griffith created the art of screen narrative almost single-handed. After *Intolerance*, there was no significant addition to film syntax until the advent of sound and of the wide screen, both mechanical rather than artistic innovations, although of course they affect the art. Acknowledging his influence, Cecil B. De Mille recently said that there is something of Griffith in every film made since his day. His contemporaries regarded him with awe, called him "The Master," and predicted an unlimited future for him after what was thought of as the temporary and accidental failure of *Intolerance*. Yet this "enigmatic and somewhat tragic figure" never fully succeeded in delivering what he had to say through the medium of which he was the virtual creator. His dream of picturing a vast screen mosaic of the American and French revolutions and the birth of modern liberty was incompletely realized; neither *Orphans of the Storm*, 1922, nor *America*, 1924, achieved the impact of *The Birth of a Nation*.

Beset by financial troubles, he was forced to turn out potboilers which boiled the pot less and less frequently. His last important film, the little masterpiece *Isn't Life Wonderful?*, 1924, revealed the source of his difficulties. The incisive realism of this study of the effects of economic inflation in Germany had small appeal to a nation hell-bent on pleasure. The 1920s, engrossed in a sort of witch hunt against everything "Victorian," regarded Griffith suddenly as dated. Why did he insist on filming social problems, why was he so obsessed with "patriotic" themes at a time when patriotism was all but a dirty word? Hard pressed for money, Griffith tried to obey his critics, but his attempts at Jazz Age films seemed the fumbling efforts of an amateur compared to the work of De Mille and his disciples. Though still nominally the dean of his profession, Griffith in the later Twenties was given the sort of respect we accord the dead.

His revenge is Time's. As fashion follows fashion with ever-accelerating speed, as the films of the Twenties and Thirties begin to look flat and superficial, Griffith's greatness emerges. His faults—flowery language, black-and-white morality, naïve cultural pretensions—we no longer judge by today's standards. Now they belong to the past, to a period in which their romanticism is appropriate. Now we can see beyond them to the profound humanity of Griffith's films—see also what we have meantime lost, a direct, naked, firsthand approach to character, psychology, and emotion. Griffith's camera searched the human countenance for "the motions of the spirit" itself.

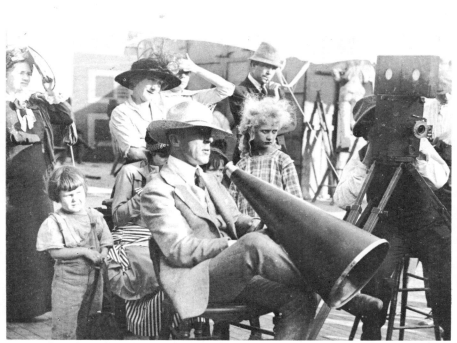

The informality of early film-making encouraged casual droppers-in. The boy to Griffith's right is Ben Alexander, co-star of the Fifties TV series "Dragnet."

D. W. Griffith demonstrates to Walter Long the correct way to strangle Miriam Cooper.

The master at the helm. In suede-top shoes and coolie hat he directs a scene for *Intolerance*, while Bitzer peers through the camera.

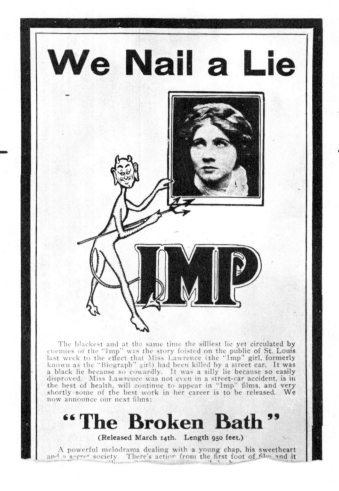

# We Nail a Lie

**IMP**

The blackest and at the same time the silliest lie yet circulated by enemies of the "Imp" was the story foisted on the public of St. Louis last week to the effect that Miss Lawrence (the "Imp" girl, formerly known as the "Biograph" girl) had been killed by a street car. It was a black lie because so cowardly. It was a silly lie because so easily disproved. Miss Lawrence was not even in a street-car accident, is in the best of health, will continue to appear in "Imp" films, and very shortly some of the best work in her career is to be released. We now announce our next films:

## "The Broken Bath"

(Released March 14th.   Length 950 feet.)

A powerful melodrama dealing with a young chap, his sweetheart and a secret society. There's action from the first foot of film and it

Florence Lawrence

# THE STAR SYSTEM

Early in 1910 Carl Laemmle electrified the industry, as was his regular custom, by publishing this advertisement (left) in the *Moving Picture World*. It purported to answer a story published in the St. Louis newspapers to the effect that Florence Lawrence, known to nickelodeon fans as the "Biograph girl," had been killed in a streetcar accident. Laemmle denounced the story as a vile slander designed by the film trust to camouflage the fact that Miss Lawrence had left Biograph's bed and board for the more uplifting surroundings of Laemmle's own company. Actually, Laemmle had planted the original story himself and his "reply" to it was designed solely to dramatize the fact that he had lured the then most popular personality in motion pictures away from her original employers: the "Biograph girl" had become the "Imp girl."

Laemmle's ad was only a minor incident in his energetic campaign to demoralize the General Film Company and blacken its name with exhibitors, but his coup portended much. The trust had refused to give out the names of its players, partly because it wished to standardize the business of film manufacture as much as possible, and partly because it rightly feared that players grown famous would also be players grown costly. But the public refused to be frustrated. When no answers came to floods of letters demanding to be told the names of favorite players, nickelodeon patrons took to such nicknames as the "Biograph girl," "the little girl

# THE
# FORMATIVE
# YEARS

with the golden curls," and so forth. (In Britain, nickelodeon operators cheerfully satisfied the curiosity of fans by making up names for American actors: Mabel Normand was known there as "Muriel Fortescue.")

As soon as the independents realized that the public disliked the trust's policy of refusing to give out the names of players, they promptly publicized the names of their own, and in doing so lured valuable actors, eager for recognition and money, away from the trust, which was finally forced to reverse itself, disclose the identity of its stars, and pay them better.

The phenomenon of star worship among stage-struck youths and maidens was not unfamiliar to the entertainment world, but now, for the first time, millions of men, women, and children lovingly discussed film players as though they were members of their own families. From then on, not acting ability or even altogether looks, but something indefinable and uniquely cinematic called "personality" became the key to success. On the day Miss Lawrence moved her make-up kit from Biograph to Imp, the star's salary became the most important single item in the budgets of most pictures.

Since the star system was the public's own creation, the first stars were players who had stood out from the anonymous ranks of the original studio "stock companies." Comparatively few had stage experience. Other qualifications were more important. Besides youth, they had to have a considerable degree of intelligence, adaptability, and stamina. The breakneck manufacture and release of two one-reel pictures every week required that they be able to play heroines one day, and maids, dowagers, or vamps the next. But most important was a strong and well-defined personality. Invariably what made them stars was some physical attribute or personal mannerism—John Bunny's jovial bulk, Mary Pickford's golden curls and sweet smile, Maurice Costello's urbanity, Clara Kimball Young's yearning eyes.

What mattered was the possession of some quality, not always at first glance the most conspicuous quality, which people could identify with or admire. The making of a movie star turned out to be a process of spotting this quality and bringing it to the fore, and it mattered little what the quality was: beauty, docility, menace, even ordinariness. The process is still followed. What Alistair Cooke wrote in 1940 about the making of a screen personality was true at the beginning and is still true:

"The most profitable screen heroine that a studio can create . . . is a heroine whose beauty is so overwhelming that it allows her own character never to come into play and therefore never to be called in question. We do not fret over the lack of social purpose, charity, humor, or anything else in such perfections of the type as Greta Garbo, Hedy Lamarr, Marlene Dietrich. But nothing is so irritating as the mildly pretty blonde whose beauty is barely acceptable in the first few feet of film and who subsequently has no other charm to offer. Those who fall between these extremes are the majority of stars who combine good looks and certain typical whimsicalities or personal traits of humor, temper, sarcasm—some single quality that is entertaining because it is effective to dramatize. Most movie-goers seem to prefer this compromise formula as a steady diet, probably because it offers superior beauty to any they are personally familiar with, but is at the same time linked up—by the chosen personality characteristic—with a life they know. Thus Jean Arthur's husky downrightness and loyalty, Claudette Colbert's tongue-in-cheek, Carole Lombard's air of honest-to-goodness exasperation, Ginger Rogers' natural acceptance of hard facts: these are the individual characteristics of current favorites who were all originally consigned to a career of solemn prettiness."

47

Constance Talmadge before she joined the Griffith company.

Norma Talmadge as a teen-age leading lady at Vitagraph.

Maurice Costello, balding and graying father of Helene and Dolores Costello, was a movie matinee idol from 1910 to 1917. In contrast to their juvenile leading ladies, male stars of the early period were often on the mature side.

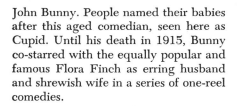

John Bunny. People named their babies after this aged comedian, seen here as Cupid. Until his death in 1915, Bunny co-starred with the equally popular and famous Flora Finch as erring husband and shrewish wife in a series of one-reel comedies.

Francis X. Bushman and Beverly Bayne, the first screen "love team," kept their marriage secret lest it deflate the illusions of their fans. (*Romeo and Juliet,* 1916)

Bessie Barriscale, seen here with Rosetta Maristini, alternately played sweet maidens and sultry vamps.

Charles Ray, perennial hick of scores of Thomas H. Ince's rural dramas. (*String Beans,* 1919)

# FAMOUS PLAYERS IN FAMOUS PLAYS

Those early movie mimes who were also professional stage actors welcomed the anonymity imposed by the trust. To work in pictures was to belong to the theatrical underworld, and no one wanted it known that poverty or unsuccess had forced him to this shabby expedient. But when the public craze for picture personalities brought fame and fortune to former prison guards, hat-check girls, and sandhogs, the prima donnas of Broadway suddenly changed their tune. After all, Adolph Zukor had already imported Sarah Bernhardt in *Queen Elizabeth,* and if the owner of the world's most golden voice was willing to act in silence, it must be acceptable for mere American stars to do like-

The famed Mrs. Leslie Carter brought her production of *Du Barry* to the screen exactly as it was produced on the stage —only without voices.

wise. Besides, William A. Brady and Dan Frohman had lent their names to the Zukor enterprise, and David Belasco was permitting the filming of his backlog of stage successes by Famous Players. When Geraldine Farrar signed with Samuel Goldwyn at $10,000 a week, the gold rush was on. Writers dreamed of selling their old turkeys and rejects for fabulous sums; stars saw themselves earning big money for work that would be, really, little more than a summer vacation in California. Pictures were still "Galloping Tintypes" to Broadway, a butt for jokes and nothing but the thinnest kind of substitute for the "legitimate" theater—but who could resist so much easy money?

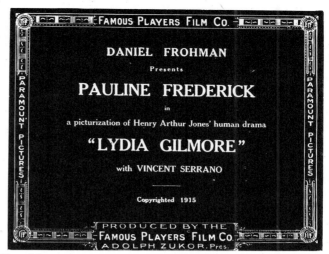

To add tone to his "Famous Players in Famous Plays" idea, Adolph Zukor got Daniel Frohman to "present" his "picturizations" of stage dramas.

To enhance the connection between his film version of *A Good Little Devil* and the original stage production, Zukor introduced the film with a scene showing the author, David Belasco, seated in his study pondering the play, while the ghosts of the characters he is creating appear in double exposure. Mary Pickford and Ernest Truex are materializing at the right.

"Watching director Arthur Hopkins trying to knead Maxine Elliott's beautiful face into the semblance of an expression" afforded amusement during the making of *The Eternal Magdalene* at the Goldwyn studio in 1918.

Zukor's first American presentation under the Famous Players banner was a stagey production with a corpulent James O'Neill of *The Count of Monte Cristo,* 1913.

# FAMOUS PLAYERS --
# THE FLOPS

Mrs. Fiske's fascinating, sinister stage performance as Becky Sharp became, in the movie *Vanity Fair*, 1915, a distressing example of an elderly lady being kittenish.

Mary Garden's operatic hauteur lent small conviction to her role as an abandoned minx in *The Splendid Sinner*, 1918.

Movie producers, conscious of their own humble origins and relative inexperience, were sure that the newcomers from Broadway would sweep the field. Even the picture players did not think they could stand "genuine" professional competition and apprehensively awaited eclipse. Nothing of the sort happened. On the stage, beauty and drama are created by suggestion, illusion; but the intimacy of the camera demands the genuine article. Deprived of their vocal assets, the stage players fell back on a pantomimic technique designed to be visible to the last row of the theater balcony but which, magnified on the screen, appeared dangerously close to caricature—and no one dared suggest to the distinguished performers that their methods might be modified. But when movie extra Monte Blue was called upon to double for Sir Herbert Beerbohm-Tree, when the ankles of a film pretty were substituted, in close-up, for the piano legs of a stage lady, the original picture people took heart. And when the first "Famous Players in Famous Plays" were released, the wave of rumor and surmise which had been seeping through the studios was fully confirmed. They were catastrophic flops. The movie public wanted no part of these aging hams. It wanted the favorites it had chosen for itself.

The case of Mary Garden is typical. Miss Garden followed her rival, Geraldine Farrar, to the Goldwyn studio at $10,000 a week for two pictures. The first, naturally, was to be a "picturization" of her greatest operatic success, *Thaïs*. As the picture had no other reason for being than its star, it consisted of little more than a series of shots of Miss Garden in the statuesque poses of opera tradition and, as a result, was a close approach to a motionless motion picture. The movie public scorned this cold stranger, trying to vamp like their Theda Bara. It was decided that for her second picture a "modern" story might put Miss Garden over more successfully. But *The Splendid Sinner* was modern only in the details of its costume and décor. The story had Miss Garden a Parisian wanton who leaped upon a table and madly played the violin to the rich moths clustered around the flame of her sex appeal. Such abandon could not go on and leave her "sympathetic" in the finale, so she atoned as a Red Cross nurse in a uniform which fitted her as snugly as cunning could contrive. But Nurse's intellectual face did not agree with the sweet compassion written into the subtitles, and Mr. Goldwyn and his backers had another load of grief on their hands.

Pauline Frederick's eloquent face and intelligent acting made her a favorite with mature and discriminating audiences long after she had passed her first youth.

## FAMOUS PLAYERS -- THE SUCCESSES

A few of the stage invaders made a permanent place for themselves on the screen. Those who did so made the grade because they threw themselves into the new, raw business of making pictures with the same zest as the humbler movie pioneers. Behind "Madam Geraldine Farrar of the Metropolitan Opera" was a vital American beauty who looked upon each new opportunity as a challenge. The studio employees who expected an icy diva were confronted instead with an eager movie actress who would face physical danger for the good of the picture, who asked innumerable questions about the camera, and herself figured out her own best "angles." Pauline Frederick was if anything more effective on screen than on stage. Her ability to project emotion with her eyes, her hands, even the set of her shoulders, made her one of the great movie actresses. Alla Nazimova, from the Crimea via Broadway, had definite theories about acting for the silent camera. She thought it comparable to the ballet. Her stylized acting and exotic beauty earned her considerable popularity until she insisted on producing, with her own money, such highbrow plays as *A Doll's House* and *Salome*. All who survived the camera test did so not because of their skill and experience but because they had sharply defined screen personalities.

Charles Ray and Frank Keenan in *The Coward,* 1915. Keenan was too old to simulate youth when he came from Broadway and found a place as a character player.

Lew Cody and Fannie Ward in *Our Better Selves,* 1919. Miss Ward's ageless beauty withstood harsh movie lighting even though she was well advanced in years.

Two brothers, William and Dustin Farnum, and their unrelated namesake, Franklyn Farnum, had played romantic costume roles on the stage. They switched to the screen by donning movie cowboy clothes.

Geraldine Farrar and Wallace Reid in Cecil B. De Mille's *Carmen*, 1915.

Alla Nazimova and Henry Kolker in *Billions*, 1920. Nazimova's "bizarre" beauty made her the popular stereotype of Continental sophistication as long as she restrained her yearning for the higher things of life.

America's Sweetheart—she really was. But this unsmiling early photograph shows a Mary the public never knew.

# "LITTLE MARY"

For twenty-three years, Mary Pickford was the undisputed queen of the screen. For fourteen of these years she was the most popular woman in the world. She was literally what she was billed: America's Sweetheart.

Why? It becomes increasingly difficult to answer the question. How far we have come from an instinctive understanding of her appeal is indicated by Alistair Cooke's remark that Miss Pickford was "the girl every young man wanted to have—for his sister." She was not. She was the girl every man wanted to have, or wished he'd had, for himself. On the screen her prettiness was often disfigured by a smudged face, tattered dresses, and pigtails, for she mostly played children—or, rather, girls in that misty mid-region between sexless childhood and buxom womanliness which seems to have had a strong and specific appeal to many American males of the early century. To hold her lead, she always had to play Little Mary, a girl on the verge of puberty, innocent to the point of idiocy of any acquaintance with the facts of life. Yet always hovering in the wings was a male admirer, frequently elderly (her biggest hits included *Daddy Long Legs* and *Poor Little Rich Girl*), and the implication dangled that someday, beyond the final fade-out, perhaps . . .

What was it that set Miss Pickford apart from all her contemporaries, imitators, and competitors? The answer can only be a guess. But her sweetness and light were tempered by a certain realism. Inevitably she played that almost-forgotten character, Pollyanna—but played her not so much saccharinely as vigorously. In spite of her creed, the Glad Girl knew that it was no cinch to make everything come out right. Nothing could have been more in tune with an era which combined limitless optimism with a belief that what was called "git up and git" was necessary to make optimism come true.

The real Mary Pickford had put git up and git before optimism. Born Gladys Smith, she was drilled by her mother in the knowledge that the little family's future depended on the professional exploitation of her good looks. The results of such experiences, so young, are indicated by a conference between the star and Adolph Zukor, after two years' work for him had demonstrated her supremacy at the boxoffice. "You know, Mr. Zukor," she said, "for years I've dreamed of making $20,000 a year before I was twenty. And I'll be twenty very soon now." Zukor learned to recognize this approach. Before long he was paying her $100,000 a year, then half a million. She knew, and he knew that she knew, that he needed her pictures as a bait to lure exhibitors into booking his less desirable features and to establish and consolidate his company's position at the top of the heap. The clincher in her successful bids for more and more money was always that she was worth it.

Finally came the moment when she asked for more than even she was worth. To get it, she was banking on her knowledge that Zukor dared not lose her to his competitors. His last-ditch stratagem to eliminate her as a factor in his war with them was described by an intimately concerned onlooker, William C. de Mille:

"With compassionate eye and throbbing voice, Mr. Zukor told Mary that she was tired, that she had been working much too hard for many years and needed a long rest. No line must ever be allowed to mar her beautiful face, nor should that face ever appear on any screen save Paramount's. Just think what Mary and Paramount had meant to each other these last few years! The thought of her going to another company, where perhaps she would not be so well loved, hurt the kindly Mr. Zukor in his deepest and most sensitive feelings. So, just for friendship and *auld lang syne*, he would give her one thousand dollars every week for five years on condition that she would take a complete rest during that period and not bother her pretty little head about pictures at all.

"Mary's large, soulful, and expensive eyes opened wide as she regarded her generous benefactor with feeling. She was much touched and deeply moved. If the thought occurred to her that, from Paramount's point of view, it was well worth $260,000 to eliminate her for five years as a competitor, she brushed it aside as unworthy. She, too, knew what friendship meant, and her affection for dear, considerate Mr. Zukor was fully as deep as his for her. But, after all, she was only a young girl just on the threshold of what might prove to be a successful career. She was a little tired, perhaps, but not quite tired enough to take a five-year vacation, at the end of which she would undoubtedly be five years older.

"Timidly, in her innocent, childlike way, she explained all this to the man who was so anxious to protect her from the hard life of professional exertion. Tempting as his offer was, she would rather work for $675,000 per annum than rest for $52,000. It desolated her to think of leaving Paramount, where she had been so happy and contented, but, after all, duty was a much nobler goal than mere happiness; so unless Mr. Zukor could see his way clear to meet these terms . . . The poor child could say no more; she was a young artist and they kept forcing her to talk about money."

Nine members of Fred Karno's London troupe, with their wives and children, shortly before their departure for America. The young man, third from the left, with the arrow pointing to his straw hat, is Charles Chaplin. The other arrow points to the youthful Stan Laurel.

Charlie Chaplin in *The Tramp,* 1915.

## "THE LITTLE FELLOW"

They were dreadfully poor. Charlie's parents were third-string strolling players. His father died early of alcoholism; his mother was often in asylums, either through drink or because of periodic mental illness. Whenever this happened, Charlie and his brothers had to shift for themselves on the streets of London. Robert Flaherty used to tell the story of one of these times: "It was a rainy winter night. Charlie, who was about eleven, had no place to sleep and was sheltering under an overhanging roof. A solid-looking man came by, took a look at the boy, and asked him what he was doing there. Charlie told his story. The man stroked his chin for a moment and said, 'Well, I've a bit to eat at my place. I've only one room, but you're welcome to stay the night if you don't mind sleeping on the floor.' They went to the man's furnished room, where Charlie slept on a pallet at the foot of his host's bed. Next morning when he woke, the man had gone, but Charlie found a note saying, 'If you've no place to sleep tonight, come here.' Charlie had to avail himself of his friend's help for many nights, but always in the morning the man had gone to his work. Charlie became curious about what that work might be. One morning he managed to wake early. The man was taking out of the closet and measuring in his hands a long, strong rope with a noose at the end of it. He was the common hangman."

Out of such experiences came the greatest comedian in the world. Chaplin came to America in 1913 with Fred Karno's "A Night in an English Music Hall" troupe. One of Mack Sennett's backers saw him, signed him to a contract at $150 a week, and shipped him west to the Sennett studio. It seemed at first that the studio had gained just another show-wise vaudevillian. But before the end of his first year with Sennett, the figure of "Charlie" had begun to emerge. His "funny" walk was based on a recollection from childhood of the pathetic shuffle of an old drunk who used to hold horses outside a London tavern. His insouciance and tattered elegance perhaps reflected the brave front which actors from time immemorial have assumed as they enter the manager's office. But no one had ever seen, before the camera showed it to them, a smile of such angelic innocence, coupled with a surprising streak of meanness, violence, and a certain deliberate vulgarity.

This equivocal, significant figure first became the favorite of children. By the time their elders discovered the little man with the derby, the cane, and the oversized shoes, the Chaplin craze was in full swing. At the end of his year with Sennett, the comedian accepted a year's contract with Essanay at $1,000 a week. At the end of that year, 1915, he demanded and received from the Mutual Film

Corporation $10,000 a week 52 weeks a year. The news of these financial pole vaults invariably reached Mary Pickford when she was discussing with Adolph Zukor, as she did so frequently, the desirability of canceling her current contract in favor of one more rewarding to her and more costly to him. For more than four years, from 1914 to 1918, if Charlie got a raise, Mary had to have a bigger one, and vice versa. Five years earlier this pair had both been obscure players. Now the astronomical sums they were receiving advertised to a world (and a Wall Street) barely conscious of pictures that the movies had become big business. They advertised, also, that the star system was the most important single factor in motion pictures. Mary and Charlie *were* their pictures, and their pictures needed nothing more to sell them to every exhibitor and virtually every movie patron in the land.

When Chaplin signed his $10,000-a-week contract with Mutual, he asked for and was given $100,000 advance on salary. His brother Sidney remonstrated at his demands, pointing out that they had no way of knowing whether the company could stand the unprecedented financial strain its new star was putting on it. Chaplin replied, "Well, even if the bubble bursts—and I agree it probably will—they can't take the hundred thousand away from me."

He's still got it.

Charles Chaplin, Mary Pickford, D. W. Griffith, and Douglas Fairbanks.

# "DOUG" AND THE BIG FOUR

Douglas Fairbanks was the most conspicuous of the invading "Famous Players" who survived the camera test, but his survival was a near thing, almost an accident. He was signed by Triangle on the basis of his modest reputation as a minor star of polite comedy on the stage, and sent to Hollywood in 1915 to appear in one of Triangle's first releases, *The Lamb*. The regular studio personnel were in the first flush of resentment over the high salaries paid the stage favorites; perhaps it is too much to call it sabotage, but certain it is that Fairbanks was murk-photographed in this first film, and that he had been given an ashen make-up which made him look ten years older than his thirty-two years. Perhaps he was oblivious of this, perhaps he was retaliating in his own way, but throughout the making of the picture he was the hail-fellow-well-met, giving his colleagues mighty slaps on the back and indulging his private penchant for athletics and acrobatics all over the set, often at the expense of the shooting schedule. These antics so pained D. W. Griffith, who was supervising the picture, that he told Fairbanks that if he had any future with the movies it would be with Mack Sennett. But two observers intervened. Anita Loos, a script writer hardly out of her

teens, but who had won Griffith's confidence in their three years of association, pointed out to the great man that this jolly, jumping-jack, off-screen Fairbanks was a far more interesting personality than the polite comedian they had signed. Miss Loos proposed that she and her husband, director John Emerson, be turned loose to see what could be done with the private personality of Douglas Fairbanks in pictures made for the public screen.

The remarkable series of comedies which Miss Loos wrote for Fairbanks established him as a popular figure only slightly below the level of Mary, Charlie, and William S. Hart. He was not the figure we chiefly remember today, the wealthy producer-star of expensive cloak-and-dagger fantasies. The Loos-Emerson Fairbanks was a happy-go-lucky fellow, a prophet of optimism, of "100 per cent Americanism" (as then understood), and, above all, of normalcy. The Loos scripts had him demolish all the current preoccupations which most people disliked or did not understand—psychiatry, Couéism, hypochondria, the craze for European royalty. He was Mr. Average Man with the powers of Superman. And that was important: his triumphs at the end of every picture were the triumphs of clean liv-

Douglas Fairbanks leaping from a tree to a window in *The Iron Mask,* 1929.

Douglas Fairbanks, supporting Charles Chaplin and Mary Pickford, 1917.

ing, noble ideals—and muscles of steel. But all this, sugary as it sounds, worked a spell (it still does when you see his pictures) not only with the provincial Americans at whom it was aimed but all over the world. A French critic wrote, "Douglas Fairbanks is a tonic. He smiles and you feel relieved."

Behind the stage star and the grinning athlete there seems to have been a third Douglas Fairbanks, an ambitious one. At any rate, a certain pattern emerges from subsequent events. Fairbanks' star was rising fast, but others still eclipsed it. Then, in 1920, he married Mary Pickford. The union of Doug, the all-American male, with Little Mary, America's Sweetheart, had a sentimental logic which thrilled the fans of both, which was nearly everybody. By another kind of logic, the marriage raised Fairbanks to a place by Mary's side and equated his official popularity with hers. Soon he made another move. At the suggestion of B. P. Schulberg, he pointed out to his wife and to Charlie Chaplin that the enormous salary raises they were successfully demanding were making the margin of profit on their films dangerously low, and that there might come a time when, despite their popularity, they

would actually constitute liabilities to their employers. Why not form—with him and D. W. Griffith, who was also getting too expensive for his own good—a company to produce and distribute their own pictures, enabling them to keep all the profits for themselves? In 1919, the United Artists Corporation was formed.

United Artists was the logical conclusion to the star system. When he heard of it, Richard Rowland, head of Metro, commented, "The lunatics have taken charge of the asylum." But the head keeper in this case was no loony. Though only one of four partners, and at first the least powerful, Fairbanks took the most active part in the affairs of the company. In the mid-Twenties, he enticed Joseph M. Schenck to head the administrative affairs of the corporation, bringing with him Norma and Constance Talmadge, who were quickly followed by Gloria Swanson, John Barrymore, and Buster Keaton. In the Thirties, when things were looking bad, Fairbanks brought in Darryl Zanuck. And when D. W. Griffith ceased to be a productive contributor, Fairbanks quietly eased him out of the partnership. So long as he was alive, United Artists made a profit.

Louise Lovely

Mary Pickford

Rubye de Remer

King Baggott

Harold Lockwood

Carlyle Blackwell

## THE HEROINE

The first requirement for the movie heroine was that she be sweet, preferably as sweet as the high priestess of them all, Mary Pickford, and if possible with a replica of Miss Pickford's golden curls. She should be fond of children and animals (she was customarily introduced to audiences in a shot showing her sitting on the lawn playing with puppies, kittens, or bunnies). That she should be pure went so without saying that it was never referred to except by the color of her dress—white—or at a moment when her purity was menaced, as it constantly was. Intelligence or lack of it was irrelevant, but it helped if her name could symbolize her leading characteristic: the early screen was dotted with Blanche Sweets, Arline Prettys, and Louise Lovelys. It was also helpful if her name was exotic, like Violet Mersereau and Muriel Ostriche, or aristocratic, which was why Olga Cronk was metamorphosed into Claire Windsor and Lucille Langehanke into Mary Astor. Probably this trend reached its climax when Erich von Stroheim introduced as the heroine of his *Foolish Wives* a lady whose lineage was reputedly so high that she must never be referred to except as Miss Dupont.

## THE HERO

He, of course, had to be as strong as the heroine was gentle. A proper hero must also be silent, kind, noble, generous, patriotic, pious, slow to anger yet quick to avenge his honor, and horse-loving. Bearing such a heavy load of virtues, it is a wonder that he ever had time to be tempted into sin, but he frequently was—and, unlike the heroine, who never found resisting sin any effort at all, it was all right for the hero to be tempted, as long as he didn't do anything about it. If he did, if he fell, the audience was on notice that at least three reels would now be consumed in remorse, penance, and atonement before he could hope to see an answering light in the heroine's eyes. And even then—well, one asked oneself, how could a sweet, lovely girl like that let any man touch her who had . . . All such thoughts ended in three dots in those days.

It was not important that the hero's name be high-sounding. A man could survive even names like Carlyle Blackwell and J. Warren Kerrigan if there was nothing, absolutely nothing about him of the sissy. The American movie hero of the early silent period was a virile, red-blooded, go-getting, rough-and-ready, he-man, Sunday-school teacher.

# THE MOVIE FAMILY

By the time the star system had established itself, there had also emerged a sort of formula movie family or standard *dramatis personae*. With rare variation, these obligatory characters were The Hero, The Heroine, Mother, The Villain, and The Vamp.

Arline Pretty, Dustin Farnum

Lois Wilson, J. Warren Kerrigan

## MOTHER

"Why must all American movie mothers be white-haired and tottering even though their children are mere tots? Does the menopause not operate in the United States?" asked Iris Barry, film critic of the London *Daily Mail*, in 1926. The answer to Miss Barry might have been that in American movies, Mother more often than not was old before her time. Her figure might be flawless, her face unlined, but gray-haired at least she must be, to brand her as a martyr, worn out by toil, her fingers worked to the bone in the service of callous husbands and unfeeling children. What deep vein of sentimentality and repressed guilt she touched in the American soul it is hard now to say, but Mother was a figure of supreme importance in the silent drama, symbolizing not only self-sacrifice but rectitude, authority, and an apron-strings world to which many perhaps longed to return. Father was by no means so important. In most movies he was either a figure of dread or of little consequence, almost obliterated by hand-wringing, tear-stained Mom. Increasingly he was obliterated.

Pauline Frederick came to specialize in agonized mothers of erring sons. *Her Honor, the Governor*, 1926, with Carrol Nye.

## THE VILLAIN

When Ben Hecht came to Hollywood to write scripts at the invitation of Herman Mankiewicz, his host gave him some friendly advice: "I want to point out to you that in a novel a hero can lay ten girls and marry a virgin for a finish. In a movie this is not allowed. The hero, as well as the heroine, has to be a virgin. The villain can lay anybody he wants, have as much fun as he wants cheating and stealing, getting rich and whipping the servants. But you have to shoot him in the end. When he falls with a bullet in his forehead, it is advisable that he clutch at the Gobelin tapestry on the library wall and bring it down over his head like a symbolic shroud."

Mr. Hecht was so appalled at this counsel that he wrote his first movie, *Underworld*, 1927, entirely around the villain.

The movie villain was more than a scapegoat for the phobias of the audience—fear of foreigners, the aristocracy, the Big City. They projected onto him all their own secret desires for luxury, skullduggery, and unlimited illicit sex. Occasionally villains reformed at the end of the picture, but it was much more satisfactory, as Mankiewicz says, to shoot them. Audiences found it hard to believe that anybody enjoying such a life as the villain led would ever give it up voluntarily.

*the* Cinema Primer

*by Robert E. Sherwood    Drawing by John Held, Jr.*

*the* Villain

The Vil-lain earns our Hiss, for he
Is of the Ar-i-stoc-ra-cy.
He wears Silk Hats, and Evil Leers;
He goes to Clubs, and drinks straight Beers;
He plays Rou-lette, and stays out Late—
In fact, a base Li-cen-ti-ate.
He gets the Mai-den in his power
And wrest-les with her for an Hour,
But when the He-ro heaves in view,

The archetypal mother, Mrs. Mary Carr, a brisk young matron adept at simulating advanced age.

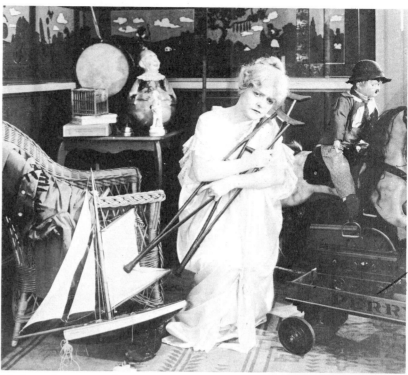

Mother also yearned over mementoes of faithless or deceased children. Elsie Esmond in *The Black Stork,* 1917.

A screen villain must be recognizable as such at first glance. James Mason, above, was much in demand.

Nobody was better at menacing virtue than Walter Long, as he is here with Marguerite de la Motte in *Desire,* 1923.

*Cleopatra*, 1918.

*Gold and the Woman*, 1916. Another of Miss Bara's wealthy

## THE VAMP

When Frank J. Powell set out to film the stage play *A Fool There Was*, he sought an unknown actress to play the aggressive *femme fatale* who ruins men and tosses them aside. He found her in dark-haired, big-eyed Theodosia Goodman, an extra player from Ohio. This "circumspect and demure" girl was at once whisked out of sight and an entirely new personality was manufactured for her. She was renamed Theda Bara, which the publicity office insisted was an anagram for "Arab Death." She was alleged to be the daughter of a French father and an Egyptian mother, to be a seeress and inscrutably but frightfully evil. A dead-white limousine at-

tended by "Nubian" footmen drove her to the Chicago hotel where she gave an unforgettable interview in a dim room hung in black velvet and filled with incense fumes. The amused press gave her a very rough time about her supposed Egyptian background, but she stood the ordeal bravely until every reporter and photographer had left. Then little Miss Goodman tore the velvet hangings from a window and gasped, "Give me air!"

The campaign, apparently the first designed artificially to create a movie star, was successful. *A Fool There Was* made Miss Bara famous overnight, gave the word "vampire" and its derivatives "vamp" and "baby vamp" to the language, and offered the sublime subtitle, "Kiss me, my fool," which was quoted for a generation. Thereafter Miss Bara was

66

Theda Bara and the skeleton of one of her victims.

Miss Bara in an uncharacteristic lighter moment.

admirers learns that the future bodes him no good.

wicked through forty subsequent films in four years. Constantly photographed with skulls and with snakes, she became the public's permanent symbol of evil. Attempts to let her play sympathetic roles were as unsuccessful with audiences as attempts to let Mary Pickford play grown-up, romantic roles. Vamp she was and must remain, until the public tired of pictures which seemed increasingly like carbon copies of one another.

After completion of her lucrative contract with William Fox in 1919, Miss Bara, unable to understand the distinction between fame and popularity, waited for further offers. None came. On the strength of her movie name, Al Woods starred her on the stage in a drama of the supernatural, *The Blue Flame*, which amused Broadway sophisticates

for months, much as the Cherry Sisters had. Finally an independent producer brought her back to the screen in a version of *The Unchastened Woman*, of which Sally Benson wrote: "When I realized that this was Theda Bara's comeback picture, and not just one of her old releases, I could hardly believe my eyes." This was in 1925. After that, Miss Bara's occasional roles in short comedies burlesquing the vamp parts she used to play in deadly seriousness only confirmed Hollywood's belief that "they never come back." Wealthy, married to a successful director, Charles Brabin, Miss Bara took up charity work and became something of a social wheel in Los Angeles. But, almost till her death in 1955, she advertised that she was "at liberty" in the Hollywood casting directory.

# THE VAMPFOLLOWERS

**the Vampire**

A Fool there was, and he paid his Coin
To a dark-eyed Dame, from the Ten-der-loin.
He took her out to a West Coast Town,
Dressed her up in a Form-fit Gown,
Filled her Eyes with Bel-la-Don-na,
And said, "Now, Kid, for-get your Hon-na,
For, Hence-forth, you're a scar-let Scamp—
A reg-u-lar, red-lipped, black-souled Vamp."
She signed his Con-tract, for she was Meek,
He made her Fa-mous with-in a Week;
And when I tell you his Pro-fits, you'll
A-gree that, per-haps, he wasn't a Fool.

Theda Bara's success brought an army of vamps to the screen. For five years the movies were overrun with female wickedness, but by 1918 the reign of the vamp was over. She had become unbelievable. The vamp films depended on public acceptance of two rigid conventions. First, that a vamp was at all times automatically, completely irresistible to all males. At the crook of her beckoning finger, a man, any man, would leave his wife, fireside, and job for the purpose of being putty in her hands. This was an absolute law which had to be accepted even when optical evidence suggested that the vamp in question was not so supremely above the ordinary

*The Kiss of a Vampire,* 1916, with Virginia Pearson and Kenneth

Louise Glaum's press agent declared that the vampire's leopard coat was "purchased in an Oriental market place."

68    Barbara La Marr, "the girl who was too beautiful." Her sultry vamping gained her stardom in the Twenties, until death cut short her career.

in beauty and sensual appeal. The other convention was that the vamp was moved by some mysterious force of evil which caused her to revel in the destruction of her victims for the sake of destruction itself. While she accepted, indeed demanded, money from her men, she did not spend it on luxury or save it against the day when she would be too old to vamp. She just wanted to ruin her victims and then laugh at them. She was *bad*.

Such motivation could be accepted only by very unsophisticated people with the narrowest experience of life. For a few years the vamp depended on suspension of disbelief among rustics, the urban poor, and the young. But the movies themselves were mass-producing sophistication on the grandest scale known in human history, and audiences were acquiring wide knowledge of life beyond their own social spheres. By the 1920s, vamps were no longer the central figures of films but sideline "villainesses." Compared to the new Woman of the World created by Cecil B. De Mille, the vamp seemed a crude and old-fashioned figure. Soon her tradition was swallowed up in the new ego-ideal exemplified for American womanhood by Pola Negri and Greta Garbo—the *femme* who is *fatale*, all right, but chiefly to herself.

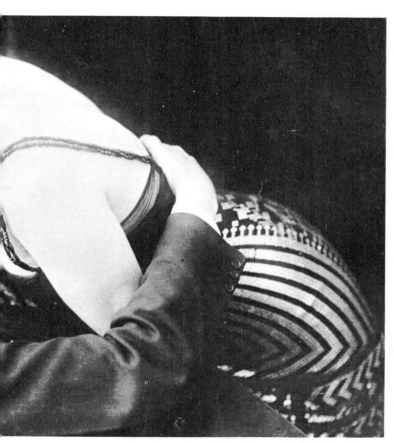

Hunter. The woman was the sexual aggressor in vampire films.

After the success of Theda Bara, Valeska Suratt transferred her vamping activities from stage to screen.

Virginia Pearson, posed here with the obligatory skull, was William Fox's second-string Theda Bara.

The screen's greatest comedienne. Mabel Normand's comedy was mostly a matter of a wry and delicate knowledge of life and human beings. Of all Mack Sennett's gifted pupils, only she and Chaplin became creative artists in their own right.

# COMEDY

## MACK SENNETT

Mack Sennett at the peak of his success in 1926.

Screen comedy began as short, knockabout improvisations. But in 1909, Mack Sennett, a former plumber's helper, wandered into the Biograph studio where D. W. Griffith was at work inventing screen narration. Sennett at once applied the principles of Griffith's discoveries in camera work and cutting to comedy. Two years later, at the head of the famous Keystone Company, he was busy creating his own private world, and in the process shaking the real world with earthquakes of mirth.

The Sennett world is inaccurately remembered today. Slapstick is in a decline, and the antics of the Three Stooges bear little relation to the ordered madness and harmless violence which Sennett made so funny. The principal feature of this master comedian's world was that nothing in it had normal consequences. Frenzied beatings caused the pain of a pinprick, hundreds of bullets produced no fatalities. In this slightly off-center caricature of the world of ordinary experience, people could do things that in real life would have the most catastrophic effects. They are the things we all wish to do, without daring to—hence the primary appeal of Sennett's work.

Nothing was sacred to Sennett and his studioful of irreverent comedians. To the primitive humors of undress and obesity he added wild ridicule of virtue, authority, romantic love, religion itself. In Sennett's world all lawyers were shysters, all pious people hypocrites, all sheriffs both stupid and venal, and in that world everybody was caught with his pants down. His mysterious knack, and it remains a mystery, was that of creating satire as sharp as a needle while simultaneously extracting the sting. Policemen all over the world guffawed as heartily as their neighbors at the Keystone Cops. Perhaps it was just the broad extravagance of such caricature that enabled him to commit his outrages with never a protest from foreign governments, organized religion, labor unions, or Rotary clubs. Deeper than that, Sennett's work said: Whatever we pretend, we're all what we are, and we're all alike. Let's take the masks off for a moment.

Ben Turpin.

Louise Fazenda, Mack Sennett, and Teddy, the Sennett trick dog.

Sheriff Polly Moran, Ben Turpin, Heinie Conklin (with sneer).

Slim Summerville and Louise Fazenda heat up the thermometer.

# A GALLERY OF GROTESQUES

Sennett enriched the screen with a great gallery of grotesques—the cadaverous Slim Summerville, the huge Mack Swain and Fatty Arbuckle, cross-eyed Ben Turpin, pop-eyed Ford Sterling, gangling Louise Fazenda, and dozens of others. The tender passion received anything but tender treatment from Sennett: pretty girls mooned over elderly gentlemen, matrimony was a comic predicament, and it was not unusual for the villain to get the girl. His actors were recruited from the ranks of vaudevillians and circus clowns to whom payday fifty-two times a year made his studio the only Eden they had known since childhood. Their heavy eyebrows, enormous mustaches, and dead-white faces gave to the Keystone universe that touch of unreality that Sennett needed.

Roscoe Arbuckle, Buster Keaton in *Good Night Nurse*, 1918.

Blackface was still a respectable form of humor in 1916.
Ford Sterling, Polly Moran, Guy Woodward in *The Hunt*.

Chester Conklin and Mack Swain.

An assignation in a film entitled *Curses! They Remarked*, 1914.

73

*In the Clutches of a Gang, c.* 1913. Sennett's finest: Ford Sterling at the desk; Al St. John, Hank Mann, and Roscoe Arbuckle in the line-up.

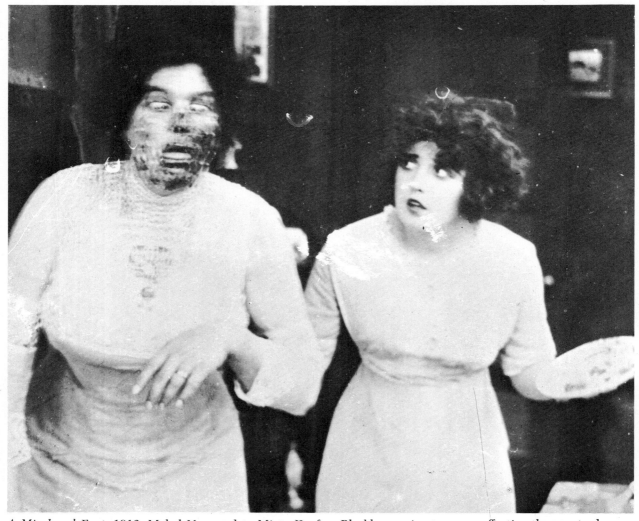

A *Misplaced Foot*, 1913. Mabel Normand to Minta Durfee. Blackberry pie was more effective than custard.

Gloria Swanson in a Sennett comedy of 1916.

## SLAPSTICK AND GIRLS

Cops, pies, and bathing belles are all that remain in public memory of the Sennett era. They didn't compose the whole range of his delicate art, but they do illustrate its leading tendencies. Cops, like all authorities, are congenital idiots, a pie the most degrading way of puncturing dignity, and the bathing beauties, alone uncaricatured in the Sennett world, the only sure good thing in life.

Chester Conklin and vintage Sennett beauties, c. 1913.

**SENNETT'S IMITATORS** *His Last Laugh,* 1916, with Mary Thurman. Everybody imitated Sennett and mostly trailed him, but here a rival decorator and costumer score a comic victory.

*Making a Living*, 1914. Chaplin as a Mephistophelean nobleman in one of the many roles he played before he developed the Tramp character.

*A Woman*, 1915. One of Chaplin's several female impersonations.

# CHARLES CHAPLIN

When Mack Sennett's backers, Kessel and Bauman, signed Charlie Chaplin and sent him out to the studio, Sennett was not much impressed. An obscure Cockney vaudevillian had come to join his troupe of equally obscure small-timers, that was all. For weeks he played snaky counts, sharpers, any odd parts that came along. Then Chaplin invented the Tramp. In costume and gait, this was just another of the funny-looking men in which the Sennett studio abounded. But out of the eyes of the Tramp looked a soul.

*The Vagabond*, 1916. The Tramp searches his pockets for a toothpick.

# CHAPLIN BECOMES THE TRAMP

After his year with Sennett, Chaplin adopted the Tramp character permanently. Now writing and directing his own films, he provided in a series of one- and two-reel comedies a chronicle of his hero's adventures so fundamentally continuous that one distributor in the Near East spliced together all the short films and called the resulting feature *Charlie's Life*. These episodes from the biography of a vagabond appealed at first to children in the millions, then to everybody. His films were shown from New Guinea to the Arctic, his name was known to savage peoples who had never heard of the founders of the world's great religions. He became in two short years the universal folk-hero of the modern world. Intellectuals lured into the movie houses in search of the source of his fame found that this world hero was a homeless tramp whose shabby elegance and careless poverty bespoke a spirit equal to life's cruelest and most humiliating blows. They found in him as many things as have been found in Hamlet. They found him sly, cruel, pretentious, disdainful, crude, witty. They found a touch of madness in him, and a bottom of hard common sense. And behind this urban lover of nature, this hopeless, hoping lover who snapped his fingers at the universe, there was something that hurt.

Emma Clifton, Charles Chaplin, Ford Sterling, and Chester Conklin in *Between Showers*, 1914.

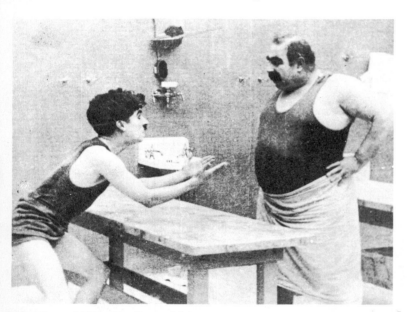

*The Bank*, 1916. Edna Purviance and Chaplin.

*The Cure*, 1917. Charlie and his masseur.

*A Night at the Show*, 1915. Chaplin with May White.

*Sunnyside*, 1919. Charlie's first fans were armies of children.

80

*The Perils of Pauline,* 1914. Scenes from this famed serial look comparatively tame in relation to those which were to come after it, but it was the spark which set off the serial craze and did much to confirm the movie-going habit.

*What Happened to Mary,* 1912, with Mary Fuller, Miriam Nesbit, Marc McDermott. The first movie serial was not one story but a series of related stories.

*Zudora,* 1915, the sequel to *The Million-Dollar Mystery.* The sun, passing through a magnifying glass, is burning off Marguerite Snow's bonds, as Donald Gallagher looks on.

# SERIALS

## TO BE CONTINUED NEXT WEEK

The movie serial was a by-product of one of America's most sensational newspaper circulation battles. In 1913 the Chicago *Tribune*, fighting desperately with blackjacks as well as black headlines to maintain its local prestige against six hungry rivals, concluded that the nickels of nickelodeon patrons were as good at the bank as those of more cultured readers.

Some unknown genius, possibly City Editor Walter Hovey, later immortalized in *The Front Page*, came up with the notion that it would be profitable to synchronize the weekly publication of a thrill-packed serial with the appearance of a screen version in the nickelodeons. The idea, like many other supposedly startling innovations, was not wholly original. About a year before, McClure's *The Ladies' World* had, as a promotion stunt, arranged for the release in the theaters of a series of two-reel films simultaneously with its publication of a group of short stories known as *What Happened to Mary*. Each story was a self-contained unit only loosely tied in with the other installments by the appearance of the same characters.

The *Tribune's The Adventures of Kathlyn,* however, was a continued story which established the unfailing formula for all succeeding movie serials: the maximum of excitement and the minimum of plausibility. Every episode ended on a high note of tension and suspense, nicely calculated to induce any audience to come back the following week to see how the heroine could possibly escape from the horrible predicament into which the villain had lured her. Written by Harold McGrath, produced by Selig, with Kathlyn Williams in the leading role, *The Adventures* was a smashing success. The *Tribune* announced a circulation increase of 10 per cent, and even exhibitors, habitually reticent for fear of increased film rentals, admitted that business was good.

For the next three years the nation was swept by an epidemic of newspaper-sponsored serials, each seeking to out-sensationalize its predecessor. The *Tribune's* second entry was *The Million-Dollar Mystery*. The name was chosen first and the story line worked out later. It starred Florence LaBadie and

James Cruze. The twenty-three chapters cost approximately $125,000, played in about 7,000 theaters, and grossed nearly $1,500,000—all fabulous figures for those days; it returned 700 per cent to its stockholders on their investment—fabulous for any day.

The serials were a godsend to the movies in their awkward age of transition from two-reelers to features. The old-line companies which feared to embark on the production of the expensive long pictures seized upon the serial as a perfect compromise, and audiences took to their hearts this thrilling hybrid fruit of machine-age culture.

THE TRIAL OF THE ORACLE

# The Perils of Pauline

There is not one exhibitor in any part of the country who is not a booster for the "Perils of Pauline." It has paid for itself in many instances on the showing of the first episode, leaving the returns from all the others as clear profit. What would you not pay for a series that forces you to turn people away from your door every time you show it. What would you not give to be able to show one that is so popular your patrons call up and ask that you issue reserved seat tickets for the evenings it is to be shown as they wanted to buy for the full series in advance. Yet this has happened in several instances. Some of the exhibitors have advertised that on the days the "Perils of Pauline" are to be shown the prices will be advanced. They had to do this to protect themselves. Do you need any better evidence of the immense pulling power of this picture?

### Pauline Pulls People—She's A Gold Mine

**THE ECLECTIC** 110 West 40th Street    **FILM COMPANY** New York City

"Pauline Pulls People—She's A Gold Mine," says this trade advertisement. The suspense of serials brought whole families back to the theaters week after week and thus built up the movie audience.

Ruth Roland in *The Timber Queen*, 1923.

Maurice Costello and Ethel Grandin in *The Crimson Stain Mystery*, 1916.

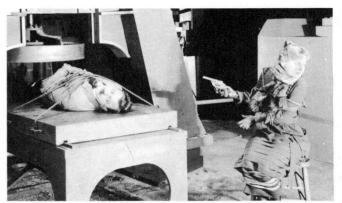

Coit Albertson, Lillian Walker in *$1,000,000 Reward*, 1919.

Hero about to be run over by wagon.

# ACTION - - ACTION - -

The serial craze made movie acting a perilous if lucrative profession. Serial kings and queens had to dangle from airplanes, sink into quagmires, leap from burning buildings, suffer imprisonment, torture, and peril from flood and fire. Action was the keynote of the serial, and in this kind of movie the star's ability to swing from a window ledge to a tree was more important than acting or beauty. The day of the professional stunt man or stunt woman had not arrived, and though doubles were sometimes used by the more timid players, most of the top serial stars actually performed the super-

Helen Greene in *The Perils of Our Girl Reporters*, 1916.

*The Mysteries of Myra*, 1916, with Howard Estabrook,

Charles Hutchison, Anne Luther in *The Great Gamble*, 1919.

## ACTION

human physical feats for which they were adored by the public. The two most popular serial queens, Ruth Roland and Pearl White, prided themselves on never using doubles for their thrilling stunts, even though their anxious producers would have much preferred to provide doubles rather than risk the lives of such valuable "properties." Audiences tended to confuse the private lives of Miss Roland and Miss White with what they saw on the screen, an illusion which producers fostered by giving their screen characters their actual names—*Ruth of the Rockies, Pearl in Peril.*

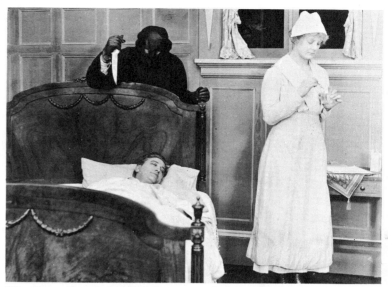

*The Great Secret*, 1917. Other exact details unknown.

Tom Mix in *3 Jumps Ahead*, 1923.

Natalie Kingston and Milton Sills in *Framed*, 1927.

featured a secret society bent on world domination.

Ruth Roland, Jenny biplane, and friends.

Buck Jones and Silver Buck

*Riding Through Nevada, 1943.*

# WESTERNS

## BRONCHO BILLY

When Frank Capra returned to Hollywood in 1945, after four years of Army service, he said, "You can't help being afraid you've lost your touch. I keep wishing I could sneak off and do a couple of quickie Westerns, just to make sure I still know how." The great director wanted to do his finger exercises in the basic movie form. The simple formula of the Western remains the foundation for all the complex storytelling rhetoric the movies have since developed. Whatever the plot is saying, Westerns move. That fact has kept them the staple movie cycle from *The Great Train Robbery* till today.

The first Western movies were descendants of the Wild West shows and dime novels which flooded the world in the days after Col. "Buffalo Bill" Cody began the international exploitation of his adventures on the Western plains. These one-reelers consisted of little more than a chase and a fight, and they were shot in the New Jersey woods and along the Palisades by men who didn't know a bowie knife from a bolo. The actors were equally innocent of life as lived beyond Times Square. One of D. W. Griffith's first movie jobs was playing an extra in a Western. His comment to his wife: "It's not so bad, you know, five dollars for simply riding a horse in the wilds of Fort Lee on a cool spring day."

The first Western star was a peculiar figure indeed. Born Max Aronson in Little Rock, Arkansas, in 1882, he adopted the stage name of Gilbert M. Anderson for his mostly unsuccessful career as a vaudeville actor, then drifted into

working for Edwin S. Porter in the days of *The Great Train Robbery*. By 1907 he had formed a partnership with George K. Spoor of Chicago in the Essanay Company, the name formed from their two initials. The Edison Company had already begun its series of lawsuits against its early competitors, and Anderson found it prudent to move half of Essanay to the West Coast. There, in a studio at Niles, California, he began producing the more than 375 one-reel Westerns centering around his own screen character, "Broncho Billy."

The appeal of "Broncho Billy" is difficult to understand today. This stolid, rather portly figure hardly suggests a product of Western life, and when he began in films Anderson could not even sit on a horse; he was thrown during the first day's work on *The Great Train Robbery*. Later on he finally learned to ride. "But I was never anything more than a competent rider," he said in 1948. "I used doubles for the sensational stunts. And as for marksmanship, heck, in those movies a blank used to turn a corner and kill a man."

Anderson never thought that Westerns changed much in later years. "They're just like I used to make, except that they talk a little. Most of them are mediocre. They all have the same formula—two guns, bullets, 'pardner,' a boy with a crooning voice, horses, and a sheriff. It's one big stew out of the same stewpot." Anderson did more than escape the Edison lawyers by moving to California. On location, the real West loomed up behind the tinpot action of the one-reel Western and overwhelmed it.

Broncho Billy

*Trailin' West*, 1936

## THE WESTERN BACKDROP

Against the great natural background of the Far West, in itself dramatic, the Western developed from melodrama toward epic. From 1911 till today, the majesty of plains, deserts, and mountains has given an importance beyond itself to the feeblest Western. Whatever plot is spinning, the background reminds us that these films are part of the national drama of the winning of the wilderness. But this was not yet apparent to the America of the Teens. It was, rather, overcultivated old Europe which first saw the Western for what it was and

what it meant. In 1919 the great French critic and film director Louis Delluc pointed out the part played in these films by their background and their physical material: ". . . bare gray plains, mountains as steep and luminous as the screen itself, horses and men in all their brute strength, the tremendous intensity of a life so simple that it has all the room in the world for beauty and harmony and contrast, and lends an incomparable spark of humanity to the simple sentiments like love and revenge which spring from it."

*Westward Ho!* 1935

*Brigham Young, 1940*

The French critic Louis Delluc wrote in 1923: "I think that Rio Jim [as William S. Hart was known in France] is the first real figure established by the cinema . . . and his life the first really cinematic theme, already a classic—the adventures of an adventurer in search of fortune in Nevada or the Rocky Mountains, who holds up the mail coach, robs the mails, burns the rancher's house, and marries the sheriff's daughter."

*The Gun Fighter, 1916*

# THE GOOD BAD MAN

The greatest of all Western stars was also the most authentic. William S. Hart was brought up in the "real" West. Born in Newburgh, New York, he was taken by his father to Minnesota and Wisconsin when those states were still inhabited by the Blackfeet and Sioux who had fought Custer in the Indian wars. At six, the boy Bill could speak Sioux and by the time he reached adolescence he had worked as a plowboy and ranch hand, learning to protect himself against the daily dangers of life in a country where knowledge of the terrain and instant readiness for self-defense were conditions of survival. Before he reached manhood, he had come to think of frontier life as the most natural and healthy, and the frontier code an iron law.

When the Harts returned to the East, Bill succumbed to an unaccountable urge to become an actor. From the early 1890s to 1914 he barnstormed the country as leading man to stars like Julia Arthur and Modjeska. Most successful at first in Shakespearean roles, he eventually found his metier in a series of plays of Western life (*The Virginian, The Squaw Man*). This was greatly to his liking. He enjoyed re-creating the experiences of his childhood and instructing Broadway dramatists and thespians in them. But the proscenium was limiting, and when producer Thomas H. Ince invited him to join the famous stage players then trekking to California, he welcomed the chance.

When Hart entered films in 1914, the familiar pattern of the Western film had been established by "Broncho Billy" Anderson and indeed appeared to have exhausted its initial popularity. To Hart, this theatrical version of the frontier was ridiculous and unreal. He determined to put the genuine article on the screen, and in the many two-reel films in which he starred for Ince a new portrait of the frontier appeared, and a new protagonist.

William S. Hart as Messala in the 1899 stage production of *Ben Hur*. Before he became a movie actor, Hart specialized in stage spectacles and in Shakespeare.

91

Hart, that "severe yet impassioned figure," not only felt strong emotions but expressed them with all stops out.

Despite his differences from them, the Good Bad Man displayed all the tricks and traits of the standard Western heroes. Here he condescendingly allows his horse, Pinto Ben, to show his affection.

## TWO-GUN BILL HART

William S. Hart created his character, the Good Bad Man, out of his own memories and experiences. In the majority of his pictures, he was an outlaw who underwent moral reformation of a kind, yet stayed outside the law. In this he embodied two conflicting tendencies of the Old West. Murder was not a major crime on the prairies and in the Rockies because rudimentary frontier justice, and often life itself, rested on quick trigger fingers. But horse-stealing, claim-jumping, or consorting with the Indians as a "renegade" were despised because they were *social* crimes—indirect threats to the whole community. Hart, the outlaw, was sympathetic because he always supported the basic code.

To his audiences the Good Bad Man was not only a sympathetic but an enviable figure. Americans of the early twentieth century had been steeped in the traditions of the frontier and fully understood the sliding-scale morality of the Hart films. The West was opened by men whose tenacity in the face of hardship was matched by a boyish desire for adventure for its own sake. As the new country developed, this latter quality became an anachronism and soon *only* an outlaw could live what formerly was the normal life of all men on

Evil Louise Glaum lured and sweet Bessie Love redeemed Bill Hart in dozens of films. Top, *The Return of Draw Egan*, 1916; above, *The Aryan*, 1916.

But, good or bad, vamp or heroine, both got the same treatment.

the frontier. In Hart's films, which represent the halfway stage in this transition, the Good Bad Man was still a glamorous character, secretly envied by all who were irked by civilized restraint. But by 1910-1920 he had to meet a tragic end. The characters *inside* the film might admire him, but the morality of a now-settled country could not permit an outlaw to escape scot-free.

Probably, pictures like William S. Hart's Westerns will never be made again. The formula of the later Western became as stylized as that of Restoration comedy. Its purpose was not to portray a way of life, but to gratify the escape impulse once served by dime novels and gaslight melodrama. Hart's films were different. They were produced by a man who understood the frontier code and could furnish it out in authentic detail. His pictures were not only more accurate psychologically, but also achieved wider and more lasting impact than the subsequent Western films could boast. People of all sorts found themselves strangely stirred by the conflict between Hart's behavior and his character. It was a conflict to which they felt linked, a cultural inheritance from the "lost, wild America" of the day before yesterday.

Nowhere is Hart's difference from the conventional Western hero of the Talkies better seen than in his treatment of women and sex. The standard cowboys

may have been allowed a final clinch with their heroines, with their horses present as chaperones, but their main concern was to rescue them from other men, not for themselves but for the noble cause of virginity. Hart expected all women to be like Louise Glaum, the seductive villainess of many of his films; his relations with them were a working arrangement involving money and sex, no questions asked, no answers given. When, to his surprise, he encountered innocence in the person of Bessie Love or Margery Wilson, he either ran from them as jail bait, or attempted—and often accomplished—seduction, followed by remorse and a tragic death of atonement. There were many tragic endings in Hart's films, unthinkable as that would be in later standard Westerns; and Louis Delluc and other European intellectuals were fascinated by the resemblance to the simplicity of classic tragedy, with Louise Glaum as a new Clytemnestra and Miss Love another Electra. The European reception of Westerns was conditioned by the Continental popularity of James Fenimore Cooper, and the French especially thought of Hart and his women as contemporary American types. Despite this confusion between nineteenth- and twentieth-century America, the French were the first to see that the Hart films were epic in style and that their material was truly cinematic.

As audiences responded to Hart's realistic Westerns, he extended their range to include every aspect of the old frontier days he knew and loved. His West was both drab and sinister. It pulsated with menace and passion. Men lied and betrayed and fought and killed. But they also loved and sacrificed.

Hart as Black Deering in *The Toll Gate,* 1920, an outlaw who, in his own words, "ain't never been any good" and doesn't intend to be. Yet he saves Anna Q. Nilsson's child from drowning at the risk of his freedom. On the frontier even outlaws supported the basic code.

Later Western heroes surged up to the bar and then ordered sarsaparilla. This is what Hart thought of anything less potent than redeye.

Hart's Western saloons were as genuine as the real thing, and as unglamorous.

# WILD AND WOOLLY

Many of the exteriors in Hart's films have the look of a Brady photograph. The characters in them were hard-bitten desperadoes of every national variety who had come to the frontier for no good. Often they were played by men Hart gathered from the last frontiers of Arizona and the Yukon. (Right, *Travellin' On*, 1921.)

*The Narrow Trail*, 1917. "The plot is nothing extraordinary, but this film contains a little masterpiece: the fight between the two men in the night. . . . In the center of a half-blinded and horrified crowd, the two figures circle. To follow them the camera draws back, moves nearer, rises higher: . . . The naked bodies, slippery with blood, take on a sort of phosphorescence. Two mad creatures are at grips, trying to kill each other. They look as though they were made of metal. Are they kingfishers or seals or men from the moon, or Jacob with the angel? Is it not some Buddha, this great naked figure which falls to its knees and dies there like a thousand little fishes in a lake of mercury? M. Ince may be proud of himself, for a spectacle such as this seems in recollection to equal the world's greatest literature."—Jean Cocteau.

"M. Ince" would certainly have been surprised.

# FIGHTS

## FIGHTING IS FUN -- IN THE MOVIES

Sir Winston Churchill's readiness to battle on the beaches and in the hills is matched by that of the movies, which are invariably prepared to fight on any provocation or pretext anywhere, any time, and in any manner. Men fight, women fight, children fight. They fight with fists, fingernails, feet, and firearms. They fight in doublet and hose, stripped to the buff, in the glamorous uniforms of the Northwest Mounted and the less glamorous ones of Alcatraz. They fight on mountain tops and under the seas; in fast-moving planes, motor boats, sleek black sedans; in bars, barges, bedrooms, and balconies adjoining said bedrooms; on horseback, on stairways, in quicksands, under tables, on tables, over tables. The good Lord apparently designed cliffs especially for individuals fighting to a finish, but man, with equal ingenuity, provided cellars for good old-fashioned free-for-alls. Any place is good enough.

With the passage of time and the continued advancement of the medium, fights have grown longer, fiercer, and, like some old Japanese drama, immutable to the last detail. The fighter felled by a blow that would kill an ox, rises promptly, like Antaeus refreshed by contact with Mother Earth; the apparent victor about to leap upon his victim encounters a terrific kick that sends him reeling backward; hero and villain alike stretch for the pistol only a few inches from their grasp, while the heroine simulates terror on the sidelines. No Western worthy of the name has fewer than three fights —one to get the picture well started, one in the middle to pick it up, and one in the last reel for a grand finale. But murder mysteries, spectacles, and smart society dramas are also well sprinkled with the thud of flying fists and some occasional happy eye-gouging.

Why do movie characters fight so much? Sometimes to promote skullduggery, sometimes to protect virtue in distress, but always and obviously to make life easier for members of the Screen Writers Guild. A poke in the nose or a half nelson is a lot less exhausting, for the author if not for the actor, than a scintillating line of dialogue. To topple over a host of pursuers by a giant swing on a chandelier requires dexterity on the part of the performer but not of the writer.

And if life is thus simplified for the author, so is it for the audience. They know that a swordsman like Douglas Fairbanks, Sr., can easily resist the onslaught of a dozen high-born Frenchmen. A peaceful stripling like Richard Barthelmess can be relied on to demolish the local bully eventually. Gangsters armed to the teeth, champions defending their titles against youthful contenders, Mexicans, Germans, Indians, Italians, and, nowadays, Russians and Chinese, all uniformly bite the dust. In a world where all is chaos and confusion, film fights represent the only certainty, an ultimate security. Villainy can never be victorious. The good man is always the best man.

Soldiers, boxers, and other real-life hard guys snicker at fight scenes in movies. They know that the handsome actor who plays the hero has a double for the in-fighting. They observe and remark on the fact that the heavy mayhem is apt to take place in long shots, while in close-up punches are visibly pulled. Thanks to the self-betrayal of the movies in their endless search for publicity, the man in the street is well aware that it is possible and easy for the film editor in his cutting room to fake a shattering blow by cutting from one camera position to the other, and in fact that the fist may belong to an actor who never met the owner of the chin he connected with. He knows that the chairs which break over the victim's head are made of yucca, a wood almost as light as paper, and that the window through which the hero crashes is made of glass as thin as a Christmas tree ornament. He is aware that the fearsome break-bone sounds of fists on flesh and blackjacks on skulls are added by the sound-effects man, *ex post facto*. He knows all this. But just the same he sits forward in his seat when the fight scene comes on and the hero faces half a hundred men single-handed. After all, if Audie Murphy could be a one-man army, maybe you could be, or I, or even that guy on the screen.

*The Spoilers*, 1914
William Farnum, Tom Santschi.

*The Spoilers*, 1922
Milton Sills, Noah Beery.

# THE SPOILERS

The classic movie fight of all time was the battle between William Farnum and Tom Santschi in the 1914 version of Rex Beach's *The Spoilers*. These fisticuffs lasted a full reel, and every subsequent movie fight has been compared unfavorably to them, while the actors in the four later versions of *The Spoilers* have been faced with the problem of surpassing not only their immediate predecessors but also the legendary melee of 1914.

*The Spoilers*, 1930. When the third version was made, Santschi and Farnum were engaged by Paramount to advise William Boyd and Gary Cooper how to restage the famous battle.

*The Spoilers*, 1930
William Boyd, Gary Cooper.

*The Spoilers*, 1942
Randolph Scott, John Wayne.

# THEY FIGHT...

*North of Nevada, 1924.*

...on balconies

...on cliffs

But wherever
they fight,
the hero can
lick the mob
single-handed.

James Kirkwood in *Luck of the Irish,* 1920.

100

*The Sea Beast*, 1926. John Barrymore in an early *Moby Dick*.

**...on ships**

*Reno*, 1924.

**...in geysers**

Douglas Fairbanks in *The Black Pirate*, 1926.

# THE NEVER-ENDING FIGHT

Through the years, Charles Starrett and Dick Curtis have fought each other in more than two dozen films. Fights remained indispensable to the movies. Three of the biggest hits of the post-war years, *From Here to Eternity*, *Guys and Dolls*, and *Shane*, climaxed in "epic" brannigans. But, some say, these boys didn't pack the wallop of the old-timers.

*Song of the Prairie, 1945.*

*Singing Guns, c. 1945.*

*Hidden Trails, c. 1945.*

*Shotgun Rider, c. 1945.*

Frank Sinatra in *From Here to Eternity*, 1953.

Jean Simmons in *Guys and Dolls*, 1955.

Martin and Osa Johnson, pioneer movie explorers, toast each other in ginger ale at the completion of *Simba*, 1927.

# THE WORLD BEFORE YOUR EYES

## THE SILENT DRAMA

At the head of the movie page conducted by Robert E. Sherwood in the old *Life* magazine stood, in the Teens and early Twenties, a drawing showing the Muse of the Cinema holding a crystal globe, while on either side stretched a panorama of all peoples, times, and climes. It was in this way that people first thought of the movies—as a Magic Carpet which could take them to the ends of the earth, range through all epochs of history, give them the eyes of a worm or a bird—in short, realize the old dream of omniscience. In particular, it could realize the dream of travel. Movie cameras had become standard equipment for explorers and globe-trotters by the early 1900s, and literally hundreds of travel films began to pour through the theaters. But feature-length "travelogues," to survive in the theaters, had to have a popular quality, usually stemming from the personalities of their makers. Of these, the most successful were Mr. and Mrs. Martin Johnson, whose hold on their audiences came from their casual air of being any American husband and wife on tour. Beginning with *Cannibals of the South Seas,* 1912, the Johnsons made innumerable pictures, and after her husband's death, Osa Johnson summed up their career with a compilation from all their films called *I Married Adventure,* 1940.

Such films continue to be made and shown for that mysterious and enduring breed, the armchair traveler. Indeed, today, on our Cinerama screens, they are more popular than ever before. But the conventional movie audience soon tired of them. It was wonderful to be whisked from Paris to Shanghai in a split second, but actual Paris, actual Shanghai, turned out to be far less exciting than most movie-goers had imagined. So they had to be replaced with those familiar dream worlds, Wicked Paris and the Mysterious East. The cameras re-turned from the ends of the earth and set to work to duplicate Paris and Shanghai in Hollywood. The duplicates were marvels of accuracy, but these meticulous re-creations were used as backdrops before which were enacted old myths.

All the locale stereotypes with which we are familiar today had established themselves in the movies by World War I, and have continued down the years as the necessities of mass-production have dictated. Sometimes one stereotype moves forward and dominates the rest, registering with seismographic accuracy some subterranean shift in popular feeling—the Sands of the Desert in the Twenties, Low Life during the depression. "We must identify ourselves with what we are," wrote Cesare Zavattini, the author of such Italian realist films as *Paisan* and *Bicycle Thief.* "The world is full of people thinking of myths." But the camera, the most marvelous means yet known of re-creating actual events, has become, by popular dictate, a device for re-creating on a colossal scale the most primitive dreams of man.

From Martin Johnson's *Congorilla,* 1932.

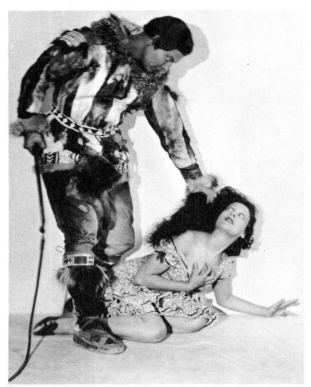

## THE FROZEN NORTH

The popularity of Jack London, James Oliver Curwood, and Rex Beach made the Frozen North a natural stereotype locale; the stories of all three authors have been filmed over and over. The Royal Northwest Mounted Police also provided and still provide an agreeable change of scene for the Western star too monotonously identified as a lone rider from Texas or Nevada. Sex, too, has its place amid the ice and snow, thanks to those long winter nights.

## THE DESERT SANDS

The white simplicity of desert sands merging with a vast sky irresistibly compelled directors of desert films to complete the composition by mustering an array of horsemen on the horizon. If a palm frond projected into the frame, so much the better. Art-minded cameramen often carried a tree branch with them just in case.

Lenore Ulric made her talkie debut as an Eskimo temptress in *Frozen Justice*, 1929.

A location shot from *Mount McKinley*, 1924.

*Beau Sabreur*, 1928. "The long line of Touaregs, about to pounce on the Great Oasis."

## THE MYSTERIOUS EAST

Defying Rudyard Kipling, East and West met constantly in screen dramas of the Mysterious East. Met and mingled, but rarely blended. Miscegenation or some hint or threat thereof hung over these films like a miasma, but it was usually unmasked or nobly renounced in the last reel. For the rest, the East was neither the emergent Asia we know nor the Yellow Peril of William Randolph Hearst's imagining, but simply a stamping ground for vice —opium dens, gambling hells, white slavery, torture cells, and the like. On the whole it was a not inaccurate portrayal of colonial Asia of three generations ago, a place where the representatives of two colliding cultures corrupted each other. And when all these excitations could be brought to America in films about the Chinatowns of New York and San Francisco, the thrill was greater than ever.

The continuing popularity of such films brought fame to several Oriental actors. The great Sessue Hayakawa was the first. Anna May Wong rose from the extra ranks to leading roles and an international career on stage and screen. For twenty years she was indispensable to any film dealing even remotely with Asia. The Japanese actor Sojin was imported by Douglas Fairbanks to play a Mongol khan in *The Thief of Bagdad* and remained to act Chinese villains (at this period Chinese were preferred to Japanese as villains) until the coming of the talkies. But for the most part, Asiatics were played by white men in yellowface.

Sojin and Anna May Wong unveil an American beauty to a visiting mandarin in the Chinatown sequence of *In Old San Francisco*, 1927.

The caption: "Having lost all her recollection of her convent-like life, Blanche de Montford (Gladys Brockwell) goes to the other extreme and becomes 'the Wildcat' of the Apaches." *The Devil's Wheel*, 1918.

## WICKED PARIS

According to a Library of Congress catalogue, the word *Paris* occurs in more film titles than any other word except *love*. As soon as experienced audiences of the silent days saw the obligatory opening shot of the Eiffel Tower, they were prepared to expect: a) Montparnasse, Apache dances, the sewers of Paris, Le Rat Mort; b) Montparnasse, ateliers, artists and models, Le Moulin Rouge; c) a wealthy American woman, overwhelmed by Continental finesse and good table manners, abandoning her husband until it is (almost) too late (alternatively, when the wife found the husband straying after Parisian cuties, she just disguised herself, went to the Moulin Rouge, and captivated the fugitive anew). Many pictures combined all four motifs with exhilarating effects. What a loss it is to science that no one in the Teens and Twenties thought to survey the opinions of Parisians themselves as to what they saw on the screen in the Hollywood version of Paris.

# SOUTH OF PAGO PAGO

South of Pago Pago! What a wonderland Polynesia opened to the studios! Dusky beauties! Beachcombers and remittance men! Drunken doctors forgetting it all! Volcanoes erupting and earthquakes quaking! Tidal waves swamping! Wild beasts menacing! There was simply no end to it all. Nor should an important variant be forgotten—the white-man-and-woman-shipwrecked-*alone*-on-a-desert-isle gambit. This was likely to be better in idea than in performance, since most of the time hero and heroine just pondered (and pondered) whether they had the right in the eyes of God and man to consummate their love—resolved, eventually, by an al fresco service, with the hero's key ring doing duty as the wedding band. After which, sad to relate, The End was likely to arrive before more than a token consummation had taken place.

But it was and is the white man and the dusky beauty who remain the central characters in dramas south of Pago Pago. Needless to say, the girls' duskiness is a matter of make-up, since they all have been played by white women, with the sole exception of the lovely Reri of *Tabu* (1931). Gilda Gray, the shimmy girl imported from Broadway for *Aloma of the South Seas* (1926), doubtless never heard of a sarong, but she started a stereotype that never fades. The particular male daydream involved here has survived the reports of returning GIs that neither Pago Pago nor the territory south of it is all it's been cracked up to be.

Dolores del Rio and Walter Pidgeon in *The Gateway of the Moon*, 1928.

Clara Bow in *Hula*, 1927.

## RUSTIC DRAMA

Before 1917, more than half of the American film dramas were played in rustic settings. Centering around the home and the church, they hymned the virtues of the simple life and, by contrast, the evils and the perils of the Big City. The heroes and heroines of these dramas were inarticulate country youths and gingham girls, the villains "city slickers." But while it depicted this Puritanism and provincialism, the movie itself destroyed the isolation which kept them alive. Even at its most circumspect, the movie urbanized, introducing a relativist gray into the blacks and whites of traditional morality and belief. What happened is well illustrated by three versions of the same film, *State Fair*. In the 1933 version, the state fair was still the symbol of agricultural pursuits and simple pleasures. In the 1945 remake, it became an affair of automobile shows, "name" bands, and radio comedians. And, of the 1962 version, with five new Rodgers tunes and three new down-home stars (Bobby Darin, Pamela Tiffin and Ann-Margret), *Variety* reported: "*State Fair* is still as American as mom's apple pie, but the pie is stale after seventeen years in the pantry." Today, the films dealing with farm life could be counted on the prongs of a pitchfork.

*The Girl Who Ran Wild,* 1921. Gladys Walton seems to rely more on her fetching smile than on her gun for protection from the whip.

*Hail the Woman,* 1922. The delicate caroling of Florence Vidor, right, would undoubtedly have been drowned out by the lusty hymn-singing of the rest of the choir, if that sort of thing had mattered in silent pictures.

*Some Punkins,* 1925. Charles Ray and Duane Thompson. Typed as the epitome of rustic shyness, Ray had to play bumbling youths into his late thirties, though in real life he ordered his shoes from London and his ties from Charvet.

## Backstage

*The Devil's Circus*, 1926. Only a cloak stands between Norma Shearer and the fate thought to be worse than death but sometimes considered better than starving. John Miljan is the devil's advocate here.

## Down to the Sea

*Old Ironsides*, 1926. The last of the sailing ships found their final haven in Hollywood, where they were used for sea fights of astounding realism. Wilson Mizner commented, "The public doesn't want to know what goes on behind the scenes. It prefers to believe that a cameraman hung in the clouds, mid-Pacific, the day Barrymore fought the whale."

# The Fall of a Nation

Defenseless, America is overcome and invaded. Blindfolded are two Civil War veterans condemned to die by the commander of the European confederation's invading army.

*The Fall of a Nation*, 1916. The Hon. Plato Barker, a thinly veiled caricature of William Jennings Bryan, presides over a meeting which opposes preparedness for war.

Hon. Plato Barker and the Rev. A. Cuthbert Pike, Peace Commissioners, repel with scorn the order that they must serve the Imperial General as potato parers in the camp kitchen.

The Peace Commissioners, who came out to welcome the invading army with flowers, are forced to the ignoble task of peeling potatoes for the Imperial General's soup.

# WORLD WAR I

## HOW TO SELL A WAR

The outbreak of the First World War in 1914 found the movies too much engrossed with their own burgeoning growth to recognize the opportunities it provided. But the arrival from Europe of films partisan to both sides of the conflict and the growing division of the American public into "preparedness" and "pacifist" camps soon opened new boxoffice possibilities. Then *The Birth of a Nation* demonstrated conclusively that the screen was an unrivaled medium for propaganda and polemics. In the autumn of 1915, J. Stuart Blackton, partly at the instigation of Theodore Roosevelt, filmed Hudson Maxim's book *Defenseless America* as *The Battle Cry of Peace.* It attacked the Germans as "Huns" and contended that only by arming to the teeth could America keep out of war. The film created an unprecedented controversy. No less a personage than Henry Ford took full-page newspaper advertisements to denounce the author of both book and film as a "merchant of death" whose real purpose was to increase the sale of his munitions stocks.

More extraordinary still was *The Fall of a Nation,* product of the unlikely collaboration of Victor Herbert and the Rev. Thomas A. Dixon. In it a leading pacifist, a thinly disguised William Jennings Bryan, persuades the country that all that is needed to defeat aggression is sweet reasonableness, with national catastrophe as the result. But such films, while appealing to the preparedness-minded, alienated pacifists and isolationists, and Thomas Ince's *Civilization* shrewdly straddled the situation by being at once antiwar and anti-German. It featured a secret army of women pledged to stop the slaughter by refusing to bear any more cannon fodder. A similar theme animated Nazimova's *War Brides,* which was abruptly withdrawn in April 1917 because "the philosophy of this picture is so easily misunderstood by unthinking people that it has been found necessary to withdraw it from circulation for the duration of the war."

The fact that *any* motion picture had to be withdrawn for reasons of national morale was startling in 1917. Movie-makers suddenly found themselves the wielders of a formidable weapon. The Democratic National Committee had credited *Civilization* with helping elect Wilson in 1916 on the "he kept us out of war" platform. *Now* the movies were to be used for exactly the opposite purpose. The Committee on Public Information created a Division of Films "to sell the war to America."

*War Brides,* 1916, with Alla Nazimova.

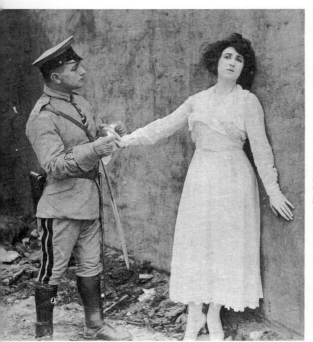

American sympathies were exploited through the plight of the children of conquered Europe. The studio caption says: "Belgian children at school under a Prussian tutor" in Cecil B. De Mille's *Till I Come Back to You,* 1918.

Rita Jolivet heroically refuses to have her eyes bandaged before she is shot as an American spy in *Lest We Forget,* 1918.

"Damn your insolence." Henry B. Walthal as a noble French peasant, or possibly intellectual, is threatened by Lon Chaney in *False Faces,* 1919 (below).

The very aspect of the hideous Hun. Walter Long as a Prussian officer in Mary Pickford's *The Little American,* 1917.

Mary Pickford in *The Little American*, 1917.

# SCHRECKLICHKEIT

Pleasurably aghast at French and British reports of German brutality and vandalism, American film-makers concocted a cinematic frightfulness which even outdistanced its supposed model. The composite portrait of the hideous Hun, usually embodied by Erich von Stroheim, George Siegman, or Walter Long, showed him a fiendish torturer and sadist who thought no more of raping a ten-year-old girl than of sweeping a priceless piece of Sèvres from the table in order to make room for his feet, in the aristocratic French château which he invariably commandeered as his headquarters. He was not quite shown bayonetting babies but the screen did not stop short of much else. Over and over—almost routinely—audiences were treated to the spectacle of the honor of innocent American womanhood saved from despoil at the very last split second. Seldom, if ever, had so much venom been channeled through the medium of the screen. But the overdose brought its reaction. After November 11, 1918, films about the war, especially those aimed at stirring up hate, became totally unsalable.

Death before dishonor. Robert Harron prepares to shoot his sweetheart, Lillian Gish, rather than allow her to fall into the hands of the Huns, in D. W. Griffith's *Hearts of the World*, 1918.

*Huit chevaux, quarante hommes. America's Answer,* 1918, one of the first and most pedestrian of the war documentaries sent home from the front.

## DOCUMENTARIES

The war documentaries and news-reel compilations which began to reach the United States toward the end of 1917 disappointed a public steeped in the synthetic horrors of Hollywood. They caught very little of the front-line fighting and seemed chiefly to feature the ministrations of the YMCA. "Viewed as drama," said D. W. Griffith of the living death of trench warfare, "the war is disappointing." Despite visits to the front, Griffith concentrated his own war film, *Hearts of the World,* 1918, on the horrors of Prussian militarism rather than on the simple horror of war itself. The great films of the war were made after the war by men who had survived the guns and the mud.

*America's Answer.* A mud-spattered YMCA canteen in a French monastery.

## WAR HUMOR

Meanwhile, in reaction to the violent melodrama of *schrecklichkeit* and to the dullness of the films of actual combat, the wartime public increasingly turned to humor as escape from monotony and anxiety. Charlie Chaplin feared that his great *Shoulder Arms* would offend people, but it became his greatest hit. In it, Charlie, by luck, pluck, and devilish ingenuity wins the war singlehanded and brings a captive Kaiser in triumph to London. The chief difference between this hilarious burlesque and some of the serious war dramas was that in Charlie's case it all turned out to be a dream.

Chaplin, disguised as a German general, clowns with Edna Purviance just before winning the war singlehanded.

Charlie Chaplin in his biggest hit, and one of the biggest of all time, *Shoulder Arms*, 1918.

Douglas Fairbanks kayoes the Kaiser with Liberty Bonds while the Devil looks on in glee. Uncle Sam was played by the actor Gustav von Seyffertitz, who changed his professional name to C. Butler Clonebaugh for the duration.

*The Eagle's Eye*, 1918. Heinric von Lertz, head of the German spy ring, with his henchmen, prepares to blow up a munitions wharf.

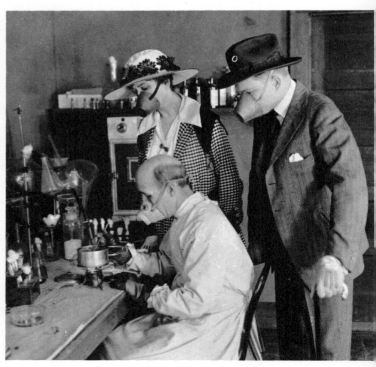

*The Eagle's Eye*. The studio caption: "Heinric von Lertz and Baroness Verbecht watch Dr. Wolf prepare a paste culture of infantile paralysis germs to infect thousands of house flies by permitting them to walk through the paste."

The war films accustomed audiences to the use of the screen for topical and propagandist purposes. Lewis J. Selznick, producer of *Bolshevism on Trial*, cabled the ex-Czar, Nicholas II, after the February revolution: WHEN I WAS BOY IN RUSSIA YOUR POLICE TREATED MY PEOPLE VERY BADLY HOWEVER NO HARD FEELINGS HEAR YOU ARE NOW OUT OF WORK GLAD TO OFFER YOU JOB WITH ME REGARDS.

Mae Murray and Robert Z. Leonard as "England" in one of the tableaux of a war relief rally in Los Angeles. Wallace Reid, who portrayed "America," at extreme right.

## THE HOME FRONT

By mid-1918, every branch of the movie industry was deeply involved in the war effort. Movie theaters were used as community centers for fund-raising rallies, producers distributed hundreds of "picturettes" urging the purchase of Liberty Bonds, and leading movie stars participated frenziedly in bond rallies, in partial atonement for the riches and freedom they were enjoying while most of American manhood was in uniform. Movies themselves were full of Red Cross nurses (including Marie Dressler in a film entitled *The Cross Red Nurse*, 1918), Gold Star mothers, heroic infantrymen, spies, and saboteurs—especially spies and saboteurs. The movies contributed more than their share to the 1918 wave of hysteria which saw sabotage in every accident and a sinister plot in any unusual occurrence. Small children fled from strangers in mustaches, since they knew from the silver screen that a stranger with a mustache was a German spy.

*The Service Star*, 1918, with Madge Kennedy.

An "artist's conception" of the Cathedral of the Motion Picture. The Roxy Theater, which opened in 1927, climaxed a decade and a half that saw the building of ever more sumptuous movie palaces. Named after the greatest of motion-picture showmen, S. L. "Roxy" Rothafel, the Roxy was the ultimate in opulence if not in taste.

# THE GOLDEN TWENTIES

## ENTER THE MIDDLE CLASS

During the course of the First World War, the middle class, by imperceptible degrees, became a part of the movie audience. The wartime need for escape and for news gradually overcame the old prejudices of the nickelodeon days. The nickelodeons themselves were fast disappearing. They were replaced not only by the Bijou Dreams but also, beginning with the opening of the Mark Strand Theatre on Broadway in 1914, by more and more lavish movie palaces. Ornamentation grew so lush that the eye was bewildered. Carpets grew so deep that they became a menace to navigation. Regiments of ushers were organized and drilled under the tutelage of West Point graduates. The more adult among the new audience professed much amusement at all this commercial splendor, but most of them secretly enjoyed it as much as the humbler movie patrons. A routine trip to a motion-picture palace now provided a pleasure equivalent to a tour of Versailles, with the added satisfaction that audiences felt *this* palace really belonged to them.

Not only in their surroundings but in their screen fare as well, the tastes of the new audience had to be reckoned with. They were changing tastes. The middle class, long the stern guardian of morality and respectability, entered the postwar decade with a gleam in its eye.

# THE GREATEST SHOWMAN ON EARTH

## CECIL B. DE MILLE

Cecil (pronounced to rhyme with *wrestle*) Blount De Mille owed to Mary Pickford his opportunity to become the most influential of all movie directors. Miss Pickford had just been offered $675,000 a year to leave Paramount for First National. If she left, Paramount would lose and First National would gain the most powerful boxoffice attraction in the industry with the possible exception of Charles Chaplin. To persuade her to stay, Paramount would have to pay her a yearly emolument likely to denude the company of all but nominal profits. Moreover, other Paramount stars would demand equivalent raises in salary. In this dilemma, De Mille convinced the heads of the company, Adolph Zukor and Jesse L. Lasky that he could make successful pictures without stars. He pointed out that it was the habit of D. W. Griffith, then the greatest name in the industry, to cast virtually unknown players, build them up toward stardom in successive films, and then, when they had attained national popularity, let them go to other companies which would have to pay them stellar salaries while Griffith repeated the whole process. Zukor and Lasky were persuaded by this argument. Miss Pickford was allowed to go, and De Mille began the production of a long series of "all-star" pictures—meaning, pictures without any stars at all.

It seemed a foolhardy step. Griffith was a "genius," and outside his portion of the motion picture realm, the star system had reigned supreme since 1912. But De Mille had something with which to replace the plus that a star name gave to a film. He possessed a type of extrasensory perception that made him aware of any approaching tidal wave of public taste long before anyone else, least of all the public itself, detected the faintest ripple—or perhaps he just knew how to take a ripple and magnify it into a tidal wave. In the prewar screen world, people had been heroes, heroines, villains, and vamps, and anyone not in one of these categories needed not apply. But in a picture De Mille made in 1916, *The Cheat*, a "good" woman was forced by the exigencies of the plot to behave for part of the time like a vamp. The favorable response to this brew convinced him that a new public was coming to the movies, one which preferred such qualities as courage and weakness, evil and good—until then neatly divided—all mixed up together in a potent cocktail of human fallibility.

Not yet was the Jazz Age, not yet the controversy over the younger generation, the eager emulation by their elders, or the open violation of the Noble Experiment. De Mille prepared the way for all three in a series of films in which he created a world peopled by charming people who did dangerous, reckless, even foolish but always exciting things against a background of luxury. His formula might have worked at any period; people have always been attracted by such daydreams. Morality, however, forbade. It was De Mille's peculiar insight that the strait-laced Puritanism of prewar days was weakening and needed only to be given lip service to be placated. He dedicated his pictures to showing people, at length and in intimate detail, what they ought *not* to do. His titles left no doubt at all of where his sympathies lay—*Don't Change Your Husband, Why Change Your Wife?, Forbidden Fruit.*

Cecil B. De Mille directing the blizzard sequence in George Melford's *Nan of Music Mountain,* 1917. The actor with the snow-rimmed beard is Wallace Reid.

# DE MILLE DISCOVERS THE BATHROOM

Having decided to demote the gods and goddesses of the screen to ordinary human beings, De Mille began to analyze ordinary everyday life and probe it for situations which could be made more than ordinarily attractive. His first discovery was the bathroom. To a generation brought up never to mention personal sanitation, he introduced bathing as an art and disrobing as a prolonged rapture. In the shrine of cleanliness, deshabille and even partial nudity were so obvious a necessity that the most godly could not object to their display on the

An advertisement of the Crane Corporation, 1930.

The caption: "When Cecil B. De Mille thinks of bathtubs he thinks hard! In addition to a glass bathtub in his new Metro-Goldwyn-Mayer picture, *Dynamite*, he presents also a 'bath-salts fountain.' Kay Johnson is illustrating the method of pouring salts into their holder."

screen. Whatever the story of a De Mille film of the Twenties, there came an obligatory point when the plot halted to allow for a lingering scene in which the heroine, or sometimes the hero, washed away grime and anointed herself in preparation for a gay masquerade ball or perhaps for some less public pleasure.

De Mille and his bathtubs became a national joke, like Ford stories—but a profitable one. The sophisticated used them as Exhibit A of movie absurdity. The less sophisticated may have laughed too, but they were also impressed. After generations of Puritanism, it was thrilling to be told that bodily beauties were not a shame and a weakness. American bathrooms, previously severely utilitarian, took on the gleam of marble, tile, and chromium, and the tactile luxury of great fuzzy towels and rugs. By the end of the golden decade plumbing corporations which had never dared mention their wares in public were taking full-page advertisements to display bathrooms frankly modeled on the De Mille splendors.

## Cleanliness Is Next to Godliness

Phases of Gloria Swanson's ablutions in *Male and Female*. First, her maids fill a receptacle above her shower with Rose Water. Next, the ceremonial disrobing. Finally, the immersion. The bath water has been artfully colored for the sake of modesty.

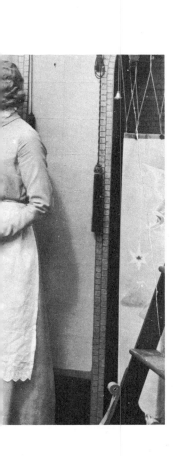

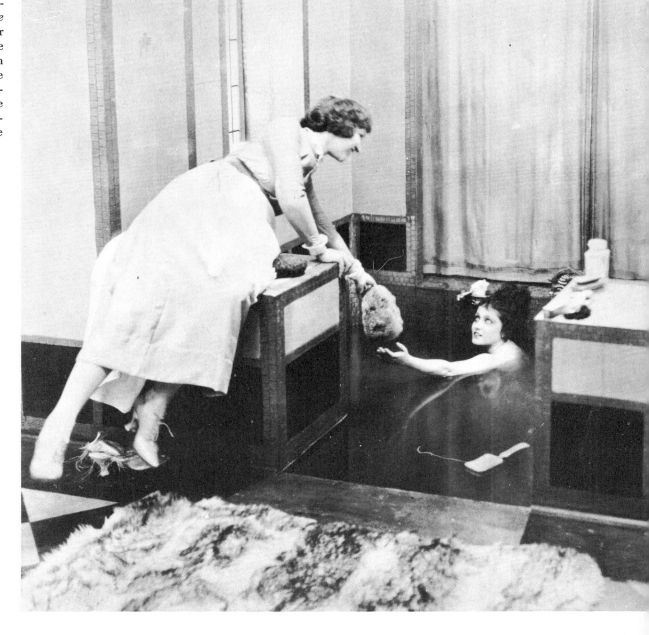

# DREAM BEDROOMS

After the bathroom, the bedroom was the chamber that interested De Mille most. Here, too, disrobing and enrobing could be carried on at length and in full view of the camera. De Mille's beds were things to dream about, although they were constructed for more practical purposes than dreaming. They symbolized many things—art, culture, style, even sleep.

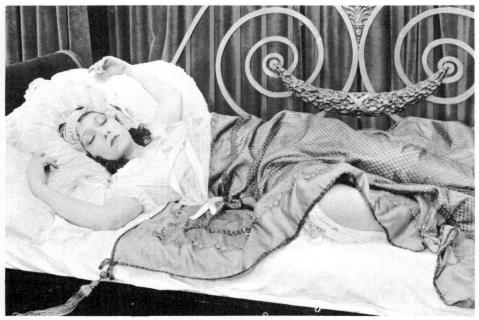

*Male and Female*, 1919. In her troubled slumbers, Gloria Swanson has inadvertently exposed one of her nether limbs.

Leatrice Joy in *Saturday Night*, 1922.

Lillian Rich in *The Golden Bed*, 1925, is the impoverished daughter of aristocratic forebears who marries beneath her to recoup her fortunes. The bed was "a gift of Louis XV" to one of her high-born ancestors.

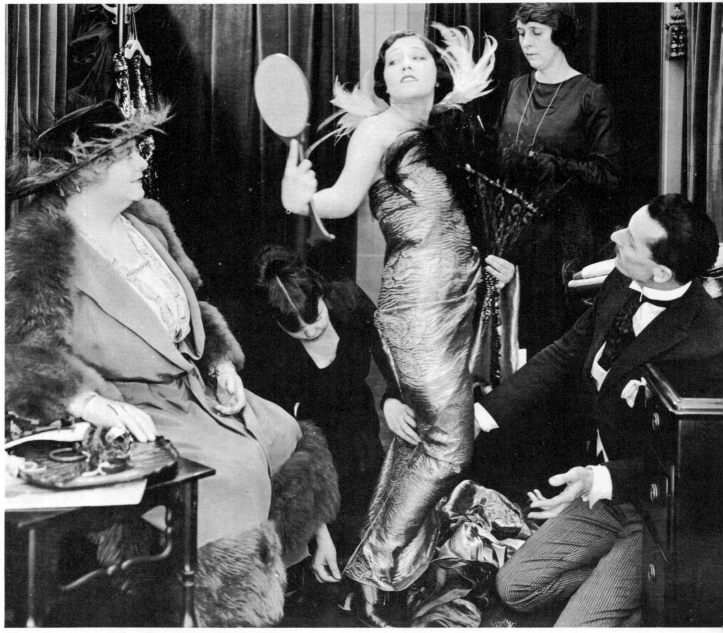

Gloria Swanson in *Why Change Your Wife?*, 1920.

# THE CLOTHES HORSE

While disrobing remained De Mille's most absorbing interest, he recognized that clothes must be worn on some occasions and he insisted that they be worth wearing. His brother William wrote of his interest in them: "Before this, Paris fashion shows had been accessible only to the chosen few. C. B. revealed them to the whole country, the costumes his heroines wore being copied by women and girls throughout the land, especially by those whose contacts with centers of fashion were limited or nonexistent. He achieved this, of course, not by accident but by engaging the best artists of dress he could find; his gowns, lingerie, shoes, hats, and

hairdressing were all done by the best Parisian and New York style experts. This was, and still is, no simple problem, as the clothing and coiffures must be designed and in use in the studio at least six months before they become publicly fashionable."

But Mr. De Mille was not really concerned so much with being fashionable as with being sensational. He knew that Paris creations existed for the movie public only in imagination and that their imagining was lurid indeed. So although he used the best designers, he instructed them to exaggerate the mode and told them that the sky was the limit. His heroines, smothered in ostrich plumes, staggered

The studio caption says: "Perfume, shoe, and hat cabinet used by Lillian Rich in *The Golden Bed*."

under the weight of their jewels, their coiffures, their extravagant gowns like sheets of metal tubing. The bizarre beauty of Gloria Swanson especially inspired him to go to extremes. She was soon stamped as a "clothes horse" in the public mind, and her gowns, and especially her headdresses, were often singled out as the great example of movie bad taste. But Mr. De Mille did not care that her satin swathings and the elaborate convolutions of her hair were copied only by rustic maidens and hash-house waitresses. The films he starred her in attracted women to movie theaters as no other films ever had.

Gloria Swanson, *The Affairs of Anatol*, 1921, *For Better, for Worse*, 1919.

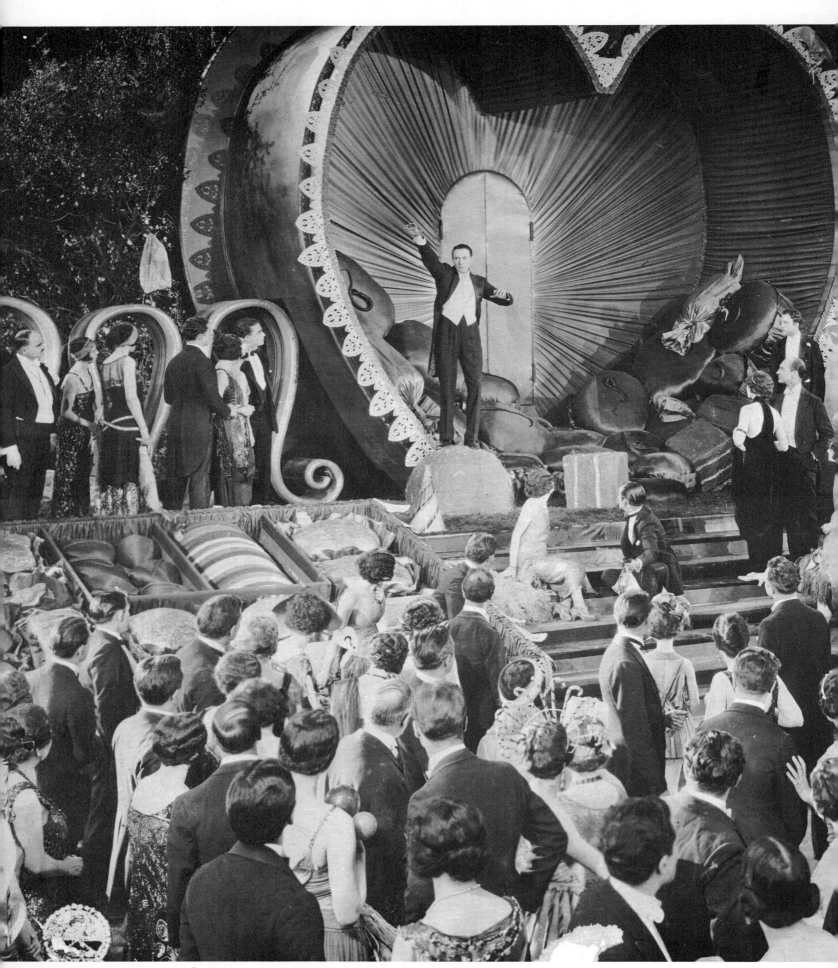

Ecstasy at its height: The Candy Ball, from *The Golden Bed*, 1925.

Detail of the Candy Ball. The studio caption says: "The Marshmallow Girl—a novelty of Flora Peake Holtz's Candy Ball, given on the eve of her husband's financial disaster."

The Swimming Pool Masked Ball from *Saturday Night*, 1922.

# ROUTS AND REVELS

Once bathed and adorned, the De Mille heros and heroines usually proceeded to balls of a magnitude and splendor unknown to Newport at its height, and featuring some titillating novelty picked up from current fads or invented for the occasion. In the subtitles De Mille deplored the extravagance and immorality of these routs, especially in *The Golden Bed,* where a ball given by his wife is the cause of her husband's financial downfall. But of course they had to be shown in order to be deplored.

## WHY/WHY NOT CHANGE YOUR WIFE/HUSBAND

What action took place against the background of the elegant De Mille world? Boy meets girl, of course, but they were considerably older boys and girls than the adolescent screen was used to. In fact, they were married couples tempted to stray from their connubial vows. Of all the innovations De Mille introduced to the screen of the postwar era, this was the most revolutionary. Before Cecil, "love" was the exclusive prerogative of the young and unmated; such married couples as were to be seen were drab, gray figures in the background. Should a prewar wife or husband seek happiness outside the home, their action stamped them automatically as minor and malevolent characters, their only function being to highlight the goodness of the principals or temporarily delay their arrival in each other's arms. De Mille suddenly presented the movie audience with husbands and wives who were human, all too human, and he began his pictures where his predecessors left off, with the honeymoon over and the man and woman sitting down to

Gloria Swanson and Elliott Dexter in *Something to Think About,* 1920.

dinner together night after night, pondering their bargain. Presently appeared the serpents in their shaky Eden. Villains or vamps they would have been earlier, on calculated malice bent, but De Mille showed them as unable to control their actions, sincerely and fatally attracted to the married hero or heroine. Who, then, was to blame for what followed?

As always, De Mille's titles rebuked his plots. *We Can't Have Everything,* 1918, and the like, upheld the sanctity of marriage and insured a last-reel return to the fold. But a wide territory had been explored in the meantime. And the explorers seemed to be saying marriage had better turn out as advertised because there are, after all, second and third and even fourth choices. Watching these films, audiences knew that somewhere the life of the emotions was organized on a more attractive scheme and that that somewhere might be the future. In 1920, the De Mille world seemed the world of tomorrow.

Gloria Swanson and Theodore Kosloff in *Why Change Your Wife?,* 1920.

Gloria Swanson, Wallace Reid, in *The Affairs of Anatol*, 1921.

Lillian Rich meets her fate.

Lillian Rich, Warner Baxter, in *The Golden Bed*, 1925.

Gloria Swanson and Thomas Meighan, in *Why Change Your Wife?*, 1920.

# DE MILLE AND THE MATRIMONIAL STATE

A trade paper of 1922, in an exultant review of *Forbidden Fruit* which praised the film's elegance, strong dramatic situations, and "human" characterizations, added primly, "There is no giddy and blatant sex appeal to prompt maidens of fifteen to ask their mothers embarrassing questions." To the extent that this was true of *Forbidden Fruit* or any De Mille film, it was true because De Mille showed sex where it "belonged." His preoccupation with the bathroom, the conjugal chamber, and the marriage bed provided opportunities for intimate glimpses of forbidden things, but since his lovers were so often married to each other it was hard for the censors to object. So maidens of fifteen saw in his films only what they might presumably see around the house. If what he chose to show of domestic felicity was over their heads, it was clear enough to their elders. Husbands and wives of the early 1920s found themselves watching on the screen experiences which they had shared but

which neither had ever dared mention to the other.

Not all De Mille heroines stayed within the bounds of licensed sex. Flora Peake Holtz (Lillian Rich) of *The Golden Bed*, whose "extravagant Candy Ball" we saw a few pages back, realizes on the night of the ball itself that she has bankrupted her husband (Rod La Rocque), and allows herself to be swept off her feet by a rich playboy (Warner Baxter) with whom she "goes away." A few months later the playboy tires of her and decamps, leaving her huddled amidst the pretties he has tossed out of bureau drawers as he packed his things. Miss Rich drew this harsh fate because of the taint of materialism in her amatory behavior. Other De Mille wives—and husbands—who "went away" with lover or mistress out of sincere emotion, simply returned to their proper mates when they realized their mistake. The interlude was presumably forgotten by both, though it was likely to leave a lasting impression on the spectator.

The Fall of Rome sequence from *Manslaughter*, 1922; the entrance of Venus.

*Male and Female,* 1919. In De Mille's version of *The Admirable Crichton,* Thomas Meighan reads Henley's "When I Was a King in Babylon" to Gloria Swanson. Follows a vision sequence in which they see themselves in ancient Babylon.

## REPENT! REFORM!

Nearly all of the De Mille moralities contained long flashbacks in which the modern characters were seen as people of ancient Rome, ancient Babylon, or even of Paleolithic times. In these flashbacks, the heroes and heroines faced much the same emotional problems as confronted their contemporary counterparts, and their solutions pointed the way of righteousness to these latter when the "vision" ended. The function of these vision sequences, besides correcting the errors of the characters' ways, was to depict Sin in some period when it was reported to have been unbridled. But in *Manslaughter,* 1922, De Mille struck a new note. The wealthy heroine in her craving for speed and excitement runs down and kills a motorcycle policeman. Her follies and those of her fellow sensation-seekers are compared in the inevitable flashback to the weakness of dissolute Rome just before its fall. This popular film sounded the first of the forebodings on the consequences of putting the nation on wheels. For De Mille it marked a turning point. He here emphatically says that the pleasures, freedom, and

The Fall ot Rome sequence from *Manslaughter;* the Goths are coming!

excitements which his films had so relentlessly celebrated might constitute a decadence that would
bring upon the Republic the fate of Rome. He continued the theme from here on in. Convictions
fortunately coincided with commercial success.

De Mille's all-star-no-star policy had paid off for
Paramount. In four years he directed 11 pictures
which cost $1,416,365 and grossed $9,719,666 for
the company. He had led toward stardom Gloria
Swanson, Bebe Daniels, Rod La Rocque, Ricardo
Cortez, Leatrice Joy—but as soon as they became
actual stars he turned them over to lesser directors
and sought new unknowns. As legends grew about
him, his breeched and putteed form superimposed
itself in the public imagination on the old-fashioned
figure of D. W. Griffith as the apotheosis of movie
directors. De Mille stood for the new age, the more
abundant life that, everybody was convinced, the
Twenties were about to usher in. "I believe that my
pictures have had an obvious effect upon American
life," he said in 1924. "I have brought a certain
sense of beauty and luxury into everyday existence,

all jokes about ornate bathrooms and de luxe bou-
doirs aside. I have done my bit toward lifting the
level of daily life."

That this form of uplift had been highly profitable was not altogether beside the point for De Mille.
But even as he spoke, he was preparing to turn a
new page. *Don't Change Your Husband,* first of
the bathtub-and-boudoir films, had cost $73,922 to
make and grossed $292,394; *Adam's Rib,* the last,
cost $408,432 and grossed $880,585. The less costly
picture made proportionally the far greater profit,
but De Mille realized that though he could avoid
using expensive stars he couldn't get around the
general rise in production costs. He had spent his
time, according to his brother William, "in figur-
ing how to make hit pictures without spending
any money." He now decided to reverse himself
and spend more extravagantly than anybody had
dreamed was possible. The form his extravagance
took showed that as usual his ear was applied very
firmly to the ground. He was going to reform the
nation his critics said he had corrupted.

Rodolpho Alfonzo Rafaelo Pierre Filibert Guglielmi di Valentina d'Antonguolla in *A Sainted Devil*, 1924.

# LATIN LOVERS

## SOUTH OF THE BOUDOIR

After November 11, 1918, war films overnight became a drug on the market. Those already made were unreleasable, those in work were abandoned. People were fed to the teeth, or so it seemed to the producers, with patriotism and sacrifice. But over at Metro, the brilliant scenarist June Mathis wondered if an *antiwar* film might not appeal to this new mood of exhausted cynicism about wars to make the world safe for democracy. She could not get it out of her head that Blasco Ibañez' anti-German but also antiwar novel *The Four Horsemen of the Apocalypse* had run into more than one hundred editions in the United States since its publication in 1919. Although Richard A. Rowland, boss of Metro, had never read the book, she converted him to her way of thinking and preparations to film the novel began. What was more difficult, she induced Rowland and director Rex Ingram to cast in the leading role a young man about Hollywood variously known as Rodolpho di Valentina and Rodolph Valentino (both severe abridgments of his baptismal name). (See opposite.)

Valentino had been playing minor roles in pictures for about four years without attracting much attention. The popular leading man Milton Sills tried to help by taking him daily to the Goldwyn commissary in the hope that he would be seen by the mighty. Geraldine Farrar was one of the few whom he impressed. After meeting him on the Goldwyn lot, she said to a friend, "Wouldn't you think somebody'd be interested in trying out that young man, to see what he could do, what he had?" No one was, and his casting in *The Four Horsemen* was thought to jeopardize an already risky venture.

There is some disagreement as to the cinematic merits of *The Four Horsemen*, but none as to its boxoffice potency. As Ingram directed it, it was more than a "war"—or antiwar—film: it introduced American audiences and especially American women to a glamorous international money aristocracy shuttling between Buenos Aires and Paris, between dives and *thé-dansants*, studios and salons. Such milieus had been presented on the screen before—but always with frowning disapproval. Nor was the Latin Lover a novelty. Probably half the villains of the prewar screen were Latin—but they were sneering, greasy, black-hearted cads. Now the same character reappeared as a romantic Apollo who treated women with courtesy and deference but whose eyes promised (what the villains had threatened) that behind the deference, and behind the bedroom door, other, more exciting qualities would emerge—skill and experience. The strong, silent, he-man, Arrow-collar heroes of the American screen were designedly awkward in their movie romancing; it was their badge of self-respect, or perhaps of virginity. The magnetic pull Valentino exerted on millions of women signaled that they were tired of awkward love-making, on screen *and* off.

This scene made history. The moment Valentino first appeared in *The Four Horsemen of the Apocalypse*, the greatest screen idol was born and a new era begun.

The tango sequence from *The Four Horsemen*, 1921. Valentino and Helena Domingues.

# THE SHEIK

Soon after the release of *The Four Horsemen,* and before Metro had had time to realize the gold mine that Valentino was to become, Paramount signed him for what was intended to be a minor film based on *The Sheik,* a British bestseller by E. M. Hull. Sheiks had been seen on the screen before this, but none so revolutionized the technique of love-making from Portland, Maine, to Portland, Oregon, as did this ex-gardener, dish washer, and gigolo. For reasons difficult for mere man to diagnose, he represented the ultimate in masculine appeal. Call it the mystery of the burning sands, the magic lure of the tropics, the titillating uncertainty of the unfamiliar, the reputed animal magnetism of the Arab aristocrat—these are mere words which leave the cult of this particular sheik unexplained. Give Valentino a burnoose, a bejeweled dirk and fancy belt,

a pair of riding boots, a luxurious tent with intimations of a harem in the background and a well-cushioned couch in the foreground, and he became irresistible. To be borne in his arms on a white Arabian steed, struggling virtuously but not too violently, was apparently the goal of nearly every woman's ambition.

Two years after its release, *The Sheik* had earned a million dollars for Paramount, and probably no one knows the exact amount it finally earned. In 1938, deep into the talkie period, Paramount reissued it with a musical accompaniment and it did surprising business. Valentino's leading woman, Agnes Ayres, then a long-time has-been, was exhumed from obscurity and sent on a vaudeville tour to capitalize on the resuscitated fame of a film seventeen years old.

## The Valentino Attack

Much of the action of *The Sheik* consisted of a menacing Valentino staring at a pleading Agnes Ayres while they warily circled each other in preparation for the clinch that was a long time coming. This famous film was largely a tease, an art at which Valentino was adept. His employer, Adolph Zukor, wrote that Valentino's acting "was largely confined to protruding his large, almost occult, eyes until the vast areas of white were visible, drawing back the lips of his wide, sensuous mouth to bare his gleaming teeth, and flaring his nostrils."

# SECOND STRING SHEIKS

The strong, specific appeal of Valentino for American womanhood obviously called for immediate imitation; it was clear that Latin Lovers were to be the order of the day and producers were quick to swing into action. In the first five years of the Twenties, any man with a Latin name or a Latin look could get a screen test. But though the looks were not hard to find and the names could always be fabricated, the essential Valentino quality was harder to come by. Jim Tully was probably the first to call it sex menace, and it was far from an exclusively Latin property, as Clark Gable and Jimmy Cagney proved a few years later.

In 1923, Valentino struck for more money and more control over stories, and walked out of Paramount. The studio got an injunction prohibiting him from appearing on the screen for any other company and set about finding a rival Latin Lover. The discovery that Jack Krantz had "bedroom eyes" led to his rechristening as Ricardo Cortez and an elaborate campaign to build him up as an ersatz Valentino. Cortez did not escape this stereotype until the talkies revealed him as a plain American.

Ricardo Cortez.

The fading career of Antonio Moreno, who entered films in 1913, received a shot in the arm when his Spanish birth and name gave him a place beside Valentino's throne.

← Ramon Novarro was built up by Rex Ingram as Metro's Latin threat. His horde of feminine fans liked to see him as nearly in the nude as the censors allowed, as here in *Ben Hur*, 1926. The studio caption says: "This picture proves rather conclusively that he has no intention of entering a monastery or taking up the profession of concert pianist."

142

When Novarro was not in the altogether, he was likely to be found in Sheik costume. Above, in *The Arab*, 1924, with Alice Terry. Right, Novarro attempted a comeback in *The Sheik Steps Out*, 1937, with Lola Lane billed as a "madcapped American heiress." But fans of the new generation didn't know what a Sheik was, nor much about heiresses either.

John Gilbert in *Arabian Love,* 1922.

Norma Talmadge as "Rose of All the World," and Arthur Edmund Carewe in *Song of Love,* 1924.

The most rewarding of the Valentino imitators was Ben Turpin, seen here with Kathryn McGuire and the Sphinx in Mack Sennett's burlesque, *The Shriek of Araby,* 1923.

Innocent lust. Rudolph Valentino and Nita Naldi in *Blood and Sand*, 1922.

Brutal.

Filial.

144

Courtly.

Pursued.

Transfigured.

# BUT VALENTINO TOPPED THEM ALL

If none of the substitute Valentinos quite managed to make the image of the Latin Lover real, Valentino himself always could. The answer perhaps was that he believed it all. A certain animal grace gave magic to all his movements, but beyond that, the crude situations of his movies rang true to him and he gave them everything he had. Adolph Zukor records an off-screen incident: "He was arguing with an assistant director—about what I did not know and did not inquire. His face grew pale with fury, his eyes protruded in a wilder stare than any he had managed on the screen, and his whole body commenced to quiver." Clearly, life was indistinguishable from the movies to him. But life, even in Hollywood, refused to measure up to the standards of dreamland, and the private loves of the greatest romantic idol of all time were anticlimactic and sometimes almost ludicrous.

# THE LEGEND AND THE MAN

In addition to his beauty and grace, Valentino had the capacity to convey to any woman by a glance or gesture that between them there existed some rare and mystic bond. But this male, so irresistible on the screen and in the fan magazines, in real life sought women stronger than himself and was something of a pushover for any woman who was really determined. He married Winifred Shaugnessy De Wolf Hudnut, who preferred to call herself Natacha Rambova, before his divorce decree from his first wife, Jean Acker, was final, thus bringing about his arrest for bigamy. Natacha, like Valentino, believed implicitly in a special occult power with which she was in close communion, but the conjunction of their astral bodies was not entirely propitious. Along with her supernatural gifts, Miss Rambova was convinced that she possessed an almost equally abnormal infallibility in matters of film production. She had been a costume designer for Nazimova, and a successful one, but she also wished to supervise the writing, direction, and acting of her husband's productions. Her interference became so persistent that the Paramount executives were almost relieved when Valentino, at his wife's command, left the company for independent production. *The Hooded Falcon,* which Natacha wrote for Valen-

tino, proved unproduceable after some $80,000 had been invested in it, and it would have been fortunate if *What Price Beauty?,* of which Natacha was sole author and producer, had also been left in limbo. Together this pair wrote a book of verses entitled *Daydreams,* of which the following is typical:

> Your kiss
>   A Flame
>     Of Passion's fire
> The sensitive seal
>   Of love
> In the desire
>   The fragrance
>   Of your caress
>
> Alas
>   At times
>   I find
>   Exquisite bitterness
> In
>   Your kiss

Natacha presented Valentino with a slave bracelet without which he was never seen in public and which aroused considerable derision among envious males. So did his Beverly Hills home, Falcon's Lair.

Every Valentino film had to have a dressing or, preferably, an undressing scene. These two are from *Blood and Sand,* 1922, above, and *Monsieur Beaucaire,* 1924.

Indeed, Valentino's publicity, once he left Paramount, was consistently bad, reaching its culmination in an editorial in the Chicago *Tribune* called "Pink Powder Puff" which urged the desirability of drowning Rudy, "the beautiful gardener's boy," before "the younger generation of American males replaced razors with depilatories and the ancient caveman virtues of their forefathers were replaced by cosmetics, flopping pants, and slave bracelets."

Although his popularity was already on the wane, Valentino's early death in 1926 evoked a worldwide hysteria. Women who had never laid eyes on him except on the screen were reported to have committed suicide. Pola Negri, who had replaced Natacha in his affections, rushed to his bier accompanied by a nurse and a publicity man. Scenes reminiscent of the draft riots of Civil War days took place in the New York streets, only the demonstrators were exclusively females, who displayed more than male fortitude as they charged the police lines surrounding the funeral chapel where their hero's body lay in state. On the day of his funeral, over one hundred thousand women lined the streets to pay homage to his funeral cortege, and his grave in Los Angeles has become the mecca of loyal if aging members of the ageless cult of the Sheik.

Turbaned Natacha Rambova leaves Los Angeles for New York to arrange for the making of her production *What Price Beauty?*, 1925, while Valentino remains behind to continue acting in a film which had to get along as best it could without his wife's bossing.

After her divorce from Valentino, Natacha Rambova starred for the first and last time in a film bluntly named *When Love Grows Cold*, 1925.

147

The studio caption says: "Mme. Elinor Glyn in the act of composing her immortal masterpiece, *Three Weeks.*"

The studio caption: "This valuable sphinx, with the body of pearl, is worn constantly by Elinor Glyn as a reminder of her creed. 'Live in the present—do not retrospect.'"

In 1928, Madame Glyn appeared in an early talking short, *What Is "IT"?*, in which she expounded the meaning of her famous discovery.

# RURITANIA

## ELINOR GLYN

Until the advent in Hollywood of "Madame" Elinor Glyn, writers had played only a small part in picture production. Stars and directors dominated the scene, while producers pulled strings behind it. True, Samuel Goldwyn had imported his "Eminent Authors," popular writers like Mary Roberts Rinehart and Rex Beach, and turned them loose to make pictures according to their liking, but the results were neither literature nor film but something less than either. Their downfall was their attempt to elevate the screen. Madame Glyn, as she liked to be called, knew better than that. Her biggest bestsellers had been written before 1914, and reflected a prewar world of stratospheric aristocracy as seen through the eyes of a servant girl. This world had been officially abolished in the democratic triumphs of 1918, but Madame Glyn, like other British authors before and since, was smart enough to see that the citizens of the United States of America were still secretly awed by titles and loved to picture the lives led by European nobility as a combination of luxury and depravity. For an industry invariably described as still in its infancy, she was just what the doctor ordered.

No sooner had Madame Glyn arrived in Hollywood than she proceeded to take charge of both its professional and social activities. She instituted the strange custom of afternoon tea as a badge of gentility, intimidated movie hostesses by her criticisms of their manners, and gave innumerable interviews to the fan magazines on the ever-popular topic, "What's Wrong with Hollywood?" Magnanimously she offered lessons in deportment to the local belles, and actually coached Gloria Swanson in the proper thing to do, something that took Miss Swanson many a year to live down. For her second protégée, Clara Bow, Madame Glyn invented the mysterious term IT, and dubbed Clara the IT Girl supreme. Stripped of her verbiage, IT proved to be our old friend sex-appeal, sieved of its concomitants, love and affection, and offered neat. Even so, IT took a good deal of explaining, and Madame Glyn was ceaselessly willing to oblige.

The authoress also insisted on supervising every detail of the films made from her books, each of which was offered as "An Elinor Glyn Production." Her dictatorship grew so irksome that the studios were forced in self-defense into a tacit conspiracy. If Metro and Paramount both contemplated productions of her works, they were likely to begin filming them simultaneously, forcing Madame to distribute her time between them.

Her vogue lasted through the Twenties, but by the time the full force of the depression struck, Madame Glyn found herself expounding IT to an unheeding audience. She returned to England where she supervised a few pictures on the strength of her Hollywood reputation. But in the atmosphere of the Thirties, Ruritania seemed long ago and far away, and no one appeared to care with Madame Glyn whether Lady Alyce had or had not dishonored the family name by marrying a common gamekeeper. It was not only that *Lady Chatterley's Lover* had put a new evaluation on gamekeepers, with or without marriage. It was also that, now, Lady Alyce, the gamekeeper, and those who had once thought no price too high for true love were exclusively concerned with the price of bread.

Madame Glyn poses to show her resemblance to Aileen Pringle, whom she chose to play the heroine of *Three Weeks*. The studio caption says: "Except for the difference of some thirty years in their ages, the two might be doubles."

149

Aileen Pringle and Conrad Nagel in *Three Weeks*, 1924.

# THREE WEEKS

*Three Weeks*, Madame Glyn's official masterpiece, told of a beautiful queen of a Ruritanian kingdom who forsakes her loveless existence for three flaming weeks on a bed of roses in the company of a youthful British aristocrat. Then she sorrowfully renounces him and returns to her duty. That was all there was to it, but it was enough. Every hour of those three forbidden weeks was fully accounted for in Madame Glyn's pages and just as extensively (though more prudently) dealt with in the movie version. *Three Weeks* definitely proved the superiority of the movies to literature. It was delicious to read about tiger skins and beds of roses. Actually to see them was rapture hardly to be borne.

To play her queen, Madame Glyn chose the then unknown Aileen Pringle. Miss Pringle spent most of the rest of her starring career prone on tiger skins, chin cupped in hand, staring at the camera with eyes that promised nameless pleasures. No more ironic example of movie typing is known. Miss Pringle, daughter of a British governor of Jamaica, was as genuine an aristocrat as Madame Glyn's were phony. She was also urbane, witty, and caustic in her comments on Hollywood, her associates, and especially her roles. She became the darling of literary lights like H. L. Mencken and George Jean Nathan, and Hollywood, quick to seize an advantage, made her a sort of official greeter. "Whenever M-G-M signed a new author," she says, "they sent me down to the station to meet him."

When the bed of roses palled, there were tiger skins (below).

The Deaf and Dumb Society reproved Aileen Pringle for this tender scene. Her lips were actually saying to Conrad Nagel, "If you drop me, you ———, I'll break your neck."

## Three and a Half Weeks

Soon after the release of her masterpiece, Mack Sennett generously presented Madame Glyn with *Three and a Half Weeks*, 1924, with a touch of Erich von Stroheim thrown in. Ben Turpin and Madeline Hurlock (Mrs. Robert E. Sherwood) are the impassioned pair.

*The Prisoner of Zenda*, 1922. Alice Terry (with Stuart Holmes) wears Hollywood's uniform for all European princesses. Any woman of noble birth could be spotted by her stand-up collar and beaded gown, both obligatory for Ruritanian heroines.

William Powell discreetly disentangles his spur from Virginia Valli's dress in *Paid to Love*, 1927.

Hauteur at its height. The studio caption says: "Lord St. Austel (Antonio Moreno) tells his bride (Pauline Starke) that she has discredited the family name." In a scene from *Love's Blindness*, an Elinor Glyn production for M-G-M.

The ultimate moment in *His Hour,* 1924, by Elinor Glyn, with Aileen Pringle, John Gilbert.

Antonio Moreno discovers Marion Davies' true sex, in *Beverly of Graustark,* the 1926 screen version of George Barr McCutcheon's romance.

## POMP AND PASSION

Ruritanian romance remained a dominant screen cycle till the end of the silent era, sometimes under Madame Glyn's auspices, sometimes drawn from such outmoded turn-of-the-century favorites as Anthony Hope and George Barr McCutcheon. Already, at the beginning of the era of democracy that World War I was supposed to have ushered in, audiences displayed a hankering for pomps and glories, the stately behavior and volcanic emotions of the prewar world. Hollywood satisfied this longing with a will: American actors and actresses loved to play it haughty and dressed up.

Buster Keaton.

154

# COMEDY IN THE TWENTIES

## LLOYD, KEATON, CHAPLIN

To Europeans, comedy is the most aesthetically satisfying achievement of the American film. In this field the sentimentalities, reticences and evasions which the national morality or its self-appointed custodians impose on the dramatic film do not operate. The irreverence of the movie comedians spared neither social and political institutions, class pretensions, nor popular beliefs. Only the flag and the pulpit remained safe from their ridicule. These licensed jesters could analyze and criticize the fabric of contemporary life on a far deeper level than was ever permitted to "serious" films. After all, it was all in fun—wasn't it?

While Mack Sennett remained king of the comedy short, a series of comedy stars, following in Chaplin's footsteps, graduated into feature films in the Twenties. Of these, Harold Lloyd, whose films are said to have earned a total of $30,000,000, was by far the most popular. His "glass character," pitifully ill-equipped to get along in the world, tackled and overcame obstacles that made strong men quail. His was the welcome message: Get hold of those bootstraps and pull!

Buster Keaton, a greater artist, had profounder things to say about the terms of modern life. His natural state is a sort of permanent incredulity. Keaton moves in the mechanized world of today like the inhabitant of another planet. He gazes with frozen bewilderment at a nightmare reality. Inventions and contrivances like deck chairs and railroad engines seem insuperably animate to him, in the same measure that human beings become impersonal. Without friends or relatives, he is generally incapable of associating with his fellow-beings on a "human" basis, but mechanical devices, though often inimical to him, are, on the other hand, the only "beings" who can "understand" him. They are the real co-stars of his films. "He always wins in the end," says Iris Barry, "not, like Chaplin, by romantically escaping from the world of machinery into a realm of human freedom, but, on the contrary, by fatalistically throwing his humanity into the whirlpool of mechanical forces. He is a hero by the grace of Un-reason and Un-feelingness, and in this respect is a very modern hero indeed." Man into machine is another way of putting it.

Through the Twenties Charles Chaplin made fewer and fewer films. The greatest artist and by far the most beloved personality motion pictures had brought forward, he seemed increasingly to withdraw from the movie industry, from the Hollywood scene, and from his adoring audience. He seemed to want to say things in his films that that audience, supremely content with his clowning, might not like. What they might be was not yet clear in *The Pilgrim* or *The Gold Rush*, but it is significant that he spent more time and care on directing *A Woman of Paris* than on any of his starring films. In this "drama of fate" he played the small part of a railway porter. It was a near-failure.

Harold Lloyd in *Speedy,* 1928.

". . . A warm-hearted understanding of the secret ambitions of ordinary people."
In *The Freshman*, 1925, Harold's tuxedo, held together only by basting, comes apart.

# HAROLD LLOYD

*Safety Last*, 1923. Lloyd's famous, spine-chilling "human fly" stunt was done without doubles or trick photography, and with only a net between him and the street below.

*Why Worry?*, 1923. In giant's shoes, and with his "slave of the lamp," Harold Lloyd breezes through a Central American revolution.

*Girl Shy*, 1924. In real life, Harold is too timid to attend the Saturday night dance.

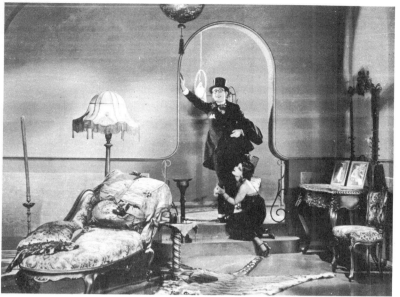

But in Harold's dreams, the Flapper, the Old-Fashioned Girl, and here, the Vamp, vainly compete for his affections.

*The Three Ages.* A De Mille flashback to the Stone Age.

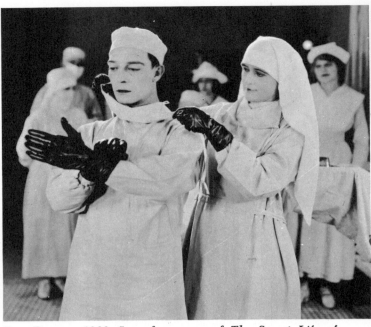

*Day Dreams*, 1922. In a forerunner of *The Secret Life of Walter Mitty*, Buster phantasies himself as a famous surgeon.

*The Frozen North,* 1922. The sheriff of Yonkers.

## BUSTER KEATON

*Day Dreams* again. Keaton as Hamlet.

*The Three Ages,* 1923. Buster, in his parody on Cecil B. De Mille, as a Christian martyr thrown to an exceedingly indifferent lion.

159

*The Gold Rush*, 1925. The haunted, haunting face of the Lone Prospector.

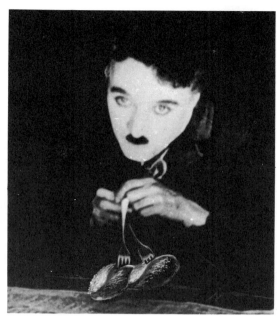

The dance of the Oceana rolls.

*The Gold Rush.* Treating the laces as spaghetti and the sole as meat, the starving prospector eats his shoe.

## CHAPLIN

The party, with favors, to which nobody came.

*The Cohens and the Kellys,* 1926. Vera Gordon, George Sidney, Charlie Murray, and Kate Price in the obligatory scene from the first of their long series.

*Atta Boy,* 1926, with Monty Banks, Fred Kelcey, Stan Laurel, assisted by a bootlegger's liquor belt.

## TYPICAL COMEDY MATERIAL

The foibles of the Twenties provided an endless supply of material for Hollywood's satirists, from the mysteries of the "beauty parlor" to the humors of the speakeasies, not forgetting the movies themselves, where every successful film was followed immediately by its burlesque—*Rob 'Em Good, One Week, Mud and Sand,* and Will Rogers' memorable *Two Wagons— Both Covered.*

*Mud and Sand,* 1922. The comics enjoyed poking fun at the undressing scenes in Rudolph Valentino's vehicles. Valentino's disrobing in *Blood and Sand* took place in a series of coy close-ups of those parts of him which extended from behind a screen. Stan Laurel was quick to see that a single long shot that should include all those close-ups would reveal an anatomical impossibility.

162

*Leave 'Em Laughing*, 1928. Stan Laurel and Oliver Hardy as usual surrender themselves to laughter prematurely, while Edgar Kennedy goes into the slow burn which never bodes him good and which made him famous.

*The Girl in the Pullman*, 1927. Harrison Ford, Marie Prevost, Franklyn Pangborn in a typical situation from one of many films modeled on *Getting Gertie's Garter*.

*Hold Your Breath*, 1924. The mishaps of pioneering days of the artificial hairwave provided unending fun in the Twenties.

*His First Flame*, 1927. Harry Langdon carries the primping Natalie Kingston to what may or may not be safety. For a few years Langdon challenged Chaplin, Keaton, and Lloyd, but his adult infantilism eventually wearied the public. A brilliant craftsman, he seemed unable to vary his technique.

*Jubilo, Jr.*, 1924. The original Our Gang—Mary Kornman, Mickey Daniels, Joe Cobb, Farina, and Jackie Condon—all now grown up and some of them gathered to their fathers, but again entertaining youngsters through their rebirth on television.

163

The Open Trail, 1925, with Jack Hoxie.

The Pioneer Scout, 1928.

164

# WESTERNS

## THE BOY FROM MIX RUN

William S. Hart's films began to earn less money after 1920. Hart himself remained personally popular but exhibitors complained that his pictures were old-fashioned. Finally, Paramount asked Hart to relinquish control over the story and direction of his films and to appear as a star in vehicles supervised by others. Hart would not agree. What they were asking him to give up was just what he had worked hard to put into his films, old-fashioned or not. He was well aware of the difference between the romantic and melodramatic conception of the Old West and his own version of it; he rejected *The Covered Wagon* on the ground that corralling a wagon train in a blind box canyon in Indian country, or swimming oxen across a river with their neck yokes on were "errors that would make a Western man refuse to speak to his own brother." Paramount, however, was firm in its insistence on a new policy and, rather than give in, Hart let his contract with them lapse. Two years later, in his own production for United Artists release, he tried

a comeback. A "one-half life size" bronze statue (opposite page) of William S. Hart was donated by the star to the best bronco buster at the 1926 Cheyenne rodeo, as a half-hearted publicity gesture for *Tumbleweeds*. It didn't help. Nothing helped. The limp reception of the film proved conclusively that the new audiences of the 1920s were no longer interested in the actualities of the old West.

The Western star who succeeded Hart in popularity was a man whose background was very much like Hart's. Tom Mix was born at Mix Run in Clearfield County, Pennsylvania, January 6, 1880, and went west at an early age. Before he was twenty-five he had been Sheriff of Montgomery County, Kansas, and Washington County, Oklahoma; a Deputy U. S. Marshal in Oklahoma; and had spent three years as a Texas Ranger. He knew his section of the West as intimately as Hart had known the Sioux country. Yet it was Mix who created the male dream world, which Hollywood sold to the world as the American West.

*The Bearcat,* 1922, with Hoot Gibson.

*The Pioneer Scout.*

*The Deadline,* 1926, with Bob Custer and Nita Cavaleri.

*The Covered Wagon*, 1923. The wagon train encamps by the trading post.

## WESTERN EPICS

The success of *The Covered Wagon* in the early Twenties brought a vogue of "epic" Westerns which momentarily eclipsed the standard Western star vehicle. Perhaps for once in the history of the movies the word *epic* should not be put in quotes in reference to these productions. In the simplicity and poetry of their images, they truly reflected the national saga of the winning of the West. In them, the pioneers crossed the plains, the daring Pony Express riders established communication with the distant East, the tarriers built the Union Pacific railroad and united the shores of the continent. In Europe as well as America they had deep appeal. Their events mirrored the strong impulse which had drawn the millions to cross the ocean in search of a new life in the New World.

*The Covered Wagon*. Ethel Wales as the mother crumbles the rich black loam of Oregon between her fingers. Jesse Lasky is credited with inserting this scene after the picture was completed, to provide emotional discharge and the feeling of triumph over the long hardships of the pioneers.

166

"Drill, ye tarriers, drill." *The Iron Horse*, 1924, John Ford's epic of the building of the Union Pacific.

*The Pony Express*, 1925. Ricardo Cortez brings the mail through during an Indian attack on a frontier town.

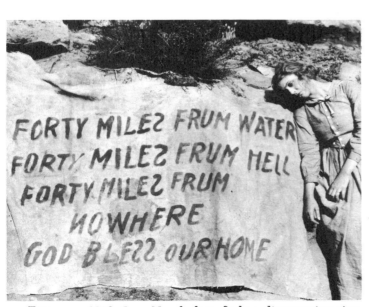

*Tigerman*, 1918. Jane Novak, lost, finds a discouraging sign.

*The Pioneer Scout*, 1928. Indians attack the wagon train.

Tom Mix in the white hat and suit he made the uniform of the Hollywood cowboy of the Twenties.

Tom Mix about the time he joined the U. S. Army to fight in the Spanish-American War in the Philippines.

## TOM MIX

Tom Mix's life of adventure began when, at the age of eighteen, he joined the Army. He saw service in the Philippines during the Spanish-American War, in China during the Boxer Rebellion, and drifted to South Africa to get in on the fun of the Boer War. It was natural when he returned to this country that he should gravitate to the wildest remaining part of the West, the Oklahoma territory. In 1910, the Selig Company came to Oklahoma to make Westerns and hired him to supply locations and cowboy extras. Soon he was acting for them. Thus three years before William S. Hart made his first film, Tom Mix was already a Western star, although a minor one.

It was not long before he became very major indeed. In 1918 he signed a contract with William Fox which, a decade later, was netting him $20,000 a week. On this salary Mix lived like a rajah of old. His vast estate eclipsed even Pickfair. He loaded his wife with jewels and showered gifts on his small daughter Thomasina in full view of the publicity cameras. His collection of fancy boots and fancier costumes reflected the tastes of a cowboy on a spree. Even at formal dinners, he wore his familiar white suit and cowboy boots. As the Twenties wore on, the off-screen personality of this "King of the Cowboys" began to merge with his professional self. The frontier community life that Hart had labored to re-create on the screen was gradually stylized into a never-never land featuring the exploits of a cowpuncher who never punched any cows and who might as well have been called Robin Hood as Tom Mix.

As the country moved further in time from its memories of the real West, and as Hollywood's West became familiar and standardized, Mix became a curious figure on the national scene. Yet publicity stills of the country's leading exponent of virile action—and spotless honor—drinking in Hollywood night clubs, hobnobbing with nobility in Europe, and dancing with debutantes did not disillusion his admirers.

When talkies came in, Westerns were prematurely pronounced dead, and Mix retired to enjoy his large fortune. Two years later Universal enticed him back to the screen, but in 1932, after a series of falls from his horse, the 52-year-old star left the screen for good. Mostly for his own amusement, he toured the country intermittently during the Thirties with "Tom Mix's Circus." In 1940 he was killed in an automobile smash-up. Thanks to a long-running comic strip that used his name, Tom Mix continued to thrill small fry born long after the end of his career.

Tom Mix, a Lochinvar of the Plains, snatches Billie Dove from her wedding in *The Lucky Horseshoe*, 1925.

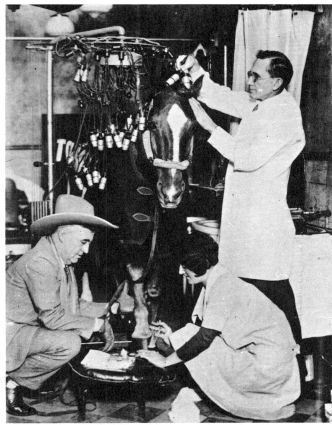

The studio caption says: "Tony, Tom Mix's horse, got a manicure and permanent wave in preparation for his appearance at the Paramount Theater, New York."

Tom Mix about 1919, with Victoria Forde, his leading woman and second wife.

*The Law Forbids*, 1924. Baby Peggy reunited Robert Ellis and Elinor

*Three Sinners*, 1928. Even Pola Negri had to yearn over children occasionally to keep audience "sympathy."

*Happiness Ahead*, 1928. The power of a good woman: Colleen Moore teaches gangster Edmund Lowe to pray on their wedding night.

Standing in the rain, bedraggled Belle Bennett watches the wedding of her daughter, Lois Moran, to wealthy Douglas Fairbanks, Jr., in Samuel Goldwyn's supreme epic of mother love, *Stella Dallas*, 1925.

Fair at the very verge of divorce. The chief function of screen moppets.

# GOODNESS

The Puritan tradition dies hard. Even in the Jazz Age, the screen continued to pay the wages of virtue, though the theme became a minor one. But kiddies from six to sixty are always with us, and for them producers continued occasionally to purvey invincible morality and ineffable domestic bliss much as they had a decade earlier.

*The Man Who Fights Alone*, 1924. The caption says: "The Miracle of Love when John Marble (William Farnum) can walk again in the woods with his wife (Lois Wilson) and their baby (Dawn O'Day)." This incredibly named tyke grew up to be the lovely Anne Shirley.

*The Man Who Had Everything*, 1921. Kindly old Alec B. Francis, who, in spite of blindness, poverty, or other handicaps, was happier than anybody and solved all problems through love and faith.

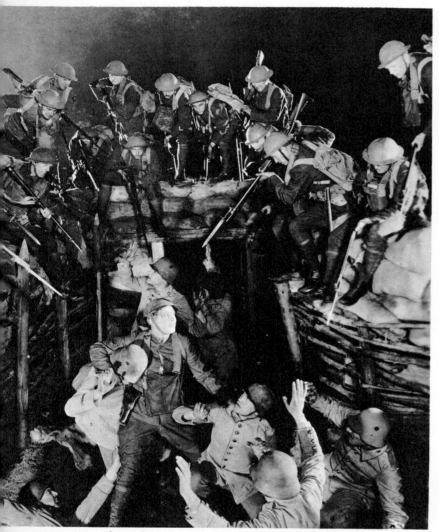

*Three Faces East,* 1926. The Kaiser rewards a beautiful double agent, Jetta Goudal, in the most famous of spy dramas. William II was as usual portrayed by Rupert Julian, who took time off from his directorial work whenever someone was needed to impersonate the monarch.

*Shootin' for Love,* 1923. Fighting Duke Travis (Hoot Gibson), pride of the A.E.F., subdues a trenchful of the Boche singlehanded, though with considerable moral support.

## The Standard Ingredients

To classify as a legitimate war picture, each film had to have behind-the-lines humor and during-the-battle heroism, even when the most poignant tragedy climaxed the story; and if you could find a way to insert some grim Prussians or beautiful spies, so much the better.

*Rookies,* 1927, with Karl Dane and George K. Arthur. Behind-the-front humor was a staple in routine war films.

# WAR
# IN RETROSPECT

The war films of 1917-18 had been filmed far from the front by men who knew little of modern war, and their routine heroics and humor were continued in formula films through the early Twenties. Only when actual veterans like Laurence Stallings, John Monk Saunders, William Wellman, and Dick Grace got into film-making did Hollywood movies begin to render the real flavor of what was to a whole generation of Americans the most overwhelming experience of their lives. Of all the films they originated, *The Big Parade* was and remains the outstanding achievement. King Vidor's filming of the battle scenes in Laurence Stallings' story so excited the producer, Irving Thalberg, that he suggested that they be lengthened and featured in the film above its romance and comedy. Vidor was deliberately trying to introduce a new view of modern war and especially of infantry fighting. From much screening of wartime newsreels and Signal Corps records, he had observed that the pace of men moving into combat has a characteristic rhythm, which he imitated for the camera, and he cut his battle sequences at the same measured pace. The result was an illusion of experience and close participation in the action still unique in fictional war films.

*The Big Parade* did not, like plays and novels written by intellectuals, debunk war or deplore its causes. Both its artistic strength and its immense popular appeal stemmed from a certain neutral outlook, the viewpoint of the ordinary soldier to whom war may be hell but who is not concerned with whether it is morally or socially wrong. Vidor himself has described the picture he tried to paint: "A man walks through the war and looks at it, neither a pacifist nor a soldier, he simply goes through and has a look and is pulled into these experiences."

In addition to the authenticity of its battle scenes, *The Big Parade* portrayed with acute realism the affection amounting to love which grows up between men under combat conditions, and the frenzy of women parted from their lovers in the shadow of death. No one who has seen it will ever forget the scene in which Renee Adoree clings first to John Gilbert's boot and then to the truck which is carrying him away, in a compulsive attempt to prevent the inevitable.

". . . In making contact with the enemy, the activity seems—to the soldiers engaged in it—brisk at the start, and then slows down as the tension grows. King Vidor has managed to suggest, with startling success, the second stage or slowing down. The long march through the woods succeeds in imitating the communal pace as it declines and intensifies into what has been called 'the ultimate loneliness of contact.' This loneliness is not actual, but grows from a state of depression intense enough to obliterate the sense of time. Most infantrymen will insist, however, that it is an absolute experience, for although friends are only a helping hand away, that hand may never be raised, since the line must keep its broken order and unbroken pace."

—ALISTAIR COOKE

In a famous scene, Gilbert, the American dough-boy, teaches the French girl, Renee Adoree, the technique of chewing gum.

John Gilbert starred in minor films for William Fox before *The Big Parade* brought out the dynamic magnetism which made him the top male star until the end of the silent era.

Tom O'Brien, John Gilbert, and Karl Dane, the three famous buddies of *The Big Parade*.

# THE BIG PARADE

"What price glory now?" cries Leslie Fenton in the famous dugout scene, while McLaglen and Lowe bind their wounded and count their dead.

# WHAT PRICE GLORY

In the Twenties two sweet old ladies attended a performance of the Broadway version of *What Price Glory.* At the final curtain, one said, "Shall we get the hell out of here?" and the other replied, "As soon as I find my goddamn glasses." This sulphurous aspect of the original was eliminated from the film version, which also often seemed less an antiwar picture than a portrayal of the amorous antics of Captain Flagg and Sergeant Quirt. In this it was so successful that audiences were given more of their adventures in subsequent films, including one of the biggest hits of all time, *The Cockeyed World,* 1929. But there's no mistaking the meaning of the famous scene in which the dying Mother's Boy, Barry Norton, cries out, "Stop the blood! Stop the blood!"

*Lilac Time*, 1928. Colleen Moore tries to extricate her lover, Gary Cooper, from his crashed plane.

*The Dawn Patrol, 1930.*

## "IT'S SHEER MURDER..."

"It's sheer murder to send a mere boy up in a crate like that" was one of countless clichés familiar to movie fans once Hollywood discovered the spectacular possibilities of airplane combat. If trench fighting was dull to look at in the hands of lesser directors than King Vidor, almost anybody could put on a big show with plenty of airplanes, money, and stunt men, many of whom had been wartime pilots, whose philosophy was that in Hollywood at least they were risking their necks for good pay.

*Lilac Time.* "Dogfights" between camouflaged planes added pictorial excitement to the airplane films, especially when assisted by the "optical effects" men. *The Dawn Patrol* (left). Ground strafing provided thrills aplenty, particularly for the stunt men.

177

*The Lone Eagle*, 1927, with Barbara Kent and Raymond Keane. The studio caption says: "Should she let him sleep peacefully on or awaken and send him perhaps to his death?"

*The Dawn Patrol*, 1930. Begrimed Commander Richard Barthelmess erases the name of a shot-down pilot from the company roster.

# ARMY LIFE, LAFAYETTE ESCADRILLE VERSION

Most of the airplane films were written by John Monk Saunders and directed by William Wellman, with assists from directors Clarence Brown and Howard Hawks, both air enthusiasts. For all four, stunt man Dick Grace risked his neck repeatedly— and broke it once. To routine ground crashes he added crashes in mid-air, crashes in treetops, on rooftops, in water. That he survived is a miracle.

Saunders, Grace and Wellman had all been wartime fliers, and from their romanticized experiences on the screen the movie public learned that the War I flyboys expected imminent death in their canvas-covered crates, that they drowned their anxieties in drink and French babes, and kept a stiff upper lip when the names of their fallen comrades were erased from the squadron roster by the Commander who was always on the verge of nervous breakdown from sending youths to their death.

The line between art and life began to blur when Saunders and Grace cannibalized their experiences in such films as *The Lost Squadron*, 1932, and *Lucky Devils*, 1933. In them, war aces bored with the monotony of peacetime seek excitement in Hollywood as airplane stunt men, and then repeat the escadrille pattern complete with erasure from the blackboard of the names of the fallen.

John Monk Saunders, author, Dick Grace, stunt man, and William Wellman, director, beside a plane which Grace has just crashed for their picture *Wings*, 1927.

*The Legion of the Condemned*, 1928. The Legion (left) drinks to missing comrades. Francis McDonald, third from left, Gary Cooper, third from right, Barry Norton, extreme right.

*Lucky Devils*, 1933. The Lucky Devils are ex-army pilots who go to Hollywood after the war to become stunt men. Here Creighton Chaney (later, Lon Chaney, Jr.), William Boyd, William Gargan, and Bob Rose gloomily drink to departed friends.

Mary Miles Minter.

Virginia Rappe, star of two-reel comedies, attended a drinking party given by Roscoe "Fatty" Arbuckle and, while there, died of a "chronic pelvic illness." Arbuckle, a former plumber's helper who had risen to great popularity as a comedian, was acquitted by three juries of any responsibility for Miss Rappe's death, but the circumstances surrounding it threw a strange light on the way the movie people spent their enormous earnings.

# THE BIG CLEAN-UP

## PRESS FIELD DAY

The movie craze drew to Los Angeles not only thousands of girls bent on acting careers, and a host of doubtful characters looking for easy money, but also and in considerable numbers free-lance journalists who smelled sensation. Strange stories involving sex, narcotics, and riotous living began to seep into the national press. Many in the new middle-class screen audiences felt a twinge of righteous resentment at the huge sums being earned by former plumbers and shopgirls turned movie stars. Their feelings crystallized when a sudden series of unrelated events turned vague rumor into startling fact. The never-solved murder of the director William Desmond Taylor revealed unsavory facts about his past life and his associations with two reigning favorites, Mabel Normand and Mary Miles Minter. Miss Minter's indiscreet love letters to the director shattered the public image of her as a girl of spotless purity. Mabel Normand's producer, Mack Sennett, stood by her and she was cleared of any connection with Taylor's death. But shortly thereafter her chauffeur, whom she had invited to join a drinking party at the home of Edna Purviance, Chaplin's leading woman, shot another male guest. That was too much, and the screen's greatest comedienne found herself banned from her profession. Even as the industry reeled from these revelations, the sordid death of Virginia Rappe brought into the limelight Roscoe Arbuckle's custom of holding continuous drinking parties, some said orgies, at the St. Francis Hotel in San Francisco. Arbuckle, like Miss Minter and Miss Normand, was forcibly retired from the screen, and the current films of all three, representing an investment of millions, were banned or withdrawn entirely.

The press had a field day. The Taylor murder case was said at the time to have sold more newspapers, everywhere in the United States, than any previous event. Clubwomen, reformers, and busy-bodies seized upon the sins of some members of the movie colony as an unlooked-for bonanza, and even the average lay citizen came to regard Hollywood as a cesspool of iniquity.

Advertisements like this for "Schools of Photoplay Acting" and tales of the quick success before the camera of untrained nonprofessionals lured thousands of young girls to Hollywood. Unable to find work even as shop-girls or waitresses, many of them drifted into prostitution. To avoid the California vagrancy laws they habitually gave their occupation as "movie extra," enabling the newspapers to announce when they got into trouble: "Three Beautiful Film Stars Arrested in Bawdy House."

Will H. Hays (center), first president of the Motion Picture Producers and Distributors of America, with the founding fathers of the organization, set up by the major studios to impose a "dictatorship of virtue" upon the screen.

## WILL HAYS

The roar of disapproval over the Arbuckle-Taylor-Minter-Normand sensations had hardly died down when fresh scandal arose in Hollywood. Wallace Reid's untimely death at the age of thirty revealed him to have been a drug addict. That this could have been true of an actor who symbolized healthy normality deeply shocked the nation. Not only zealots but nearly everyone agreed that something would have to be done about Hollywood before it became a national disgrace. The movie magnates were worried and duly penitent. Engrossed in cut-throat competition with one another, they had ignored the intensity of American moral standards.

Recognizing now their own inexperience, they turned to the citadels of righteousness. Acting on the analogy with baseball, they appointed Presbyterian elder Will Hays, then Postmaster-General in Harding's cabinet, as a "czar" with absolute authority to police the morals of the industry and to reform, or rather establish, its public relations.

Hays cleaned house swiftly. The studios inserted "morality clauses" in their contracts which permitted cancellation if players were so much as accused of immorality, while those whose behavior was beyond reform were promptly exiled from the screen. Hays established the Central Casting Agency, through which alone extras can find employment at the studios, and where applicants for registration must pass the scrutiny of a staff of professional sociologists. At the same time that he inaugurated a campaign to induce the press to report Hollywood news without exaggeration, he made it clear to everyone in pictures that their lives must be able to withstand public scrutiny.

In his effort to rehabilitate the industry, Hays then turned to his most powerful weapon, the screen itself. At his suggestion, James Cruze directed for Paramount a fascinating picture called simply *Hollywood*, a Cinderella story in reverse in which the beautiful girl comes to the picture capital and does *not* become a star. Mrs. Wallace Reid's attack on the dope habit, *Human Wreckage*, doubtless also owed something to Hays's inspiration. His most influential ally, however, proved to be none other than Cecil B. De Mille, who had introduced sex to the screen, and who now sought to use pictures as a pulpit. "Having attended to the underclothes, bathrooms, and matrimonial irregularities of his fellow-citizens," said his brother William, "he now began to consider their salvation."

LEFT TO RIGHT:
E. W. Hammons
J. D. Williams
Winfield Sheehan
Cortland Smith
Carl Laemmle
Rufus Cole
William E. Atkinson
Will H. Hays
Robert H. Cochrane
Samuel Goldwyn
Marcus Loew
Adolph Zukor
William Fox
Lewis Selznick
Myron Selznick

*Human Wreckage,* 1923. With the covert assistance of Will Hays, Mrs. Wallace Reid set out to avenge her husband's death by producing and starring in this anti-narcotics film. Encouraged by its boxoffice success, Mrs. Reid sought further sores on the body politic which required melodramatic disinfection. She pictured the horrors of modern youth in *Broken Laws,* ripped concealing veils from prostitution in *The Red Kimono,* then unaccountably left us to get along as best we could with the evils that remained.

# THE TEN COMMANDMENTS

De Mille was the ideal director to rescue the screen from contamination. As a tract for the times, *The Ten Commandments* could not have served the industry's public relations needs better if the script had been written by Will Hays himself. In it, De Mille used his tried-and-true technique of the sermonizing flashback with a new twist. The picture began with an awesomely spectacular retelling of

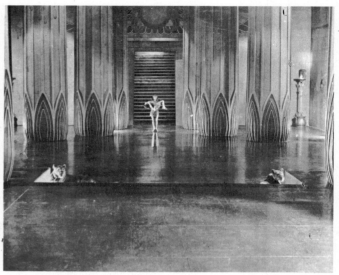

**1.** *The Ten Commandments*, 1923. Moses (Theodore Roberts) tells Pharaoh (Charles de Roche) that all the first-born of Egypt will die if Israel is not permitted to depart.

**2.** Later, Pharaoh wanders through his palace with the body of his son.

**3.** Miriam (Estelle Taylor) adores the Golden Calf.

the flight of the Israelites from Egypt and the engulfing of Pharaoh's pursuing army. This was followed by a modern story which wagged a stern finger at contemporary Americans who had forsaken the Mosaic tenets for the fleshpots of industrial civilization. De Mille's 1956 *Ten Commandments* told only the Biblical story, leaving contemporary movie-goers to tease out the moral as best they may.

**4.** The giving of the Law.

**5.** Moses denounces Miriam for sacrilege and announces the Commandments of God to Israel.

**6.** De Mille's ancient Egypt was bigger, if not more awe-inspiring, than Griffith's Babylon in *Intolerance*.

185

**7.** John MacTavish (Richard Dix), Mother MacTavish (Edythe Chapman), Dan MacTavish (Rod La Rocque), and a waif of the streets (Leatrice Joy) whom the MacTavishes have taken in. Dix, a carpenter, is much under the influence of his Bible-reading mother, but La Rocque, who worships the golden calf of quick millions, decides to leave the religious atmosphere of her house, taking Miss Joy with him as his wife.

**8.** Sally Lung (Nita Naldi), a "Eurasian adventuress," wheedles a costly bauble from La Rocque, who has grown rich and neglectful of his wife, Miss Joy. Only the audience knows that Miss Naldi has escaped from the leper colony at Molokai.

**12.** Temporarily hidden from the police in his wife's bed, La Rocque is later killed in a speedboat accident as he races for the Mexican border.

**11.** Meanwhile, La Rocque, who has contracted leprosy from Miss Naldi, shoots her and flees.

**9.** Dix tells La Rocque that the sustaining fibers he intends to use in constructing a new cathedral are shoddy, but the latter scoffs.

**10.** When Mother MacTavish visits the new cathedral, it collapses upon her and kills her. Leatrice Joy, Edythe Chapman, Richard Dix, and Rod La Rocque behold the warning of the Lord's vengeance.

**13.** The repentant Miss Joy is lectured to by Dix on the folly of breaking the Commandments and worshiping the Golden Calf.

**14.** Miss Joy and Dix clinch atop a building which Dix is constructing, in a fade-out curiously anticipatory of the final scene of Ayn Rand's and King Vidor's *The Fountainhead*, 1949.

# THE
# KING OF KINGS

Cecil B. De Mille's first attempt to top his *The Ten Commandments* (his last was to remake it) was to film the life of Christ, *The King of Kings,* 1927. Here he was on dangerous ground, and he took all possible precautions. He kept H. B. Warner, who played Christ, secluded in his dressing room when not actually before the cameras, and with the other players he went much further than did the morality clauses of Mr. Hays. "It would never do," said William de Mille, "to have the Virgin Mary getting a divorce or Saint John cutting up in a night club. Therefore they all signed legal documents which underwrote their behavior and their chastity, it being clearly understood that, although breaking solemn vows taken at the altar was only human, breaking a contract with the Company was really important."

William Boyd as Simon the Cyrenian, takes the cross from the Christus, H. B. Warner

# BEN HUR

*Ben Hur,* 1926, was filmed for purely commercial reasons, but its religious motif accorded well with Will Hays's campaign. Production was begun in Italy under the old Goldwyn company, but when Louis B. Mayer took charge of the merged Metro-Goldwyn-Mayer corporation, he scrapped most of what there was and reshot it at the M-G-M studio. It cost five million dollars and was generally regarded in the United States as the summit of screen art.

The virtuous Ben Hur maddened by the lure of the siren. Carmel Myers and Ramon Novarro.

Carmel Myers as Iras, Francis X. Bushman as Messala.

De Mille was unable to resist the temptation to elevate St. Mary Magdalene (Jacqueline Logan) from streetwalker to elegant courtesan.

The chariot race—Novarro vs. Bushman.

Clara Bow, the IT Girl,
epitome of razz-ma-tazz,
everybody's dreamboat from 1925
to 1930. Alice White (below) was
Clara's closest rival.

Alice White.

Louise Brooks.

Sally O'Neil.

190

# BUT FLAMING YOUTH FLAMED ON

## SHEIKS AND SHEBAS

Hollywood's housecleaning did not extend to the movies themselves. Though Will Hays might impose a code of decorum on the (public) conduct of the public's idols, only the boxoffice's message was on-screen behavior, and the boxoffice's message was unmistakable: anything goes. The movies had made themselves a fast transmission belt for Jazz Age ideas, and nothing could arrest the process. In spite of censorial and ministerial protests, the young knew what they wanted to see on the screen, and many of their elders, despite their protestations, wanted to see the same. In a review of the film version of Scott Fitzgerald's *The Beautiful and the Damned, Photoplay* editorialized: "If he depicts life as a series of petting parties, cocktails, mad dancing and liquor on the hip, it is because he sees our youthful generation in those terms . . . it is our youthful fascisti possessing its measure of money and knowledge, fighting against the swing of the pendulum which has brought us the you-must-not era." In short, the said youthful fascisti no longer

cared whether their idols were damned as long as they were also beautiful.

As Valentino's twentieth-century *The Sheik* incarnated the desirable male for American boys, so Betty Blythe's *The Queen of Sheba* captured the imagination of their girl-friends. In an impressive example of the process of popular myth-making, American youth equated these two figures in time —though they were actually separated by two thousand years—on the simple score that both were Oriental and, therefore, ardent and unashamed in their sexuality. After 1921, the former "drugstore cowboy" (the phrase was coined during the earlier vogue of the Western hero) was metamorphosed into a Sheik, and his date became a Sheba. As parents watched their young cultivate sideburns and spit curls, the more reflective among them came to a startled realization that the old molding influences —home, church, school—had been superseded by the silver screen. The rest wished they were young enough to be Sheiks and Shebas themselves.

Donald Keith.

Malcolm McGregor.

Lawrence Gray.

## The Stacomb Boys

The hallmark of a home-grown Sheik of the Twenties was hair that was hard and shiny with Brilliantine.

Publicity for *Prodigal Daughters*, 1923. Gloria Swanson proclaims the new creed of youth to her father, Theodore Roberts.

## "THE MODERN GENERATION"

The chasm which opened between parents and children during the Twenties was without precedent in American culture. Men and women reared by prewar tenets of morality simply could not understand "the modern generation" which regarded the pursuit of pleasure as life's major purpose and challenged the values of chastity and self-restraint. The parents were not only bewildered but weaponless—authority had departed. The heavy father of tradition might still order his wanton daughter out, out into the storm, but he was more apt to receive a wisecracking comeback than the tear-dimmed repentance in which Lillian Gish had once specialized. All this the movies zealously highlighted in dozens of pictures depicting the conflict of the generations, with ample spicing of the unholy orgies into which Daughter wandered in her search for "freedom from conventions."

Generally she "went too far," and had to be saved and forgiven by Papa in the last reel, but it was a cinch she wasn't going to resume the Victorian shackles Papa held out to her.

*Prodigal Daughters.* The studio caption says: "J. D. catches his daughters in the act of returning from a ball *after midnight.*"

*Prodigal Daughters.* "After she has been saved from a shameful fate, Mrs. Forbes clasps a repentant Elinor in her arms while J. D. says, 'Praise God from whom all blessings flow.'" Theodore Roberts, Gloria Swanson, Louise Dresser.

Clara Bow, second from left, and Donald Keith, next, look on at a fraternity initiation in *The Plastic Age*, 1925.

A ukulele was a more indispensable part of a collegian's equipment than a fountain pen in the Golden Twenties. Eddie Phillips in *The Collegians*, 1929.

# "YES, WE ARE COLLEGIATE"

If going to Hollywood was the beau ideal of American youth as the booming Twenties boomed on, going to college was a more immediately attainable goal—college conceived not as an institution of learning but as a playground, night club, or as Woodrow Wilson said of Princeton, the best country club in America. Certainly that was the way it looked on the screens of America, and the image received eager acceptance. After all, practically anybody could go to college if he could get the cash or played a good game of football. If not he could always work his way through selling subscrip-

tions or waiting on table as did the hero of *The Collegians*. This remarkable series of two-reel shorts ran uninterruptedly on the screen every week for four years, 1926-1930, to the delight of the Jazz Age adolescents. To their unspoken question—What do you go to college for?—*The Collegians* gave a highly acceptable answer: You go there to learn things—how to drink, how to pet, how to win the big game, and above all, how to meet people who will be useful to you when at last the four years of hedonistic freedom are over and you have to put your nose to the grindstone and make your pile.

The studio caption says: "Reckless youth runs a race with death on their way to a party with Joan Crawford being chauffeured by Douglas Fairbanks, Jr., in her first starring picture, *Our Modern Maidens*, 1929."

## SPEED-CRAZY

Of the three principal ingredients of the Jazz Age cocktail—gin, jazz, and gasoline—gasoline was the most novel. The inventors of the horseless carriage thought they were simply improving transportation, but American youth, aided by the screen, soon discovered that the automobile could be turned into a mobile party, petting or otherwise, where illicit activities would be safe from the prying eyes of elders, and where the thrill of speed would heighten those of liquor and sex. "Thanks for the buggy ride" became a typical feminine sneer, and "walking back" and "mad money," realities not to be scoffed at. To-

day's hot-rodders are the sinister, yet rather pallid, descendants of these reckless, feckless, possibly witless speedsters, tearing around bound for nowhere. And just as films about hot-rodders today stir doubts of their social value, so pictures about speeding drew feeble censure in the Twenties. But youth wanted to see speed on the screen, and youth was served, not only because it more and more constituted the main body of the movie audience, but, also more and more, because nearly everybody wanted to be young. Apparently the best way to be young was to be foolish.

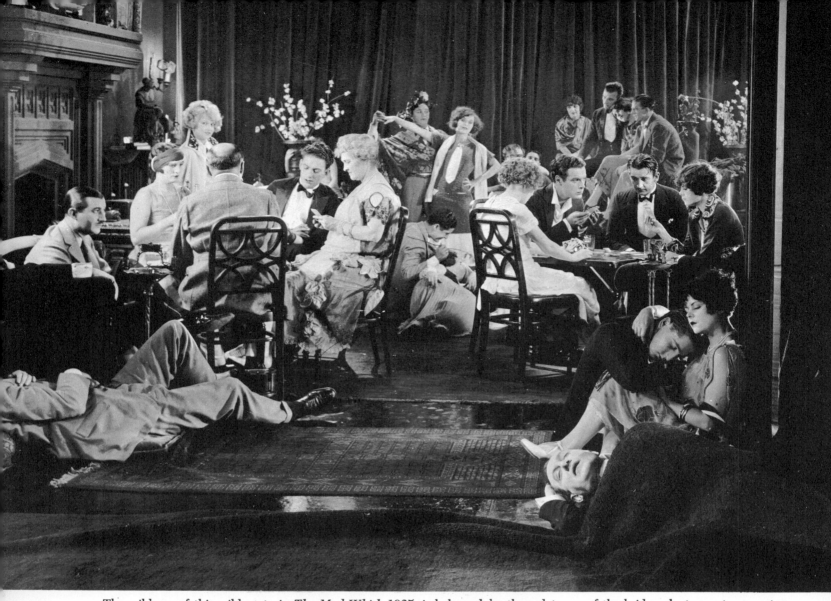

The wildness of this wild party in *The Mad Whirl*, 1925, is balanced by the sedateness of the bridge-playing matron, center.

# WILD PARTIES

"Wild parties" on the screen were distinguishable from "orgies," that other institution of the Twenties, by the fact that they were attended by healthy American youth rather than decadent aristocrats in Wicked Paris or Imperial Russia. They featured a great deal of drinking, dancing, petting, and what must have been an immense amount of noise; it is a mercy that their popularity on the screen did not outlast the silent era. Their structure never varied. As ecstasy reached its height, the screen dissolved into a montage of dancing legs, moaning saxophones, popping corks, and groping hands, followed by a second montage of dead cigarette butts, spilled wine, and guttering candles. The participants were invariably depicted as nursing horrendous hangovers the following day, but quite ready to attend another party scheduled for that very evening, if not afternoon. One thing must be said for the screen's wild parties: nothing staged in real life ever approached them in wildness, as moviegoing youths must have discovered to their disappointment.

Sally O'Neil takes a casual swig from her hip flask as Alice White looks on in a roadhouse scene from *Mad Hour*, 1928.

Joan Crawford holds a "lingerie party" on her yacht in *Dance, Fools, Dance*, 1931.

William Haines assists Mae Murray in whatever she is doing with the punch bowl in *Circe the Enchantress*, 1924.

Malcolm McGregor and Jacqueline Logan make a razz-ma-tazz entrance in *The House of Youth*, 1924.

Florence Vidor and Lew Cody struggle with that amazing innovation, the radio, in *Husbands and Lovers*, 1924.

Phyllis Haver takes a mud bath. *The Perfect Flapper*, 1924.

"Roll 'em, girls, roll 'em," was the "message" of a popular song of 1926, and of *Rolled Stockings*, 1927, with James Hall and Louise Brooks. According to Miss Brooks, who says she refused to pose for the picture, the legs shown here and advertised as hers actually belonged to Nancy Phillips.

Dorothy Mackaill's "bee-stung" lips, in *The Next Corner*, 1924, exceeded even those of Mae Murray, who claimed exclusive copyright.

## FADS AND FASHIONS

The changes which the industrial revolution made possible in American morals and manners were speeded up more by the screen than by any other agency except possibly the automobile. Especially did the movies accelerate the emancipation of women. Cigarette smoking by females was, until about 1900, confined to loose ladies and divorcées. At the end of World War I it was no longer a certain stigma of the sinful life, but was still rigidly confined to the fast and flighty. By 1928 it was a commonplace among flappers even in small-town America; the movies had licensed it. Bobbed hair and short skirts, a moral issue in 1920, were five years later close to compulsory. As women reached out for freedom and power, as the sense spread through the United States that everyone was on the threshold of a richer, freer, and much more exciting life, the movies fed these unformed expectations from a cornucopia of novelties which, trivial in themselves, nevertheless symbolized luxury, adventure, all the values loosely grouped around the word "modern." As soon as one fad lost its freshness another was provided, until at last the only thing distinctive about these ephemeral crazes was their similarity. But the appetite for them did not noticeably diminish during the Twenties. The abundant life was still too new and too shiny.

The airplane wedding was a movie commonplace by the time of *High Flying George*, 1927.

Joan Crawford does her famous Charleston in *Our Dancing Daughters*, 1928.

*Moral:*
He who would change the face of the world must build first the little circle of his own home; who does this in perfect love has then the whole world at his feet.

The final "art" subtitle in *The Face of the World,* c. 1921.

# SCREEN ART

## "WHY DO THEY DO IT?"

"In her last picture, Leatrice Joy got thrown from her horse and dragged about a mile. When she got up she wasn't even dusty." Such was a typical contribution to the "Why Do They Do It?" department, which ran in *Photoplay*, a leading fan magazine. Audiences of the Teens and early Twenties were constantly confronted with heroes who emerged immaculate from fist fights, heroines rescued from drowning with dry clothing and beautifully marcelled hair, characters who entered the drawing room in evening clothes and left it in golf costumes. Such errors were understandable in this early day, when it was usually necessary to shoot pictures out of sequence. The complicated marvel of "matching" scenes had barely begun.

But what roused the ridicule of the more sophisticated was not the upstart movie's innocent mistakes but its still more naïve pretensions to pictorial artistry and significance. "Bad taste" was the hallmark of the movies in the eyes of many urbanites whose own taste was perhaps of recent acquisition. "Symbolic" scenes and flashbacks, beloved of Mr. De Mille, impressed the hinterland but moved the highbrows to laughter, as did subtitles, which Hollywood, in an effort to mitigate a necessary evil, decked out with moralizing and "art" backgrounds. The seemingly rigid rule that all characters who were ill must wear head bandages regardless of the nature of their malady paid the rent for many a professional jokester. To an objective observer it would have been apparent that these crudities were inevitably part of the growing pains of a new art. But American intellectuals have never been distinguished for kindliness or critical restraint. It was the fashion to despise everything popular and profitable, and the movies were joyously seized upon as Exhibit A of American materialism and ingenuousness. Till the middle of the Twenties, to identify oneself as connected with the motion picture industry was to invoke pained reserve or open ribbing.

A symbolic scene depicting the sacrifice of Mae Murray on the Altar of Dollars in *The Right to Love*, 1920.

The composition and design of this scene from *Flesh and the Devil*, 1927, reveal the influence of German taste and studio craftsmanship on American films of the Twenties.

# THE GERMAN INVASION

In 1919, defeated Germany's first bid to regain her export market was with films. Hungry Berliners furnished cheap extras for mob scenes and ambitious young directors were given free rein to create films designed to lead the world in artistry and at the same time to out-Hollywood Hollywood in all that was *kolossal*. So great was the distaste for all things German that the first of these films to be imported into the United States were labeled "Scandinavian" by their distributors, but the advanced techniques and bold sensationalism of the German productions found their intended marks. For most of the Twenties, German films were the vogue with such of the American intelligentsia as did not despise the movies in toto, as well as, for a time, with general audiences.

There arrived first a series of "historical" spectacles—*Passion, Gypsy Blood, One Arabian Night*—directed by Ernst Lubitsch and usually starring Pola Negri and Emil Jannings. In them, the cynical Lubitsch used history merely as a backdrop for boudoir intrigue. But in an era when history was being debunked by everyone from Lytton Strachey to Henry Ford, these films were thought to "humanize" delightfully the stiff and wooden figures of historical personalities. The second wave of German films was much less to popular taste. Somber, unrelieved, they reflected the pessimism of a disintegrating society. But their use of arresting camera angles and of a mobile camera as a leading stylistic motif worried Hollywood. By their side, the best American product looked standardized and rigid.

Studio heads, smarting under the criticisms of the eggheads of the Twenties and the invidious comparisons between Hollywood vulgarity and German taste and skill, decided that if you can't lick 'em, jine 'em, or better still get them to jine you. Lured by what appeared to them incredible salaries, German artists and artisans crossed the Atlantic in a steady stream. Pola Negri led the van, quickly followed by Ernst Lubitsch, Dmitri Buchowetzsky, F. W. Murnau, Carl Mayer, Emil Jannings, Lya de Putti, Conrad Veidt, Erich Pommer, Michael Curtiz, and many others. Besides enriching the American roster of talent, this had the beneficial side-effect of weakening the German studios, sole effective rivals of U. S. films in the world market. The German "invasion" of Hollywood was really more like an elegant kidnaping.

Meanwhile, Hollywood absorbed and surpassed

*"Expressionismus"—The Cabinet of Dr. Caligari*, 1919. Hailed as the first truly "artistic" film, it owed its artistry more to stage expressionism than to the cinema.

Typically bad camera angle. *The Thirteenth Chair*, 1929.

the German technical advance by osmosis. The chief features of the Teutonic style were a continuously moving camera and unusual camera angles. Both devices were designed to make the audience identify with the protagonist, to share his point of view on the screen. American film-makers at first copied both indiscriminately and without regard to their dramatic purpose. The camera would follow an actor as he got up, shaved, dressed, breakfasted, and walked out the front door, though the only significant part of the action was his leaving the house; cameras peeked at actors from lampshades, bookcases, chests of drawers, and especially from the floor, leading Robert E. Sherwood to say of one film, "The camera angles throughout afford an excellent and uninterrupted view of the heroine's nostrils." But the eager artisans of California learned fast. They soon relegated camera movement and camera angles to their proper place in the repertory of film devices, and as rapidly absorbed the German lessons in design and lighting. Sets remained luxurious but became less "busy" with ornament, costumes achieved an expensive simplicity, light and shade were used for dramatic purposes. From about 1927, few technical boners appeared in American films.

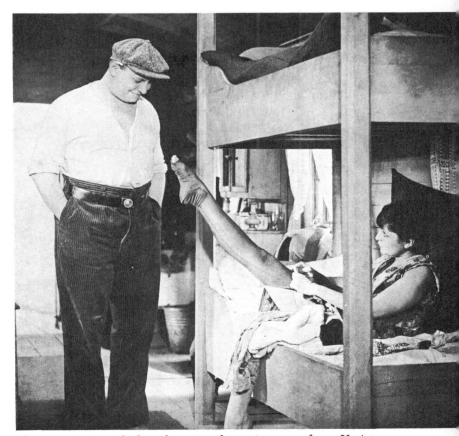

The censors passed this charming domestic scene from *Variety*, 1926, only on condition that Lya de Putti be transformed into Emil Jannings' wife, rather than his mistress.

203

The scent of her furs conjures up a vision of Thomas Meighan's inamorata, Bebe Daniels, while his lawful wife, Gloria Swanson, desponds, in Cecil B. De Mille's *Why Change Your Wife?*, 1920.

William S. Hart plays his own twin brother in a not entirely successful example of double exposure.

Her husband's aristocratic ancestors look sneeringly at the humbly born heroine in this "vision scene" from *Saturday Night*, 1922.

## MOVIE MAGIC

The discovery, in early movie days, that the exposure of the same strip of film twice would result in the second image being superimposed on the first opened a hitherto closed door to the world of fantasy and the supernatural. Directors went hog-wild. Not only "straight" fantasies but perfectly ordinary dramas and comedies were filled with instances of this kind of movie magic which obliterated the boundaries of time and space. Cecil B. De Mille especially delighted in inserting highly symbolic and moralistic "vision scenes" in his gorgeous photoplays. Any girl in any picture about to take her first false step was likely to be visited by the shadowy image of her mother, hands clasped in prayer. Any boy about to succumb to the lure of a woman of ill repute was apt to find the outlines of his childhood sweetheart superimposing themselves over those of the seductress. Anybody at all whose furrowed brow denoted deep thought might fade from view beneath the acting-out of his thoughts.

The public gradually led Hollywood away from this tricky use of the powers of the medium. In silent films, double exposure was useful, often indispensable, in conveying ideas which only dialogue could have transmitted otherwise. But even in silent films, full-scale fantasies were rarely successful, and they were completely incompatible with the hundred-per-cent realism introduced by sound. The reaction went so far that even horror films of the Thirties continued to avoid double exposure. Its last conspicuous use was in Hal Roach's *Topper* series (*Topper*, 1937; *Topper Takes a Trip*, 1939; *Topper Returns*, 1941) where, after long disuse, it pleased through novelty and skillful application.

# MOVIE MAGIC

In the early Twenties cameras were taken to any and every location, no matter how distant or dangerous, for the sake of an effective scene. Later, as the German influence grew, it became more customary and often less costly to re-create exterior scenes in the studios.

A train wreck is re-created in the studio for *The Crash*, 1928.

Shooting a horse race for *Silks and Saddles*, 1928.

George Fitzmaurice directing Colleen Moore and Gary Cooper in a love scene from *Lilac Time*, 1928, while musicians play "mood music."

First National achieved the seeming ultimate in movie magic with *The Lost World*, 1925 (right). Clay miniatures of prehistoric animals appeared larger than humans.

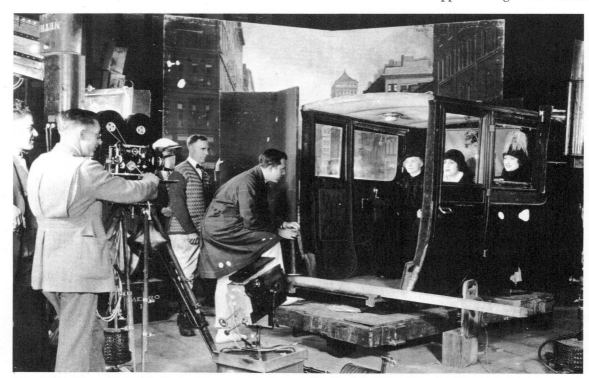

King Vidor directing Edith Yorke, Laurette Taylor and Hedda Hopper in *Happiness*, 1924.

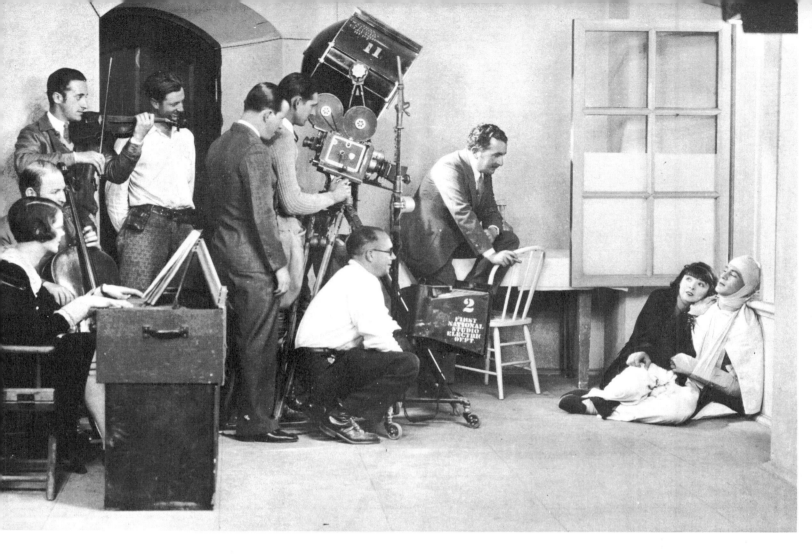

# DECLINE OF D. W. GRIFFITH

As the mechanics of film-making progressed throughout the Twenties, they seemed to pass by a lone figure which once had dominated the entire screen. D. W. Griffith began the decade with great expectations. Freed of past obligations, a partner in United Artists, he sold stock to the public in his own company, D. W. Griffith, Inc., built an elaborate studio at Mamaroneck, and set out to surpass his own unbeaten record. He wanted to make films of weight and substance, films which would realize the instructional and propagandist possibilities which he had been the first to divine in the medium. Through motion pictures, history would come to life—he would film the French Revolution, the American War for Independence, and watching these films the millions would learn the origins and sacredness of their liberties. Master of the craft, he determined to consecrate it to its highest function.

But to finance all this, it would be necessary to make a few potboilers first. He began by buying the rights to the antique stage melodrama, *Way Down East*, for $175,000. For this he was ridiculed; people said that filming it would be "like trying to make a grand opera out of 'The Old Oaken Bucket.'" But the Old Master turned out to be right after all. *Way Down East* swept the country. In it he again at-

tained the vitality, pace, and structural magnificence of *The Birth of a Nation* and *Intolerance*. *Way Down East* proved, or seemed to prove, that it did not matter how leaden the subject matter, the Griffith touch would transmute it to pure gold.

Among the films of weight and importance, *Isn't Life Wonderful?*, 1924, was a remarkable topical picture about current inflation and unemployment in Germany, filmed on the spot. Forcibly it conjured up the tragedies of defeat and hunger in Central Europe after the First World War, but its financial failure ended Griffith's independence. Before it, he had made a series of films, including his saga of the French Revolution, *Orphans of the Storm*, 1922, and his tribute to our own Revolution, *America*, 1924, into which he had injected successively stronger doses of melodrama, violence, and a rather unpalatable kind of sex.

Was history, after all, not enough? If not, what was giving this increasingly unfashionable and even distasteful shape to the Griffith films of the Twenties? James R. Quirk of *Photoplay* magazine thought the cause was Griffith's isolation from Hollywood and from contemporary film-makers and film-making. In 1924 he boldly addressed Griffith in an editorial: "You have made yourself an anchorite at

## "Out, out, into the storm!"

This classic group from *Way Down East*, 1920, includes, left to right, Burr McIntosh, Kate Bruce, Lowell Sherman, Lillian Gish, Mary Hay, Creighton Hale, Edgar Nelson, Richard Barthelmess, and Porter Strong.

Mamaroneck . . . your pictures shape themselves toward a certain brutality because of this austerity . . . your refusal to face the world is making you more and more a sentimentalist. You see passion in terms of cooing doves or the falling of a rose petal . . . your lack of contact with life makes you deficient in humor. In other words, your splendid unsophistication is a menace to you—and to pictures."

But Griffith's "splendid unsophistication" was nothing new. It had always been a leading characteristic of his style and was largely responsible for his early success. It was audiences that were changing. Even the DAR, the American Legion, and other representatives of the upper middle class on whose support he had counted, seemed more interested in films called *Dancing Mothers* than in films called *America*. The end was nearing. A casting up of accounts in 1924 revealed that D. W. Griffith, Inc., was living on the great profits of *Way Down East*. All subsequent films had incurred losses—losses due in part to the proud but uneconomic practice of maintaining a costly studio for the production of one picture a year, with the overhead rolling merrily along when no pictures at all were in progress.

Bank loans for further productions were no longer forthcoming. Griffith shook himself, abandoned Ma-

maroneck, signed with Paramount, and set out to regain his receding prestige. If "jazz" pictures were what "they" wanted now jazz pictures he would give them. The result was films which looked like slick copies of the work of his juniors and inferiors.

Further humiliation was in store for the Master. In 1927 he returned to United Artists, no longer as a producer but as a glorified wage-slave working for his former partners. In 1930 he turned to history again for his first sound film, *Abraham Lincoln*, and his talent flared up one last time. This sober film, remarkable in this transition period, earned him selection as the best director of 1930, an honor he had been without for many a year. But *Lincoln* did not appeal to audiences of the first year of the depression, and United Artists refused to finance further pictures. In desperation, Griffith rounded up what money he could and produced *The Struggle*, 1931. A contemporary reviewer wrote: "It's a struggle to have to report that D. W. Griffith, who directed some of the greatest pictures, now presents one of the worst."

To save what could be saved of Griffith's reputation, United Artists withdrew *The Struggle*. But it was too late. The sound era was in full swing. D. W. Griffith—who's he? Oh yes, of course . . .

*Nanook of the North,* 1922.

*Moana,* 1926.

# ROBERT FLAHERTY

In 1921, a blond young giant from the north descended upon the New York offices of the film companies. Robert Flaherty, an explorer for mineral deposits, had spent twelve years with the Eskimos of the Hudson Bay country, and at the end of that period had made a film of their life. Travelogues had already been relegated to a minor place on the screen bill of fare, and nobody listened when Flaherty insisted that his picture of Nanook the Eskimo would open a new world to movie audiences. More by accident than by design, the redoubtable Roxy booked *Nanook of the North* into the Capitol Theater as the lower half of a double bill which featured Harold Lloyd's *Grandma's Boy*. He was stunned by the reviews. Nanook not only opened a new world, it was a new kind of film. Previous travelogues had sketched random aspects of the lives of primitive people. *Nanook* went to the heart of Eskimo life simply by chronicling the day-to-day struggle for existence of one man and his family. The timeless, classic flavor of this unique picture is most fully suggested by Flaherty's explanation of it to the people of the island of Sava'ii, when Jesse Lasky sent him to Samoa to make a film of Polynesian life like the one he had made of Eskimo life. To explain his purpose to the Samoans, Flaherty wrote a booklet about *Nanook* which was translated -into the native tongue. Retranslated from the Samoan, his words were:

"This picture tells the story of the conduct and daily lives of the Eskimo people who live in a country where the water is frozen and covered with snow, near to the North Pole, as our own country is near to the equator. That country has no trees, no fruits or eatable plants. The animals which creep on the frozen sea, these the people kill every day to keep them alive.

"This chief, Mr. Flaherty, lived with Eskimos and imitated their customs and their conduct and dressed in their kind of clothes, made of the skin of the great white quadruped known as the bear of the North Pole. He made this picture because love overflowed in his heart for the people of this country, on account of their kindliness and their bravery, and also on account of their receiving him well, and because they look very happy every day of their lives, in a life most difficult to live in the whole world.

"The high chiefs in New York, the big village in America, they saw that Mr. Flaherty had made a very useful thing; so they gathered together in council and expressed themselves like this: 'Such pictures as this will create love and friendship among all the people of the world. Then misunderstanding and quarrels will end.'

"Then the council of high chiefs in New York prepared a great feast for Mr. Flaherty and told him to make a picture like the picture of the story of Nanook. And so Mr. Flaherty has come here to Samoa to find the genuine descendants of the pure Polynesian race of ancient times, and also their good customs, as they were in the days before the missionaries and traders came to spread their customs in Samoa."

Such an elevated view of the mission of motion pictures was not shared by everyone. The aforesaid high chiefs were daunted by *Moana*, the picture which Flaherty brought back from Samoa. The drama of Nanook's struggle to live had been as clear and strong as the contrasting blacks and whites of the old orthochromatic stock on which it was made. The structure of the new picture, instead of "another *Nanook*," was as delicate as the range of tones in its panchromatic photography. *Moana* failed to find an audience comparable to the one which had responded so warmly to *Nanook*. Still impressed with that first picture's record, Hollywood gave Flaherty several chances to adapt himself to the boxoffice but he was both unwilling and unable to compromise. He wanted to film the life of the peoples of the earth and that was all he wanted. Soon there were no more jobs for him in the United States.

But in England, the Scotch educator John Grierson, infatuated with the possibilities Flaherty had opened up, coined the term "documentary film" to describe the new kind of picture which the former explorer had created. Invited abroad by Grierson, Flaherty found the chance to make his great *Man of Aran* and *Elephant Boy*. Returning to America, he made *The Land* under New Deal auspices and *Louisiana Story* under those of Standard Oil, before his death in 1951. Meanwhile, under Grierson's leadership, a world-wide "documentary film movement" had grown up. Scores of young men dedicated themselves to the use of the Flaherty method for purposes of social enlightenment, and Flaherty found himself, considerably to his amusement, "the father of the documentary film."

Documentary films came into their own in World War II, but on the record to date no other maker of them has yet approached Flaherty's success in exploring and disclosing the basic patterns of human existence. He has left behind him not only the grand gallery of his films and the romance of a life led with proud distinction, but also an insistent sense that he and he alone has used the motion picture camera to its fullest capacity.

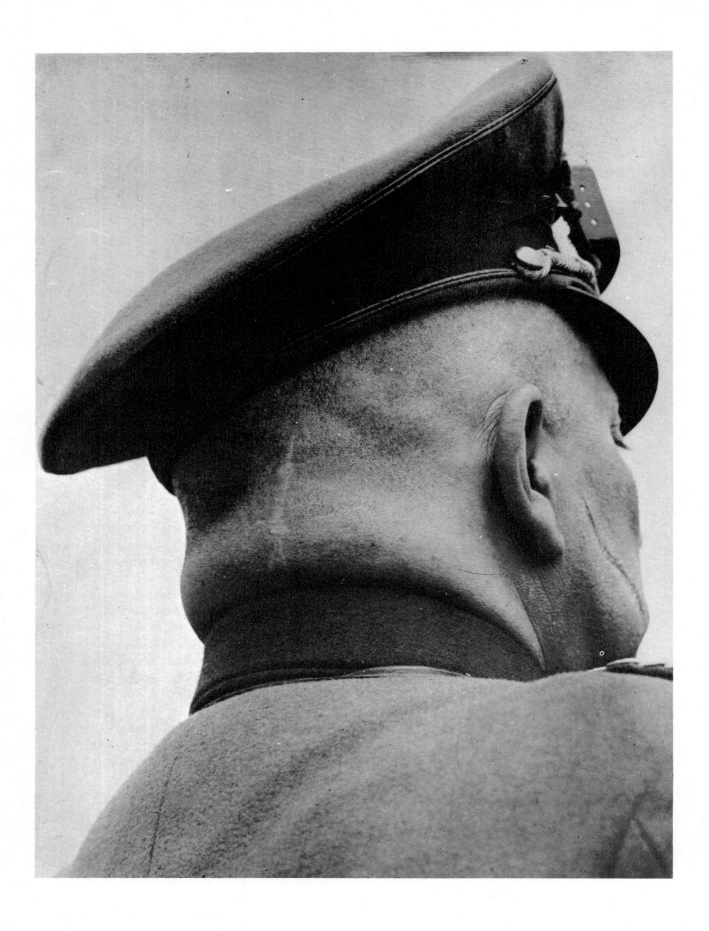

# ERICH VON STROHEIM

Erich von Stroheim's origins are not clear (he claimed to have been a member of Franz Joseph's Imperial Guard). It is a fact that, for reasons best known to himself, he emigrated to the United States about 1913 and earned a precarious living as dishwasher, trackwalker and package-wrapper while he learned English. He turned up in Hollywood in the middle Teens, where Griffith gave him work as an extra and technical adviser. World War I was a bonanza to him because, though Austrian to the core, he could play Prussian officers to the life. To millions of Americans he became "the man you love to hate," the very image of the hideous Hun.

When the war ended there seemed little future for him. Somehow he persuaded Carl Laemmle to permit him to star in and direct his own story, *Blind Husbands*, 1919. It was at once apparent that an important talent had arrived. Stroheim's handling of his actors, his camera placement and cutting derived from Griffith, but here was an insistence and intensity which bespoke an individual vision of the world. That vision was certainly a novelty to movie audiences. They were familiar enough with the wickedness of Paris, the desperations of Monte Carlo, and the infidelities of *Alt Wien* as routinely portrayed by Hollywood, but Stroheim's versions of these worlds had a detailed, firsthand intimacy which carried new conviction. This was, obviously, the straight dope on European decadence. His films portrayed successively the prewar world dancing heedlessly on the volcano; the blindness and confusion of wartime society; and finally, pleasure-mad postwar Europe in full disintegration.

Stroheim's first two pictures were profitable. They also cost a good deal. When Stroheim began *Merry Go Round*, 1923, Irving Thalberg, then rising to power at Universal, decided to keep a sharp eye on proceedings. He found Stroheim insisting that, when a bell-pull was required for a scene, the pull be wired to a real bell which actually rang for the silent camera. He discovered that the director had ordered silk underdrawers with the monogram of the Imperial Guard for the Guardsmen in his picture, even though they would never be shown in less than full uniform. When Thalberg heard that Stroheim had (reputedly) spent three days teaching the Hollywood extras who played these Guardsmen how to salute in the correct Austrian manner, for a shot that would last a few seconds on the screen, Thalberg halted production, fired Stroheim, and turned over the direction to Rupert Julian, who finished *Merry Go Round*. In the released version, it was possible to tell accurately which scenes were Stroheim's and which Julian's.

As actor, Stroheim created an image of the lascivious, cruel, elegant German officer which both repelled and attracted postwar audiences.

As director, Stroheim would spend days teaching Hollywood extras like these how to salute in the correct Austrian manner for a minor scene.

213

# "THERE'S A MADMAN IN CHARGE"

For reasons wrapped in obscurity, the Goldwyn Company next hired Stroheim and, even more incomprehensibly, gave him carte blanche to realize his old dream of filming Frank Norris' novel, *McTeague*. Stroheim was determined to film the novel exactly as written, page by page. He took his company to the actual location, San Francisco, where he bought a lodginghouse to use as his principal set, tearing off the outside walls of the rooms in order to shoot by natural daylight.

This amazing experiment emerged from the cameras in some fifty reels. Stroheim reduced it to twenty-four reels—about four hours' running time —and announced that it was finished. His employers were stunned. While production was under way, the old Goldwyn Company had merged with the Metro and Mayer picture companies, and Louis B. Mayer was in effective control of the studio. He had hired Stroheim's old nemesis, Irving Thalberg, as his second in command and Thalberg once more took the director's picture away from him. He reduced it to a neat ten-reel feature called *Greed*. Stroheim never saw *Greed*.

This ten-reel released version is an abrupt and fractured film. Continuity gaps are bridged by long subtitles, and the characters of Trina and Mac develop jerkily. But they are Trina and Mac, two living people, to everyone who saw the film. It quivered with vitality, with love and hate for the human condition. Though only a fragment of what Stroheim intended and realized, *Greed* is numbered among the screen's few masterpieces.

With the possible exception of *Intolerance*, it was also the screen's greatest flop d'estime. Audiences were not indifferent to it or bored by it—they actively hated it. People felt strangely threatened by it. As Paul Rotha wrote, "Americans frankly disliked it; its moral that money was worthless either roused their consciences uncomfortably or was passed over unseen."

Irving Thalberg showed his caliber when, after jettisoning *McTeague*, he continued to employ Stroheim. He proposed that he direct *The Merry Widow*, with Mae Murray and John Gilbert. Stroheim loaded every rift with Stroheim ore. Much that he shot had to be excised from the finished version of *The Merry Widow*. He protested, and Thalberg again fired him. *The Merry Widow* was a great success, but Stroheim was jobless.

P. A. Powers then picked him up and let him film his own script, *The Wedding March*. *The Wedding March* probably came closer to realizing Stroheim's ideal of what he wanted to put on the screen than any of his other films. Intended to be the last

word on the degeneracy and resulting collapse of Austria-Hungary, it was just that. But, again, he shot it in thirty reels, before production was halted by his alarmed backers. And, again, the picture was taken out of his hands and edited down to less than half its proposed length before release.

Things grew grim. Nobody was quite willing to chance it again. Then Gloria Swanson hired him to direct his own script, *Queen Kelly*, starring herself. For years they told conflicting stories of what happened. Stroheim says that all went swimmingly until one day, at the end of a scene, Miss Swanson said, "Excuse me, I have to make a phone call," left the set, and never came back. The star says that she was so eager to be directed by a man who apparently could get a great performance out of anybody that she bought the story unfinished and began production with the end not yet in sight. It concerned a pretty girl in prewar Germany who was seduced by an army officer destined to be the consort of the queen of a petty principality. Their amour discovered, the queen drives Miss Swanson from the palace in her nightgown. This much had been shot when the star inquired of her director-author what came next.

He explained. It seems that Kitty Kelly was next to learn that her dear old aunt in German East Africa had died and left all her worldly goods to her forsaken niece. When Kitty goes to Dar-Es-Salaam to collect, she discovers that her inheritance is a chain of brothels. The star-producer says that when she learned this she realized that even if the picture was completed it could not be shown in the United States, and phoned her backers that she must stop production because "There's a madman in charge."

That was about the end. Once more, in the early talkie years, Fox entrusted Stroheim with the direction of a film, *Walking Down Broadway*. It was finished in 1932, in thirty-some reels. *Walking Down Broadway* was largely reshot by another director and released in 1933 as *Hello Sister*, without directorial credits.

For several years thereafter Stroheim existed precariously in Hollywood, selling a few ideas, acting a few parts. It was hand to mouth. In 1935, he cabled desperately to Sergei Eisenstein, CAN YOU GET ME A JOB IN MOSCOW? Shortly thereafter, Jean Renoir brought him to France to play the prison commandant in the brilliant *La Grande Illusion*. He made Paris his headquarters, starring in French films and occasionally returning to Hollywood. Stroheim received the French Legion of Honor shortly before his death in 1957.

→

Death in the desert. In the final scenes of *Greed*, Jean Hersholt and Gibson Gowland find themselves without water, their packhorse dead, in the middle of Death Valley.

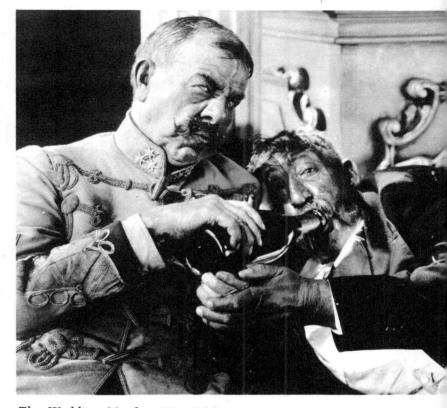

A corseted Stroheim bites the hand of one of his partners in crime in *Foolish Wives*, while she attempts to remove his ear. She is none other than "the ever-popular Mae Busch."

The details of Stroheim's *ancien régime* were realistic to absurdity. Everybody wore corsets, chin reducers, and mustache pressers; most women smoked cigars.

*The Wedding March*, 1928. While Erich von Stroheim makes love to a cafe entertainer in a rose garden, his father, the Archduke, meets with Vienna's corn-plaster king in a brothel to arrange a marriage between the Archduke's son and the magnate's lame daughter, ZaSu Pitts. The two scenes are intercut throughout this sequence. Too drunk to stand, the Archduke and the magnate crawl to a corner with a champagne bottle. The Archduke complains that his toe hurts. The corn-plaster king takes out a box of his wares and proceeds to apply one. Between swigs from the bottle, the two old men haggle over the amount of the dowry the magnate must deliver to buy his daughter's way into the aristocracy. As their bargaining goes on, the director brings his camera closer and closer to reveal the sweaty cheeks, broken veins, and bloodshot eyes of these two members of the wedding.

Georgia Hale, George K. Arthur, Baby Bruce Guerin. The motionless movie, *The Salvation Hunters*.

## REALISM

As the commercial pattern of the movies developed, it proved, or was thought to prove, that the surest path to success lay in pictured daydreams, and most directors strove to identify themselves with this kind of wish-fulfillment. The development of screen art, considered apart from mechanical progress, lay chiefly in the hands of comedians like Chaplin, Keaton and Langdon, whose laugh-provoking abilities were boxoffice insurance even when they turned their comedy toward "dangerous" themes, such as satire or social criticism. But a few brave spirits persisted in the belief that the raw material of American life as it was actually lived by movie audiences themselves was fit subject matter for a popular art.

The most conspicuous attempt to turn the movie camera on everyday life was a true experiment, conducted outside the industry. Josef von Sternberg, a film editor, produced with little capital and unknown actors *The Salvation Hunters*, 1925, which Fairbanks bought for United Artists release and which Chaplin proclaimed a masterpiece. But it did little to endear the idea of screen realism to audiences. It was the dreariest picture on record. Silent pictures were usually full of ceaseless activity: things had to be kept moving at all costs. Sternberg decided to explore the contrasting effect of complete immobility. *The Salvation Hunters* consisted of a series of scenes in which groups of characters stood or sat around without moving a muscle, looking extremely depressed and not even blinking their eyes. From time to time Sternberg cut in a shot of

the real star of the picture, a symbolic dredger which dipped into a harbor and brought up a load of slime. All this to express the idea that nothing ever happens in the lives of ordinary people. Audience reaction was, in substance: even *our* lives are not so drab as this, and if they are we don't want to know about it. Asked to comment on the failure of a film he had praised so highly, Chaplin said, "Well, you know, I was only kidding. They all take everything I say so seriously I thought I'd praise a bad picture and see what happened."

The fate of Sternberg was ironic. This devotee of the lower depths spent most of the rest of his career directing "glamour" vehicles for his profitable discovery, Marlene Dietrich.

Aside from this offbeat film, most attempts at realism were the occasional ventures of directors of standing who could not seem to get it out of their heads that an instrument like the camera, which could reproduce reality with such wonderful fidelity, should sometimes be used for this purpose. In striking contrast to his younger brother Cecil, William C. de Mille was continually poking into the seamier side with such dramas as Zona Gale's *Miss Lulu Bett*, and Owen Davis' *Icebound*. His most daring break with convention was in casting Lois Wilson in a picture called *Only 38*, which defied the law that all movie heroines should be no more than twenty years old and behave as if they were much younger. The elder de Mille had a theory that in concentrating exclusively on youth and youth's interests, the movies were losing their hold on older

The ant-heap. King Vidor probed the drabness of metropolitan life in his isolated masterpiece, *The Crowd*.

people, and he sought to recapture this vanishing audience. He was right oftener than his employers were willing to admit. His wife, Clara Beranger, records: "When the executives saw *Miss Lulu Bett* in the projection room they were not enthusiastic, but the picture went on to make a great deal of money, leading William to remark, 'Nobody likes this picture but the public.' "

King Vidor's autobiography, *A Tree Is a Tree*, reveals a drive to explore and disclose the patterns of life in the United States and the typical experiences of its people. He deliberately set out to build a reputation as a top boxoffice director in order occasionally to get his way. Sometimes he could combine doing what he liked with doing what the studio wanted. *The Big Parade*, 1925, was a boxoffice hit, and it was also the first realistic drama of World War I. Vidor's *The Crowd*, 1928, attempted to dissect the unconscious regimentation of metropolitan life; his hero was a digit in the incalculable total of city office workers. For years Vidor tried to persuade M-G-M to let him make a film about the American Negro with an all-Negro cast. When sound arrived, he insisted that this was the moment to act, since Negro music would greatly enhance the appeal of the film. To Nicholas M. Schenck, president of M-G-M, he offered to work without salary if the studio would let him make the picture. The offer appealed to Mr. Schenck's gambling instinct. "If that's your spirit," he replied, "I'd let you make a picture about whores." Vidor's *Hallelujah*, 1929, was a memorable screen achievement.

Gloria Swanson's *Manhandled*, 1924, depicted a day in the life of a salesgirl in Macy's basement with hilarious accuracy.

Richard Barthelmess brings the mail through in *Tol'able David*, 1921, the most brilliant of the regional dramas.

Gloria Swanson

Pola Negri

# GLORIA AND POLA

While Mary Pickford at one end of the spectrum and Greta Garbo at the other have known greater popularity, it is Gloria Swanson who embodies most completely the genus Movie Star. Her camera-proof face, which can be photographed successfully from any angle, conforms to no known specifications of beauty, but the prognathous jaw, dished nose, and abnormally large eyes somehow blend into a bizarre loveliness which made her for years the idol and model of millions of women in the flapper era. But it was not her strange beauty alone that made Miss Swanson the dominant star of the Twenties. To women, she was a symbol of growth, of what a woman can make of herself. Allene Talmey described the process in 1927: "Her dignity is paralyzing. It is that dignity which makes her so magnificent and for which Hollywood can never quite forgive her. There in Hollywood hover the ghosts, always remembering that the cool Marquise de la Falaise de Coudray came as an extra, as a flat-figured girl in a Mack Sennett bathing suit of black and white checks. Hollywood, with its disturbing memory, can still see the haughty Swanson of the days of the De Mille society pictures, a funny impossible girl in her crazy clothes, an overdressed Chicago kid whose hair was black and hard and shiny with Brilliantine. She did not care that the elaborate fashionings of her hair were only copied by hash-house waitresses; she did not care that her satin swathings, clinging to her as sharply as a lobster shell clings to its white meat, were just further evidences of the impossibility of that Swanson girl. With her bad posture, her Illinois twang, her gamin toughness, the movie magazines posed her as the smartest dressed woman in Hollywood; and she loved it.

"But Gloria Swanson is acquisitive. She began to discard the crudities which had made her the great example of movie bad taste. She reserved those satin swathings, which she still loves and wears, for only those moments in her own bedroom when the eyes of Hollywood cannot peep in. Lessons taught her how to carry herself, how to enunciate properly. Her time came at a dinner at the Park Lane Hotel, given her by officials of Paramount when she returned from Europe several years ago, bringing with

# STARS
# OF THE TWENTIES

her the film *Madame Sans Gêne* and her new husband, a docile nobleman with a reckless taste in spats. After the usual publicity spasms of superlatives, the daughter of Capt. Joseph Swanson, U.S.A., and the former wife of actor Wallace Beery and businessman Herbert Somborn stood up in front of those paunchy, bald-headed men who remembered a hard-faced Sennett bathing girl and a spit-curled De Mille vamp. They saw a formal, cool woman, the Marquise de la Falaise de Coudray, magnificent in her re-creation of Gloria Swanson."

When this was written, her success was so great that she had become an independent star-producer at United Artists, the Everest of movie fame. *Photoplay* bubbled: "Ten years ago she was an extra girl waiting outside the casting office. Today, she is a Marchioness whose salary is $20,000 a week." *The New Yorker* said, "Gloria Swanson's greatest achievement is her own face in repose." But from her pinnacle, the greatest star of them all had some insight into the future. At a studio party given in her honor, she was heard to say faintly amidst the hub bub, "All this is very nice. But it's over at thirty-five And that's not a hundred years off."

Miss Swanson reached thirty-five in the year 1933, two years after the release of her last successful vehicle, *Tonight Or Never*. But it was not age that dimmed her popularity. The by then ex-Marquise de la Falaise had stopped growing. To a depression-struck audience, she still symbolized the lost and discredited Era of Wonderful Nonsense.

Imported by Paramount because of her success in German films, Pola Negri automatically challenged Gloria Swanson's supremacy at their studio, and the Swanson-Negri feud was on. It perhaps consisted of little more than mutual snubs, but it was troublesome enough to cause Adolph Zukor to put a continent between the warring divas, the Swanson productions being transferred to Paramount's Astoria studios while Miss Negri (or, as she preferred to be called, Madame Negri) held forth in Hollywood.

Pola lost the feud, not through any lack of ingenuity in pursuing it but because that infallible umpire, the boxoffice, decided against her. This was in part the fault of her studio. The fiery Pola had an enormous following when she arrived in the United States, but it was gradually dissipated by mishandling. The better she was photographed, the more lavishly she was coiffed and gowned and sleeked and groomed, the more standardized she became, until in the studied attitudes of stylized acting in her last films nothing was discernible of the highly individual heroine of *Passion* and *Gypsy Blood*. Paramount, in dismay, hired expensive writers like Carl Van Vechten, Joseph Hergesheimer, and Michael Arlen to try to provide her with "suitable" vehicles that would restore her popularity, but to no avail. "We try and try," said a Paramount executive, "but everything we do is wrong." By 1928, exhibitors were refusing to feature Miss Negri's name in advertising her pictures.

In part this extraordinary personality alienated her public by her off-screen behavior. Miss Negri made no effort to conceal her opinion that her German films were superior to her American productions, or that the cultural climate was not such as she had been accustomed to in Berlin. Worse, her efforts to sell herself were more appropriate to the era of Gaby Deslys than to the wisecracking Twenties. When she interrupted the filming of *Hotel Imperial* to rush to the funeral of Rudolph Valentino, a cynical press decided that it was just a publicity gag, and photographs of the black-swathed Pola fainting at Valentino's bier provoked laughter instead of the sympathy they were intended to arouse. A certain humorlessness was apparent in her behavior pattern. Vicki Baum has speculated that her affair with Valentino was based less on mutual attraction than on the following line of reasoning: I am Pola Negri, therefore I deserve the best man in the world. The best man in the world is generally conceded to be Rudolph Valentino. *Q.E.D.* The same lack of contact with reality is evidenced in an interview she gave in 1936 when she was once more starring in German films, rumored at the instance of Hitler himself. Reporters asked if this were true. She replied, "Why not; after all there have been many important men in my life—Valentino for example." Hitler did not say whether he was flattered by the comparison.

Mary Pickford and Douglas Fairbanks "dedicate" a new link of the Pacific Highway. The crowned heads of Hollywood, always called out to officiate at cornerstone layings, their popularity toward the end of the Twenties was perhaps more official than real, but none challenged their royal status as long as silence lasted.

Corinne Griffith was famed as "the orchid lady of the screen" and as its most beautiful woman, but her uncharacteristic appearance here in *Moral Fibre*, 1921, suggests opposite qualities. Today she is a Boadicea of big business.

Of the veteran stars, Norma Talmadge kept the steadiest hold on her legion of fans. Miss Talmadge was given to roles in which she aged a great deal and wept even more. She is seen here as Donald Keith's mother in *Secrets*, 1924.

# THE GREAT CELEBRITIES

Nearly all movie star contracts of the silent days were written to last for five years. This was based on the universal belief that the life of the "average" star's career was five years, after which time the public presumably had had enough. By and large this theory held, at least for silent days. Such once raging favorites as Theda Bara, Clara Kimball Young, Carlyle Blackwell, and Maurice Costello had faded out by the early Twenties. But certain of the great celebrities of the pioneer days held their reputations and their fans down to the coming of sound and even beyond.

Mae Murray in *The French Doll*, 1923, at the time when she was building the reputation for eccentricity of behavior, pose, and costume which eventually was fatal to her career.

Pedro de Cordoba and Marion Davies in *Young Diana*, 1922. Miss Davies' popularity as a romantic heroine was long a figment of William Randolph Hearst's imagination, but she eventually won a following as a comedienne.

Lillian Gish with Ronald Colman in *The White Sister*, 1923, her biggest hit after she left Griffith.

Rex, "The King of Wild Horses," was an admirably trained tame one.

"Mortgage-lifter" Rin-Tin-Tin in *Rinty of the Desert*, 1928.

## ANIMAL STARS

Probably the first non-human movie star was "Jean, the Vitagraph Dog," a collie owned by Larry Trimble. By the Twenties, everything that ran, hopped, crept, or crawled had found a place in films. The winning spontaneity of animal players saved many an otherwise anemic film. The simple device of cross-cutting, added to superb training, gave to movie dogs supercanine and even superhuman intelligence. The first great dog star was Strongheart, owned and trained by Jane Murfin, the author of *Lilac Time*. He was succeeded in popularity by Rin-Tin-Tin, known to exhibitors as "the mortgage-lifter" because of his infallible box-office draw. He was the screen property of the Warner Brothers and their chief solace in the years before sound when most of their time and energy were spent in staving off creditors. "Rinty" had two successors on the screen and a lineal descendant on television.

Effective as animals are on the screen, all is not smooth sailing in getting them there. The late William C. de Mille once complained: "Probably every director in the world has noticed the ghoulish glee with which writers introduce dogs, flies, monkeys, mice, bees, ants, fish and babies into their plots.

They are so easy to write; so humorous on paper. A bee buzzes into the scene at exactly the right moment; an ant crawls upon a table exactly on his cue; a mouse dashes across the bed just as the lady is about to retire; these are incidents which no writer will pass up if he sees his chance to work them in. What does he care how long it takes to make the fly drunk enough to crawl in the right direction and not take to the air? He doesn't have to direct the mouse or make the baby stop crying and begin to smile. No; a simple sentence and it is done—as far as the writer is concerned. This is one great advantage which the author accepts as his special privilege. He gets away with it because the public loves animals on the screen and the director knows it. It is usually a good picture, but it is one reason why directors frequently look a bit driven."

Mr. de Mille had further cause to complain of animal stars. When his stage success *Strongheart* (the name of an Indian youth) was adapted to the screen, its title had to be changed to *Braveheart* to avoid confusion with the reigning dog star. Mr. de Mille commented, "The public liked the dog better than my play. *Cave Canem.*"

Jackie Coogan, greatest of the child stars, in *Daddy*, 1923.

Freckle-faced Wesley Barry as a Penrod of the early Twenties.

## CHILD STARS

It was Douglas Fairbanks who first observed that children and animals make the best movie actors. From the beginning children played a more important part in pictures than they ever had in the theater, and many became stars in their own right. Of these by far the most beloved was Jackie Coogan, around whom Chaplin centered his peerless *The Kid*, 1920. Coogan's parents, small-time vaudevillians, were sharp enough to realize at once the immensely valuable property they had in their son, and bargained for his services with a rapacity which astounded even Hollywood. After his discovery, the five-year-old Jackie was signed to a starring contract which netted him a fortune of $4,000,000, and he remained a top favorite until he outgrew little-boy roles.

The fate of this infant gold mine was not uncharacteristic of show business. His performances of adolescent roles, especially in *Tom Sawyer*, 1930, demonstrated that young Coogan was a genuine artist, not just a cute bundle of mischief and pathos. But in maturity he could find no place on the screen. Nor did he enjoy a penny of his vast childhood earnings. When he turned twenty-one and asked for his money, his mother, who had remarried after the death of Jack Coogan, Sr., found a California law which held that the earnings of a minor are the absolute property of his parents, and refused her son any part of the fortune which had supported her in luxury for years.

The long-forgotten Baby Peggy was a prototype of Shirley Temple.

Daughter of the pioneer movie star, Maurice Costello, Dolores Costello had a madonnalike beauty that caused John Barrymore to demand her as his leading woman and later as his wife.

Billie Dove and Ben Lyon in *An Affair of the Follies*, 1927. Miss Dove's beauty and her

## THE YOUNGER

From the founding of the star system on, the search for new stars has been constant and intense. Every girl of striking beauty, in any walk of life, anywhere in the world, soon became familiar with the "You ought to be in pictures" routine. Fallen aristocrats, society beauties down on their luck, athletes, and beauty contest winners all made the trek to Hollywood to face a screen test. Though few survived, everyone was welcome. No one could

Joan Crawford, playing her first screen role under this name, in Jackie Coogan's *Old Clothes*, 1925. Born Billie Cassin, known on stage and in her first movie, *Pretty Ladies,* as Lucille LeSueur, Miss Crawford has had the longest career of any woman star, including Mary Pickford.

Constance Bennett was rapidly climbing to favor as an ingenue when, in 1926, she married the wealthy Philip Plant and retired. Four years later, with a divorce and a million-dollar marriage settlement, she returned to Hollywood to become one of the most sensational stars of the Thirties.

figure made her a prime favorite with men in the latter part of the Twenties.

## GENERATION

tell where the lightning would strike.

In the middle Twenties, the quest for star material intensified. The movies had hit one of their periodic slumps. From 1925 to 1927, a large new crop of "discoveries" appeared. In keeping with the spirit of the times, their common denominator was youth. Producers pushed them fast, little dreaming that within two years they would face a test for which youth did not equip them—sound.

The studio caption says: "Dolores del Rio, Mexico's heiress-social leader, who recently arrived in Hollywood with $50,000 in shawls and combs, is . . . said to be the richest girl in Mexico." (The money was her husband's.)

Myrna Loy's career was mostly confined to Oriental enchantresses until the talkies made her a star. Here she is seen in blackface with Tom Wilson in *Ham and Eggs at the Front,* 1927.

Norma Shearer, far from 100 per cent photogenic, fought her way to the top through executive ability as well as talent. She is seen here with Jack Holt in *Empty Hands,* 1924.

Greta Garbo as a Spanish peasant in her
first American film, *The Torrent*, 1926.

*Wild Orchids*, 1929. Her dream-haunted eyes fixed on
some unknown, Garbo mystified while she fascinated.

The invitation direct.
*Flesh and the Devil*, 1927.

"Well . . . ?" Greta Garbo with Conrad Nagel in *The Mysterious Lady*, 1928.

Garbo in 1928.

# GARBO

Though Theda Bara spelled Arab Death, though Jetta Goudal let it be believed that she was the daughter of Mata Hari, the greatest screen siren of them all made no attempt to cloak in glamour the simplicity of her origins. Greta Garbo was born in Stockholm (1905), the daughter of a poor laborer. In her early teens she worked as a lather-girl in a barber shop, played extra in a few Swedish films, was discovered by the director Mauritz Stiller, and came to Hollywood in his entourage at the age of nineteen. That was about all that her early interviewers could pry out of this impassive, faintly scornful girl who held the public of 1926-30 in a vise of fascination. For the old, bold movie vamp, Miss Garbo substituted a more complicated and credible charmer—doomed, neurotic, torn by inner conflicts. She was poison to men and to herself, yet held in her eyes the promise of Cleopatra.

After Mauritz Stiller returned to Sweden, a failure in Hollywood, Miss Garbo shut herself off from society. Displeased by the inaccuracies of reporters, especially by the distortion of her one-sided romance with John Gilbert, she refused all interviews. Her relations with her co-workers at M-G-M were and remained rigidly formal, and she earned the lasting respect of Louis B. Mayer by conducting their business affairs with an icy candor which concealed no stratagem. Was she a sphinx without a secret? Yes, said her legion of detractors, who scoffed at her "pose" of mystery, her (supposed) big feet and thick accent, and her threats to go home to Sweden unless she got her way; while her legion of fanatical adorers, rightly called "Garbomaniacs," insisted that she dwelt apart because she was a woman apart, and found in her most trivial films, indeed in her slightest gestures, intimation of an acting talent greater than any the screen had yet produced. The battle between them was good for business, and there was no doubt where the victory lay when, by 1929, even the chubbiest American girl was wearing the shoulder-length bob and slouch hat which Miss Garbo had made synonymous with legendary beauty.

Vilma Banky and Ronald Colman in *Two Lovers*, 1928—roles they played under various names through five films.

Janet Gaynor and Charles Farrell were the sensations of 1927 in *Seventh Heaven;* they co-starred for over seven years.

Greta Garbo and John Gilbert in their first film together, *Flesh and the Devil*, 1927.

## LOVE TEAMS

The first movie "love team" was Francis X. Bushman and Beverly Bayne, whose off-screen marriage was concealed from the public lest it take the edge off their movie love scenes. After their success, producers were ever on the alert for players who struck sparks from each other and who could be featured in a series of dramas which centered around Love and nothing else but. The most ravishing of all these teams consisted of the glamorous John Gilbert and the mysterious Greta Garbo—the most sensationally successful of all the younger generation. By their time, lip service to personal privacy (at least for screen stars) had been abandoned: their studio saw to it that the public was well aware of the fact that Gilbert was wooing Garbo in real life, that he had got as far as taking out a marriage license, that she had balked at the altar but continued to waver. After all this, seeing a Gilbert-Garbo film was like eavesdropping on their private life.

Reviewing *Love,* the 1927 version of *Anna Karenina, Photoplay* said: "It isn't Tolstoy, but it is John Gilbert and Greta Garbo, which, after *Flesh and the Devil,* is what the fans are crying for. And if you think there is even a hint in the picture of the romance of Kitty and Kostia Levin, you are nothing but a silly. The movies have separated the wheat of sex from the chaff of preachment." Gilbert and Garbo made only three silent films together, but the intensity of their screen love-making plus the rumors of their romance identified them in the public mind as the supreme symbols of screen sex. Nothing mattered in their pictures but numerous, prolonged, close-up embraces. Not everyone was swept away by this make-believe lechery. One heretic called their behavior "Gilbo-Garbage," a sobriquet that pleased the disgruntled. He added that their acting in the clinches was less suggestive of uncontrolled passion than of acute indigestion.

The first subtitle from *The Last Command,* 1928.

Polly Moran, Dorothy Sebastian, Louella O. Parsons, Estelle Taylor, Claire Windsor, Aileen Pringle, Karl Dane, George K. Arthur, Leatrice Joy

Seventeen stars assembled in the M-G-M

# "HOLLYWOOD IS A STATE OF MIND"

Hollywood, the tiny suburb of Los Angeles where the movie pioneers established themselves, was soon outgrown by the giant film factories and the burgeoning movie colony. Stars and magnates built their homes in Beverly Hills and Malibu Beach, and by the middle Twenties the mansions and bungalows of the film people were creeping up the canyons which fan out from Los Angeles. Yet all these widely scattered localities and their denizens were and are known to the public by the generic name Hollywood. "Hollywood's not a place, it's a state of mind," said Wilson Mizner, the wit, promoter, and gambler who had come there to end his roistering days selling script ideas. The Hollywood of the Twenties was just that.

Its heterogeneous, rootless population had nothing in common except the fact that they were all in pictures, or wanted to be. They had come from everywhere, selling their specialties—writers, actors, painters, contortionists, cowboys, bankrupt aristocrats, bunco artists, promoters, "idea men"—and they hoped never to leave. Success had come by accident, it might leave just as accidentally, so why not live for today? Moreover, they lived under the world's most powerful spotlight, and in its unreal glare it was hard for them to distinguish their own drives and emotions from those staged by their press agents for the fan magazines and the gossip columns.

With six-figure salaries to back their whims, they staged the most spectacular display of libido on the loose since ancient Rome faded into the darkness. In this their instincts served them well. Hollywood in the Twenties was garish, extravagant, ludicrous, acquisitive, ambitious, ruthless, beautiful—which was just what its world public wanted it to be. Its very unreality was protective of the illusion. Dream worlds are not supposed to be lifelike.

Renee Adoree, Rod La Rocque, Mae Murray, John Gilbert, Norma Talmadge, Douglas Fairbanks, Marion Davies, William S. Hart

commissary for a single scene in *Show People*, 1928

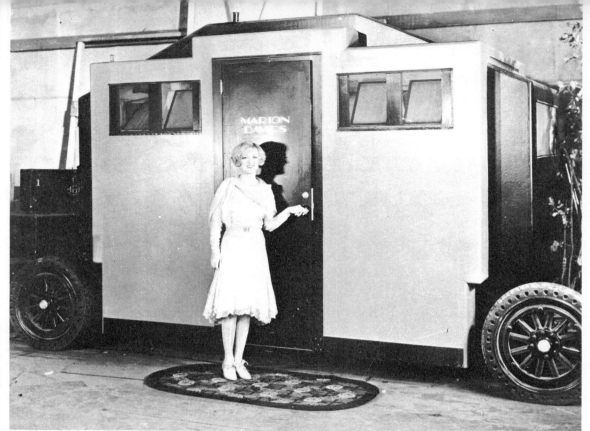

Marion Davies was one of the first to achieve a portable dressing room which could be wheeled to any corner of the M-G-M studio where she happened to be working. She seems also to have a special alighting-mat.

Every studio was compelled by law to maintain special schools where child actors could continue their studies while appearing in pictures. Here Olive Borden hovers over the juvenile cast of *The Auctioneer*, 1927.

## STUDIO "LIFE"

Twenty-six fan magazines and "special correspondents" from all over the world, aided by an army of press agents, reflected and amplified the universal interest in Hollywood's doings. The smallest details of studio routine became fodder for the insatiable publicity maw, and when they did not

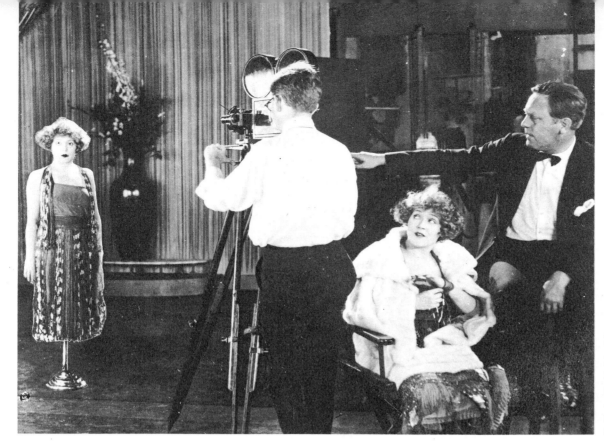

An ancestress of the stand-in. This dummy substituted for Mae Murray during camera rehearsals for double-exposure scenes in *Peacock Alley*, 1921. Miss Murray's husband and director, Robert Z. Leonard is seated beside the star.

Louis B. Mayer turns over to Lon Chaney the flag presented to M-G-M by the Marine Corps. Chaney raised it in the picture *Tell It to the Marines*, 1927. Left to right: Mr. Mayer, Hunt Stromberg, Harry Rapf, director George Hill, and Chaney.

exist, it was necessary to invent them. Audiences became as familiar with what was purported to go on behind the scenes as with what they saw in their theaters. Nor did this disillusion them. The portrait they received of the picture-making colony was even more fascinating than on-screen romance.

# HOME LIFE
# OF THE GODS

As publicity departments increasingly halved the public and private lives of the stars, a sort of double-image of the darlings of the screen was gradually built up for audience edification. All were the quintessence of remote glamour, yet all were homebodies too, plain as an old shoe, just like your next-door neighbor. At the same time, their cultural attainments were bounded only by the limits of their press agents' imaginations. Ramon Novarro's interest in philosophy was as well known to his fans as Douglas Fairbanks, Jr.'s painting and Jetta Goudal's genius at costume design. To feed the needs of the rapacious publicity machine, these gorgeous, homey, cultured creatures were continually photographed in fantastic poses which often made them seem to belong to some other species.

The caption says: "Dolores del Rio has placed the photos of her screen idols on her comb but has left the center space for the Great Unknown." Curiously Ben Lyon, Lloyd Hughes, Lewis Stone, Milton Sills, Ronald Colman, and Richard Barthelmess all belonged to her own studio.

### A Day with Pola Negri

It was axiomatic that anyone gifted enough to be a movie star was gifted in more than one way, nor was it considered odd that the stars' creative aspirations seemed always to be on display in full view of the publicity department. Pola

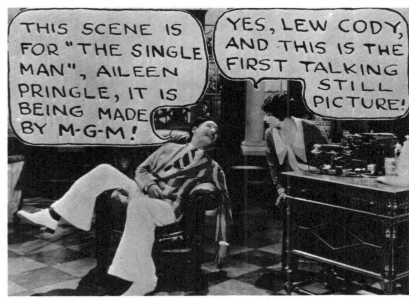

Publicity for *The Taxi Dancer*, 1927, with Joan Crawford.

Publicity for *The Single Man*, 1929.

Negri's cultural pretensions made her particularly good copy as an exponent of the arts. Here we see her blue-penciling a new script, playing the organ, playing the violin, and modeling in clay.

The Marquise de la Falaise de Coudray (Gloria Swanson) and her husband greet Sir Henry and Lady Wood as Sir Henry arrives to guest-conduct at the Hollywood bowl.

# THE BATTLE
# OF THE TITLES

When Pola Negri arrived in Hollywood, she had already married and divorced a Polish count. This enabled her to be referred to as the Countess Dombski, when she was not calling herself "Madame" Negri. That she was the only Hollywood star with any claim to a title was a sore point in the Swanson-Negri feud at Paramount, and Miss Swanson, an expert in one-upmanship, soon married the Marquis Henri de la Falaise de Coudray, thus putting herself far out in front in the Almanach de Gotha sweepstakes. She installed footmen in powdered wigs and knee-breeches in her home and issued invitations in the name of "Madame la Marquise."

This was intolerable to her fellow-divas. Something had to be done and Mae Murray did it; she became the first to corral one of the "marrying Mdivanis," thereby becoming a princess. Whether a genuine marquise was ranked by a doubtful princess (the status of the Mdivanis in their native Georgia has never been well defined) was a question which agitated Hollywood. In any case, however, Pola Negri, a mere ex-countess, was bested, and she

was too entangled in her romance with Valentino to do much about it. But less than a year after Valentino's death she rectified matters by marrying the remaining Mdivani, Prince Serge, thus becoming (though not for long) both an ex-countess and a dubious princess. A few years later a fan magazine wrote: "Pola Negri sailed for Europe with a prince and a contract. Now she has neither."

As Leo Rosten has pointed out, the behavior pattern of the stars of Hollywood follows that of Eastern plutocracy, but with a time-lag of about a quarter of a century. The Misses Swanson, Negri, and Murray had begun their pursuit of European titles a bit too long after the Henry James era for comfort. Miss Swanson read the danger signals when she found herself referred to as "la Marquise de la Etcetera," or sometimes as simply "the Marquise de Gloria," and parried by referring to her husband as "Hank."

Vital statistic: The Marquis de la Falaise married Constance Bennett when the latter succeeded Miss Swanson as queen of the boxoffice.

Mae Murray's marriage in 1926 to Prince David Mdivani. Among the group in the wedding party are, left to right: Pola Negri, Rudolph Valentino, Kathlyn Williams, Miss Murray, Prince Mdivani, Manuel Reachi, and Agnes Ayres. Miss Negri and Valentino were matron of honor and best man, and were then at the height of their romance.

## Super-Wedding

A wedding of indigenous Hollywood aristocracy was that of Vilma Banky and Rod La Rocque, staged by Miss Banky's producer, Samuel Goldwyn, in a style so spectacular that no one has ever dared try to surpass it. But Mr. Goldwyn's fluent showmanship backfired when a reporter at the wedding feast bit into a papier-mâché turkey and discovered that many of the elegant comestibles were props.

# THE END OF THE SILENT ERA

*Queen Elizabeth,* 1912. Sarah Bernhardt saw the film versions of her famous vehicles as "my one chance for immortality," but insisted on filming them as they were on the stage, "speaking my lines as usual."

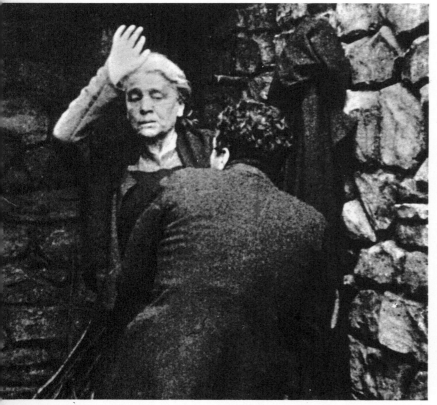

*Cenere,* 1916, with Eleonora Duse. "Something quite different is needed."

The spoken word has been the actor's principal vehicle for expressing emotion since the days of Greek drama, when the actors' faces were hidden behind huge masks. The effect of its absence can be studied in a cruel light in the several film versions of Sarah Bernhardt's standard vehicles—*Camille, Queen Elizabeth,* and others. Bernhardt thought of the screen as a visual equivalent of a phonograph record of her stage performances and made no effort to adapt her technique to it, but without the "golden voice" to give them point, her stagy gestures seemed labored and meaningless. Eleonora Duse, on the other hand, thoroughly understood the difference between the old medium of which she was mistress and the unknown new one. She had hoped for much from her first film but when she saw it she said, "I made the same mistake that nearly everyone has made. But something quite different is needed. I am too old for it, isn't it a pity?"

Few shared her insight. Griffith had early discovered that under the merciless eye of the camera it is better not to act but to *respond,* but even before his time the directors and actors of workaday film-making had already arrived at the compromise which in the main ruled as long as the silent film lasted. They adopted the repertoire of conventional stage gestures and exaggerated it to compensate for the absence of speech. The majority of movie actors "registered" their emotions rather than felt them.

"Registering" was a curious business, seen from this distance. Specific gestures and grimaces were thought to convey equally specific meanings and it was not overwhelmingly difficult to get them all by heart and thus become a movie actor. Many of these devices did double duty. A widening of the eyes and parting of the lips expressed terror, but with slight modification also indicated passion. A certain yearning look, suggesting deep intestinal distress, was known as "soulful." Grief or anguish generally led in close-up to a thrown-back head and hand pressed to forehead, clutched to throat, or raised despairingly to Heaven. A pointing finger accompanied by tightly compressed lips represented the mood accusatory, while kneeling or groveling on the floor signified a wide range of feelings, from remorse to appeal. Ingenues were wide-eyed, while vamps and villainesses invariably betrayed their character by narrowing their eyes to slits.

The movie public rapidly learned this dictionary of the passions and the majority were convinced and even moved by it. But the fact that they never encountered such behavior in their own lives led Americans to revive the archaic word *emote* to suggest the difference between people on the screen and the people in front of it.

Gloria Swanson.

Barbara La Marr, Lionel Barrymore.

Alan Hale, Jacqueline Logan.

Pola Negri, Conrad Nagel.

# EMOTE
## "v.i. To exhibit emotion"

Pola Negri.

Unknown players.

Mae Murray.

Ronald Colman, Vilma Banky.

Bebe Daniels.

# THE WARNER BROTHERS

In his flat Midwestern voice, Will H. Hays spoke from the screen and introduced the first Vitaphone program on August 6, 1926, with a timid prediction that sound would usher in a new era of "pictures and music."

In the middle Twenties, the movie boxoffice sagged. Something seemed to have gone wrong; except for the big pictures, the audience was staying home in increasing numbers. In furious quest of novelty, exhibitors added vaudeville acts, "prologues," condensed operas, and musical comedies to their programs until the nominal feature, the movie itself, seemed in danger of getting lost in a huge variety show. Among the novelties available was a device called the Vitaphone, which the engineers and technicians of the Bell Telephone system had been working on since the days of Edison's early experiments with sound films. But when the Vitaphone was offered to the screen's major companies, they rejected it.

There were those who were not so cautious, perhaps because they were not so comfortable. The Warner brothers, Harry, Jack, Sam, and Albert, had fought their way up from the nickelodeons to the ownership of exchanges and, after World War I, had graduated into production itself. Their capital and everything they could borrow was all invested in their studio program, and as the battle for theater ownership developed, they found themselves unable on the one hand to secure access to the first-run theaters of their competitors or on the other to obtain sufficient backing to buy theaters of their own. No matter how good their pictures, slow death was the only prospect before them under this setup. Then the owners of the Vitaphone patents finally came to see them. With an enthusiasm born of desperation, the Warners contracted for the exclusive use of the Vitaphone device, rounded up their remaining capital, and began a grim race with time. The issue was simply whether they would be able to complete and market enough sound pictures before their silent pictures had disappeared from first-run screens and their ledgers turned from black to red. The industry stared aghast at this foredoomed gamble. How could these minor producers, sunk in debt, back a project which their mighty competitors had rejected? The strain must have

# THE
# TALKIE REVOLUTION

been tremendous. Sam Warner died under it.

The first public performance of the Vitaphone was held August 6, 1926, at the Manhattan Opera House in New York. The program consisted of shorts featuring musical celebrities like Mischa Elman and Giovanni Martinelli, and a silent film, John Barrymore's *Don Juan,* with recorded musical accompaniment. To the opening night audience, the principal novelty seemed to be that the music came from behind the screen rather than from musicians in the orchestra pit, and it was a "canned" substitute for orchestral accompaniment that Harry Warner tried to sell to economy-minded exhibitors. Few of them were inclined to install his expensive equipment, and for a year after *Don Juan,* sound languished as an unproved gimmick in isolated theaters which showed only those "Vitaphone shorts."

But attendance at these few theaters was so consistently good that the Warners were encouraged to pursue their experiment. Trying to hang on to what little cash they had, they sought to induce Al Jolson to accept stock in their company in lieu of salary for his appearance in *The Jazz Singer.* Jolson demanded cash, and thereby turned down a fortune. *The Jazz Singer* was a mediocre silent picture with a shopworn theme, and mostly told its story with titles, but it contained three Jolson songs and a snatch of dialogue. That was enough. Once it was released, in October 1927, the revolution was under way. Exhibitors, watching the long lines before the Warner Theater in New York, decided to get in on the bonanza and ordered sound equipment, only to find that the manufacturers were already swamped with orders.

A tremor of uneasiness went through the industry when this fact became known. Most producers and exhibitors were watching the fortunes of the Warners but had not made up their own minds whether they would invest in the "novelty." Might they not wait too long? More and more Warner sound films were reaching the market; William Fox (whose Movietone sound-on-film device eventually supplanted the Vitaphone sound-on-disk method) had added sound to his newsreels and some of his short subjects. By the end of 1927 even the industry skeptics could no longer deny that any sound film, by whatever process made, was attracting large crowds to any theater that showed it.

By the spring of 1928, in any given community, the worst sound film would outdraw the best silent picture. This was genuinely alarming to the movie community. If talkies were not merely to exist side by side with silent films, but entirely replace them, a great many vested interests would be imperiled. Many of the mighty, among them D. W. Griffith, suggested a sort of conspiracy to suppress talking films, at least until they were perfected. But they reckoned without the public. Audiences took the bit in their teeth and demanded sound films—and there were the hungry Warners ready to supply them. Gradually the sober fact dawned that the 32-year-old silent motion picture medium was doomed.

Al Jolson in *The Jazz Singer,* 1927.

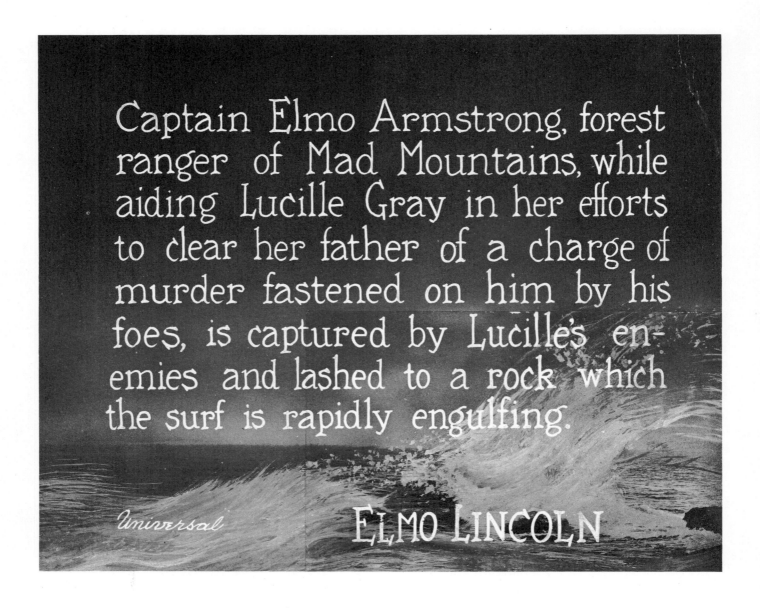

Captain Elmo Armstrong, forest ranger of Mad Mountains, while aiding Lucille Gray in her efforts to clear her father of a charge of murder fastened on him by his foes, is captured by Lucille's enemies and lashed to a rock which the surf is rapidly engulfing.

*Universal*

ELMO LINCOLN

## THE VANISHING SUBTITLE

Whatever headaches lay in store for the veterans of silent pictures, there was one adjunct of silence which none of them regretted losing—the caption or subtitle. This necessary evil consisted of "voice of God" editorial comments on the action, supplemented when expedient by "spoken titles"—lines of dialogue printed on the screen. By the end of the silent era everything possible had been done to reduce them to a minimum. Dialogue scenes were carefully photographed to enable the editor to cut away from the actor to his "spoken title" at the moment he opened his mouth to speak, cutting back to his image just as he finished. Good editors could often obtain the illusion of actual speech by this device. But in spite of such skill, the subtitle was an irritating reminder that, because of its silence, this primarily visual medium had to rely on the crutch of words at crucial moments in the narrative. Moreover, the subtitle was a weapon in the hands of the producer against the director, if the former decided the latter had done his work poorly or had overstepped the bounds of decorum. He then merely hired a good cutter and a clever title-writer to tighten up the film or alter it completely. Actors were astonished to find that lines they had mouthed as "Get that harlot out of my house" emerged on the screen as "I think the lady had better leave," or that the mistress of the villain had been transformed by the title-writer into his maiden aunt. One of these professional title-doctors advertised his calling in the trade magazines with the slogan: "All bad little films when they die go to RALPH SPENCE."

Steve Blighton, with all the fear of the actual crook in his heart, is determined to procure the papers for himself—to destroy them and so fasten for all time the guilt on John Gray, one of his employees.

UNIVERSAL

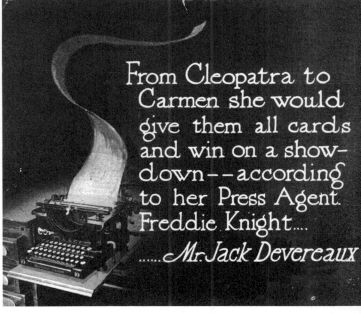
From Cleopatra to Carmen she would give them all cards and win on a showdown—according to her Press Agent, Freddie Knight....
......Mr. Jack Devereaux

Lucille 'dolls up' in the outfit provided by Blighton, hoping thereby to lull his suspicions and outwit him.

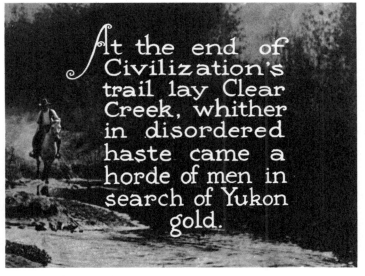
At the end of Civilization's trail lay Clear Creek, whither in disordered haste came a horde of men in search of Yukon gold.

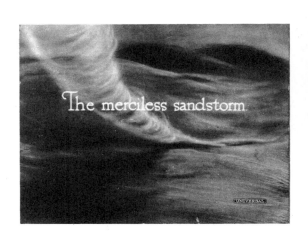
The merciless sandstorm

UNIVERSAL

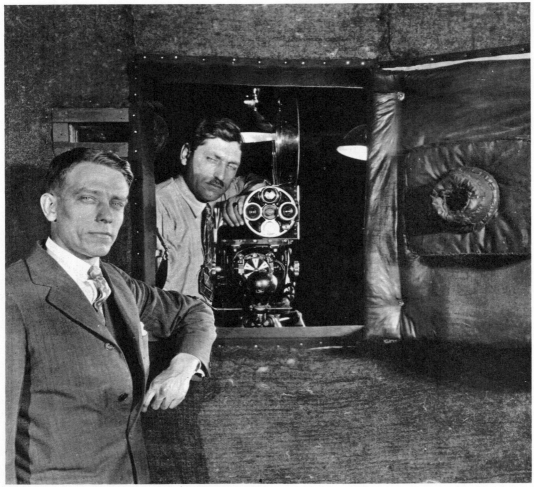

The Vitaphone camera which photographed *The Jazz Singer* had to be enclosed in a soundproof booth so that the whirring of the camera would not be recorded. Since air-conditioning was unknown then, the cameraman could remain in his prison only a few minutes at a time and usually emerged dripping wet.

## KING MIKE

By mid-1928, all the great studios faced three stark realities. To survive, they had to re-equip their studios for sound without a moment's delay; they had somehow to salvage their stock of silent films which were rapidly becoming unmarketable; and they had either to retread or jettison their expensive contract players who had proved their worth in silent pictures but whose future was now an unknown quantity.

Chaos and panic swept Hollywood as the companies moved to convert to sound. Recording problems obsessed producers and directors whose whole efforts had for years been focused on doing without sound. The free-flowing action and continuity of silent films was abruptly displaced by a static, stage-like technique, both because the microphone was at first immovable and all action and "business" had to be geared to its location, and because the cameras, immured in soundproof booths, could no longer move about freely. Concealing the microphone so that it would not be photographed presented a daily problem. Directors tore their hair in frenzy when their most cherished dramatic effects were vetoed by the sound engineers—laboratory men trained by the telephone industry whose chief concern was that voices be distinct and that all conversation be conducted at one voice level. Gradually these mechanical difficulties were overcome and the fluidity of screen technique restored, but for more than three years the microphone was king, and an overbearing monarch at that.

Meanwhile there was the problem of the com-

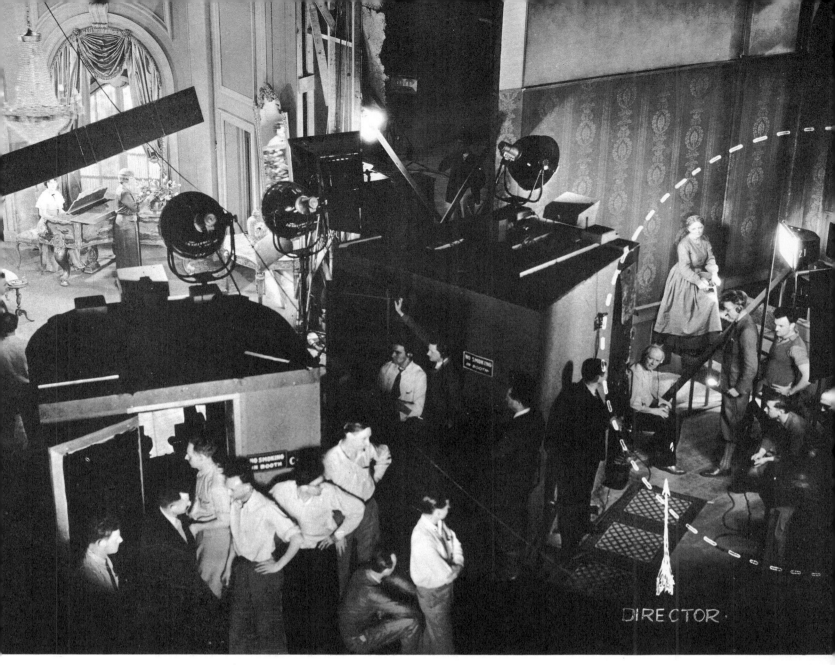

DIRECTOR.

Before "dubbing." For this scene in *Lummox,* 1930, director Herbert Brenon, seated, right, wanted heroine Winifred Westover, right, to listen to her daughter singing in another room. Since sound tracks could not yet be "mixed," the two scenes had to be photographed and recorded simultaneously.

pleted silent films which still awaited release—millions of dollars worth of merchandise which, in the eyes of the talkie-conscious public, had suddenly become as antique as *The Great Train Robbery.* Producers solved the problem as best they could by introducing sound in some form into their remaining silents so that exhibitors could advertise that their pictures made noises. Fans quickly became adept at deducing from the ads the degree to which silent films had been made into audible ones. "Sound effects and music" meant a recorded orchestral accompaniment plus various bell-ringings and door-knockings introduced into the otherwise silent action. "With sound and dialogue" usually meant that the players remained silent for five reels, became briefly but excessively loquacious in the sixth, and

relapsed into silence in the seventh. There were extraordinary variants: *After* the final clinch in Cecil B. De Mille's *The Godless Girl,* 1929, the hero and heroine sat down on the curbstone and talked about the weather for ten minutes in order that the picture might be billed as "part-talking." The public was remarkably patient with these weird "goat-glands," as they were called in the trade, tolerating and even welcoming them until the time—about the middle of 1929—when the legend "all-talking" could be applied to all pictures.

"King Mike's" reign was toughest on the players. Even experienced stage stars suffered from the crudities of early talkie recording. As for the legendary favorites of the silent screen, many of them had not spoken in public since first-grade assembly.

245

## Too Rich to Be Bothered

Some stars, the ones who had spent it as they made it, had no choice but to struggle on, whether or not they were equipped for sound. But those who had taken advantage of their huge salaries and low taxes to invest their earnings had to decide whether they would risk the possibility of failure in the talkies or take the sensible course of retiring while their laurels were still green. Since death is ordinarily the only retirement an actor will accept, most of them merely wavered.

A fan magazine used this publicity still of Norma Talmadge on its cover in 1929, but painted out the number 5 on the mike and substituted *13*. A veteran of twenty years of the movies, Miss Talmadge had grown a little bored with stardom, but the talkies seemed to challenge her and after more than a year of voice instruction she made a successful sound debut in *New York Nights,* 1930. But her second talkie, based on Belasco's *Madame Dubarry,* evoked from a critic: "She speaks the Belascoan rodomontades in a Vitagraph accent." Her sister Constance, already retired, wired her, "Leave them while you're looking good and thank God for the trust funds Momma set up." A few years later a fan asked Miss Talmadge for her autograph. "Get away, dear," the ex-star replied, "I don't need you any more."

Colleen Moore was making $12,500 a week in 1929. She had appeared in two successful talking pictures, but with the vogue of the flapper waning, her employers let her contract lapse. She then financed and starred in a Broadway play. When no movie offers resulted, she returned to Hollywood in some alarm and signed for $2,500 a week, commenting, "I'm just getting a button compared to my old salary, but I'd work for nothing, it's so good to be back." Miss Moore showed her skill and versatility in the offbeat role of a timid schoolteacher in *The Power and the Glory,* 1933, but the picture failed to re-establish her. She could have cemented her comeback in any of four opportunities Hollywood gave her. She had the looks, the talent, the intelligence. She was too rich really to care.

"So she took the $250,000" was *Photoplay's* epitaph on the fourteen-year career of Corinne Griffith. Of her *Lilies of the Field,* 1930, *Time* had said: "Pretty Corinne Griffith talks through her nose in her first sound film." Miss Griffith released her studio from their contract with her on condition that she receive her full salary, and said, "Why should I go on until I am playing mother roles? I have plenty of money. I want to improve my mind. Most of the time you'll find me bobbing around in Europe." Miss Griffith not only improved her mind but changed it: she made one picture in England and several times fruitlessly attempted comebacks on the American stage and screen. Today she is one of the wealthiest of ex-stars, active in politics, the author of several books.

## KAPUT

Secure in their long-term contracts, their incredible salaries, and their still more incredible fan mail (20,000 letters a week for Clara Bow), the silent-picture stars were at first unable to take sound seriously. But as the Jolson films swept the nation, as even the worst silent films garnered big box-office through the addition of a few talking sequences, the big stars had to face the facts. It was hard to start all over after they had reigned so long. How did you learn to "talk"? And without sacrificing what had made you talked about?

Some of them suffered cruelly. Even Dorothy Parker was compassionate about the fate of May McAvoy, one of whose lines in *The Terror* emerged as "I am thick of thutth thilly antickth." Miss McAvoy decided not to study with a voice coach on the ground that "the public would rather hear me speak in my natural voice." The public quickly decided it would rather not hear her speak at all.

Others whose voices did not fit their visual personalities were temporarily more fortunate. Marie Prevost's years of stardom as a romantic come-

# No Spik

A favorite device of imported European stars who were dissatisfied with their roles, their salaries, or their studio prestige was suddenly to "forget" how to speak English, with resulting suspension of production until they could be bribed to remember. In 1928 they discovered that production could be suspended indefinitely for all their bosses cared.

Though most of the public thought that the talkies put an end to the American career of Pola Negri, actually she had already exhausted her once great popularity. In the early Thirties RKO reimported her, hoping to duplicate the success of Marlene Dietrich as a husky-voiced, German-accented singer of sexy songs. Miss Negri went her rival one better, since her singing voice recorded as basso profundo, but her comeback picture, *A Woman Commands,* 1932, was so badly made as to end her hopes. From 1935 to 1939 she starred in German talkies but left Hitler's Germany at the outbreak of war and arrived in America, penniless, after the fall of France. Today she lives in Texas, where she has inherited a great fortune and recently published her long-awaited memoirs.

Even as he received the Academy Award for the best performance by an actor for 1928, the great Emil Jannings knew he was finished as an American movie star. His studio had decided that his English was too Teutonic to be acceptable in the talkies, and as soon as he had attended the Academy dinner and got his Oscar he left for Germany. He made one attempt to recapture his American audiences with a poorly made English version of *The Blue Angel,* filmed in Berlin, but even the presence of Marlene Dietrich couldn't put it across in the United States. He remained the reigning star of the German screen until his death in 1951.

Vilma Banky had just been elevated to stardom by Samuel Goldwyn when the talkies arrived. Mr. Goldwyn, with high hopes for his beautiful star, set voice coach Jane Manner to work on smoothing out her guttural Hungarian accent. But her coaching took more than a year and the results were not impressive. Rumor had it that Miss Banky was too lazy to work at her voice chores, although they took place in full view of the publicity department. M-G-M gave her one chance at the talkies, in a screen version of *They Knew What They Wanted* called *A Lady to Love,* 1930. Her accent was in keeping with the immigrant girl she played, but still at odds with her romantic appearance. She made a few subsequent pictures in Europe with her husband, Rod La Rocque.

dienne ended when her voice recorded like Judy Holliday's in *Born Yesterday,* but there was still demand for her services as a gum-chewing soubrette in supporting roles. Miss Prevost took her demotion hard. She sought to drown her disappointments in Scotch, and died in 1934.

There were of course the hopeless ones, the silent favorites who could not even remember their lines or delivered them as "The govment is gonna do some very ineressin things in Febewary." Some few had the sense to cut their losses, like the blonde who invoked the Act of God clause to obtain release from her contract. When her producer objected, she said, "A New York millionaire wants to marry me, and if that ain't an act of God, you tell me what is." The rest were the really damned. F. Scott Fitzgerald accurately described their fate in *The Last Tycoon,* with his portrait of the woman who saw her five years of silent stardom as a God-given birthright and the rest of her life as a dim and unjust limbo. "I had a beautiful place in 1928," she laments. "All spring I was up to my ass in daisies."

John Gilbert's first talkie was *His Glorious Night*, 1929, based on Molnar's *Olympia*. In torrid love scenes with Catherine Dale Owen he spoke the flowery dialogue in an actory tenor that brought snickers from audiences which a year earlier had hailed him as the greatest lover of the screen.

## "WHITE VOICE"

The case of John Gilbert was classic. Inheriting the mantle of Valentino, Gilbert had been the screen's top male star for four years when, early in 1929, M-G-M renewed his contract for four years at a total fee of a million dollars. The huge sum was a reward to Gilbert for staying with the studio at a time when it needed his boxoffice power. Three months later his first talkie was released. It was the star's professional death warrant. Audiences which had idolized him in his silent days refused to accept his florid yet inexpert delivery of romantic dialogue. Gay and charming, a veteran of many years in the movies, he was popular in Hollywood and both his friends and his employers tried hard to help him. He was said to be suffering from a malady christened "white voice" which time, coaching, and improvements in sound recording would eventually cure.

The world outside the barricade thought otherwise. Of his third talkie, a critic wrote: "It is getting so that reviewing a John Gilbert picture is embarrassing. One wants to be considerate of him and fair to one's readers. Also a certain reportorial instinct must be served. Amidst three fires, it is nevertheless true that *Way for a Sailor* is an indifferent picture and Mr. Gilbert is the same, more interesting as a reminder of the past than a present joy. Why this is so is just another proof of the microphone's capriciousness. It isn't that Mr. Gilbert's voice is insufficient; it's that his use of it robs him of magnetism, individuality, and strangest of all, skill. He becomes an uninteresting and inexpert performer whose work could be bettered by hundreds of lesser-known players. True, he hasn't

much of a picture to improve, but it often happens that a star is better than his vehicle. Mr. Gilbert isn't."

After the release of *Way for a Sailor*, it was clear that Gilbert had no future and the studio tried to buy up his expensive contract at its full value. Like Corinne Griffith, he could have had a fortune with no further effort, but he grimly insisted that M-G-M fulfill the contract to the letter. Through a ghastly three years the movie world was treated to the extraordinary spectacle of the production and distribution of five not inexpensive films which no audience wanted to see. At the end of this long ordeal, Gilbert was ready to capitulate, but his former co-star Garbo insisted that M-G-M re-engage him to play opposite her in *Queen Christina*, 1933. For a moment hope flared. But as before, audiences found a glaring contrast between the way Gilbert looked and spoke. His fate seemed doubly sealed.

Then Columbia, which was at that time the refuge for fallen stars, cast him for a featured role in *The Captain Hates the Sea*, 1934. He gave a brilliant performance as a drunken Hollywood script writer, and his dialogue, the common speech of his everyday life, came from his lips with total conviction. The thin voice that could not carry "I love you, darling, I love you" was eloquently ironic in delivering "If you believe it, it isn't so." Gilbert died before his future could be determined, but his performance in this picture established a paradox. The talkies were for those who could create a new personality-image in keeping with their voices—but this was apt to involve professional demotion rather than progress.

# SOME STARS SURVIVED, OTHERS EMERGED

Some of the silent players made the most of their native vocal equipment. Gloria Swanson and Bebe Daniels, neither of whom had had stage experience, triumphantly emerged with singing as well as speaking voices, and Gary Cooper's monosyllabic Montana speech matched his screen image perfectly. There was universal suspense about Greta Garbo, who was said to be handicapped by a thick Swedish accent and a low, husky, almost masculine voice. M-G-M, in spite of the total victory of the talkies, continued to star her in silent pictures the success of which was a startling exception to the public's verdict in favor of sound. Meanwhile Miss Garbo worked hard on her accent. Finally she took the plunge as Eugene O'Neill's Swedish-American heroine, Anna Christie. Her fans first sighed with relief,

Once a Broadway favorite, Ruth Chatterton was idling in Hollywood in 1928, where her husband, Ralph Forbes, was climbing to silent stardom. The talkies reduced Forbes to supporting roles, but swept the supposedly passé Miss Chatterton into the position of "First Lady of the Cinema" at half a million a year. She is seen here in *The Laughing Lady*, 1930, with Clive Brook, whose fortunes were also advanced by sound.

GARBO TALKS was the simple slogan with which *Anna Christie* was advertised when it was finally released in 1930, two years after the coming of sound. The first words the star spoke from the screen were, "Gif me a viskey, ginger ale on the side —and don't be stingy, baby."

Jeanne Eagels, the sensational star of *Rain*, made an equally sensational talkie debut in *The Letter*, 1929, followed quickly by *Jealousy*, 1929 (left, with the youthful Fredric March). Miss Eagels promised to become one of the screen's leading personalities, but she was already near death from drugs, as the painful thinness of her forearm reveals.

then swooned with delight. For her voice fitted her strange personality, and she used it with an eloquence beyond skill. In fact, speech humanized the "woman of veiled thought and unpredictable mood" which had been her silent image.

"Humanness" indeed turned out to be the touchstone of success in talking pictures. Ruth Chatterton used the same la-de-da "stage English" accent which caused the public to turn thumbs down on many stage imports, but the warmth of her characterizations won over audiences in spite of it. In mysterious contrast, the famed Ina Claire struggled in vain to become a favorite, perhaps because she was cast in sophisticated comedies, while Miss Chatterton established herself with time-tested tear-jerkers like *Madame X,* 1929.

## ALL TALKING, ALL SINGING, ALL DANCING

No sooner had the "all-talking" picture been universally accepted than it was superseded by the "all-talking, all-singing, all-dancing" extravaganza which was likely to be in color too. Hollywood went music-crazy in 1929. Stars of stage musical comedy, vaudeville hoofers, ukulele artists, ballerinas, and low comedians descended on California by the trainload, and the only Hollywood stars who did

not take singing or dancing lessons were Garbo and Rin-Tin-Tin. The song-writing industry established new headquarters in the film capital, and "voice coaches" were a special colony. Antique operettas were dusted off for the cameras, wheezy gags got new laughs from hinterland audiences. Every studio made pictures offering its entire roster of stars in "novelty" numbers, which meant that every actor

The "Pageant of Lovers" scene from *Glorifying the American Girl*, 1929.

was featured in some specialty he wasn't good at.

As suddenly as it had begun, the craze for musicals died, for the simple reason that they had been done to death. In the somber autumn of 1930, audiences found that not even musicals could take their minds off the depression, especially when they were dated operettas featuring unknowns from the stage whose vocal qualifications failed to make up for

their visual inadequacies. By 1931, a reviewer was saying of *Safe in Hell:* "Here is a reminder of the dear dead days that we thought beyond recall. For this is a musical extravaganza, replete with prancing chorines, low comics, and 'backstage' stuff. The picture must have been long delayed in release, for all its much-touted principals have by now gone back to the obscurity from whence they came."

Paul Whiteman's "Melting Pot" number in *The King of Jazz*, 1930.

Dixie Lee in the "Crazy Feet" number from *Happy Days*, 1930.

## ALL TALKING, ALL SINGING, ALL DANCING

Marie Dressler as Venus rising from the sea in a burlesque ballet from *The Hollywood Review of 1929*. A minor comedienne in silent films, Miss Dressler became one of the greatest stars of the talkies.

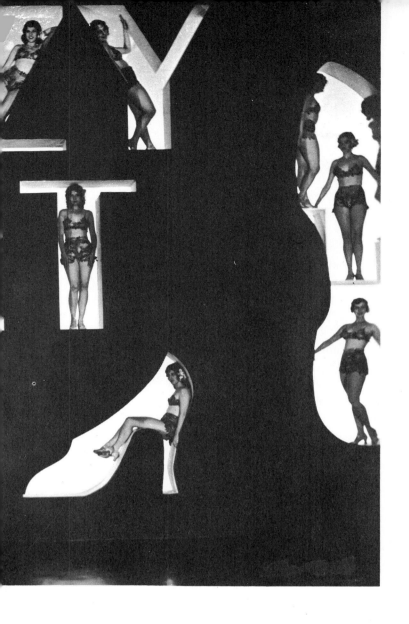

Composer Nacio Herb Brown played his perennial hit, "Singin' in the Rain" for the first time in *The Hollywood Review of 1929*.

Even Mary Pickford succumbed to the craze for all-talking, singing and dancing films, in *Kiki*, 1931.

# TEACUP DRAMA

Many, in Hollywood as well as Broadway, assumed that once the screen had found a voice, picture production would consist largely of canning stage hits on celluloid, using the original players with little or no adaptation of the plays to movie terms. Many producers acted on this assumption, and a wave of drawing-room comedies and dramas swamped the screen, monopolizing it along with the musicals. But the new stage plays and their performers, despite their much-heralded "sophistication," were rejected by movie audiences in little over a year. Nicknaming the photographed plays "teacup drama," movie fans complained that nothing ever happened in them, that they left their characters where they found them, and that what passed for action in them consisted exclusively of hand-kissing, cigarette-lighting, and an eternal pouring and serving of tea. The fact that many of these plays took place in Mayfair did not help them. Mayfair in terms of sweet Elinor Glyn was one thing, but the real article bored movie-goers who found British repression less than amusing. By 1931 it was clear that a movie still had to move, and that the major job in filming a play was translating talk into action.

Norma Shearer and Robert Montgomery in *Private Lives*. 1934.

Ina Claire and Robert Ames in *Rebound*, 1931.

A typical stage grouping in the screen version of *The Last of Mrs. Cheyney*, 1929. Left to right: Cyril Chadwick, Madeline Seymour, Moon Carroll, Maude Turner Gordon, Herbert Bunston, Hedda Hopper, George Barraud, Norma Shearer, and Basil Rathbone.

Clive Brook's manner as the hero of *The Laughing Lady*, 1930, with Ruth Chatterton, was so stiffly formal that one critic pretended to mistake him for the butler.

*The Cockeyed World,* 1929. Edmund Lowe, Lili Damita. This sequel to *What Price Glory?* was a boxoffice smash not only because of its racy situations but also because its actors under Raoul Walsh's direction achieved a free-and-easy speech and manner in marked contrast to the stilted behavior which had characterized "teacup drama."

*Hallelujah!,* 1929. King Vidor waited five years for the chance to realize his cherished dream of a drama of Negro life with an all-Negro cast before the talkies finally gave him his chance.

*All Quiet on the Western Front,* 1930. Lew Ayres in his finest role, Raymond Griffith as the dying French soldier. Griffith, a stellar comedian of silent films, retired at the advent of the talkies because of a vocal affliction which made him unable to speak above a whisper, but returned for this last role in which he did not have to utter a word.

*Morocco,* 1930. In this extraordinary mixture of sophistication and naïveté, Josef von Sternberg told his story in pictures, with sound and dialogue merely a supplement to the visual rather than the major vehicle of the narrative. Here are Marlene Dietrich and Gary Cooper.

Lon Chaney's deformed cripple, seen here with Betty Compson in *The Miracle Man*, 1920, made his reputation.

# THE GRIM THIRTIES

## HORROR

Instead of true horror, what chiefly substituted for it on the screen of the optimistic Twenties was a species of mystery-comedy borrowed from the contemporary stage—*The Bat*, *The Cat and the Canary*, and *The Gorilla* were typical of both the stage and screen manifestations of this vogue. In them mysterious events were conjured up as much to amuse as to terrify, and all the apparently supernatural occurrences—clutching hands, ghostly apparitions, flashing lights, ringing bells—invariably turned out to be the elaborately engineered work of an archcriminal bent on concealing his nefarious designs. Incredible though it may seem from this distance, it more often than not *did* turn out to be the Butler whodunit.

The supernatural explained away is only momentarily frightening. The genuine supernatural produces a deeper tremor. In true horror films, the archcriminal becomes the archfiend, the first and greatest of whom was undoubtedly Lon Chaney.

No screen pantomime has been more eloquent than Chaney's, and it is conceivable that he might have become the finest actor in the motion picture medium. It turned out otherwise. Chaney's first important role was that of the cripple in the great hit, *The Miracle Man*, and his success in it convinced producers and the actor himself that his future lay in the creation with make-up of a succession of horrendously monstrous or mutilated characters designed to frighten the public out of its wits. To support his studio-coined title "The Man of a Thousand Faces," Chaney shunned publicity as much as possible, keeping his own personality concealed behind the series of grotesque masks he concocted for his professional roles. Make-up was not his only resource. He twisted his body into agonizing positions to simulate deformity or mutilation, playing a legless man in *The Penalty*, 1920; the title role in *The Hunchback of Notre Dame*, 1923; an "armless wonder" in *The Unknown;* a one-eyed man in *The Road to Mandalay*, 1926; and a paralytic in *West of Zanzibar*, 1929.

As his career progressed, it became obvious that Chaney's popularity was not dependent on his virtuosity at the make-up table. The most terrifying of all his disguises was the simple white wig, spectacles and shawl in which he impersonated an old lady in *The Unholy Three*, 1925, and his straight roles as top sergeant in *Tell It to the Marines*, 1927, tough detective in *While the City Sleeps*, 1928, and aging railroad engineer in *Thunder*, 1929, were liked by the public as much as his grotesques. But the actor (or his studio) seemed driven to conceal his sensitive and somewhat tragic features behind a series of sinister and ever more inhuman masks. He joined forces with a director, Tod Browning, who shared his taste for the outré, and together they packed their films with as many horrid details as they could concoct. In spite of their fascination with the ghostly, however, they seemed to fear audience skepticism and their pictures, like the orthodox "mysteries" of the day, always in the end explained apparently supernatural phenomena as the product of some human agency.

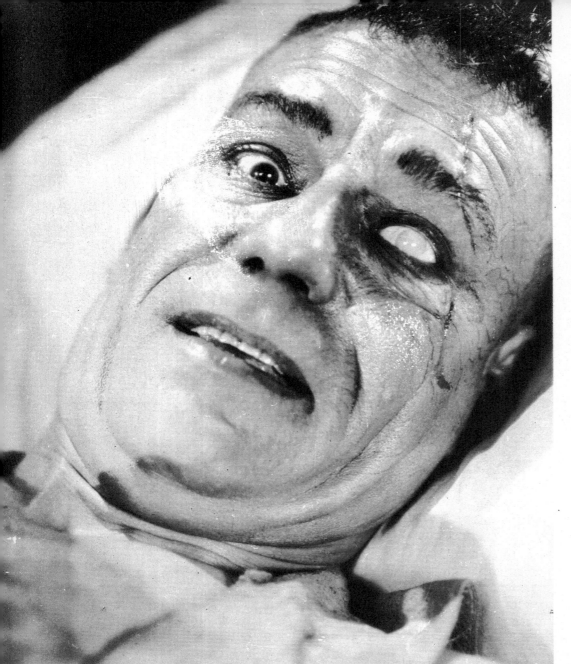

Road to Mandalay

Mr. Wu

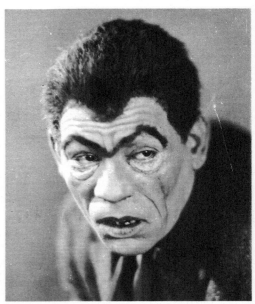

The Octave of Claudius

The Hunchback of Notre Dame

The Phantom of the Opera

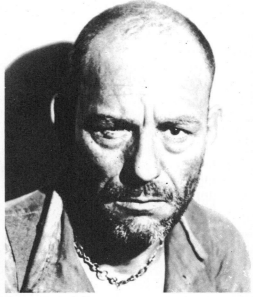

West of Zanzibar

In his only talkie, the 1930 remake of *The Unholy Three* (far right), Chaney, disguised as an old woman, gives him-

# THOUSAND FACES

West of Zanzibar

Laugh, Clown, Laugh

Mockery

Where East Is East

West of Zanzibar

London after Midnight

Tell It to the Marines

self away in the witness box when his voice inadvertently drops to his natural deep tones. With John Miljan.

Count Dracula's three sisters, also vampires, sleep in coffins in the dungeons of Castle Dracula.

## DRACULA AND

The year Lon Chaney died, his director, Tod Browning, filmed *Dracula* and therewith launched the full vogue of horror films. What made *Dracula* a turning-point was that it did not attempt to explain away its tale of vampirism and supernatural horrors. Something in the air of the early Thirties made audiences believe and enjoy believing what they would have scoffed at ten years earlier. *Dracula's* success led to a wild rummage through Edgar Allan Poe, Robert Louis Stevenson, medieval demonology, pseudo-science, and classic horror tales like Mary Shelley's *Frankenstein*, which, filmed with great skill and taste by James Whale, created an even greater sensation than had *Dracula*. These two films made stars of Bela Lugosi and Boris Karloff, and figures of popular mythology out of the characters they played. Eventually one enterprising exhibitor conceived the repulsive idea of double-featuring these two horror attractions, and they were rebooked everywhere with doctors, nurses and ambulances available for stricken patrons.

*Dracula*, 1931. Bela Lugosi as the vampire is not a figure in masquerade but a fiend who actually sucks the blood of humans, in this case Helen Chandler's.

264

This terrifying yet pathetic scene was cut by the censors of several states. Through the child who does not fear him, the monster discovers his own humanity. Yet he kills her.

# FRANKENSTEIN

*Frankenstein,* 1931. The synthetic monster is raised to the top of Frankenstein's tower, where the play of lightning will infuse him with "electrical life."

Baron Frankenstein's sadistic assistant torments the monster with fire, the only thing he fears. Eventually it destroys him.

# THE SONS AND DAUGHTERS OF FRANKENSTEIN AND DRACULA

Dracula, Frankenstein, and the other assorted creatures of the horror cycle, achieved a curious kind of commercial if not artistic immortality. There is a limit to human invention (though there seems to be none to human credulity), and it was necessary to resurrect these monsters, no matter how thoroughly they had been killed off in the preceding film. They "returned" either as themselves or as their "sons" or "daughters" or "ghosts." By the 1940s the public had supped full on horrors, and it became necessary to double the charge: wolf-men, vampires, and zombies were co-starred in the later chiller-dillers. Finally the cycle expired in self-burlesque, with such films as *Abbott and Costello Meet Frankenstein*.

Ironically, the star of many of these latter-day minor horror films was the son of the great Lon Chaney of the Twenties. Known as Creighton Chaney, he had set out to make his own name by serious acting, but the studios could not resist the temptation to trade on his father's fame, and he was billed first as Lon Chaney, Jr., and then simply as Lon Chaney—becoming, to a new generation born after his father's death, the only Lon Chaney there was. That an important talent was thus wasted by Hollywood is evidenced by his work in *High Noon* and *Of Mice and Men*.

*The Mummy's Ghost*, 1944. The studio caption says: "Determining by her weird birthmark that she is the reincarnation of the Egyptian Princess Ananka, 3000 years dead, Kharis (Lon Chaney) carries Amina (Ramsay Ames) off to the deserted mine shack where Youssef Bey awaits."

In *Bride of Frankenstein*, 1935, the pathos of the monster's distorted humanity was emphasized. His obliging creator makes him a woman of his own who takes one look at her prospective mate and screams in horror. Elsa Lanchester is the synthetic woman.

*Ghost of Frankenstein*, 1942. Boris Karloff having graduated to less strenuous parts, Lon Chaney, Jr. assumed the role of the monster in the fourth Frankenstein film. Evelyn Ankers, Sir Cedric Hardwicke, and Janet Ann Gallow are seen with him.

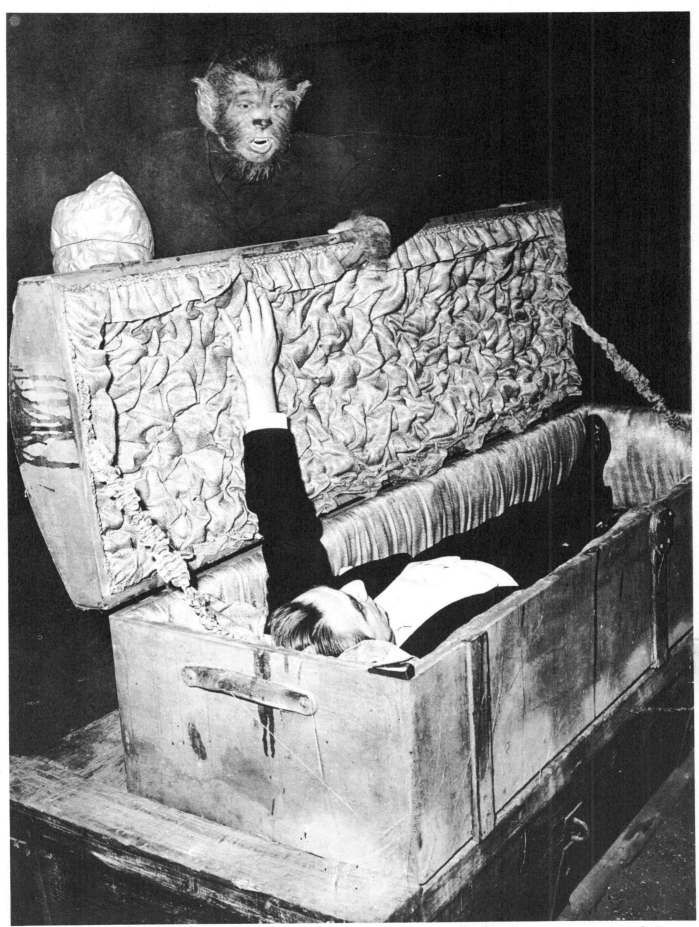

*The Return of the Vampire*, 1944. The Wolf-Man, Matt Willis, tenderly opens the coffin bed of the vampire, Bela Lugosi, apparently for the purpose of delivering a package.

# THE
# GANGSTER FILM

## RAW MEAT

In 1930, Darryl F. Zanuck, newly appointed production head of Warner Brothers, let it be known that his production policy henceforth would be planned around headline news. By that decision he brought the gangster film, a minor cycle since the success of *Underworld* in 1927, to stage center. For gang warfare, and the impunity with which gangsters flouted the laws, especially the Prohibition laws, were hot news in the early Thirties. In focusing the camera on this "shame of the nation," Zanuck correctly sensed that the Great Depression audiences were in no mood for the unreal glamorous worlds Hollywood had been showing them. They wanted the raw meat of reality, and he was prepared to give it to them. It is startling, in this day of cautious disclaimers, to recall that the gangster films usually bore a prefatory note: "Every event shown in this film is based on an actual occurrence. All characters are portraits of actual persons, living or dead."

The aesthetic and sociological importance of gangster films in the history of motion pictures is frequently overlooked. They rescued the movies from the dialogue doldrums of the photographed play, and they themselves made a truly functional use of sound. The terrifying chatter of machine guns, the squealing of tires, and the grinding of brakes—all acted as physical stimulants on audiences. Newspapermen like Ben Hecht, John Bright, and Kubec Glasmon, steeped in the notorieties of Chicago, were brought to the Coast to write the gangster movies, and they enriched the dialogue of the screen with the argot of the streets. Such expressions as "So what?" and "So you can dish it out but you can't take it" became part of the language. A corps of knowing players, mostly from Broadway— Edward G. Robinson, Spencer Tracy, James Cagney, Joan Blondell, Warren Hymer, Warren William, Ruth Donnelly, Glenda Farrell and many others—furnished out the portrait of the underworld. To the gangster himself they added the

racketeering night-club proprietor, the gold-digging moll, the strong-arm henchman, the moronic hanger-on. These films showed "a certain section of America to itself against a background of poolrooms, stale beer, cigarette smoke, alleys, bare electric-light bulbs, cities at night. There was never any doubt that the setting was an American city of the Prohibition period."

In 1931 the gangster film dominated the movies. By the middle of the next year it had entirely vanished from the screen, though not because of any lessened popularity. It was suppressed. That sensitive litmus paper, Will Hays, turned blue with alarm at the torrent of protest which the gangster pictures evoked from the Daughters of the American Revolution, the American Legion, and that greater legion of women's and business clubs which run the machinery of community life in the United States. It was useless for Mr. Hays to reply that the gangster films moralized against crime and were grim object lessons that it did not pay. The small-town civic leaders knew, what indeed everybody knew, that Edward G. Robinson in the title role of *Little Caesar*, 1930, had become an ideal for emulation by hordes of young hero-worshipers. Nor did it help to argue that one of the purposes of the gangster films was to arouse the public to a consciousness of the prevalence of wrongdoing. There was in these topical films entirely too much evidence that existing government agencies weren't acting at all, perhaps because they were being paid off. But what probably most alarmed the respectable were certain assumptions, critical not of the breakdown of American institutions but of the institutions themselves. Spencer Tracy, the hero of *Quick Millions*, 1931, says that he is too nervous to steal and too lazy to work, but that a man is a fool to go into legitimate business when he can clean up by applying business methods to organizing crime. These films implied that during the depression the American get-rich-quick instinct could only lead to crime.

← 

**Little Caesar**

It was against everyday settings such as this that the gangster film was enacted, linking crime with the ordinary life of audiences. (Top) Little Caesar (Edward G. Robinson) is shot in the street. (Bottom) Little Caesar about to commit the first of his murders.

**1.** James Cagney and his pal, Edward Woods, sneer at Cagney's older brother, who was fool enough to fall for the flag-waving and enlist in World War I where he was permanently disabled.

**2.** As boys, Cagney and Wood fall in with Murray Kinnell, a small-time sharper, who wins their loyalty by teaching them dirty songs. Then he graduates them to his school for petty thieves.

**5.** A milestone on the way to the big time is the first tuxedo.

**6.** Rival gangsters ambush the boys, killing Woods.

## CASE HISTORY OF A CRIMINAL

*The Public Enemy,* 1931. This "biography of a criminal," featuring the virile, magnetic, and sinister personality of James Cagney, illustrates the extraordinary factual objectivity which the journalist authors introduced into the writing of gangster films. Its screenplay is as clinical as a case history. Cagney plays a boy whose lower-middle-class environment and shabby-genteel family offer him no

**3.** When Kinnell double-crosses them, the boys track him down and shoot him in cold blood.

**4.** The boys induce a speakeasy owner to buy their brand of beer.

**7.** James Cagney helps Mae Clarke to some grapefruit.

## Rough Stuff

The gangster films provided an innovation in courtship techniques for the emulation of young America. When Clark Gable slapped his leading ladies, and Jimmy Cagney pushed the historic grapefruit into Mae Clarke's face, girls longed for a brutal lover who would treat 'em rough and make 'em like it. Mae Clarke's career was probably one of the most strenuous any actress has ever had to endure. Heroine of countless gangster films, she was slapped, kicked, pushed, knocked down, and dragged by the hair for reel after reel.

future other than a threadbare respectability. Rebelling, he falls in with petty criminals. The ward-heelers, fixers, and saloon-keepers of his Chicago district watch his progress in crime with the benevolent approval of school superintendents handing out prizes for perseverance. His life as an adult is detailed with a realism new to the screen. In danger more from rival gangsters than from the police, he moves uneasily from apartment to apartment, his surroundings at once luxurious and sordid, his women women and nothing more. Toward the end of the film, Cagney indicates his boredom with his current mistress by pushing a grapefruit in her face. A few minutes later, his befouled corpse is delivered to his mother's doorstep as though it were the day's supply of meat.

*Scarface*, 1932. "This is an indictment against gang rule in America and the careless indifference of the government. . . . What are you going to do about it?"

These words prefaced this last and most brutal of the big gangster films. Modeled on the career of Al Capone, *Scarface* depicted the St. Valentine's Day massacre and the hospital murder of "Legs" Diamond. Vince Barnett, to the left of Paul Muni above, supplemented his income as an actor by hiring out at dinner parties as a fake waiter who insulted the guests and "accidentally" spilled food on them. This singular form of humor was much prized by Hollywood hostesses.

*The Last Mile,* 1932. George E. Stone takes the final walk. Since gangsters—even Prohibition ones—saw the inside of prisons, movies about them spent a good deal of time there, too.

# THE UNDERWORLD ON TOP

*G-Men,* 1935. Barton MacLane and Russell Hopton torment a captured Fed, William Harrigan, while their molls look on. After 1935, the gangster cycle was cautiously revived. Its rehabilitation in the eyes of the respectable was predicated on the canonization of the G-man whose somewhat unorthodox methods of capturing criminals were shown to succeed where normal law enforcement and juridical procedures fail. The public horror over the Lindbergh kidnaping had by then created a mood which tolerated wire tapping, third degree and other violations of civil rights.

Tear-stained Helen Twelvetrees was "betrayed" by no fewer than five men in Donald Henderson Clarke's *Millie*, 1931, each step down in moral degradation being also a step up in her standard of living. But the floods of tears Miss Twelvetrees shed over her betrayals clearly proved that it was all right to have ill-gotten gowns and furs if you didn't *enjoy* them. Here she is weeping in *Panama Flo*, 1932.

# THE
# CONFESSION FILM

## THE WAGES OF SIN

The second talkie cycle to follow "teacup drama" was, like its predecessor, depression-inspired. At least as impressive as the violence of the gangster films was their implication that legal ethics and business honor were disintegrating, and now the "confession" film proclaimed that American moral institutions, under the stress of economic panic, were also falling apart. The collapsing institution here documented was female virtue.

The composite heroine of the confession films of the early Thirties was a woman who gave up her chastity in cold blood. Sometimes she did it for money, sometimes—very often—out of self-sacrifice, sometimes she was simply talked into it, but she rarely did it for the fun of it and she always got paid off in some fashion. True, she too paid, for even on the depression screen your sin must find you out. But her payments grew smaller and her gains greater as the cycle rolled on. In fact, making these films became an elaborate game in which the problem was to invent new ways for the heroine to eat her cake and have it too.

These stories were lineal descendants of the servant-girl tales which have been a constant factor in American and English popular literature since the days of Richardson, and today are a genre by themselves in the field known as "confession magazines." Wish-fulfillment for shopgirls and stenogs, they reached the screen sporadically through the Teens and Twenties. When the depression struck, they suddenly gained a much wider audience acceptance. They were an answer to the frustration of the middle-class woman to whom industrial civilization had given a taste for luxury and adventure and who could see no way of achieving either in the economic world of the Thirties except by trading on her sex. But she needed the sanction of morality too, and the movie version of the confession tales neatly resolved her conflict. Watching her favorites on the screen, she learned that you accepted money and a penthouse from a man because you "trusted" him to do right by you. Was it your fault if he turned out a cad, and you were forced into a life of idle sin through the loss of your "reputation"? Obviously not. Obviously someone else was to blame.

The Confession Girl at the crossroads—Norma Shearer pleads with Chester Morris not to leave her merely because she has had an affair with Robert Montgomery. This became the obligatory scene in all confession films, beginning with Miss Shearer's *The Divorcee*, 1930, based on Ursula Parrott's novel, *Ex-Wife*. At first glance it appeared to be a continuation of This Freedom theme of the Twenties: a wife detects her husband's affair, condones it, but goes off on her own with another man for a while. There, ten years earlier, the tit-for-tat situation would have ended. But now the wife has to learn, through loss of her husband and a series of affairs, that sexual freedom may be theoretically accepted but is in practice rejected by the male. This salutary lesson learned, the husband relents and all is hunky-dory.

# BENNETT'S BOXOFFICE BULL'S-EYE

Norma Shearer's extra-marital adventures took place from start to finish in high life, while Helen Twelvetrees did most of her weeping in the underworld or in the "gutter." For the feminine audience which so readily responded to this kind of fiction, something of identification and therefore of wish-fulfillment was lacking in both milieus and their central figures. The formula which satisfied the lack was developed around the unlikely person of Constance Bennett. Miss Bennett had starred in two photographed plays, *Rich People*, 1930, and *This Thing*

*Called Love*, 1929, in which her glazed smartness was an asset. Then she appeared in a talkie version of Cleves Kinkead's old tear-jerker, *Common Clay*, 1930. Miss Bennett seemed miscast in this parlor-drama of a maid seduced by the scion of the house and abandoned by him. Audience response, however, demonstrated that the ladies believed in her and that feminine martyrdom was to be the essential ingredient in the developing pattern of the confession film.

Swiftly Miss Bennett was martyred in a series of

## Some confession girls strayed because

. . . they liked nice things, like Constance Bennett (with Adolphe Menjou) in *The Easiest Way* (below) . . . or maybe they were tricked into becoming artists' models, with shocking results, like Constance Bennett in *The Common Law* (right).

## Some were animated by the purest motives

. . . like Joan Crawford, who, in *Possessed*, 1931, is a factory heroine who achieves luxury as the mistress of wealthy Clark Gable. He is a candidate for the gubernatorial nomination, and when Miss Crawford learns that their affair may spoil his chances she pretends she has only been playing him for a sucker. When he discovers her noble deception he insists on taking her back, even though they still cannot be married. (It wasn't made clear whether he got the nomination under those circumstances, but what the heck.)

such films—*Sin Takes a Holiday*, November 1930; *The Easiest Way*, March 1931; *Born to Love*, April 1931; *The Common Law*, July 1931; and *Bought*, August 1931—five seductions in less than a year. The star used her ten-week vacation from RKO to farm herself out to Warner Brothers at $30,000 a week. (When informed that taxes on such a salary would be ruinous, she replied to Warner's, "Oh, then you will have to pay the tax for I must have thirty thousand clear.") This display of financial acumen underlined the quality which made her queen of the confession films. In most of her pictures Miss Bennett was seduced by a rich man and left to her fate. Far from weeping by the wayside, after the manner of Helen Twelvetrees, she fought for her man so resourcefully that she eventually won a wedding ring from him. Brittle, articulate, and ingenious, Miss Bennett was unbelievable as the victimized stenographers and artists' models she played, but this very superiority to type helped her audiences believe that she would get out of traps that would hold them fast.

The early confession girls lost their virtue for fun, for luxury, or for nobly self-sacrificial motives. But as the depression continued, films began to touch on a more basic motive for streetwalking: staying alive. In the first of these, *Faithless*, 1932, Tallulah Bankhead is an heiress so wealthy that she refuses marriage with an impoverished $20,000-a-year executive (Robert Montgomery) because he insists that they live on his salary alone. When both are wiped out by the depression, Miss Bankhead in order to go on living in the style to which she is accustomed, becomes the mistress of a rich boor (Hugh Herbert). When she can no longer stand his ill-treatment, she seeks out the penniless Montgomery and they agree to marry and start over. But Montgomery is badly injured in a labor riot and his desperate wife dashes out into the night and hails the first man she meets, as the only way of keeping them going. She is picked up for streetwalking, but the kindly Irish cop relents and sends her home instead of to jail.

Another martyr was Irene Dunne in *Back Street*, 1932. Miss Dunne falls in love with John Boles, who is married and has children. He proposes that she became his mistress, which she does, and so is condemned to live out her years on a side street which he visits secretly. Through the years Miss Dunne ages and ages and changes her clothes, and sentimentalizes over the children she can never have, but she remains faithful to the end.

*Common Clay*, 1930. Lew Ayres, Constance Bennett.    *Common Clay*. Constance Bennett and baby.

*Born to Love*, 1931. Constance Bennett, Joel McCrea.    *Born to Love*. Constance Bennett and baby.

*Rockabye*, 1932. Constance Bennett, Joel McCrea.    *Rockabye*. Constance Bennett and child.

*The Blonde Venus,* 1932. Cary Grant, Marlene Dietrich.     *The Blonde Venus.* Marlene Dietrich, Dickie Moore.

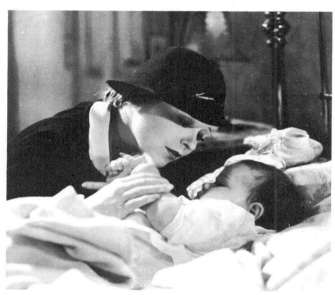

*Call Her Savage,* 1932. Clara Bow, Monroe Owsley.     *Call Her Savage.* Clara Bow and baby.

# BABIES--JUST BABIES

As might have been anticipated, babies were all too frequently the by-products of the illicit love affairs which the confession film featured. Once a figure of shame, the unwed mother now asked for and presumably received the sympathy of her audiences. She always ended, of course, either in the arms of the father of her child or in those of some complaisant male willing to take his place. Constance Bennett had the most screen offspring (with Joel McCrea usually fathering them, so that it was no shock to the movie public when they beheld in 1933 a title credit which read: "Constance Bennett in *Bed of Roses,* with Joel McCrea"). Miss Bennett's

children came in handy for many plot purposes, including breach-of-promise suits, marriages in name only, and the foreswearing of promising careers.

By the end of the confession period, babies were used to motivate just one thing—prostitution. Deserted by husbands and lovers, Marlene Dietrich and Clara Bow had to take to the streets in order to buy food for their young, thus ensuring them an even richer harvest of sympathy than Tallulah Bankhead reaped by sacrificing her honor for the sake of her sick husband. Miss Dietrich added a novel twist by taking her young son along when she went on the prowl for customers.

*I Am a Fugitive from a Chain Gang,* 1932. A jobless veteran, Paul Muni (top), tries to pawn the Congressional Medal of Honor he won in the A. E. F., but they're a drug on the market. He is framed for a robbery he didn't commit, and finds himself in a chain gang at four o'clock in the morning, headed for work on the roads. Edward Ellis is at his right.

# TOPICAL FILMS

Though the gangster film temporarily disappeared from the screen in 1932, it left a permanent legacy. Audiences had become conditioned to seeing contemporary life dealt with from a critical point of view. This new attitude, along with speedy continuity, idiomatic dialogue, and naturalistic acting remained characteristic of films of the Thirties.

The policy of basing films on spot news, which had produced the gangster film, also resulted in the topical film, for many years the specialty of Warner Brothers although imitated by the other studios. Ostensibly these pictures did no more than capitalize on topics of current interest. But as the pattern emerged, as writers grew bolder and players more accurate in their reflection of character, the topical film, like the two cycles which preceded it, became a mirror of the subterranean discontent with the American social structure which slowly rose through the depression years.

Individual films in this genre usually attacked the special case and absolved the system as a whole. Frequently their critical tone was veiled by comedy. *The Dark Horse* displayed the naive mechanisms of American electioneering in terms all too familiar to the citizen. The stupid candidate for governor, "Hicks, the Man from the Sticks," is a tool in the hands of his campaign manager, who has him photographed in fishing togs, newsreeled awarding blue ribbons to prize bulls, and made an honorary chief of an Indian tribe. The film was released during the 1932 presidential campaign, as was a similar satire, *The Phantom President*. Both pictures painted politics as a racket, public officials as hypocrites, and many voters as venal fools purchasable with flattery and government jobs. In like serio-comic vein *The Mouthpiece*, 1932, argued that lawyers were to be had for a price and were the bulwark of organized crime, while *Night Court*, 1932, chronicled the misdemeanors of a grafting judge. News reporters will commit almost any crime for the sake of a story, according to *Scandal Sheet*, 1931, *The Front Page*, 1931, and *Five Star Final*, 1931. *Is My Face Red*, 1932, *Okay, America*, 1932, and *Blessed Event*, 1932,

were films based on the career of Walter Winchell, depicting the rise of a newspaper columnist who grows rich by ruining reputations—and who is adored by the public. *American Madness*, 1932, informed disappointed speculators that banking was a confidence game in which the honest man was left holding the bag.

The majority of topical films were crude snapshots of American life. *I Am a Fugitive from a Chain Gang*, 1932, the apotheosis of the cycle, dealt directly with social abuse, but no picture could afford to be thus uncompromising unless it confined itself to so narrow a field as prison brutality. Nevertheless, the topical films succeeded in voicing a blanket indictment of depression America because their effect was cumulative. *It's Tough to Be Famous*, 1932, *Love Is a Racket*, 1932, *Beauty for Sale*, 1933—what wasn't a racket, what couldn't be bought, in the third year of the depression? Nothing, answered the topical films, which found a sordid story behind every newspaper headline. They were a reflexive and unconscious response to the despondency of a nation.

The giant Negro strikes off Muni's shackles.

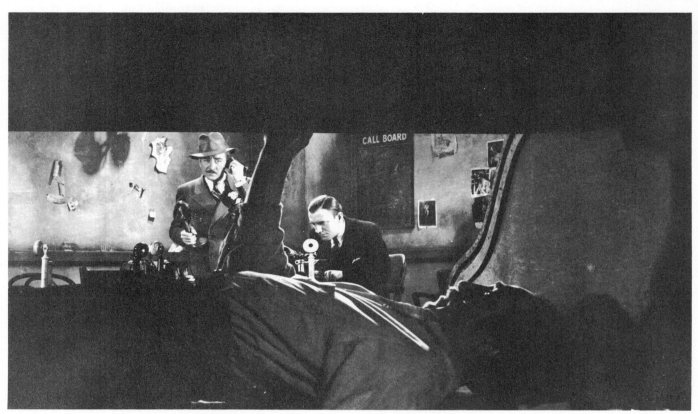

*The Front Page,* 1931. Editor Adolphe Menjou and reporter Pat O'Brien conceal the escaped murderer, George E. Stone, in a rolltop desk while they scoop the rest of the nation's newspapers with his story.

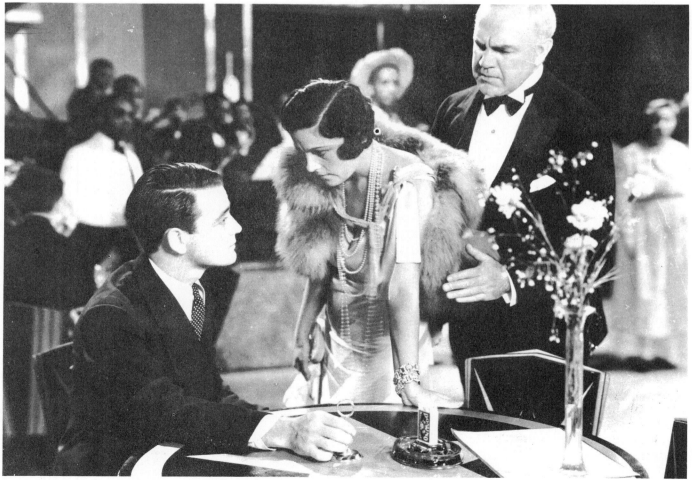

*Okay, America,* 1932. A victim of famed gossip columnist Lew Ayres threatens to kill him for ruining her reputation, but he is unmoved.

*Life Begins,* 1932. Nurse Aline MacMahon gives her baby to Gloria Shea while the father, Frank McHugh, looks on. This film, which took place entirely in a maternity ward, was typical of many hospital pictures of the early Thirties, in which audiences were familiarized to the point of burlesque with scalpels, anesthetics, and pulsating oxygen bags.

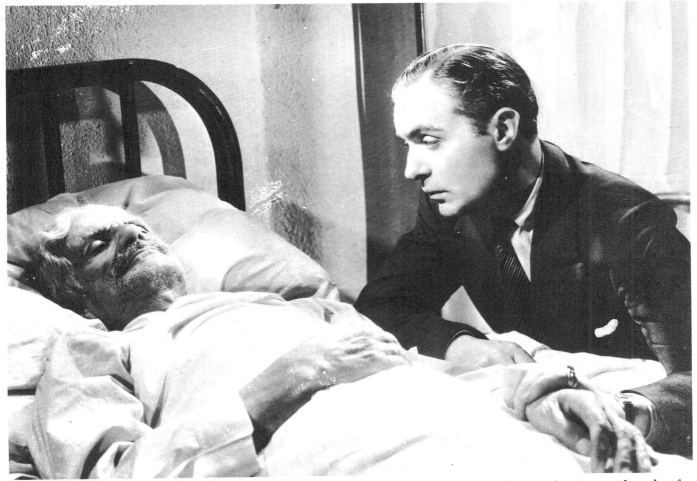

*Private Worlds,* 1935, dramatized mental illness. Here psychiatrist Charles Boyer comforts a dying Arab patient, and speaks a few words to him in his own language.

## THE DEPRESSION

The movies ignored the depression as long as they could. But by the end of 1931, prosperity just around the corner had become the grimmest of jokes, and the boxoffice was saying that films which faced the facts of life under the depression paid off. Some films, like *One More Spring*, tried to make light of conditions by picturing the joys of freedom from property and humdrum work, but the jest was

*One More Spring*, 1935. Jobless singer Walter Woolf King, and penniless producer Warner Baxter, delicately roast a partridge in their new home, Central Park.

*Heroes for Sale*, 1933, with Richard Barthelmess.

*American Madness*, 1932. Bank president Walter Huston tries to calm a panic-stricken mob that is making a run on his bank.

sour. Increasingly there appeared on the screen of the Thirties bonus marchers, Hooverville shacks, bank failures, governmental paralysis, embittered veterans. Few films dealt directly with the economic crisis, few placed direct blame for it or offered any precise solution. But in 1932 and 1933 the depression peered out from around the corners of even the brightest and shiniest romance.

*Framed*, 1930. Robert Emmett O'Connor, the archetypal detective, supervises the wrecking of a speakeasy, essential to every cops-and-robbers film.

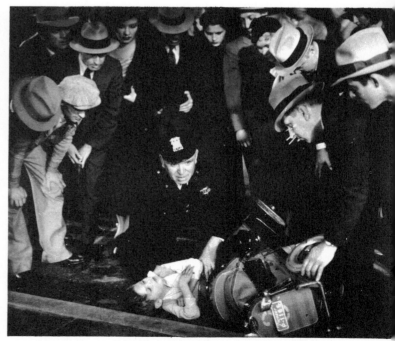

*The Devil Is Driving*, 1932. In opposition to the glorification of speed in the Twenties, some movies warned the public that gasoline and alcohol won't mix.

*Lawyer Man,* 1932. William Powell demonstrates to Joan Blondell his ideas about justice.

*Hard to Handle,* 1933. A survival of the wacky Twenties, marathon dancing was pictured as a racket in the Thirties.

*Female,* 1933. Surrounded by her executives, tycoon Ruth Chatterton firmly makes a world-shaking decision. As potent a day-dream figure for women as the confession gals, Miss Chatterton played the self-made president of a giant corporation who refuses to marry because she does not want to share her power. Instead, she asks her male subordinates to come up and see her some time, only she always sets the time.

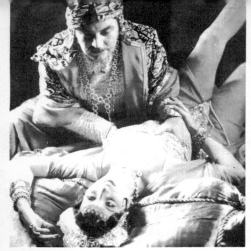

*Kismet,* 1930.
Sidney Blackmer and Mary Duncan.

*Kept Husbands,* 1931.
Joel McCrea and Dorothy Mackaill.

*The Night Watch,* 1928.
Billie Dove and Donald Reed.

*Framed,* 1927. The studio caption says: "Milton Sills and Natli Barr in a perfervid scene wherein she vamps the hero." The scene was removed from the film by the censors of several states.

# DECENCY

## THE GATHERING STORM

In theory Will Hays was czar of the movies, but his authority was by no means as absolute as that of the real czars who lay down the ground rules in the field of sports. He could, of course, have imposed his will by threatening resignation if the studios failed to obey his rulings—a resignation which would have signaled that the movies were not keeping their implicit bargain with the public. He chose not to exercise so autocratic a sway. Instead he used the arts of persuasion and cajolery, reasoning that gradual amelioration was preferable to brute dictatorship.

In truth his task was much thornier than those of his fellow-monarchs in baseball and elsewhere. Cleaning up Hollywood was one thing, but protecting the public by removing from pictures what most of the public paid to see was quite another. To simplify his task he caused to be gathered together a codification of all the regulations imposed by state and municipal censor boards upon motion pictures. Between 1927 and 1930 these were combined into a single instrument and promulgated as the Code of the Motion Picture Industry. This was designed as a guide for producers to enable them to anticipate the objections of local censor boards and thus avoid that variegated mutilation which hitherto had been the fate of a number of films. In the course of time the Code came to be regarded as a sort of gentleman's agreement between the Hays Office and the studios, binding the latter to good conduct in accordance with its provisions. But its principal targets were sex and violence, and sex and violence were just what most film-makers regarded as boxoffice insurance. Many an expensive but weak picture, approved in script form by the Code officials, emerged with scenes of undress or brutality added at the last moment to bolster its doubtful pulling power. How easily Mr. Hays's rulings could be evaded was shown in the case of the play *Rain*, which Gloria Swanson wanted to do but which had come under his ban. Miss Swanson simply purchased the original Maugham story and released her film, still substantially *Rain*, as *Sadie Thompson*.

*Dante's Inferno*, 1924.

*Grand Slam*, 1933.
Paul Lukas and Sally Blane.

When the depression struck Hollywood, evasions of the Code multiplied. Aside from the brutality and animalism of the gangster films, quite ordinary films increasingly featured "horizontal" love-making, risqué situations, and off-color dialogue, while the camera lingered more and more lovingly over the details of the heroine's preparations for retiring. Hollywood did not deliberately set out to scandalize the nation. Producers simply could not think of anything else as effective for the ailing boxoffice.

*Breach of Promise*, 1932.
Mary Doran and Eddie Borden.

*Beauty for Sale*, 1933.
Charley Grapewin and Una Merkel.

*Red Hair*, 1928, with Clara Bow.

*Bachelor Apartment,* 1931.
Irene Dunne, Mae Murray, and Lowell Sherman.

*The Cockeyed World,* 1929.
Edmund Lowe and Victor McLaglen.

*A Royal Romance,* 1930.
Pauline Starke and Buster Collier.

*A Farewell to Arms,* 1932. Gary Cooper and Helen Hayes in a scene excised from the film when it was reissued after the formation of the Legion of Decency.

*Grand Hotel,* 1932. Wallace Beery, Joan Crawford.

*The Sins of the Fathers,* 1929. Emil Jannings, Ruth Chatterton.

*Sadie Thompson,* 1928. Gloria Swanson, Raoul Walsh.

# THE GATHERING STORM

The same constellation of civic-minded persons, reformers, and busybodies who had frowned on the gangster film watched the growing license of the movies of the Thirties with mounting alarm. They objected not only to leg art, lingerie, and love-making, but also, and even after Repeal, to what they considered excessive drinking in pictures, and to the purchase of novels and plays which by their frankness or realism were thought unsuited for the screen.

Perhaps most of all they disliked the irreverent, cynical, and increasingly critical tone of what was

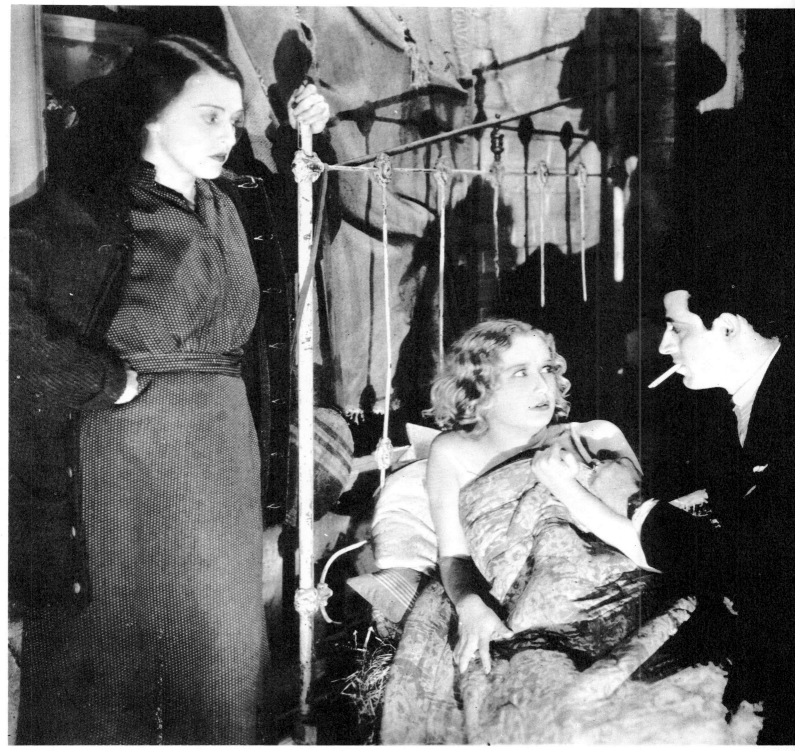

*The Story of Temple Drake,* 1933. Florence Eldridge, Miriam Hopkins, and Jack La Rue. Women's clubs recoiled in horror when Paramount bought William Faulkner's *Sanctuary,* even though the film was released under a disguising title. Sexual abnormalities were removed from the story, but reformers complained that it still condoned murder, though this one was as condonable a murder as ever was.

coming out of Hollywood. So long as the country lay prostrate under the depression, there was little they could do. They represented a "respectable" viewpoint which was then deeply discredited in the eyes of the country at large. But with the inauguration of the New Deal and the rebirth of hope, they took courage. It needed only a single incident to set them in motion. Chance provided not one but two. The first was the publication of the results of the Payne Fund studies of the influence of motion pictures in a sensational book called *Our Movie Made Children.* The second was Mae West.

*She Done Him Wrong, 1933.*

Mae West and production assistant Boris Petroff discuss "shooting script."

## MAE WEST

How far the bars had been lowered is clear from the fact that Mae West was brought to the screen at all. Her stage play, *Sex,* was considered in the theater to be the next thing to straight pornography. Though she toned down her performances for the movies, she left little to the imagination with such bawdy-house songs as "I Wonder Where My Easy Rider's Gone" and "I Like a Man Who Takes His Time." But her success was phenomenal. The nation roared at "Come up and see me some time," "You can be had," "Beulah, peel me a grape," and "It's not the men in my life that counts—it's the life in my men." What delighted everyone, or nearly everyone, about Mae was her honesty. She didn't pretend, like the confession gals, that she had been tricked into turpitude, or that she hated the luxury that went with it. Nor did she atone or reform. She just had a royal good time, and picture's end found her wealthy, wicked, and well loved.

Mae was the last straw. Mary Pickford, apostle of virtue, who however had been around show business long enough not to be shocked at ordinary ribaldry, was quoted as saying: "I passed the door of my young niece's room—she's only about seventeen and has been raised, oh, so carefully—and I heard her singing bits from that song from *Diamond Lil*—I say 'that song' just because I'd blush to quote the title even here." Exactly six months after the release of Mae's first starring picture, *She Done Him Wrong,* the Episcopal Committee on Motion Pictures was formed in October 1933.

*She Done Him Wrong*, 1933. "I collect diamonds," says Mae West to Gilbert Roland, "it's m' hobby."

*Goin' to Town*, 1935, with Tito Coral and Mae West. "Mae West eyed a man from head to foot. All the time you knew she was evaluating him in terms of virility, as James Cagney eyed a woman."—LEWIS JACOBS.

*Night after Night*, 1932. Alison Skipworth with Mae West in Miss West's screen debut. It is in this movie that the hat-check girl says, "Goodness, what lovely diamonds," and Mae replies, "Goodness had nothing to do with it, honey."

# THE LEGION OF DECENCY

The Episcopal Committee on Motion Pictures denounced the American motion picture of the Thirties as tending to promote immorality. Such denunciations had been heard before, but the Catholic bishops took action as well. In 1933 they formed the National Legion of Decency, the function of which was to review all new films before their release and classify them under the headings "Passed," "Objectionable in Part," and "Condemned." These findings were announced from pulpits. Communicants of the Catholic church were exhorted to stay away from "partly objectionable" films, and were told that attendance at those "condemned" by the Legion would constitute a venial sin. Jewish and Protestant organizations joined with the Legion in what was intended as a mass boycott aimed at forcing Hollywood to discontinue its exposures and sensationalisms and make what were vaguely described as "good" films. In the big cities, especially those with a large Catholic population, the widely publicized campaign did cause decrease in theater attendance.

Appalled, Will Hays sought help. The old Production Code of 1927-30 was dusted off and rewritten by Father Daniel A. Lord working in close co-operation with Martin Quigley, prominent Catholic layman who also happened to be the publisher of the important trade journal, *Exhibitor's Herald-World*. A branch of the Hays office, the Production

A CODE

TO GOVERN THE MAKING

OF MOTION AND TALKING

PICTURES

the

Reasons Supporting It

And the

Resolution for Uniform

Interpretation

by

Motion Picture Producers and Distributors of America, Inc.

JUNE 13, 1934

The Motion Picture Code as amended in 1934, whose provisions govern the making of all films produced by the members of the Motion Picture Association.

Code Administration, was set up in Hollywood under the supervision of a young Catholic newspaperman, Joseph I. Breen, to enforce the Code and, in effect, to police the production of every film from first screen treatment to finished product. All producers, whether or not members of the Motion Picture Association, could submit their films for precensorship and all had to abide by the Code Administration's rulings, on pain of a fine of $25,000. Perhaps more painful than the fine was the knowledge that the leading theater circuits were at that time controlled by members of the Motion Picture Association, who were not likely to book films lacking Mr. Hays's seal of purity.

The dictatorship of virtue, toward which Mr. Hays had worked for twelve years, was established. For the next three decades, the Code was evaded, strictly enforced, or more honored in the breach than the observance, depending on box-office fluctuations. As it edged toward "liberalization" in the late Fifties, the Code's more sympathetic critics urged its alteration in keeping with the changing times, while abolitionists contended that under the cover of imposing decency on films, it prevented or discouraged the frank treatment allowed plays and books of many phases of modern life.

When the promulgation of the Code was announced in 1934, Mae West was about to embark on the production of her third film, *It Ain't No Sin*. Among other alterations made necessary by the new dispensation, the title was changed to *I'm No Angel*. Someone whispered at the time that all would have been well if she had simply called her picture *It Is A Sin*.

When the Production Code Administration was set up in Hollywood in 1934, a Jean Harlow picture called *Born to Be Kissed* was in the making at M-G-M. In a panic, the studio changed the title to *100% Pure*. Calm, if not logic, finally prevailed and the film was released as *The Girl from Missouri*, with Miss Harlow and Lionel Barrymore.

*Little Women*, 1933. Left to right: Jean Parker, Joan Bennett, Katharine Hepburn, Douglass Montgomery, Frances Dee. The success of this vibrant version of the Alcott classic, starring the new favorite Katharine Hepburn, helped the forces of Decency prove that the public really did want "good" films.

# THE
# NEW
# DEAL

# SWEETNESS AND LIGHT

Under the regime of Decency, Hollywood, with considerable grinding of gears, dragged its cameras away from their fixation on contemporary life and turned them on a sweeter and safer day. Charles Dickens, Louisa May Alcott, and Sir James Barrie were the spiritual, as they were often the actual, authors of the stories on which the screenplays of 1934, 1935, and 1936 were based. Victorian England and America, reconstructed with all the skill and care of which the makers of talking pictures were now capable, replaced the penthouse, the gangster, and the shady lady. The favorable audience response to these nostalgic memorabilia caused the trade to reflect that the public might possibly be glutted with sophistication. More likely is that the gradual return of confidence brought about by the early days of the New Deal made it possible for people to believe in goodness again.

*David Copperfield,* 1935. Frank Lawton as David; W. C. Fields and Jean Cadell as Mr. and Mrs. Micawber. With a bow to Decency, David O. Selznick brought this version of Dickens to the screen, and provided W. C. Fields with his best-loved role.

*Little Lord Fauntleroy,* 1936. Freddie Bartholomew, who had played the young Copperfield, as Fauntleroy, and C. Aubrey Smith as his grandfather, in another Selznick tribute to the new era.

## "FAMILY"

Gangster and topical films had appealed to male audiences; the confession gals had supplied wish-fulfillment for women. Now producers initiated

*Love Finds Andy Hardy*, 1938, with Judy Garland and Mickey Rooney. Based on a play by Aurania Rouverol, the first film about Judge Hardy and his family was produced as an inexpensive "B" picture. Its success led to a series of immensely popular Hardy films featuring the adolescent antics of Mickey and Judy and the father-image of Lewis Stone.

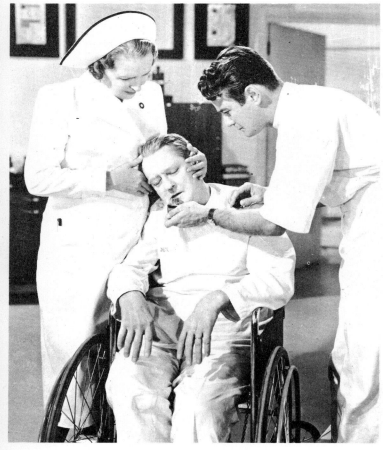

*Blondie*, 1938. The popular comic strip successfully transferred to the screen with Penny Singleton; Arthur Lake as Dagwood.

The "collapse sequence" from *The Secret of Dr. Kildare*, 1939, with Alma Kruger, Lionel Barrymore, and Lew Ayres. From his wheelchair, the all-wise Lionel Barrymore supervised the activities of Lew Ayres as Dr. Kildare—until it became known that Ayres was a conscientious objector, whereupon Dr. Kildare's shingle was replaced overnight by Dr. Gillespie's.

# PICTURES

films designed for the whole family. Often they were *about* families as well, and were made in series—the screen equivalent of soap opera.

The endearing personality of Jackie Cooper and the calculated hominess of Chic Sale had begun to please audiences even before the dawn of the new era. *When a Feller Needs a Friend,* 1932.

*Pepper,* 1936. 20th Century-Fox teamed Irvin S. Cobb with Jane Withers in a vain effort to replace the late Will Rogers.

*Little Miss Marker,* 1934, with Shirley Temple and Adolphe Menjou. Displacing Janet Gaynor and Greta Garbo as top star of the Thirties, Shirley Temple achieved greater screen popularity than any child since Jackie Coogan.

301

*Gold Diggers of 1933.* Joan Blondell sings "Remember My Forgotten Man" to a chorus of the unemployed, while behind her in silhouette we see the same men when they were fighting in World War I for the country which neglects them now.

# CONFIDENCE

"The only thing we have to fear is fear itself." The President's magic words made "Confidence" the slogan of the hour, and Hollywood hastened to do its bit toward restoring belief in the future. The musical film, a neglected corpse since it was done to death in the "all talking, all singing, all dancing" days, was now suddenly resuscitated. Besides providing licit escape from the importunities of landlords and grocers, it was a fitting setting for the fantastic view of New Deal economic panaceas which the movies offered. In *Stand Up and Cheer,* 1934, a Department of Amusement was added to the President's cabinet, its purpose to laugh the country out of the depression; and many musicals of the period featured Forgotten Men and choric hymns to the NRA. Little by little the strictly escapist began to dominate the sermonizing elements in these blithe films. In *Broadway Melodies, Big Broadcasts,* and *Gold Diggers,* Busby Berkeley disposed chorus girls in floral and geometric patterns photographed from above, while musical "fashion shows" exhibited fashions no woman would dare to be seen in. These pictures were merry and tuneful, provided vicarious luxury to the deprived, and were a nice way of "passing the time while waiting for the New Deal to get down your way."

"Hall of Human Harps" from *Fashions of 1934*. A critic observed, "The theme song of mothers of stage-struck daughters might well be, 'I Didn't Raise My Girl to Be a Human Harp,' but the chosen young ladies probably regard it as a royal road to stardom."

*The Kid from Spain*, 1932. The Goldwyn Girls.

# ONE HUNDRED PIANOS, ONE HUNDRED

*Dames*, 1934. A Busby Berkeley production.

One hundred girls play one hundred pianos in *Gold Diggers of 1935*.

*Rosalie*, 1937. Nelson Eddy in the distance, back there up on the steps somewhere.

*The Big Broadcast,* 1932, with Bing Crosby, Stuart Erwin, Leila Hyams. Soon after the beginning of the talkies, radio started to cannibalize Hollywood talent. It offered stars huge sums for brief appearances on the air, to the great distress of movie exhibitors who claimed that people would rather stay home and hear their favorites than pay to see as well as hear them. Soon the screen returned the compliment, beginning with *The Big Broadcast,* which made a star of crooner Bing Crosby and also featured such radio personalities as Kate Smith, the Boswell Sisters, the Mills Brothers, Burns and Allen, and Arthur Tracy, the Street Singer.

*Naughty Marietta,* 1935. By 1931 operetta had been pronounced officially dead as a screen cycle. The camera emphasized the absurdity of its conventions too cruelly. But in 1935, Irving Thalberg and W. S. Van Dyke found a way to naturalize the marriage of song and plot. *Naughty Marietta* made singing co-stars of Nelson Eddy and Jeanette MacDonald through a decade's worth of mellifluous films.

*One Hundred Men and a Girl,* 1937 Fifteen-year-old Deanna Durbin's pure soprano enthralled the nation and helped bring "serious" music closer to public acceptance. She was aided by Leopold Stokowski and his musicians.

*One Night of Love*, 1934. Grace Moore sings the title song while pelting the populace with apples as she rides through the streets of Venice with Lyle Talbot. Miss Moore had made her screen debut in 1930 in *A Lady's Morals* and *The New Moon*, but fans decided that her prim dignity was better suited to the Metropolitan Opera. Determined to conquer the movies she returned in 1934, glamorized and jazzed up and in her first picture was a sensation. Thanks to the marvel of rerecording, she sang, or seemed to sing, better on the screen than she ever had at the Metropolitan. But the public soon found her acting limited and monotonous.

## THE OPERATIC

*I Dream Too Much*, 1935. Lily Pons's coloratura soprano provoked the rude remark that her picture should have been called *I Scream Too Much*.

*Here's to Romance,* 1935. Nino Martini in a snippet of *Tosca,* Anita Louise in the wings. Operatic scenes on the screen were tolerated by the public only if they were brief, and the histrionic or physical inadequacies of the opera stars militated against their achieving popularity.

# INVASION

*Rose of the Rancho,* 1936. The Metropolitan's Gladys Swarthout, here teamed with established movie singer John Boles, made four films in a doomed attempt to become a favorite.

*Carefree*, 1938. The dance-poems of Fred Astaire and Ginger Rogers are among the cherished memories of the screen, and their films are as brightly burnished when seen today as they were thirty years ago. Astaire was the first to revolt against the Busby Berkeley tradition of photographing dancers from a variety of odd angles in order to exploit "cinematic" opportunities. Astaire insisted that his full figure be kept on camera throughout his dancing, and that it be presented from an audience-eye view, thus unconsciously following in the footsteps of Chaplin.

*Second Fiddle*, 1939. The movies' unending search for novelty led to the acquisition of Sonja Henie as a skating star of musical films. Miss Henie acquired something too—new millions to add to those she already had.

*Born to Dance*, 1936. Eleanor Powell in Cole Porter's brilliant musical. Miss Powell came from Broadway to take over as queen of dancing stars.

Thelma Todd, Jimmy Durante, Buster Keaton, and Hedda Hopper in *Speak Easily*, 1932. A reviewer wrote about it, "Buster Keaton's farewell to M-G-M gives major opportunities to Jimmy Durante, but we needn't inquire into that." There was indeed no need to. It had been obvious for two years that M-G-M was building up the Schnozzola at Keaton's expense.

# COMEDY AND COMEDIANS

Of the great silent comedians, Lloyd and Keaton had voices well suited to their screen characters, but dialogue slowed their dizzy pace and blunted the fine edge of their miraculous timing. When they spoke, they ceased to be universal clowns and were automatically identified with the particular time and place which their words—often considerably less than inspired—conjured up. Lloyd, independently wealthy and his own producer, continued to make films as long as it pleased him, but Keaton was dispensed with as soon as his contract, signed in the silent days, expired.

No one took their place. There was no longer any nursery for new comic talent. In the first years of the talkies, Mack Sennett carried on in the grand tradition, "discovering" Bing Crosby and re-discovering W. C. Fields, but the growth of the depression-fostered double feature system hurt the short comedy, and the increasing popularity of Disney's cartoons finally killed it altogether. Sennett retired in 1933. Meanwhile screen comedy was in the hands of transients from the stage and vaudeville—stock comics using stock two-a-day material. By the middle Thirties, "slapstick" had become a dirty word. The talking screen had to evolve its own new comedy form.

Ginger Rogers and Joe E. Brown in *You Said a Mouthful*, 1932. Of the talkie newcomers, Brown was nearest the innocent clown of silent days.

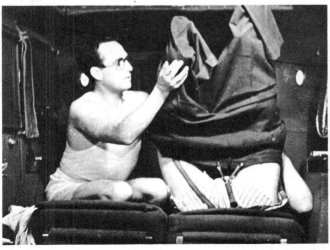

*Professor, Beware*, 1932. Harold Lloyd repeated his sight gags for the talking camera with fair success for some years, but his brilliant handling of dialogue was not revealed until Preston Sturges made *Mad Wednesday* in 1946.

Robert Woolsey, Bert Wheeler, and Raquel Torres in *So This Is Africa*, 1933. Among the hundreds of vaudevillians drawn to Hollywood by the talkies, Bert Wheeler and Robert Woolsey made an immediate hit and afflicted the screen for five years with wheezy vaudeville gags.

All show business predicted that the screen rights to George S. Kaufman's and Moss Hart's side-splitting *Once in a Lifetime* would never be sold. But Carl Laemmle of Universal bought the play, filmed it without change, and prefixed it with a subtitle congratulating himself on his own courage in doing so. The film, like the play, burlesqued the nondescript stage hangers-on who flooded Hollywood as "voice culturists" during the early days of the talkie panic. Mr. Glogauer, Gregory Ratoff, head of the studio, introduces his prize vamp and ingenue to the voice culturist, Aline MacMahon.

Veteran Ben Turpin instructs novice Stu Erwin in the art of pie-throwing, in *Make Me a Star*, 1932, the talkie version of *Merton of the Movies*.

Mack Sennett's parody of a Western star at the world premiere of one of his pictures in a small-town theater. Harry Gribbon as the star, Marjorie Beebe as his girl-friend, Andy Clyde as the theater owner in *A Hollywood Star*, 1929.

## SATIRE

William de Mille once proposed the formation of a syndicate to purchase an island on which a new state should be erected, to be named Villainova. The inhabitants could be supported in luxury by a tax on Hollywood studios, which in return would receive the right to make the heavies in all their pictures Villainovans. In this fashion they could hope to avoid the protests of foreign governments and domestic pressure groups when one of their nationals or members, fictitious or real, was portrayed on the screen in a less than favorable light.

Lacking a Villainova, the picture industry has solved its problem by making Hollywood itself the major butt of cinematic satire. From *A Vitagraph Romance* of 1912, to *Myra Breckenridge* of 1970, every facet of picture-making has taken a ribbing, the more acute because the ribbers knew their material at first hand.

Sound provided fresh material in the form of the crudities not only of the early talkies but also of the movies' most formidable competitor, the growing giant of radio. The rivalry of the two great industries had reached a standoff by the early Thirties, and their warfare was merciless. The movies had the advantage, since they could satirize the idiocies of sponsored entertainment visually as well as orally, while radio could only tell funny stories about the goings on in Southern California.

*Six of a Kind*, 1934. Fields and his famous crooked cue stick. He had an idea that it was funny if an object merely bent when it was expected to break. He was right.

*Never Give a Sucker an Even Break*, 1941. Fields's deep-rooted suspicion of children always turned out to be founded on fact.

*Never Give a Sucker an Even Break*. Mr. Fields absent-mindedly blows the head off an ice-cream soda.

*The Old-Fashioned Way*, 1934. Courtly love-making to an unlovely dame was a Fields specialty.

# W. C. FIELDS

Micawber, Major Hoople, Monsieur Verdoux, Cagliostro—all have strong affinities to the character which, for lack of a single name, must be called after its creator, William Claude Fields. The character Fields portrayed was essentially the same in all his films, as, were the characters created by Keaton and Lloyd. Originated on the stage in dialogue, Fields extended it by inspired pantomime on the screen into one of the inimitable figures of our time. Martini-drinking, child-hating, gifted with the strange ability to make even humdrum fact seem wildly implausible, the line betwen Fields's actual self and his screen creation was a blurred one. He became a popular idol as well as the center of a highbrow cult. At the time of his death he was working on a new screen play, *Grand Motel*.

*Modern Times.* (Paulette Goddard's eye, lower left.)

*Modern Times,* 1936. Assembly-line Charlie: man into machine.

*Modern Times.* Machine into satyr.

*City Lights,* 1931. Genteel tramp and symbol of labor.

*Modern Times.* Man-eating machine.

# CHAPLIN

Charles Chaplin knew that his Charlie the Tramp could not survive speech, and he refused to put him into talkies. His films of the Thirties had musical and sound accompaniment but no synchronized talk. But though Charlie was not put to the test of speech, he was called upon by his creator to face the greater ordeal of survival in a world much more recognizably contemporaneous than the caricatured world of his early adventures.

*City Lights,* which when it was revived in 1950 *Time* called the greatest film of that or any year, began the process. Here for the first time Charlie was allowed a serious romantic attachment. It was right that his girl should be blind; right that she fall in love not with Charlie but with her imagining of him; not right, in the eyes of many of Chaplin's more critical admirers, that she should recognize him when she regains her sight. This nice question is still being argued.

Five years later, *Modern Times* was still more arguable. It begins with a shot of sheep going down a runway followed by a shot of workers entering a factory. Charlie is set down in the midst of industrial civilization, which is dominated by machinery and in which men are organized into mechanical units, Capital and Labor. Charlie's real enemies are no longer the Cop or the Boss, with whom he can always enter into some human relation, but a vast impersonality, invisible and invulnerable.

*Modern Times* offered a variety of minor attractions: it featured Chaplin's wife, Paulette Goddard; it had wonderful gags; it indulged in tricks of sound which came to the very brink of being dialogue. But what did the picture mean, what was it trying to say? Because Chaplin charged his usual enormous percentage for it, and because of foreign receipts, *Modern Times* made money, but exhibitors were not happy at the limited audience turnout. For the majority, the new Charlie was too serious; for the minority, not serious enough. Since the picture seemed to be about the dehumanizing effect of machinery, intellectuals called upon Chaplin to join them in reorganizing machine culture to some more human scale of things. Off the screen, Chaplin said nothing. On the screen, his anarchic enmity for any kind of machine culture expressed itself in scenes like that in which Charlie is fed by a machine and that in which, crazed by the assembly line, he runs into the street, his arms moving convulsively like two pistons. Charlie the rebel, Charlie the poet, Charlie the invincibly human, had been turned into a machine.

*A Day at the Races*, 1937. Chorus: "This woman is mine."

*A Night at the Opera*, 1935. Sig Rumann, Margaret Dumont, Groucho.

# THE MARX BROTHERS

Margaret Dumont recalled that in her first appearance with the Marx Brothers, in the stage version of *The Cocoanuts,* the moment arrived for her entrance but she received no cue. Peering out from the wings, she realized that the Brothers had long since abandoned the script and were improvising scene after scene. Since this could not go on all night, she entered without cue and stood apprehensively awaiting the Brothers' next move. Seeing her, Chico and Harpo made an unceremonious and unexplained exit. Clearly Groucho had no idea of what came next, but he met the situation characteristically. "Ah, Mrs. Rittenhouse!" he said. "Won't you—lie down?"

The reminiscences of other associates, such as S. J. Perelman, on the futility of writing scripts for Marx Brothers comedies, underline the fact that screen historians can contribute nothing to an understanding of the Brothers. The Brothers just exist—Harpo, mutely eloquent, poetic, musical, and fond of blondes; Chico, Greek chorus to the foibles of the others but blind to his own; lamented Zeppo, ineptest of straight men; and the great Groucho, whose conversation "sees to it that no idea gets anywhere, or, if anywhere, that its destination will be of maximum unimportance to the human race." Their pictures create the anarchy Chaplin yearned for. He would have been happier in their world than in that to which another Marx beckoned him.

"There ought to be a statue erected," wrote Cecilia Ager, "or a Congressional Medal awarded, or a national holiday proclaimed, to honor that great woman, Margaret Dumont—a lady of epic ability to take it, a lady whose mighty love for Groucho is a saga of devotion, a lady who asks but little and gets it. Surrounded by brothers who are surely a little odd, she does not think so. To her, her world of Marx Brothers pictures is rational, comprehensible, secure. Calmly she surveys it, with infinite resource she fights to keep on her feet in it." *Animal Crackers,* 1930.

*Horse Feathers,* 1932. Professor Quincy Adams Wagstaff (Groucho Marx), President of Huxley College (its closest rival is called Darwin), confers with two of his colleagues in the higher learning, E. J. Le Saint and E. H. Calvert.

# THE MARX BROTHERS

*A Night at the Opera.* Harpo temporarily substitutes a trombone for his usual musical weapon.

*A Day at the Races.* "Get your tootsie-frootsie ice cream" is Chico's siren song to gullible Groucho in search of a sure thing.

*A Day at the Races*. Groucho in "disguise" eludes Chico with tray and Harpo with seltzer.

*It Happened One Night*, 1934. The Walls of Jericho are trembling! Claudette Colbert and Clark Gable.

## SCREWBALL COMEDY

Two seemingly routine films of 1934 revolutionized film comedy in the Thirties. The first was a purported murder mystery, the second, one of a short-lived cycle of pictures about bus travel. But both *The Thin Man* and *It Happened One Night* featured something new to the movies—the private fun a man and a woman could have in a private world of their own making. A new image of courtship and marriage began to appear, with man and wife no longer expecting ecstatic bliss, but treating the daily experience of living as a crazy adventure sufficient to itself. And if what went on in these private worlds was mostly nonsense, what sense could be found in the great world outside, where economic crisis and the threat of approaching war barred all the conventional roads to achievement and happi-

ness? It is hard to describe today what these films meant to a depression-bred generation, and it is not surprising that the "screwball comedies," as they came to be called, usually ended in slapstick or violence. They mirrored a world of frustration.

In this context William Powell's suave irony found ideal expression. So did Claudette Colbert's tongue-in-cheek manner and Carole Lombard's air of honest-to-goodness exasperation, while Myrna Loy's calm acceptance of the inevitable in her spouse made her suddenly, after ten years of playing "inscrutable" Oriental sirens, everybody's ideal wife. The brilliant dialogue and violent clowning of these Alice-in-Wonderland comedies held the screen until the onset of war, when the frustrations of the Thirties were replaced by an entirely new set.

*The Thin Man*, 1934. "This is the best Christmas present you ever gave me," says Private Eye William Powell to Myrna Loy, as he casually picks off the Christmas-tree balls with his new air pistol.

*My Man Godfrey*, 1936. Dizzy matron Alice Brady proudly shows off her protegé, Mischa Auer, doing his monkey imitation, while her husband and daughter, Eugene Pallette and Carole Lombard, look on.

*The Mad Miss Manton,* 1938. Hattie McDaniel welcomes Henry Fonda as instructed by her mistress, Barbara Stanwyck.

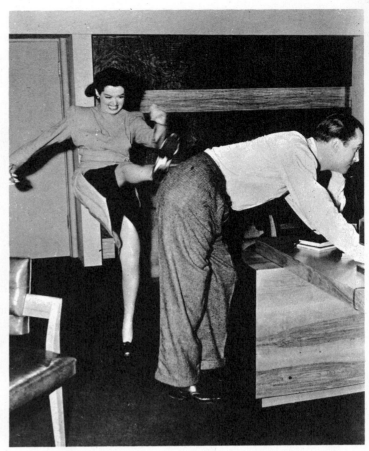

*Hired Wife,* 1940. Rosalind Russell expresses her opinion of her employer-husband, Brian Aherne.

**SCREWBALL**

*Nothing Sacred,* 1937. Lombard vs. March: the battle of the century. March scores a kayo in Ben Hecht's and David Selznick's brilliant satire on publicity stunts.

*After the Thin Man,* 1936. William Powell and Myrna Loy give Asta his dental inspection. Next to Fala, Asta was the most famous dog of the Thirties.

*Bringing Up Baby*, 1938. Paleontologist Cary Grant tries to bring Katharine Hepburn up to his intellectual level.

*Friends of Mr. Sweeney*, 1934. Charles Ruggles helps Fred MacMurray cool off after one too many cocktails.

# COMEDY

*You Can't Take It with You*, 1938. Left to right, Isobel Elsom, James Stewart, Jean Arthur, Samuel S. Hinds, Halliwell Hobbes, and Donald Meek hymn the joys of the simple life.

*Joy of Living*, 1938. Douglas Fairbanks, Jr. impersonates an Indian brave for Irene Dunne in a Tyrolean beer garden.

*Topper*, 1937. Roland Young stares aghast at the materializing Constance Bennett and Cary Grant. Trick photography gave a new twist to the screwball comedy. As ghosts, Grant and Miss Bennett could indulge in zany antics with even greater impunity than the fleshly screwball heroes and heroines.

*The Invisible Man*, 1933. Claude Rains orders the helpless William Harrigan to do his will. In his film debut in this movie, Rains's face wasn't revealed until the final shot.

# RETURN TO SPECTACLE

*King Kong*, 1933. Brains (plus brawn) vs. brawn. King Kong defeats a Tyrannosaurus while Fay Wray screams from the treetop.

## WHITE MAGIC AGAIN

Temporarily suspended by the technical problems of the early talkies, both trick photography and spectacle began to return in the Thirties, with such films as Cecil De Mille's *The Sign of the Cross*, 1932, Cooper and Schoedsack's horrendous *King Kong*, and Universal's thriller, *The Invisible Man*. Gradually the two genres combined into the superproduction, which joined camera wizardry to colossal sets and catastrophes of nature in the hope of recapturing the big grosses of an earlier day.

# THE SUPER-PRODUCTION

*A Midsummer Night's Dream,* 1935. James Cagney as Bottom embraced by the enamored Titania, Anita Louise. Literature proved disappointing as a source for superfilms. Warner Brothers' production of Max Reinhardt's version of William Shakespeare's play, though staged with all the wizardry of the studios, did not find public favor.

*Lost Horizon,* 1937. With Shangri-La a household word, Frank Capra's version of the celebrated James Hilton novel could not miss at the boxoffice. But Capra's, or his set designers', Tibetan paradise was architecturally unconvincing and strangely unattractive. Jane Wyatt as the ageless girl, and Ronald Colman as the intrepid visitor.

# THE SUPER-PRODUCTION

*The Good Earth*, 1937. O-Lan and Wang Lung find their food reserve exhausted. Four years in the making, with much background footage shot on Chinese locations, *The Good Earth's* spectacle and catastrophe impressed the public less than the strong and moving story of one Chinese family. Luise Rainer won an Academy Award for her touching O-Lan.

*Mutiny on the Bounty*, 1935, with Charles Laughton, Clark Gable, Donald Crisp. This sweeping sea story founded on fact had the bite of veracity in its handling of both ships and men. Laughton's Captain Bligh became one of the legendary villains of the twentieth century.

*Romeo and Juliet*, 1936. Far more successful than *A Midsummer Night's Dream*, M-G-M's *Romeo and Juliet* had the great advantage of performers like John Barrymore as Mercutio and Edna May Oliver as the Nurse. Norma Shearer and Leslie Howard seemed youthful when compared to the mature, sometimes venerable, players who traditionally have enacted the lovers on the stage, but the intimacy of the camera hardly helped the illusion of extreme youth.

*San Francisco*, 1936. The 1906 earthquake stunningly re-created by movie magic.

*Disraeli*, 1929, with George Arliss and Anthony Bushell.

*Old English*, 1930. George Arliss.

## The Man of One Face

Brought back to the screen by the talkies, George Arliss was hailed as a distinguished actor by nice old ladies and other such judges. According to Arliss, Disraeli, Voltaire, Richelieu, and even Alexander Hamilton all looked exactly alike, except for details of costume, and all were crafty but benevolent old gentlemen who spent most of their time uniting unhappy young lovers.

# MESSAGE PICTURES

*Cardinal Richelieu*, 1935. George Arliss pronounces the Curse of Rome.

## BIOGRAPHY

Screen biography consisted chiefly of George Arliss tinkering with the course of history until the mid-Thirties, when Warner Brothers, who had adopted the slogan "Good films—good citizenship," began the production of a remarkable series of biographical films including *The Story of Louis Pasteur*, 1935; *The Life of Emile Zola*, 1937; *Juarez*, 1939; *Dr. Ehrlich's Magic Bullet*, 1940; and *A Dispatch from Reuter's*, 1941. Usually starring Paul Muni or Edward G. Robinson, these films shed the light of realism on the contributions to democratic life of healers, research scientists, newspapermen, and humble revolutionaries. Laid in the past, smelling a bit of the lamp, they nevertheless were forceful arguments for enlightenment and rational human progress such as the screen had not previously known. Their modest success encouraged the Warners to permit their writers and directors to take up similar themes in a contemporary setting.

The result was a startling and artistically as well as sociologically admirable series of films which came to grips with such national issues as strikes and strikebreaking, lynching, slums, sharecropping, vigilantism, and migratory workers. All that had been learned about the making of sound films was used to force audiences to recognize the scene as *their* scene and the problems as *their* problems. Vivid and direct, these films were the real social literature of their time. They remain among Hollywood's greatest achievements.

Such films, made by liberals who wanted to use the power of the screen for liberal causes, came to be known as "message" pictures and provoked considerable controversy and criticism within the industry. "When I send a message, I use Western Union," was a common wisecrack of the opposition, and Terry Ramsaye, the embattled editor of the *Motion Picture Herald*, wrote, "If they want to preach a sermon, let them hire a hall." Even Jack Warner said, "Voltaire, Voltaire, all these writers want to be Voltaire." But he continued as long as it remained profitable to encourage Voltaires on the Warner lot—at least.

*Rasputin and the Empress,* 1932. Lionel Barrymore as Rasputin, John Barrymore as Prince Paul Chegodieff, Diana Wynyard, center background, as Natasha. M-G-M assembled three Barrymores, Ethel, Lionel and John for this lavish, exciting, reasonably factual resumé of Rasputin's assassination and the downfall of the Russian Imperial family. But the widow of the leader of Rasputin's assassins successfully contended in British courts that this retelling of events which she did not deny as true caused her extreme anguish. She received an immense settlement and the film was withdrawn from circulation. The incident made the studios more cautious than ever about filming actual events and real persons in any but the most laudatory terms.

*Viva Villa!*, 1934. Stuart Erwin seen as an American newspaperman, with the dying Pancho Villa, Wallace Beery. This effective, realistic account of Villa's career revealed comedian Wallace Beery for the great actor he was.

*The Story of Louis Pasteur*, 1935. Paul Muni as Pasteur confronts the skepticism of Dr. Rossignol (Porter Hall). The Sheridan Gibney-Pierre Collings script concentrated on Pasteur's researches and discoveries and his controversies with his fellow-scientists, with practically no love interest.

# AMERICAN OR UN-AMERICAN?

The press hailed Warner Brothers for bringing the art of the screen to maturity with these films in which the materials of the past were used to create a new affirmation of the democratic faith. A decade

**MUNI** *The Life of Emile Zola,* 1937. "By all that I have done for France, by my works—by all that I have written, I swear to you that Dreyfus is innocent. May all that melt away—may my name be forgotten, if Dreyfus be not innocent. He *is* innocent." Paul Muni as Zola at the trial.

later, Jack Warner, appearing before the House Committee on Un-American Activities, heard the same films described as insidious, Communist-inspired propaganda.

*Juarez*, 1939. Paul Muni as the Indian president who liberated Mexico from the Austrian-born emperor Maximilian and Carlotta and their French supporters. For his work as Pasteur, as Zola, and as Juarez, Muni was acclaimed the screen's greatest actor, a new Jannings.

*Mr. Smith Goes to Washington,* 1939. James Stewart learns from telegrams that the public, far from supporting him in his dispute with the corrupt "Silver Knight," Senator Claude Rains, sides with Rains. Later, of course, it rallies to Stewart. Frank Capra's immensely popular message pictures argued that all would come right with the nation if we replaced politicians with idealists. His message was, Turn the rascals out, but he was somewhat vague about how to do it.

*Black Legion,* 1936. Humphrey Bogart takes the oath of fealty to the Legion, which he has joined because of resentment at the promotion of a fellow-worker who happens to be foreign-born. More than half of this extraordinary film was devoted to detailing the mentality, frustrations, and origin of the kind of man who would be attracted by a terroristic society.

# MESSAGE PICTURES

*Fury*, 1936. The faces of ordinary citizens. Only here they are not ordinary citizens but a mob in front of a jail, bent on lynching an innocent man falsely accused on hearsay evidence. Behind his scenes of melodrama, of mobs and jail-burnings, director Fritz Lang brilliantly cross-sectioned the secret life of a small town, uncovering in gossip (left) the seeds of credulity, ignorance and hate which grew into the lynching.

## SOCIAL REALISM

*How Green Was My Valley*, 1941. The crowd at the pithead receives news of the trapped miners, in John Ford's production based on Richard Llewellyn's novel of the Welsh depressed areas.

*The Grapes of Wrath,* 1940. The Joad family about to set out on their journey to distant California (right). Jane Darwell, Russell Simpson, Eddie Quillan and Henry Fonda say good-by to John Carradine, in John Ford's monumental epic of the Okie migrations. (Above) Russell Simpson, Henry Fonda, player.

### Reaction:

Millionaire Walter Connolly looks inquiringly at his butler as his daughter holds a political meeting of her college friends in the living room in *Soak the Rich,* 1936. Most message pictures were frankly New Dealistic, but a few, such as this by Ben Hecht and Charles MacArthur, derided or deplored the rising tide of liberalism and radicalism. In an ad for this film which pained the more sobersides radicals, Hecht and MacArthur were depicted singing: "We're the boys who wrote the yarn/ And here's what it's about/ Class ideas don't mean a thing/ When love kicks 'em out."

*Dead End,* 1937. The great single set of Samuel Goldwyn's impressive version of Sidney Kingsley's drama of crime-breeding slums. The Messrs. Kingsley's and Goldwyn's humanitarian and reformist intentions in this film had a singular outcome. The famous Dead End Kids, seen in the foreground with Humphrey Bogart, won such popular favor that they were starred in a long series of cheap pictures the "message" of which, if any, was that it was a whale of a lot of fun to be a Dead End Kid.

*Little Man, What Now?*, 1934. Douglass Montgomery and Christian Rub in Frank Borzage's exposition of the roots of Nazism, one of the first such.

## ANTI-FASCIST

The only "ism" in which Hollywood believes, Dorothy Parker once remarked, is plagiarism. But as the Thirties advanced, as writers increasingly influenced Hollywood culture, as outside events like the depression and the approach of war began inevitably to impinge on the charmed city beside the Pacific, a change became apparent. Theatrical folk traditionally "do not want to be counted," but players, writers, and directors joined anti-fascist committees, sent ambulances to Spain, food to China, urged the boycott of Nazi and Japanese goods, and sought to persuade the conservative producers to enable them to use the entertainment screen to further these ends. The producers were reluctant. Many of them were as violently opposed to fascism as they were to communism or any but the mildest liberalism; their opposition to producing political pictures was not itself political

*Blockade*, 1938. Henry Fonda and Madeleine Carroll in the ruins of Madrid. With the outbreak of the Spanish Civil War, Hollywood liberals turned from their preoccupation with domestically oriented message pictures and sought to use the screen to warn of foreign dangers in store. Walter Wanger dared to film the Spanish conflict itself, but his cautious script made it difficult to decide who were the good guys and who the bad. Fearing that the picture would prove a flop, a zealous publicity man reported that it had been banned in Spain. Franco promptly took the hint and banned it.

*Confessions of a Nazi Spy*, 1939. Francis Lederer and player, Nazi spies, heil the Fuehrer with his secret representative, George Sanders.

## PICTURES

but an outgrowth of their rooted belief that people came to the movies to forget just the things which the writers and directors wanted to remind them of. And there were also foreign markets to worry about. Still, yielding to a sense that the times were urgent and ordinary policies might temporarily be suspended, they cautiously permitted the making of pictures which attacked the Nazi, Japanese, and Fascist dictatorships. Although sufficient at a later date to cause them considerable tribulation with Congressional investigating committees, what actually reached the screen was mild indeed.

The one exception was *Confessions of a Nazi Spy*, which, founded almost wholly on fact, used a brilliant blend of documentary and fictional techniques to report to the nation in vivid terms an espionage plot of which few were aware.

Edward G. Robinson as an FBI man in *Confessions of a Nazi Spy* arrests a spy against the background of an actual munitions plant.

Gene Autry (with Smiley Burnette in *Sunset in Wyoming*, 1941) triumphed with vocal and equestrian prowess.

*Cimarron*, 1931, restored the epic sweep of the old-time Western. The land rush into the Oklahoma Territory was its high spot.

# WESTERNS
# OF THE THIRTIES

In spite of the success of the two early talkies, *The Virginian,* 1929, and *In Old Arizona,* 1929, Hollywood believed that Westerns were washed up when sound came in. Sound-recording problems did initially make outdoor shooting difficult, but with the release of *Cimarron* it was clear that the old-time Western epic would hold the same important place in sound that it had in silence. What did decline to the vanishing point was the routine Western, once the mainstay of the cinema program. Stars like Ken Maynard, Hoot Gibson, and Tim McCoy continued their careers, but in cheaper and cheaper pictures for more and more obscure companies. Then the situation changed overnight with the screen debut of radio singer Gene Autry. Autry still dislikes riding a horse, but his singing of pseudo-hillbilly ballads brought back to the screen the rural audience it had lost to radio. Soon he was joined by singing stars Tex Ritter and Roy Rogers, also from radio and equally innocent of experience as cowboys. William S. Hart, Tom Mix, and other Western stars of the Twenties were actual Westerners, and what they put on the screen had real relation to the West of the nineteenth century; their dramas had the classic simplicity of myth. The world of the new singing cowboys was a strange never-never land where the social conditions of 1880 rubbed shoulders with the costumes and dialogue of 1935.

Ken Maynard belligerently proclaimed his faith in the future in an advertisement in the trade press.

*Destry Rides Again*, 1939. The off-type casting of James Stewart as a nonviolent sheriff and Marlene Dietrich as a very violent saloon songstress turned this old Tom Mix vehicle into a subtle burlesque on Westerns, and bailed out Miss Dietrich's floundering career.

*Jesse James,* 1939. Mr. Howard's victim. Tyrone Power as Jesse James is shot as he nails "God Bless Our Home" to the wall.

*Stagecoach,* 1939. The coach, followed by cavalry, winds through the desert. John Ford gave this film the shape and unity of *The Covered Wagon* by focusing on the adventures of a single stage and its occupants.

William Boyd, idolized as the rugged Hopalong Cassidy, began his career as a romantic and marcelled leading man in the costume dramas of Cecil B. De Mille and D. W. Griffith. Here he is in Griffith's *Lady of the Pavements*, 1929, with Jetta Goudal and Lupe Velez.

Anticipating standard television practice, advertisers of the Thirties used stalwart Western stars to induce small fry to buy their products. Here Buck Jones whoops it up for Moxie.

As Western stars increasingly became not only idols but models of conduct for their young audiences, they had to cast their private lives in the im-

After a long career in romantic roles, William Boyd was considered "through" when Harry Sherman cast him as Hopalong Cassidy in several cheaply made films. Since Boyd had detested playing the matinée idol, he gladly adapted not only his screen but his private personality to the new role of Hopalong.

# WESTERN

age of rectitude, particularly in view of the publicity cameras. Here Roy Rogers reads grace from the Bible to his family.

While the Western heroes of the Thirties were only actors who got paid for doing a job, their fans expected them to be what they pretended to be, and the line between reality and fiction grew blurred. Here Charles Starrett in an off-screen moment is supposedly ribbed for using make-up by his colleagues, Allan Brook, Clem Horten, and Iris Meredith.

# STARS
# OF THE THIRTIES

## GARBO

Greta Garbo's eagerly awaited talkie debut settled affirmatively the question of whether the spell she wove stemmed from some trick of personality or from great acting talent. But her immediate triumph in talking pictures hastened a serious crisis: the unfortunate effect of the maturation of her talent on her boxoffice draw.

Overshadowed by her later prestige as the screen's greatest actress, Garbo's potent sex appeal in the silents and early talkies has now largely been forgotten. There was in her eyes in those days a look that said to men that for her sex was beside

the point, that indeed she held it so unimportant that she didn't mind if she did. In that derisive gaze was invitation without responsibility, from a woman obviously much too proud to be beholden to a man or ever call him to account. Pride was perhaps indeed the sphinx's secret; the early Garbo was in the literal sense an adventuress of life and love. But Miss Garbo grew older, and something happened to that amused, self-sufficient look. Alistair Cooke has well described the change and its consequences:

"This is the spirit of tragedy, where all is already inevitable before the curtain goes up, and imper-

*Grand Hotel*, 1932. Greta Garbo and John Barrymore were the top stars of this famous all-star film. Barrymore considered Miss Garbo the screen's greatest artist.

*Queen Christina*, 1933. The Swedish queen seemed the ideal role for the great Swedish actress, but though the picture marked the exact peak of her popularity it was also the beginning of its decline.

ceptibly, without conscious intention on anyone's part, she moved toward tragic roles as the Thirties wore on, and in tragedy lost her original masculine audience. It was hard to feel the dominant male with this superior woman whose eyes saw and discounted everything in advance. The women remained faithful for a time to this woman who held men so lightly, and they even preferred her films to have tragic endings."

"Garbo was the only one we could kill off," J. Robert Rubin of M-G-M remembers. "The Shearer and Crawford pictures had to end with a clinch, but the women seemed to enjoy watching Garbo die." Even so, the artistic queen of the screen (so regarded by her fellow-players) was in boxoffice trouble by the time of her greatest prestige success, *Camille*, 1936. For one thing, her films were becoming more and more expensive, what with her salary of $250,000 per picture which had to be paid before a camera turned, and her insistence on the best in cast, sets, and especially camera-work. Only her supreme European popularity compensated for the poor domestic returns. Her successful comedy debut

under Ernst Lubitsch's direction in *Ninotchka* turned the tide for a while, but audiences of the late Thirties were slowly withdrawing from this increasingly remote and, to them, somewhat inhuman figure. When the war cut off the European market, Miss Garbo left the screen without officially retiring from it. She could have continued in cheaper films at a lesser salary. She chose the pinnacle or nothing.

Renewed offers have come her way since the war, both in Europe and America, but she has responded seriously to none. She is said to lack confidence in any producer or studio other than M-G-M. She is said to have refused to appear on the stage unless the first fifteen rows of the theater are kept clear of spectators, something no producer could afford. She is said to have rejected fabulous television offers on the ground that she doesn't like to watch television and therefore wouldn't want to appear on it. All this is hearsay and conjecture. Miss Garbo has revealed her mind to no one. Some years ago reporters asked her plans. In the most explicit reply she has ever made to any question, she said, "I don't know, really. I suppose I'm just drifting."

*Ninotchka*, 1939. Greta Garbo and Melvyn Douglas. By the late Thirties, Garbo had become too austere and remote for average audiences. *Ninotchka* cleverly exploited this by making her a humorless Communist drawn to laughter and love under the spell of Paris.

*Camille*, 1936. By now the legendary face had both hardened and softened into a mask of tragedy.

Spencer Tracy and Freddie Bartholomew in *Captains Courageous*, 1937.

Mae West and George Raft in *Night after Night*, 1932.

Ann Harding and Thelma Hardwick in *The Right to Romance*, 1933.

Phillips Holmes in *An American Tragedy*, 1931.

# GLAMOUR VS. HOMESPUN

Glamour and sophistication were the watchwords of the early Thirties, in terms of screen personalities. But the femmes fatales who crowded the screen in feeble imitation of Garbo, Dietrich, and Mae West

Marlene Dietrich in *Morocco,* 1930.

*Tarzan and His Mate,* 1934, with Johnny Weismuller, Maureen O'Sullivan. Edgar Rice Burroughs' fantastic character made Olympic champion Weismuller a durable movie star of the depression days.

Gary Cooper and Jean Arthur in De Mille's *The Plainsman,* 1936.

Carole Lombard and James Stewart in *Made for Each Other,* 1939.

soon faded out. In sound as in silence, the audience preferred for daily diet stars who were not too goddess-like for personal identification. Carole Lombard, Jean Arthur, Claudette Colbert, Norma Shearer among the women, like Clark Gable, Gary Cooper, Spencer Tracy, and James Stewart among the men, were earthy enough to provide lasting ego-images. Most of them lasted well into the Forties.

*Grand Hotel,* 1932. Joan Crawford, John Barrymore, Lionel Barrymore, Lewis Stone. Beginning with this famous film, M-G-M, with "more stars than there are in heaven," revived the all-star film, which flourished throughout the Thirties, climaxing in *The Women.*

*Ruggles of Red Gap,* 1935. Charles Laughton, Charlie Ruggles, Maud Eburne, Zasu Pitts.

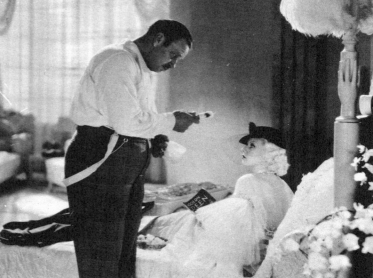

*Dinner at Eight,* 1933, with Wallace Beery and Jean Harlow.

*Cavalcade*, 1933. Clive Brook, Diana Wynyard, Irene Browne.

Shirley Temple and Gary Cooper in *Now and Forever*, 1934.

*Lightnin'*, 1930. Until his untimely death, Will Rogers upheld the homely virtues against the tide of sophistication and sex.

*The Women*, 1939. Rosalind Russell, Joan Crawford.

Mary Pickford and Leslie Howard in *Secrets*, 1933. The last of Miss Pickford's starring vehicles, after which she voluntarily retired from the screen and devoted herself to producing.

Marie Dressler and Wallace Beery in *Min and Bill,* 1930.

Katharine Hepburn made her sensational screen debut in *A Bill of Divorcement,* 1932, in which John Barrymore gave his finest screen performance.

After a slow start, Bette Davis struck her screen stride as Millie, the venal waitress in *Of Human Bondage,* 1934, seen here with Reginald Sheffield, Reginald Denny and Tempe Piggott.

*Hold Your Man,* 1933. Clark Gable and Jean Harlow attracted a huge public in a

# OF THE THIRTIES

Henry Wilcoxon and Claudette Colbert in Cecil B. De Mille's *Cleopatra*, 1934.

*Girls About Town*, 1931. Lilyan Tashman and Kay Francis competed for the fashion crown of Hollywood until the former's death in 1934.

series of sexy comedies until Miss Harlow's death ended their association.

Janet Gaynor, Fredric March, and Adolphe Menjou in the first version of *A Star Is Born*, 1937.

## HEDDA VS. LOLLY

After the fabulous and reckless Twenties, pressure was brought to bear on Hollywood's merrymakers to draw in their horns. The depression was no time to flaunt sudden wealth or unconventional behavior, especially as Will Hays sought to take over control of fan magazine publicity at the same time that his Production Code imposed its standards on the content of films. Outright scandal was now not available to the more than 200 newspaper correspondents centered in Hollywood, and innuendo perforce took its place. The successive news that Mr. X and Miss Y were "feeling the glow," "smoldering," and "on fire" chronicled their supposed progress toward bed.

Louella O. Parsons, veteran Hearst journalist, proved herself supreme at this form of oblique reporting, and many were the tall tales of her abil-

Playing herself in the movie *Hollywood Hotel*, 1937, the high priestess of movie gossip, Louella O. Parsons, comforts a star, Lola Lane, in a moment of stellar crisis.

The sudden advent late in the Thirties of the veteran player, Hedda Hopper, as gossip columnist and radio chatterer challenged the reign of Louella Parsons as arbitress of the rise and fall of movie careers. Miss Hopper's candid and sometimes acid wit came as no surprise to those familiar with the smartly knowing society women she had played in more than a hundred films.

# HOLLYWOOD IN THE THIRTIES

ity to make or break careers, and even affect the destinies of studios. Her supremacy was suddenly challenged at the end of the Thirties by Hedda Hopper. The rivalry between the two produced a distillation described by S. J. Perelman as "sugar and strychnine," but which, however poisonous, became the favorite tipple of an army of fans, perhaps for want of better. For want of better, also, the stars were now seen and photographed exclusively on the set or in night clubs, more intimate glimpses being officially tabu. (The vogue of nightclub photographs of stars was no doubt due to the advent of the candid camera, whose cruelties applied to everyone and therefore were tolerated by all.) The game of seeing and being seen in Hollywood hot spots eventually became as elaborate and as compulsory as a court minuet. Many a player

longing for bed because of a 7 A.M. shooting schedule had to make the weary round of the *boîtes;* many the stars who, with absolutely nothing in common, were seen and photographed together in public by studio decree for the sake of ephemeral mention in the columns.

The public, except the very youthful public, was not really deceived by all this. The pitiless glare which had beat on Hollywood so long had revealed every publicity device for what it was. But if people no longer dreamed of movie stars as gods and goddesses of legendary romance, they could still identify with them as successful Americans whose professional secrets they knew and whose private lives were a façade behind which they did as they pleased, which was pretty well understood to be what you and I would please, if we were they.

Nightly, lonely appearances in movieland cabarets were the almost-forgotten D. W. Griffith's last bid for the attention of Hollywood. He gained the attention of few besides veterans such as W. S. Van Dyke, director of *The Thin Man* and *San Francisco,* who had served his apprenticeship with the Master on *Intolerance,* and is shown here with Griffith.

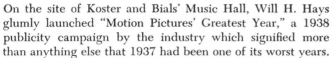

On the site of Koster and Bials' Music Hall, Will H. Hays glumly launched "Motion Pictures' Greatest Year," a 1938 publicity campaign by the industry which signified more than anything else that 1937 had been one of its worst years.

Jeanette MacDonald finger-blends her lipstick while Allan Jones looks on on the set of *The Firefly*, in full view of a disillusion-proof public.

Movie stars in person retained their fascination in the Thirties. Here Tyrone Power and Henry Fonda are ogled by a crowd in Pineville, Missouri, while on location for *Jesse James,* 1939.

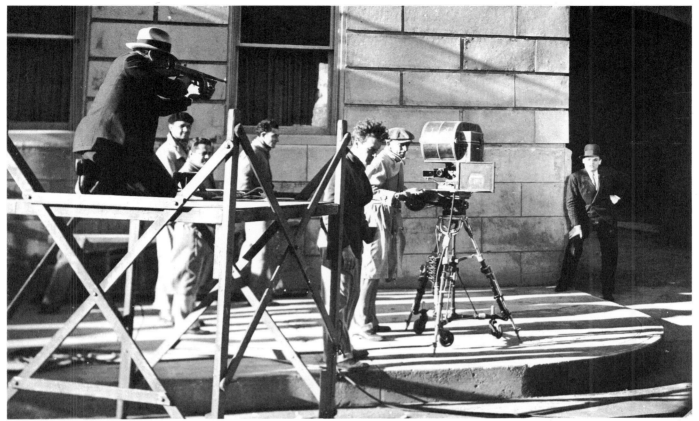

Movie magic reached its zenith in the 1930s. Here an expert marksman prepares to fire a sub-machine gun at a point a few inches from James Cagney's head so the camera can photograph the slugs hitting the building. For *The Public Enemy*, 1931.

Hollywood consolidated its influence over American everyday taste as the decade wore on. Sets like this from *Top Hat*, 1935, invariably furnished and decorated in white, were dubbed "Hollywood modern" by a contemporary decorator and set the national standard for modern elegance.

"Dish Night" and its concomitants, Screeno and Bingo, were doubtful boxoffice panaceas in the slumping Thirties.

In the teeth of the slumping boxoffice the courageous Samuel Goldwyn produced Ben Hecht's and Charles MacArthur's admirable screen version of *Wuthering Heights*, 1939, with Laurence Olivier and Merle Oberon. The Brontë classic did not earn back its cost until it had been reissued twice. Mr. Goldwyn's *The Little Foxes*, 1941, on the other hand, with Bette Davis as the tarantula played on stage by Tallulah Bankhead, earned profits commensurate with its intelligence and dramatic excitement.

# INTERLUDE

## THE SLUMP BEFORE THE STORM, 1939-1941

Movie tycoons on the eve of American participation in World War II believed that they were suffering all the pains flesh and the screen are heir to. Leading stars were demanding stratospheric salaries. Clark Gable's pay zoomed to $7,000 a week. Garbo received $250,000 per picture, Irene Dunne $100,000. Ann Sheridan, justly indignant at a beggarly $600 a week, fought and eventually won her one-woman war for $2,000 every Friday night. Educators complained that Hollywood treated the public as though it had a twelve-year-old mentality. Reformers bewailed the movie-makers' reluctance to depict the less agreeable aspects of American economic and social life, while Congress proceeded to investigate them as warmongers because of their occasional timid explorations of totalitarian tyranny and brutality. Double features were under attack by clubwomen, clergymen, and crackpots—indeed by everyone except picture patrons who continued to attend them in preference to single films. A Federal court decree banned block booking, the practice of selling at one time a studio's projected output for an entire year; no picture could be merchandised unless it was first displayed to theater owners. But the exhibitors, understandably reluctant to sit through what they would eventually have to play whether they liked it or not, stayed away from the ordained screenings in large numbers.

What was worse, the public stayed away from the subsequent theater showings. According to a Gallup poll, movie attendance, formerly estimated by the Hays office at 85,000,000, had shrunk by 1941 to 55,000,000, and even such tried-and-true boxoffice stimulants as Screeno, Bingo, and Bunko failed to revive the fabulous invalid. Indeed, *Fortune* reported that 79 per cent of the public preferred listening to the radio to movie-going. Incidentally, Mr. Gallup described the typical movie fan as being 27 years of age, earning $28 a week, and strongly averse to patronizing pictures which dealt with the causes or probable consequences of the war. His or her favorite actor was Mickey Rooney.

The highly successful M-G-M musical, *The Wizard of Oz*, 1939. Ray Bolger, Jack Haley, Judy Garland and Bert Lahr.

The only big new star to emerge at the end of the Thirties was Hedy Lamarr, introduced by Walter Wanger in *Algiers*, 1938, with Charles Boyer. The picture itself introduced the diehard catch-phrase, "Come with me to the Casbah."

The burning of Atlanta. Rhett Butler rescues Scarlett, Melanie, the baby, and Prissy. Scarlett is the figure beside Rhett; the others are lying down in the wagon.

Vivien Leigh as Scarlett O'Hara in the famous traveling camera shot of the makeshift hospital in the railroad station, the biggest attempt to reproduce Civil War carnage since *The Birth of a Nation*. From the depths of his involuntary retirement, D. W. Griffith issued a parting shot: "Chaplin says I got the same effect with a close-up of a few corpses."

Louisa Robert, Susan Falligant, and Alicia Rhett, three of the more than a thousand Southern "belles" tested by David O. Selznick for the role of Scarlett O'Hara in *Gone with the Wind*. The book's hordes of fans agreed with Mr. Selznick that an unknown should be found to play Scarlett, but they unanimously decreed that Rhett Butler must be played by Clark Gable. In order to get him, Selznick had to agree to release the picture through his studio, M-G-M.

# GONE WITH THE WIND

The faltering Thirties achieved a Gargantuan climax when David O. Selznick's *Gone with the Wind,* destined to gross over $70,400,000, opened in Atlanta late in December 1939. It had taken three years, thirteen scenario writers, three directors, and close to $4,000,000 to translate the 1,037-page colossus of a novel into an even more colossal picture. Four hundred and seventy-five thousand feet of film had been shot, but by dint of Herculean Selznickian efforts these had been cut to 25,000—three and three-quarter hours of epic entertainment. The world had been ransacked for a suitable Cinderella to play the brash and bitchy Scarlett O'Hara. At just the correct moment she was unearthed, not among the unknowns, but in the person of a minor though well-known British film actress, Vivien Leigh.

Even Sherman did not take Atlanta as overwhelmingly as did *Gone with the Wind.* Two thousand of its most eminent citizens were granted the privilege of purchasing expensive seats for the première. Even the critics had to pay and, possibly as a consequence, shouted tumultuous hosannahs. The Mayor declared a three-day festival and urged the city's manhood to raise sideburns or goatees and to wear tight-fitting pants and beaver hats, while its womanhood was admonished to appear minus rouge and abbreviated eyebrows, in hoop skirts and pantaloons. The less distinguished proletariat lined the streets for seven miles to welcome the movie aristocracy with cheers and confetti. As the band blared "Dixie," the delectable Miss Leigh is reputed to have remarked, "How sweet of them to be playing the theme song of our picture." In 1968, *Gone with the Wind* had its face lifted. Stretched to 70mm. proportions and reissued, it raced neck and neck with *The Sound of Music* for the title of box-office champion of all time.

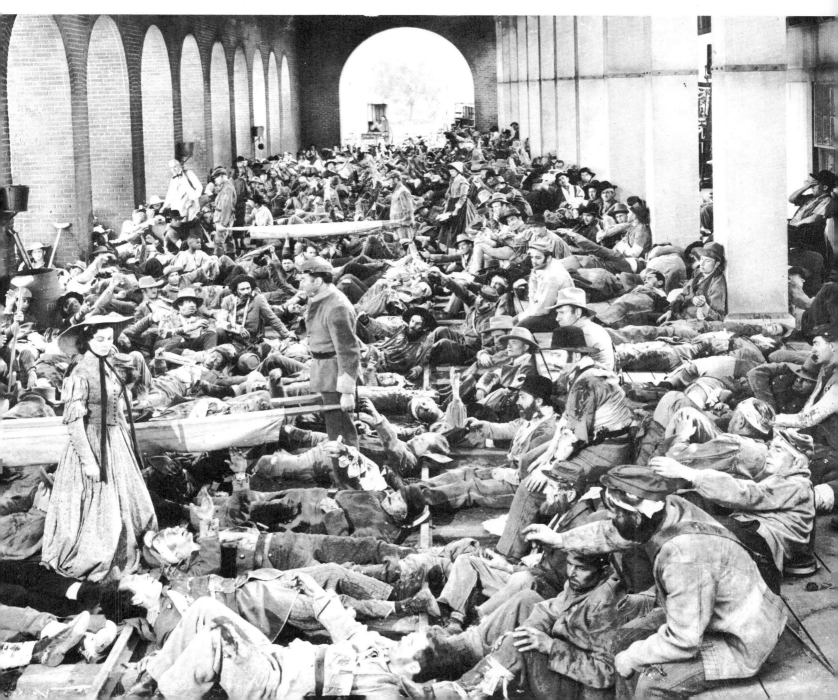

# ORSON WELLES

After he had unintentionally hoaxed the citizens of New Jersey half out of their wits with his documentary-style radio version of H. G. Wells's *The War of the Worlds,* it was inevitable that Orson Welles should be sought by Hollywood. RKO gave him an extraordinary contract as producer-writer-director-actor, with control over his material and, apparently, *carte blanche* in the matter of expense.

His first film, *Citizen Kane,* was widely believed to be a thinly disguised treatment of the life of William Randolph Hearst, and as such was denounced sight unseen by Louella O. Parsons in the Hearst papers, which also refused to accept any advertising for the picture. The resulting notoriety aroused widespread expectations, and the reviews were for the most part ecstatic. "It's as though you'd never seen a movie before," said the veteran Cecelia Ager. Foreign critics such as Cedric Belfrage were even more enthusiastic. "No one," he wrote, "will be quite the same after seeing *Citizen Kane* as he was before. It is as profoundly moving an experience as only this extraordinary and hitherto unexplored medium of sound-cinema can afford in two hours—you become dizzy trying to recall all the good things in it—lighting, composition, direction, dialogue, acting, makeup, music and sound, editing and construction." With the passing of the years the admiration of most movie commentators and buffs has not diminished. In 1962 *Kane* was voted by a group of critics "The Best Picture Ever Made." Arthur Knight, however, has substantial reservations and finds *The Magnificent Ambersons* "a good deal more inventive but in subtler, more cinematic ways." Stanley Kauffmann is considerably more critical of Welles' talents than most of his confreres. Writing of *The Trial* he says, "Welles stands where he stood, a spoilt big baby prodigy who cannot resist showing off and who would be unbearable except that his showing off is so magnificent—he is not capable of dedicating himself to an author, he just wants chances for virtuosity—he lacks the controlling artistic intelligence of an Antonioni or Kurosawa. Which means ineluctably that he has no view of life that he wants deeply to state, no vision to convey, no relation with his world of which his films are an expression. He is a scene and sequence maker, not a film-maker."

Following *Citizen Kane,* Orson Welles embarked on the production of Booth Tarkington's once-famous, long-forgotten novel *The Magnificent Ambersons* and of Eric Ambler's thriller *Journey into Fear.* He played no part in the first but was Col. Haki in the second. Both pictures were in the cutting stage when a shake-up at RKO resulted in the abrupt cancellation of Welles's contract. Announcing that their future slogan would be "Showmanship in place of genius," the new studio managers released the two Welles films as cut by others. Whether their poor showing at the box office would have been bettered had Welles been permitted to put in the finishing touches remains conjectural.

A genius fired is more recognizably a genius than ever, and Welles stayed on in Hollywood, acting a few roles from time to time, notably a bravura Rochester in *Jane Eyre,* 1944. After the war he was permitted to direct two films, *The Stranger,* 1946, and *The Lady from Shanghai,* 1948—the latter starring his then wife, Rita Hayworth. Both were disappointments to Welles because he was not permitted to finish them the way he wanted—even so, they were highly entertaining thrillers. Then Herbert Yates of Republic gave Welles the chance to film *Macbeth.* This production ended his Hollywood career. Welles went into temporary exile in Europe, where he was canonized by the intellectuals as a victim of American materialism and indifference to cultural values.

With the usual avenues of production closed to him, Welles continued to accept occasional acting assignments—in *The Third Man, Moby Dick,* and *Compulsion,* to mention his more memorable performances—and produced two films on his own in Europe, with great financial difficulty. Neither his novel version of *Othello,* 1951, nor his ruthlessly cut (by his backers) *The Confidential Report,* 1955, a return to the theme of *Citizen Kane,* lived up to the hopes of his admirers. When Albert Zugsmith at Universal gave him another chance, Welles returned to his native land to make *Touch of Evil,* 1958, set in a Mexican border town. A melodramatic thriller turned into a study of shades of evil, *Touch of Evil* came nearer the level of accomplishment of *Citizen Kane* and *The Magnificent Ambersons.* Once again, Welles went back to Europe to produce *The Trial,* an unsatisfactory attempt to reproduce in visual terms the nightmare world of Kafka's novel, and another Shakespearian film, *Chimes at Midnight,* 1966, which combined the various Falstaffian episodes from the several plays. Welles may not have been the best of all Falstaffs, but he was certainly the fattest.

*Citizen Kane.* Kane, played by Welles, launches his unsuccessful campaign.

*Macbeth,* 1948. Orson Welles, in the title role of this "arch-aeologically correct" rendering, wore the horns and furs of ninth-century Scotland.

*Mission to Moscow,* 1943. Walter Huston as Ambassador Joseph E. Davies, Manart Kippen as Josef Stalin. Three pictures made in 1943 with the laudable intent of aiding the war effort eventually proved embarrassing to their producers: *Mission to Moscow, North Star* and *Song of Russia.* Later they appeared to many either subversive or naïve, or both.

*Foreign Correspondent,* 1940. Joel McCrea, player, Eduardo Cianelli. Walter Wanger had been preparing to film Vincent Sheean's *Personal History* for five years when the war enabled him to give a new, grim, and timely slant to the adventures of American newsmen in Europe. It seemed a cry for help from a submerged continent.

*Casablanca,* 1942. Conrad Veidt and Humphrey Bogart. Another lucky break for Hollywood: Warner's *Casablanca,* which was made without knowledge of the American landings in North Africa, was released just a week after the landings took place in Casablanca itself.

*Mrs. Miniver,* 1942. While Hollywood was deciding how the actual fighting should be treated, it rehearsed the events of the preceding three years, with the Continent succumbing to Hitler while Britain held fast. *Mrs. Miniver* gave eloquent expression to Americans' indignation over the terror-bombings of London. Here Greer Garson and Walter Pidgeon protect their children in the shelter.

# WORLD WAR II

## THE FIRST DAYS

Picture-making, like gestation, ordinarily requires nine months from conception to delivery. Europe was hit by the Second World War in the fall of 1939 but nothing tangible emerged from Hollywood until midsummer of 1940.

Hollywood's two most ambitious early war efforts were 20th Century-Fox's *Four Sons,* 1940, which attempted to depict the effect of Nazism on the individual members of a Sudeten family, and Metro's *Mortal Storm,* 1940, which far more effectively illustrated the grim realities of life in Nazi Germany. Both of them unfortunately proved boxoffice failures, discouraging further serious efforts of this nature. Much more popular were *Foreign Correspondent,* in which Hitchcock's capacity for creating suspense and excitement prevailed over fourteen script writers, and *Escape,* 1940, taken from a hair-raising suspense novel that cost M-G-M $60,000, a considerable sum at the time. The outstanding war picture of 1941, and also its major boxoffice attraction, was *Sergeant York,* the tender and touching biography of the number-one hero of World War I, a man who, in his simplicity, courage, and religious nature, typified the democratic virtues which we were arming to protect.

Although Hollywood was not particularly successful with its early war efforts and though its major wartime sacrifice, made with tight-lipped gallantry, was the abandonment of the Santa Anita racing meet, the war refused to overlook Hollywood. While the blitz of Britain was at its height the London *Mirror* instructed its California correspondent to cable full details of Ann Sheridan's feud with Warner Brothers, and as the Australian troops in North Africa marched across the desert sands of Libya they lifted their voices to sing a refrain from *The Wizard of Oz.*

The most popular picture of 1942 happened also —this occurs occasionally—to be one of its best. *Mrs. Miniver* dealt honestly with the impact of war upon the life of a middle-class English family, reflecting the inner significance of the great struggle rather than its outward trappings. It happily grossed over $6,000,000.

In all, eighty pictures of 1942's output, most of them of little merit, touched in some fashion or other on war if not The War. For a time, the demand for combat titles clogged the machinery of the Motion Picture Association. Six companies sought simultaneously to establish priority on "Remember Pearl Harbor" and three promptly registered "Send Us More Japs," when the Wake Island commander cabled this defiance. After a gallant flyer named Kelly sacrificed his life, one producer wanted to make "Kelly of the U.S.A.," another "Tribute to Kelly" and a third "Kelly the Third."

One of the great sleepers of movie history came out of Hollywood at this time. *Hitler's Children* was produced on the proverbial shoestring but was publicized with the first all-out radio campaign ever tried for a movie. It worked itself up into a high lather and even higher receipts by exposing such tidbits of Nazi brutality as the flogging of lovely damsels with well-developed (and uncovered) torsos for their refusal to cohabit with Prussian supermen.

*Hitler's Children,* 1943, with Bonita Granville and Tim Holt.

*The Story of G. I. Joe,* 1945. Robert Mitchum at the left.

*Battleground,* 1949. Player, Van Johnson and Richard Jaeckel. The Battle of the Bulge re-created four years after.

# BLOOD, SWEAT, TEARS--AND PROFITS

War, like crime, may not pay, but it certainly helps the boxoffice. By 1942 everybody not in the army was working, making more money than ever before, and looking for an agreeable way to spend it. What with gas rationing, the automobile was worthless for speeding to roadhouses or necking on lonely lanes. Night baseball was out for the duration. TV was as yet only a faint disturbance on the distant air waves. Few new homes were available, and there were no refrigerators or washing machines to make the few that were available homelike. So that, though the bright lights of the theater marquees were browned out on Broadway and Main Street, the absence of illumination did not diminish the public's appetite for what was inside the theaters. Exhibitors gaily quipped, "You can open a can of sardines and there's a line waiting to get in."

But although the theater owners gloated, an ominous gloom permeated Hollywood. Rumor followed distressing rumor, most of the rumors bearing as little relation to reality as the pictures in production did: the government planned to set up under the OWI a dictatorship over all motion picture production; film raw stock was to be rationed; double features were to be banned. When a maximum of $5,000 was actually established for the

use of new materials in any single set, everybody agreed that this spelled finis to smash musicals and super spectacles, but in a brief time it was discovered that the skill and ingenuity of studio technicians made the regulation only a minor inconvenience. The proposed $25,000 ceiling on salaries, later raised to $67,000, set all movieland in a dither. What executive or star could be expected to labor for so beggarly a sum! Apparently, however, there was little cause for anxiety, for the Treasury tax report for 1942 indicated that Mr. L. B. Mayer of M-G-M had received a salary of $949,765.

By 1944 the movie producers had conspired, wisecracked Nunnally Johnson, that "no writer should get under $250,000 for a script." In the meantime most of the male performers, directors, and technicians had of their own accord taken themselves off the studio payrolls and transferred to Uncle Sam's less generous one. One hundred members of the Screen Writers' Guild alone were in the Signal Corps. The Army, Navy and Air Forces were bursting with cameramen. And the older the star, the more eager he was to join the armed forces and to demonstrate his patriotism, to say nothing of his youth and virility. Most of the big names—Gable, Power, Fonda, Montgomery, Stewart, etc.—man-

*Sands of Iwo Jima,* 1949. Amphibious landing craft, most important war engine of the Pacific conflict.

*Action in the North Atlantic,* 1943. Humphrey Bogart cries, "Abandon ship!" in Warners' fearsome account of the perils of the Merchant Marine.

As combat footage and firsthand accounts of the fighting filtered through to Hollywood, war movies took on a convincing toughness which sometimes made it hard to believe they were filmed in a studio. Just as happened after the First World War, several of the best were made by returning veterans who knew the smell of battle.

aged however to get a picture or two under their civilian belts before they replaced them with military ones.

New faces, not to mention new bodies, became an absolute necessity. With the shortage of other handsome young males Van Johnson, M-G-M's fair-haired boy, was the reigning favorite of Hollywood, particularly after his stellar performance in *Thirty Seconds Over Tokyo,* 1944. Lauren Bacall's sultry personality gave *To Have and Have Not,* 1944, something sexy well worth having. Twelve-year-old Elizabeth Taylor raised *National Velvet,* 1944, from a pleasant racing film to an earthy, tender story of a girl who loved and knew how to handle a horse (as well as a disreputable but lovable boy, Mickey Rooney). Esther Williams made her first film dive in *Bathing Beauty,* 1944, and remained on the crest of the wave of popularity for ten years. Jennifer Jones emerged from the *Bernadette* cloister in *Since You Went Away,* 1944, to prove that she was not only a devout girl but a very glamorous one. She played opposite her estranged husband, Robert Walker, whose premature death a few years later was to deprive Hollywood of one of its most promising young performers. June Allyson scored her first musical success in *Music for the Millions,* 1944,

with more than an assist from little Margaret O'Brien. Danny Kaye, fresh from his Broadway triumphs, exercised his fast feet and even faster tongue in Goldwyn's movie version of *Up in Arms,* 1944, and another eastern exile, Frank Sinatra, created a riot among the bobby-soxers upon his arrival in Los Angeles if not in his first important screen appearance in *Step Lively,* 1944. To all intents and purposes the deft and debonair Clifton Webb was also a newcomer when he returned to the screen in *Laura,* 1944, after an absence of twenty years.

When quality of story and performance became less than adequate, Hollywood turned hopefully to quantity. Never before had so large a percentage of pictures sought to atone for their limited merits by the length of their screen footage. *The Story of Dr. Wassell,* 1944, a tale told originally by F.D.R. to Cecil De Mille, and surely told more briefly and cogently, ran 136 minutes. *Dragon Seed,* 1944, dragged on for two and a half hours and *Thirty Seconds Over Tokyo* lasted 138 minutes. As for *An American Romance,* 1944, an epic of the steel industry, it proved that it was an epic by running over two and a half hours. One cynic remarked of *Mrs. Parkington,* 1944, which ran 121 minutes, that "it is two hours too long."

## THE WAR DOCUMENTARIES

The American people watched World War II from a grandstand seat without parallel in history. Thanks to the bravery of combat cameramen and the increasing skill of the military film-makers, the war documentaries provided a panorama of the world conflict in a manner which suggested that the cinema was destined to become the history book and the pulpit of the future. The outlook for documentary films seemed unlimited in 1945. But its promise went unfulfilled. In sharp reaction to their widespread showing in wartime, the postwar public turned abruptly back to escapist films.

*The True Glory,* 1945. Garson Kanin's and Carol Reed's vast record of the liberation of the European continent.

*The Life and Death of the U.S.S. Hornet,* 1944. "Old Glory" still flies from the staff of the U.S.S. *Hornet,* after a Japanese dive bomber has crashed on the signal bridge of the carrier.

*The Battle of the Beaches,* 1943. American audiences grew accustomed to seeing their soldiers in scenes of exotic beauty and of unimaginable horror as the Army and Navy attacked and captured one Pacific island after another.

*The Fighting Lady,* 1944. Filmed in color by the renowned and venerable photographer, Edward Steichen, this saga of an aircraft carrier was one of the most beautiful and honest films of the war.

*The Battle of San Pietro,* 1944. The bodies of American soldiers (right). Major John Huston's commentary says, "These lives were valuable—valuable to their loved ones, to their country, and to the men themselves," a suggestion unprecedented in a culture which habitually evaluates war casualties in terms of their damage to the feelings of female relatives.

*The Great Dictator,* 1940. Charles Chaplin as Der Phooey, Adolf Hynkel, contemplates the object of his affections. Chaplin began this hilarious spoof of the Nazis in the Thirties, but by the time it reached the screen audiences found the subject of Hitler too grim for laughter.

*Caught in the Draft,* 1941. Bob Hope, Eddie Bracken, and Lynne Overmann do perfunctory justice to the familiar humor of army life in a typical wartime comedy.

*Pardon My Sarong,* 1942. Marie McDonald, Bud Abbott, Nan Wynn, Lou Costello. The wartime need for primitive humor sparked the popularity of Abbott and Costello.

# COMEDY IN WARTIME

Aside from combat documentaries and war dramas, the wartime screen afforded space for little other than comedies and musicals. A few of these, such as *The Great Dictator* and *The More the Merrier,* tried to

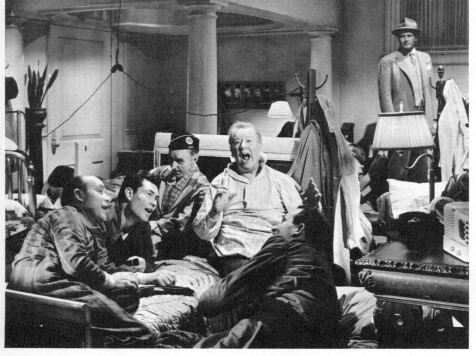

*The More the Merrier,* 1943. Charles Coburn, center, Joel McCrea, right. Garson Kanin's account of the hazards of housing in war-crowded Washington.

*The Road to Morocco*, 1942. Dorothy Lamour, Bing Crosby, and Bob Hope in one of the best of their successful "road" series.

find fun in the exigencies and ideologies of the war, but most of them ignored the struggle completely. Hollywood was performing its old function of providing an emotional refuge for the nation.

*The Miracle of Morgan's Creek*, 1944. William Demarest, Betty Hutton, Diana Lynn. Preston Sturges brilliantly revived the slapstick tradition.

*Stage Door Canteen,* 1943. Katharine Cornell and Aline MacMahon serve the soldiers.

*Babes on Broadway,* 1941. Judy Garland and Mickey Rooney in the Hoe Down.

*Meet Me in St. Louis*, 1944. Judy Garland and Margaret O'Brien.

*Yankee Doodle Dandy*, 1942. James Cagney and Joan Leslie.

*This Is the Army*, 1943.

## WARTIME MUSICALS

In the years immediately preceding the war, the old-fashioned musical with its hackneyed backstage story serving merely as a pretext for introducing a series of interminable specialties ("clambake shows" in movie gobbledygook) was waning in popularity. A new era was ushered in by *Alexander's Ragtime Band*, 1938, which played a different and irresistible tune—or rather thirty tunes all culled from the six hundred compositions of Irving Berlin. The lyrics were as familiar to American audiences as the stilted story, but together they constituted a cavalcade of the preceding quarter of a century brimming over with sentiment, nostalgia, and patriotism.

The best musical of 1942 and one of the year's highest grossing pictures was *Yankee Doodle Dandy*. It was not only an affectionate, melodious biography of George M. Cohan but a nostalgic evocation of a colorful era in the American theater. *This Is the Army*, 1943's super-duper musical, was a melange of flag-waving, star-singing, fast-stepping hokum showmanship tied up into an unbeatable bundle of boxoffice allure with seventeen smash Berlin songs. By 1943, 40 per cent of the year's films were musicals, and this percentage was maintained for the remainder of the war. Musicals provided escape from war worries and at the same time they permitted the expression of vigorous and unabashed patriotic emotion.

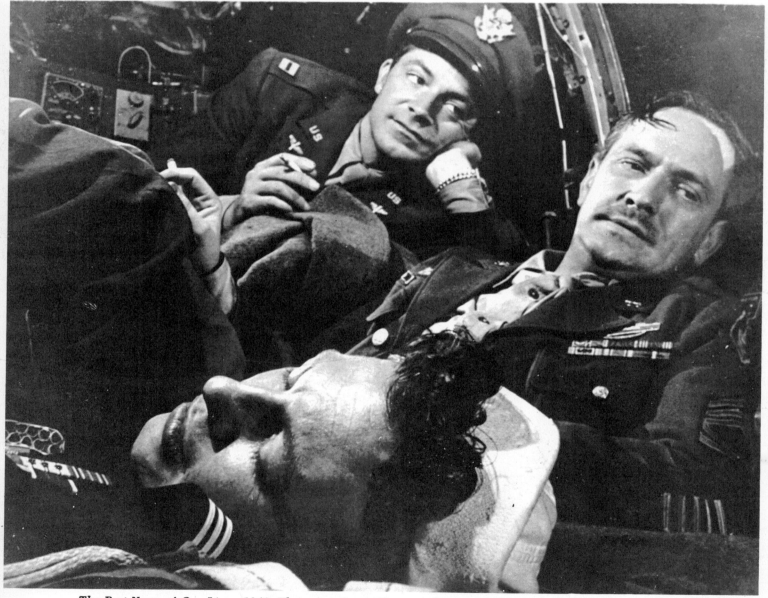

*The Best Years of Our Lives*, 1946. Three Americans. Captain Dana Andrews, Sergeant Fredric March, and 1st-Class Seaman Harold Russell in the nose of the bomber that is taking them back home.

# THE POSTWAR DECADE

## "MATURE" FILMS

Through the years the intelligentsia has bitterly criticized "Hollywood" for its failure or refusal to make "mature" films about social and economic problems of national importance. In vain did industry spokesmen reply down through the years that all the evidence showed that the movie audience consisted primarily of children and adolescents of all ages, and that the minority of grownups who said they wanted grown-up films were too casual in their movie attendance to make the production of such films anything but the riskiest of gambles. But the modest success of "message" pictures in the Thirties and the flood of wartime documentaries encouraged hopes that after the war the liveliest and most popular of the arts would assume the responsibilities its more serious-minded well-wishers wanted to confer on it. The men of Hollywood had seen service in all parts of the world and had once again rubbed shoulders with their fellow-Americans. They wanted—or said they did—to project what they had learned onto the screen. There was a general air of expectancy in 1946 that the future of the movies would be very different, and more mature, than their past.

*The Best Years of Our Lives* seemed to fulfill all these hopes. This American masterpiece, the crowning achievement of Samuel Goldwyn's long career, came as near perfection as popular art contrives to be, from its beautifully equivocal and suggestive title to the magnificent performance elicited by William Wyler from the nonprofessional amputee Harold Russell. Goldwyn had enlisted the services of novelist MacKinlay Kantor, playwright Robert Sherwood, and director William Wyler, all of whom had been involved in the war effort. Their film epitomized both the dream and the reality of the postwar world. This intimate engagement with the psychological facts of American life gave it an almost universal audience. But, unlike contemporary and preceding "message" pictures, it was not a preachment. It showed Americans as they are, presented their problems as they themselves see them, and provided only such solutions—partial, temporary, personal—as they themselves would accept. The picture's values are the values of the people in it.

*The Best Years of Our Lives.* Ex-flyboy Fred Derry (Dana Andrews) in the airplane graveyard.

The Lost Weekend, 1945. Ray Milland in d.t.'s.

The Song of Bernadette, 1943.
The apotheosis of Jennifer Jones.

## REST, REST, PERTURBED SPIRIT

The stresses of war gave rise to a generally heightened consciousness of the loneliness of the individual in the modern world, and of his search for anodyne. Three panaceas of the solitary spirit—alcohol, religion, and psychiatry—were examined, suddenly and intensively, by the movies just as war was turning to peace. Charles Brackett's and Billy Wilder's magnificent *The Lost Weekend* chilled and titillated the nation but distillers reported no notable reduction in their profits; in fact it was noted that audiences coming out of theaters where this appalling object lesson was being shown headed straight for the nearest bar. The short-lived spate of psychiatric films, of which the best was Anatole Litvak's *The Snake Pit*, were not particularly scientific in their approach to the growing national problems of neurosis and psychosis. In fact they treated psychiatry as a form of new sorcery, and while they were successful enough in depicting the nightmares of mental disease, all the hopes they held out for its speedy cure were completely unconvincing. Only the religious cycle, that began with *The Song of Bernadette* and reached its climax with *Going My Way*, 1944, and *The Bells of St. Mary's*, 1945, has continued fitfully into the Fifties.

The Snake Pit, 1948. Olivia de Havilland in the depths of her pit.

# "SEMI-
DOCU-
MENTARIES"

The thousands of documentaries produced and shown during the war years were not entirely without influence on subsequent commercial motion picture production. Louis de Rochemont's *The House on 92nd Street* was the first tangible evidence of their impact on the entertainment film. Using many of the techniques he had already developed with "March of Time," and basing his story on FBI files, he told, at a time when the telling could still arouse surprise and consternation, of the operations of an enemy spy ring in our midst. Because it used actual locations and unknown or little-known actors, it escaped from the old-fashioned cloak-and-dagger fustian into the honest excitement of real places and real people.

Its success encouraged such films as de Rochemont's *13 Rue Madeleine*, 1946, *Boomerang*, and Henry Hathaway's memorable *Kiss of Death*, 1947. But these exciting semi-documentaries died in childhood. Their documentary approach had grown out of purposes more serious than plain film-making or money-making. Detached from the inspiration of those purposes, the task of teasing a dramatic pattern out of the materials of everyday life soon came to seem too hard. And, after all, the studios were still there.

*Boomerang*, 1947. The assassination of a priest.

*The House on 92nd Street*, 1945. The files of the FBI.

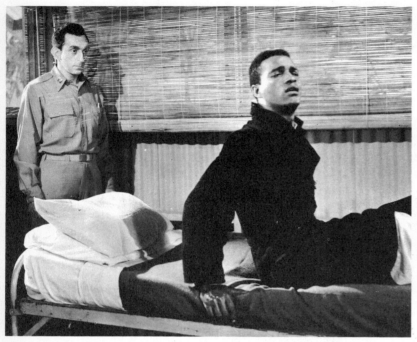

*Home of the Brave,* 1949. "Walk!" Army psychiatrist Jeff Corey tries to get Negro GI James Edwards to overcome his phobias and walk.

*Pinky,* 1949. Jeanne Crain, a Negro girl passing as a white, seeks the consolation of her grandmother, Ethel Waters, after she has fallen in love with a white doctor.

*Intruder in the Dust,* 1949. Claude Jarman, Jr. and Juano Hernandez in the last and best of the Negro dramas, Clarence Brown's version of William Faulkner's novel, which failed to attract a public surfeited with racial films.

# HOLLYWOOD LOOKS AT THE MINORITIES

In the late Forties, a sudden spurt of films arguing for racial justice evidenced a considerably greater degree of courage in Hollywood than Hollywood's detractors are willing to grant it. Unfortunately these films also illustrated the almost insuperable obstacles which have to be hurdled by any film-maker who wants to make an honest social statement. In 1946, the literate Dore Schary bought Richard Brooks's wartime novel, *The Brick Foxhole*, for reasons nobody could understand since the book dealt with the tabu subject of homosexuality. Schary changed its theme to the almost equally tabu subject of anti-Semitism. The resulting excellent film, *Crossfire*, 1947, had considerable success. Shortly thereafter the youthful Stanley Kramer, a veteran of Signal Corps "nuts and bolts" films, bought the play *Home of the Brave,* which attacked anti-Semitism. Kramer substituted a Negro for the Jewish hero. *Home of the Brave,* quickly and cheaply made, earned a lot of money, elevated Kramer into the position of the fair-haired boy of the industry, and entirely failed to incite predicted race riots.

Schary and Kramer had realized that the tradi-tional tabus against public discussion of racial and religious injustice had weakened, and they had had the courage to act on their belief. Then the inevitable happened. The studios attacked the newly freed theme with righteous frenzy. The resulting films, of which the most notable were *Gentleman's Agreement, Intruder in the Dust, Pinky, Lost Boundaries,* 1949, and *No Way Out,* 1950, varied widely in quality. Some hedged, some spoke out plainly against the unresolved dilemma of race and religions. But the flood of such films speedily exhausted public interest in what had been a fresh as well as a brave screen subject. The abrupt end of the cycle again indicated the precarious nature of "mature" films in an industry which had fashioned its mass appeal to a primarily immature audience. At that, the cycle achieved to some extent the social effect so desired by the champions of adult films. Intellectual Negroes boggled at the compromises and evasions in the race films, but no Negro can have been unaware that the fact of his second-class citizenship, so long concealed or denied, was at last being shown on the public screen for all to see.

*Gentleman's Agreement,* 1948. Gregory Peck, Celeste Holm, and John Garfield in the climactic scene.

*Johnny Belinda*, 1948. Doctor Lew Ayres introduces the deaf mute Jane Wyman to music.

*From Here to Eternity*, 1953. Monty Clift blasts it.

*Come Back, Little Sheba*, 1952. Burt Lancaster, Shirley Booth, Richard Jaeckel, and Terry Moore. Miss Booth's triumphant screen debut in Daniel Mann's admirable version of her stage vehicle.

# HOLLYWOOD LOOKS AT BOOKS AND BROADWAY

Hollywood has never had much faith in its own procreative processes. It tends to rely on the seal of success achieved in kindred arts. In its postwar search for "mature" material, it turned, as it had so many times before, to popular current plays and books, and to Broadway for new faces such as Marlon Brando, Judy Holliday, Shirley Booth, Paul Douglas, Richard Widmark and Montgomery Clift.

*A Place in the Sun,* 1951. Elizabeth Taylor and Montgomery Clift. For the love scenes between this attractive pair, director George Stevens used huge close-ups which "sent" youthful intellectuals who knew not the days of Vilma Banky and Ronald Colman. Told about this, Stevens said, "They'll fall for anything."

*All the King's Men,* 1949. Broderick Crawford in Robert Rossen's much-praised version of Robert Penn Warren's novel based on the rise of Huey Long.

# HOLLYWOOD SEES RED

The presidents of the major companies were thoroughly alarmed at the investigation of the "Hollywood Ten" script writers by the Committee on Un-American Activities of the House of Representatives. Believing that the best way to counter the charge that the movie colony was infected with communism was to make anti-communist films, the magnates turned to their writers and directors and said, in effect, "All right, you're so anxious to make message pictures, and to use the screen for serious purposes—be serious about this."

The craftsmen duly sought to be serious, but the

results were weak, routine cloak-and-dagger stuff or imitations of the old Nazi spy melodramas. It was as though the film-makers could not really believe in the menace of communist espionage. Their pictures had the unreality and languor of a command performance. The one obviously honest one, Leo McCarey's *My Son John,* proved the most distasteful. Its hatred of communism seemed mingled with a hatred of everything intellectual. It also implied, probably unconsciously, some curious things about the role of American motherhood and family life in creating future left-wingers.

*My Son John,* 1952. Robert Walker swears on the Bible to his mother, Helen Hayes, that he is not a Communist.

# HOLLYWOOD LOOKS AT THE STARS

The public's enduring fascination with the private lives of actors is shared by actors themselves, and indeed by everyone with whom they are professionally concerned. As a result, every period of Hollywood's history has seen the recurrence of a cycle of films about show business. The mid-century revival produced two of the best pictures of that decade, *Sunset Boulevard* and *All About Eve,* both released in the same year, 1950. *Sunset Boulevard*, Charles Brackett's and Billy Wilder's mordant study of the old and the new Hollywood, brought the great Gloria Swanson back to the screen, after many years of absence, in the role of a rich but forgotten star slowly moving toward madness as she broods over her vanished fame. The conviction Miss Swanson achieved in this role is the more remark-

*All About Eve,* 1950. Bette Davis in a prize display of temperament. Anne Baxter, Gary Merrill, Celeste Holm, Miss Davis, Hugh Marlow.

able in that she herself has never ceased to fight for her place in the sun, even after the end of her screen career.

*All About Eve* dealt with that older forcing-bed of animosities, the theater, where another aging star, Bette Davis, was threatened with the loss of both her career and her man to a scheming new-comer, Anne Baxter. A very funny picture, it had nothing in it quite so novel or quite so penetrating as the contrast in *Sunset Boulevard* between the barbaric grandeur of the silent days and the slick, sharp, safe playing of more recent days. The dia-logue in *Sunset Boulevard* was really unforgettable. "You were a big star once," Joe Gillis says to Norma Desmond. She replies, "I'm still big. It's the pictures that got small."

*Sunset Boulevard*, 1950. Gloria Swanson recounts her past glories to an embarrassed William Holden.

Clara Bow, the IT girl of the Twenties.

Jean Harlow, reigning sex-queen of the Thirties.

## Hot Sex

*The Outlaw*, 1943 (right). Jane Russell in all her glory and in the hay. Miss Russell's first picture, Howard Hughes's *The Outlaw*, was completed before the war but not released until 1947. Meanwhile, publicity stills of the star-to-be were adopted as pin-ups in every theater of war and Miss Russell was world-famous before she ever appeared on the screen.

## Violence

*Detective Story*, 1951 (right). William Bendix watches Kirk Douglas get it. This film's serious portrayal of police routine did not lessen its brutality. The public had acquired a taste for violence and even sadism from wartime films which could be satisfied only by a revival of the gangster film.

*Public Enemy*, 1931.

*The Maltese Falcon*, 1941.

*Double Indemnity*, 1944.

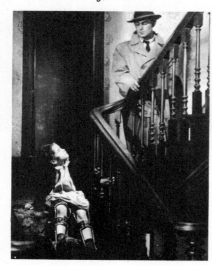

*This Gun for Hire*, 1942.

# OLD RELIABLES

Despite their desire to bring the movies out of their infancy with mature films on new subjects, American film-makers had to consider the desires of their audience as the Forties wore on. The peacetime cornucopia was pouring forth new cars and new housing, television was racing across the nation, and, above all, Americans were suffering from a sort of "ideological fatigue" after so many years of sacrifice and dedication. Those who had predicted that the movies would never be the same after the war were amazed at how very much the same they were turning out to be. Major emphasis on sex and violence, those basic appeals, speedily reappeared. Tragic romance returned to the screen with *The Heiress,* 1949, and even Ruritanian romance reared its long-forgotten head in *Roman Holiday,* in which Audrey Hepburn presented as lovely and appealing

a princess as the movies had ever offered. Location trips to Italy and Africa were much in vogue, with luxury-loving stars enduring physical hardships to bring the public spectacular thrills. A particular sign of the times was the renewed cultivation of the small-town audience, generally ignored by the major studios in lush periods. *Ma and Pa Kettle,* 1949, was designed for what is insultingly known as the family trade. Costing less than $500,000 and exhibited in the less imposing theaters, it grossed an amazing $2,300,000 and ushered in the seven-picture series of Kettle adventures. Another successful Universal release in the low-bracket field, introducing an almost equally profitable series, was *Francis,* 1949, the comic adventures of a mule who talked and acted more intelligently than most two-legged performers.

*Thirty Day Princess,* 1934, with Sylvia Sidney.

*Three Weeks,* 1924, with Aileen Pringle.

*Roman Holiday,* 1953. Gregory Peck and Audrey Hepburn.

**RURITANIAN
ROMANCE**

*The Swan,* 1925, with Frances Howard Goldwyn.

*The Swan,* 1930, with Lillian Gish, O. P. Heggie, Marie Dressler.

*The Swan,* 1956. Sophisticates of the Thirties and Forties thought Ruritanian romance belonged to as remote a past as *Where Is My Wandering Boy Tonight* until Audrey Hepburn made *Roman Holiday* and Miss Grace Kelly, of Philadelphia and Hollywood, married the reigning Prince of Monaco, thus one-upping Pola, Gloria, Mae, and all the other title snatchers of the Golden Twenties. By stunning coincidence, M-G-M released Miss Kelly's new version of Molnar's old Ruritanian play, *The Swan,* just before the big wedding.

*High Noon,* 1952. The symbol of integrity. Though he had been in pictures thirty-five years, the lines which settled in Gary Cooper's face seemed imposed by the physical and emotional climate of his native Montana rather than of Hollywood. Made out of the most ordinary materials of the familiar Western formula, *High Noon* achieved the shape of a democratic allegory which reached people in much the same way and for the same reasons that *The Best Years of Our Lives* had done. Its cutting suspense was the hallmark of director Fred Zinneman's mastery of the movie medium.

Brandon de Wilde and Alan Ladd in *Shane*, 1953.

*The Treasure of Sierra Madre*, 1948. The last moment. Humphrey Bogart surprised by the bandit chief who he knows will kill him.

## WESTERNS

For some forty years Hollywood was sustained by the knowledge that, in good times or bad, a Western, any Western, will play in a minimum of 6,000 theaters and will be gratefully welcomed by a host of fans. But those 6,000 did not include the top-grossing first-run houses of the big cities. Essential to small-town exhibitors, Westerns were believed to be boxoffice poison in the big theaters. But when John Wayne became the nation's top male favorite, it was clear that Westerns were becoming as popular in the first-runs as they had always been everywhere else. This subtle revolution in audience tastes was further pointed up by *The Broken Arrow*, 1950, with its $3,500,000 gross, and *Shane*, 1953, with earnings of more than $8,000,000. The return to the oldest of movie genres meant not so much that films were rounding on their own past but that the country at large was hankering after a vanished America, where danger was the tangible menace of physical combat rather than the fear of losing a job or of an invisible death from the sky. The new vogue of Westerns not only rolled up big grosses, but also permitted the making, within the Western formula, of two great films, *The Treasure of Sierra Madre* and *High Noon*.

Gary Cooper in a 1929 Western, *Wolf Song*, with Lupe Velez.

# POSTWAR MUSICALS

*On with the Show,* 1929.

The great genius of the postwar musical—dancer, singer, actor, choreographer, and film director—is Gene Kelly. Here he is in *An American in Paris,* 1951, and (center) in *Take Me Out to the Ball Game,* 1949, with Frank Sinatra.

Joan Blondell and chorus in *Gold Diggers of 1937*.

What slapstick was to the silent screen, the Hollywood musical was to moviegoers and movie-makers of the Forties and Fifties. Sometimes the story meant something, sometimes it got lost and stayed lost; in any case, the blithe carnivals just kept rolling along. Because they were nearly always about show business show men loved them. They loved to bring back the old songs and corn of vanished theater and vaudeville days and brightly polish them for a new audience. These musicals disarmed even the sophisticates because they were fundamentally so innocent.

*Easter Parade*, 1948. Judy Garland and Fred Astaire dance to Irving Berlin's "When the Midnight Choo-Choo Leaves for Alabam'." Officially retired, the indestructible Astaire has let himself be lured back before the cameras time and time again to show modern audiences what a really great dancer is like.

*Sitting Pretty*, 1948. Clifton Webb introduced a genuinely novel character with the omniscient Mr. Belvedere. He is shown here in a scene that would have delighted the late W. C. Fields.

*The Chaser*, 1928.

*His Wedding Night*, 1917.

*Born Yesterday*, 1950. Broderick Crawford and Judy Holliday in the superb gin rummy scene. Miss Holliday's—and Garson Kanin's—dumb but all-wise blonde was another novel character creation.

## POSTWAR COMEDY

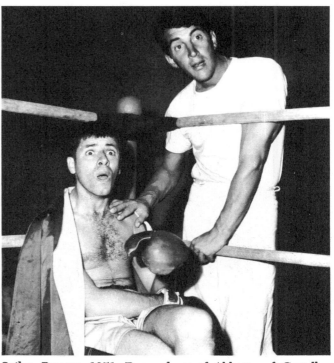

*Sailor, Beware*, 1951. Descendants of Abbott and Costello, of Wheeler and Woolsey, Martin and Lewis were the supreme box-office comedy team of the early and mid-Fifties.

The former puppet film producer, George Pal, initiated the Fifties vogue of science-fiction films with this modest descendant of Méliès's *A Trip to the Moon* of 1902. Not really very different from the old "mad scientist" horror films, they were given a new look by the improved gadgetry and a wider appeal by the spread of technological knowledge. To the satisfaction of the industry, their success relegated the cheaper science fiction to TV. Then, after the genre had suffered a decade of neglect, sci-fi proved its potential popularity through the success of Stanley Kubrick's *2001: A Space Odyssey*, 1968.

*A Trip to the Moon,* 1902.

**SCIENCE FICTION**

Robby the Robot combs Anne Francis' hair. M-G-M's *Forbidden Planet*, 1956.

*When Worlds Collide*, 1951. George Pal's staging of the inundation of New York.

*Noah's Ark,* 1929.

# SPECTACLE

*Samson and Delilah,* 1949.

When business turns bad some industries economize, but Hollywood found it paid to spend more—and the most expert of all more-spenders was the late Cecil B. De Mille. *Samson and Delilah* was his 1949 answer to all that was wrong at the box office. Its huge popularity demonstrated once again that the Bible is the picture-maker's best friend, a never-failing source of spectacle, sex and sadism that no censor could dare to suppress and no movie-goer could afford to miss. It was the direct precursor of such incredibly costly and successful "epics" as *The Robe, Quo Vadis?* and De Mille's last and greatest spectacle, *The Ten Commandments*, which held the record as the biggest box-office blockbuster of all time. Yet when De Mille died in 1959, it appeared that the art of the successful Biblical spectacle died with him.

*Male and Female*, 1919.

*The Greatest Show on Earth*, 1952. Only De Mille could top De Mille. His circus picture grossed over $12,000,000.

# STARS
# OF THE FORTIES
# AND FIFTIES

The traditional canon of five years as the life-span of a movie star's career was shattered by the amazing survival capacity of many favorites of the 1930s. It would almost seem that American audiences were beginning to develop the same kind of lifetime loyalty which enabled Bernhardt and Mistinguette to remain stars for half a century in Europe; Ponce de Leon was looking in the wrong place:

The Fountain of Youth
was in Southern California.

Cast as a cryptic bum or tough in the early Thirties, Spencer Tracy hit his stride as the Portuguese fisherman in *Captains Courageous*, 1937, and remained a firm but benign father figure ever after until his death in 1967. Here he is in *The Old Man and the Sea*, 1957.

Put out to pasture by M-G-M under its pension plan, "The King" no longer officially reigned on his own lot, but continued to make pictures until, over-exerting himself on the production of *The Misfits*, he died in 1961.

Gregory Peck as Captain Ahab in John Huston's respectful version of *Moby Dick*, 1956. This was Peck's admirable but unsuccessful attempt to escape the limitations of his roles as the handsome romantic leading man.

The longest record as a man-of-action probably belongs to John Wayne; his career in action films runs from the beginning of the Thirties right through the end of the Sixties. He was the rugged individualist of a line of John Ford and Howard Hawks films. Here he strides vigorously through *Hondo*, 1954.

Lauren Bacall's request for a light set aflame a celebrated romance on screen and off, in her introduction to movies and to her future husband in *To Have and Have Not,* 1945. Marcel Dalio observes the effect on Bogart.

## BOGART

It seemed that only the end of life itself could put finish to some actors' careers, until Humphrey Bogart proved to be indestructible even in death. The tough guy died of cancer in 1957, but in the following decade his films were revived not only on the late show, but in the theaters of college towns, where those too young to have seen most of his films when they first appeared made an anti-heroic cult figure of him. They pinned his pictures to their dormitory walls and quoted his snarling dialogue: "Drop the gun, Louie," "You're good, you're really good," "Play it again, Sam." In France, Jean-Luc Godard produced a tribute in *Breathless,* when Jean-Paul Belmondo gazed at a poster featuring Bogart in *The Harder They Fall,* and ran a thumb across his mouth in a gesture copied from his prototype.

Bogart began his career as a stage juvenile said to have been the first to utter the immortal line, "Tennis, anyone?" In the mid-Thirties, his success on stage as Duke Mantee in *The Petrified Forest* led him to his subsequent movie career as a cynical, rough-mannered good guy or gangster. His disillusioned, ugly, scarred face, which Warner Brothers had thought fatal for a movie star, looked irresistible to his leading ladies and movie fans.

Alistair Cooke put it well, "Here was a universal type of our rebellious age but one that never appeared in life quite so perfect: never quite so detached in its malice, so inured to corruption, so self-assured in its social stance before the diffident, the pompous, and the evil...a touchy man who found the world more corrupt than he had hoped, a man with a tough shell and a fine core."

Bogart and Peter Lorre in *Casablanca,* 1942. A game of chess well symbolized the relentless logic of the Bogart character's relations with friend and foe.

The inimitable Philip Marlowe encounters Harry Jones (Elisha Cook, Jr.) in *The Big Sleep,* 1946.

The confrontation of Katharine Hepburn at her most spinsterish and Bogart as a drunken river boat captain made *The African Queen*, 1951, a popular sensation, thanks to John Huston's flair for the bite of off-type casting.

Billy Halop, a good kid, was led astray and into prison by Bogart in *You Can't Get Away with Murder*, 1939. Bogart didn't.

In John Huston's playful spoof of thrillers, *Beat the Devil*, 1954, Bogart is captured by Arabs. He gains release by promising the Captain (Manuel Serano) to fulfill his life-time dream of meeting Rita Hayworth, the Captain's favorite pin-up.

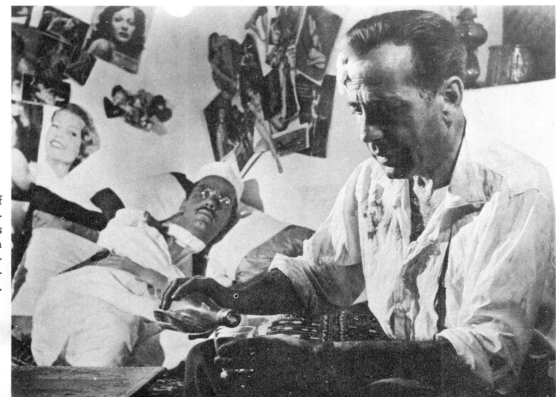

The vulgarity with which Jayne Mansfield's phenomenal natural equipment was exploited is well exemplified here. Every era has to have its gimmick star, but the gimmickry with which Miss Mansfield was surrounded, on and off screen, was on a low imaginative level, and her non-career was a sad one.

Grace Kelly, the epitome of the well-bred Philadelphia girl, in *High Society*.

Besides beauty and sex appeal, the Kim Novak of 1955 seemed to have inborn camera personality—that arresting, appealing flair that cannot fail. But mistaken casting cruelly revealed her acting limitations, while paradoxically preventing her from realizing her full potential within them.

Blessed with bone structure that allowed her face to age interestingly, Katharine Hepburn continued her career through the Sixties. Here she is in *The African Queen*, 1951, and *The Madwoman of Chaillot*, 1969.

The American career of Marlene Dietrich, which began in 1930, has been pronounced finished no less than three times by industry wiseacres, but nobody told Marlene. She is the permanent symbol of sex appeal. She is seen here in *A Foreign Affair*, 1948.

*Monsieur Verdoux*, 1947. Charles Chaplin in his penetrating "comedy of murders."

# THE GREATEST STAR OF THEM ALL

Abandoning for the first time his character of Charlie the Tramp and creating the new and intriguing one of Monsieur Verdoux, Charles Chaplin subtitled his first film in seven years "a comedy of murders." This was meant to shock, as was the picture's attack on war and on capitalism as the source of war, not to mention its ironic sidelights on Christianity—but to shock us to our senses. *Monsieur Verdoux* managed to shock the American middle class, but not in the way its maker had intended. The public connected the distasteful message of this "crazy" film with vague memories of scandals in Chaplin's personal life and his supposed left-wing leanings. *Mon-*

*sieur Verdoux* was a disaster at the American box-office and was promptly withdrawn from release. The screen's greatest actor, its most important creative figure, the most famous man in its history, known to more of his contemporaries than even the central figures of the great religions, Chaplin for the first time tasted defeat and failure.

*Limelight,* which appeared five years later, was booked into only 3,000 theaters instead of the 12,000 which in earlier days had always been eager for any Chaplin film. This debacle had nothing to do with the quality of the picture but stemmed from the efforts of pressure groups which, incensed at Chaplin's defiance of accepted moral and economic standards, exerted all their power to persuade exhibitors not to show and the public not to attend

*Limelight*, 1952. Chaplin and the beautiful Claire Bloom in what may prove the final appearance of the "Little Tramp" at least in films distributed in the United States.

it. Only its tremendous European success, as in the case of *Monsieur Verdoux,* saved it from financial catastrophe.

But bigotry and hate were not the only reasons for the failures of these two highly personal confessions. They are the films of a man who has withdrawn to a distance to observe the human comedy, and it is from a distance that he sends us his messages. Their Sophoclean irony and detachment are matched by a latent savage anger and an infinite compassion. They deal in high style with our highest concerns. Above all they seek to speak the truth, not the acceptable truth, not necessarily the whole truth, but the truth as an aging man leaving illusions behind sees it. If they have a film counterpart, it is Von Stroheim's *Greed,* and, pressure groups or

no, they were bound to meet the fate of *Greed.*

When Chaplin sailed for Europe for the premiere of *Limelight,* the State Department effectually barred his re-entry to the country where he'd triumphed and contributed monumentally to the world supremacy of the American film. The U.S.S.R. invited him to make films in Moscow, but he remained in Switzerland. Twice he emerged, to produce *A King in New York* and *The Countess From Hong Kong,* neither critical nor commercial successes. At the end of an early film, *The Pilgrim,* Charlie finds himself between the United States and Mexico, unwanted and menaced in both countries, doomed to straddle the border forever. Perhaps that is where Chaplin stands today. Perhaps that is where he has always stood and wanted to remain.

*Paris,* 1926.
Joan Crawford with Charles Ray.

*Our Dancing Daughters,* 1928.
Joan Crawford, John Mack Brown.

"The greatest star of them all," the phrase with which Erich von Stroheim appeased the crazed Gloria Swanson in *Sunset Boulevard,* has been applied by every female star's admirers to every female star. Professional longevity would seem to be the most objective test of this, and by that yardstick Joan Crawford wins hands down. Mary Pickford's screen career lasted twenty-four years; Miss Crawford began in 1925 and today makes at least a picture a year. As good an explanation as any of her amazing survival value has been her inventiveness and adaptability. Every year the "new" Joan Crawford has looked out from the pages of the fan magazines. Beginning as an ingénue, she made her mark as a jazz baby, became a leading exponent of the "God, the pain of it all" school, turned café society élégante, and ended (for the moment) in her present incarnation of tough-minded career woman fighting for success and love. She has the priceless knack of seeming to create fashions in heroines rather than to follow them.

Only three times in thirty-two years has Miss Crawford's foot slipped, the first when she made two pictures, *Rain,* 1932, and *Today We Live,* 1933, which were beyond her dramatic reach and outside the interests of her fans. She quickly turned the tide with a smash-hit musical, *Dancing Lady,* 1933. Four years later, after a string of undistinguished pictures, an exhibitors' poll listed her among other stars as "boxoffice poison." Such a statement by theater men could be damaging indeed to a studio with unreleased Crawford pictures on its hands, and M-G-M ostentatiously gave her a new contract to prove their faith in her future. But the new contract provided nothing new in the way of story material or handling, and in 1943 Miss Crawford announced that her eighteen-year tenure at M-G-M had been severed by mutual agreement and that she was mov-

*This Modern Age,* 1931.
Joan Crawford with Pauline Frederick.

*Rain,* 1932.

*Dancing Lady,* 1933.
Joan Crawford with Clark Gable.

# DAME OF THEM ALL

ing to Warner's. There she remained idle for almost two years while the Warner storysmiths tinkered with possible vehicles for her, and rumors began to fly that she was being gently eased onto the skids. Advised of this, Miss Crawford replied with flashing eyes, "Let them try it!" Evidently "they" didn't dare, for Miss Crawford emerged triumphant in 1945 with one of her biggest hits, *Mildred Pierce*.

"Let them try it!" The bugaboos of Hollywood have no terrors for Lucille Le Sueur, née Billie Cassin, who fought her way up from an ugly and poverty-stricken childhood to the Broadway chorus line and to what then seemed an inauspicious screen debut. Her screen name was chosen for her by a Rochester housewife in a contest conducted by *Photoplay* magazine. Her screen manner, a sort of subdued gutsiness, was achieved after many and sometimes ludicrous experiments, amid the ridicule of the sophisticates. Blessed with bone structure which made her a perfect camera subject, she has continued to mold and remold the outlines of her face with the assiduity of a sculptor seeking unattainable perfection. Her first three marriages ended at the first sign of conflict with her career. She has achieved and enjoyed a sort of marginal motherhood by adopting four children. Miss Crawford's original fans of the dancing-daughter days are balding, graying nonmovie-goers now, and no one knows what segment of the audience supports her pictures. Perhaps the entire audience, and Hollywood itself, feels a sort of religious awe at the spectacle of a woman who has exemplified the American dream by fighting for success, holding onto it, and loving every minute of it. As Miss Crawford stood drinking in the applause after the premiere of *Mildred Pierce*, the ladylike Greer Garson said to her, "Well, none of us should be surprised. After all, my dear, you're a *tradition!*"

*Autumn Leaves*, 1956.
Joan Crawford with Cliff Robertson.

*Sudden Fear*, 1952.
Joan Crawford.

*Mildred Pierce*, 1945.
Joan Crawford with Zachary Scott.

*Ice Follies of 1939.*
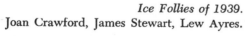
Joan Crawford, James Stewart, Lew Ayres.

*What Ever Happened to Baby Jane?*, 1962.

# PIN-UPS
# AND
# SWEATER GIRLS

Although the public was unaware of it, Rita Hayworth's career lasted about three times as long as those of most stars considered her contemporaries. Brought up in show business from childhood as a member of the troupe known as the Dancing Cansinos, little Rita Cansino began as a plump movie ingénue in Westerns of the early Thirties. Columbia changed her name, streamlined her figure, and launched her on a career in which she became, with Jane Russell and Betty Grable, one of the favorite pin-up girls of the armed services. Originally a favorite with men, Miss Hayworth endeared herself to feminine audiences too through a spectacular private life reminiscent of the glamour queens of the Twenties, and especially through her marriage to the Ali Khan, in which she beat Grace Kelly to the post in the revived title sweepstakes.

Lana Turner in her brunette days.

Jane Russell in *The French Line*, 1954.

A strong contender for first place among the pin-up sister-hood, Betty Grable was top star of the 20th Century-Fox musicals for more than a decade. She is seen here with her admirers in *Meet Me After the Show*, 1951.

During the production of *The Seven Year Itch*.

# PIN-UP GIRL SUPREME

Marilyn Monroe hit the star-starved screen with the impact of a tidal wave. "It's Jean Harlow all over again," deliriously declaimed 20th Century-Fox's casting director, Ben Lyon, when he first laid eyes on her. What matter that her acting talent appeared limited to a capacity for manipulating her hips and eyelashes simultaneously, half-closing her eyes, opening her moist lips, and speaking in a high-pitched baby voice? Other less intuitive Fox executives disagreed. After they previewed *Scudda-Hoo, Scudda-Hay*, the first Fox film in which Marilyn appeared, she disappeared. Her role had consisted of one word, "Hello."

They acquired a clearer understanding of dramatic values when, two years later, M-G-M introduced her in a minor part in *The Asphalt Jungle*. To those with their ears to the ground and their eyes on fan mail, it was immediately clear that America's favorite legend, the Cinderella story, was about to be re-enacted on the flamboyant scale that only Hollywood can achieve.

Born June 1, 1925, Norma Jean Martenson was an illegitimate child. Her mother, deserted by both husband and lover, suffered a nervous breakdown; a crazed neighbor tried to smother the baby; at six she was raped by a friend of the family. She was boarded out with no less than twelve indigent families; was sent to an orphanage where for her services scrubbing dishes and toilets she was paid five cents a month. She grew up without affection, education, or self-confidence; but nature had blessed her, in addition to her physical endowment, with a hard inner core of courage, common sense, and resiliency.

Twentieth Century-Fox also had resiliency. After *Asphalt Jungle,* they re-engaged her at six times her previous salary. Five pictures of less than world-shaking consequence in 1953 and 1954 promptly propelled her to the head of the boxoffice parade. Sixteen magazines simultaneously selected her as their cover girl. Psychiatrists wrote lengthy dissertations about the little waif who, deprived of a normal home life, turned to men for love and understanding. The Communists denounced her as capitalism's latest opiate for the masses. Gossip columnists came up with one juicy bit of gossip: Marilyn had posed in the nude for a calendar. Such exposure might have been fatal to anybody else, but Marilyn simply explained that she had needed the money and all was forgotten and forgiven while the sales of the calendar vaulted to six million copies. "Didn't you have *anything* on?" quizzed one sob sister. "Oh yes," answered Marilyn, "I had the radio on."

Other pertinent replies to impertinent questions might have conveyed to the observant that another popular folk myth was in the remaking—the dumb dizzy blonde who is far from being dumb or dizzy. "Is it true you wear falsies?" asked an interviewer. "Those who know me better know better," was Marilyn's succinct reply. "Is it true that you are having trouble with the Johnston Office?" she was queried. "Their trouble," she answered, "is that they worry whether a girl has cleavage. They ought to worry if she hasn't any." In *Gentlemen Prefer Blondes* she gave her first intimations of a gift for light comedy. One critic asked her to explain how she interpreted her role. "I cannot define Lorelei's character," she replied. "I know what's in her mind." About a favorite subject of many of her admirers, she once said, "Sex is part of nature, and I go along with nature."

The studio executives recognized in Marilyn the perfect replacement for Betty Grable and were nonplused when they discovered that she aspired to study Stanislavsky. (When in a radio interview she discoursed for twelve minutes on the Stanislavsky method, her press agent was accused of ghosting the material for her. He replied, "What press agent knows that much about Stanislavsky?")

In 1955, after she had finished her part in *The Seven Year Itch* (as well as her marriage to baseball's Joe DiMaggio) she told the studio what it could do with her contract and flew east to study at the Actors Studio in New York, read the world's best books, be analyzed and mingle with the intelligentsia. Hollywood was convulsed with laughter—until Marilyn announced the formation of her own production company whose first film would be *The Prince and the Showgirl* with Laurence Olivier as co-star and director. Joshua Logan called it "the best combination since black and white."

Fifteen months after her departure, Marilyn staged a triumphal return to Hollywood accompanied by the accolades of egghead directors such as Kazan and Strasberg, and Pulitzer Prize-winner Arthur Miller as a husband, not to mention a handsome bonus from 20th Century-Fox and a voice in her future stories and directors. Her performance in *Bus Stop,* 1956, indicated that she was on her way to becoming a deft and skillful performer and that an acquaintance with Freud was not necessarily fatal to sex appeal. Indeed, these achievements only seemed to add a bit more luster to the already firmly established legend of Marilyn, the sex goddess supreme.

Tom Ewell and Marilyn Monroe in *The Seven Year Itch,* 1955.

# TRAGIC SYMBOL

Then tragedy began to haunt the legend. Marilyn's playwright-husband wrote a screenplay for her, the ill-fated *Misfits*, and by the time the picture was finished, their marriage had broken up. Twentieth Century-Fox fired her from the cast of *Something's Got to Give* for failing to show up on the set. By then it was clear to both the studio and the press that Marilyn was in deep trouble with herself. A few months later, early in August 1962, she took an overdose of sleeping pills and became permanently enshrined in that Valhalla the public reserves for its favorites who die young. After her death, the image suffered a sea change. She was no longer the polished sex-symbol, but a lonely and sensitive waif, buffeted by this harsh world, suffocated between the crassness of Hollywood and the adoration of the mob. The legend was nurtured not so much by the garden-variety fan as by the intellectuals. Poems were written about her, artists were moved by the symbolism of Monroe to create paintings and sculpture, and early in 1968 the Sidney Janis Gallery was able to collect fifty-two of these works in an "Homage to Marilyn Monroe."

The aging King and the doomed Queen: Clark Gable and Marilyn Monroe in *The Misfits*, 1961.

Tony Curtis (yes it is) and Marilyn in *Some Like It Hot*, 1959.

On their way to Valhalla. Within five years of the taking of this picture on location for *The Misfits*, Montgomery Clift, Marilyn Monroe and Clark Gable were all dead, two of them suicides. In the back row, Eli Wallach, Arthur Miller and John Huston.

# JAMES DEAN

Even briefer than Marilyn Monroe's, James Dean's career left trails of glory. In his only year in Hollywood, this moody, intense, 24-year-old Indiana farm boy, reminiscent of Brando but with a sensitivity and capacity to express emotion distinctively his own, starred in three films, *East of Eden, Rebel Without a Cause,* and *Giant.* A week after the completion of *Giant* he was killed in an auto collision, a loss the commercial movie world he so despised could ill afford, but which enshrined him forever as the idol and symbol of a restless, confused, but fundamentally idealistic younger generation.

James Dean in *Giant*, 1956.

The mask of rebellion. James Dean in
*Rebel Without a Cause*, 1955.

Kim Hunter and Marlon Brando in *A Streetcar Named Desire*, 1951.

Marlon Brando and Elizabeth Taylor in *Reflections in a Golden Eye*, 1967.

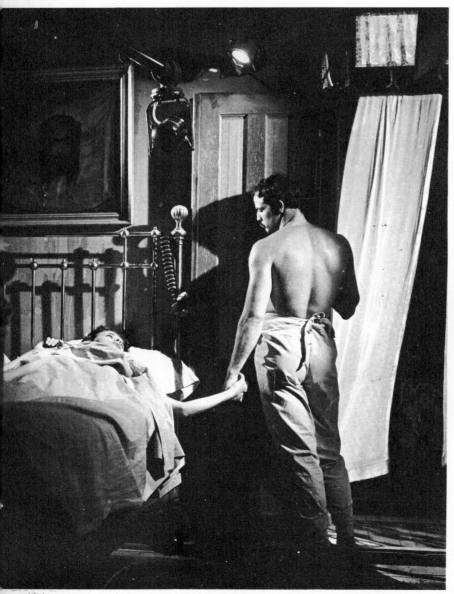

Marlon Brando in *On the Waterfront*, 1954.

Marlon Brando and Jean Peters in *Viva Zapata*, 1952.

Marlon Brando as Marc Antony in *Julius Caesar*, 1953.

## MARLON BRANDO

Carefully type-cast by Elia Kazan and tailored to the role which he played in both stage and screen versions of *A Streetcar Named Desire*, Marlon Brando gave a portrayal of the brutish Stanley Kowalski which fascinated while it repelled. To his elders, Brando's performance was an accurate exposition of D. H. Lawrence's instinctual man, but carried no more significance than that. But the young man's combined savagery and inarticulateness struck flaring response in teen-agers, to whom they mirrored their own frustrations at a society they could not understand or participate in. Overnight a new Hollywood white hope was born. This accidental success happened to a young intellectual who, however reserved and withdrawn, took his profession seriously and would not revise his own aims to follow the standard routine of the climbing movie star. He refused interviews, or gave brief and rude ones; the middle-aged as well as the adolescents were inwardly delighted when his rebellion against the system took the form of turning up in sloppy clothes at Hollywood soirées. He was equally intransigent in professional matters. He allowed Stanley Kramer to cast him as a teen-age cut-up in *The Wild One*; but, for the most part, he cut his teeth on roles as varied as Zapata, Antony, Napoleon, Sky Masterson in *Guys and Dolls*, and Sakini in *Teahouse of the August Moon*. Although the depth and bite of his acting suffered somewhat through these strenuous efforts at versatility, it was evident Brando did not consider acting to consist of making over traditional characters into the image of Marlon Brando.

By 1960, however, Brando was saying in an interview: "Acting is fundamentally a childish thing to pursue. Quitting acting—that is the mark of maturity." This was at the point when he first tried his hand at direction, having taken over from Stanley Kubrick on the Brando production of *One-Eyed Jacks*. The experiment was not a great financial success, and Brando continued to take on intermittent acting jobs. But something seemed wrong. Some of his admirers thought of him as an example of how Hollywood could ruin great actors, trading on star qualities rather than on acting talent. To others, he seemed to be marking time. Reaching middle age, this one-time symbol of adolescent rebelliousness appeared increasingly uncertain about his goals.

Vivien Leigh and Marlon Brando in *A Streetcar Named Desire*.

# THE REVOLUTIONARY SIXTIES

## HOLLYWOOD TODAY

### THE NEW PROCESSES

The 70mm. width for motion-picture film was used as early as 1897 by the Veriscope camera, especially made to photograph the Corbett-Fitzsimmons fight at Carson City, Nevada. It was only by accident that the 35mm. width became the industry standard until the 1950s.

As television took hold of the country's imagination (and its rooftops) in the late-Forties, the picture industry tried at first to ignore its menace. In the impending battle between entertainment at home free of charge and at theaters where it had to be paid for, the movies seemed hopelessly handicapped. Moreover the leadership of the industry appeared ill-qualified to cope with the emergency. Most of the company heads dated back to the early pioneer days. The years seemed to have undermined the energy and initiative which had enabled them to build their empires.

But the industry was not so superannuated as it appeared. The movie tycoons remembered how the coming of sound had once saved the movies from a similar threat and above all how the American public has always responded to the novel, the bigger and perhaps the better. They dusted off half-forgotten three-dimensional and wide-screen processes to create giant theater screens which, they hoped, would dwarf the home screen into insignificance.

Cinerama was the first of these new techniques using three projectors to throw a tripartite image on a huge wide-angle screen to give a realistic illusion of depth. Much as audiences back in 1896 had ducked the onrushing Empire State Express, in 1952 they held their breath in pleasurable horror as they seemed to zoom down Coney Island shoot-the-chutes. Some of the original magic and mystery that had endeared it to millions had returned to the screen.

Among the new processes, Todd A-O, utilizing

70mm. film, afforded the most dramatic sense of depth and clarity of definition, and Paramount's VistaVision, in which the film ran through the camera horizontally rather than vertically, thus substantially increasing the size of the negative, was the most agreeably proportioned. Twentieth Century-Fox's CinemaScope was, however, the best publicized and the most boldly handled. Consequently it quickly outdistanced its competitors. Spyros Skouras, the dynamic head of the company, guaranteed skeptical exhibitors that although no feature had ever been made in CinemaScope it would be exclusively utilized for all of his future productions.

Actually, CinemaScope too was only an adaptation of an anamorphic process designed by Professor Henri Chrétien of France in the early Twenties. By means of distorted wide-angle lens, a compressed image is registered on the film and subsequently corrected by a compensatory lens on the theater projector in such a fashion as greatly to extend the range of vision and to suggest a sense of depth to a picture two and a half times as wide as it was high. Cinema-Scope was, so to speak, the poor man's Cinerama and was rapidly adopted by American exhibitors, rich as well as poor. It did not require three cameras or three projectors. It could be installed with stereophonic sound in practically any theater, with no loss of seats, for about $20,000. It made its initial bow with the opening of *The Robe* at the Roxy Theater and promptly proceeded to smash the house box-office record there and everywhere else it was shown. By early 1957 *The Robe* had earned domestically $30,000,000, putting it next to the all-time movie high of $33,500,000 established by *Gone with the Wind*. It made a contribution to show history as memorable as that of *The Jazz Singer* twenty-six years previously.

By the Sixties, the wide-screen ratio dominated the industry. Movie theaters everywhere were equipped with projectors which could show both 35mm. and 70mm. widths, and with big wide screens, many of them curved to add to the sense of depth. Cinerama, originally a three-camera, three-projector system, de-

veloped a one-camera-one-projector combination which somewhat reduced its original illusion of depth and participation but which was much more practical to install in theaters. Lightweight 70mm. cameras were developed which made location shooting once more possible. New processes were announced every day, but in time most of the industry settled down to a wide image and a slight illusion of depth.

At first the Hollywood craftsmen, from stars to directors, were dismayed by the preoccupation of their overlords with all this technical gimmickry at the expense of traditional dramatic values. From her retirement Pola Negri egocentrically commented, "Hollywood has gone from Pola to Polaroid." When the authors asked Josef von Sternberg his opinion of the wide screen, the veteran director replied, "Suppose you were filming *Gulliver's Travels*. Cinema-Scope would be excellent while Gulliver is pinned to the ground, but when he arises to extinguish the fire in the palace by the most readily available means, he becomes a problem." But, just as they did when sound arrived, the artists and technicians soon buckled down to overcome the limitations of the expanded medium and to explore the opportunities it provided. Among these, they made some unexpected discoveries. For some, film-making had already begun to move in the direction of a style less dominated by montage, a style in which camera movement is as important to the composition as editing. As early as 1938 Jean Renoir had said, "The more I advance in my craft the more I feel it necessary to have the scene set in depth in relation to the screen; the less can I stand actors placed carefully before the camera as if they were posing for their photographs. It suits me rather to set my actors freely at distances from the camera, to make them move about." And in 1955, Antonioni was still employing the old ratio for *Le Amiche* when he observed, "I want to show my characters in their context, not to separate them by montage from their daily environment—the interaction of people with each other and with their surroundings is much more subtly expressed by showing them simultaneously."

This frame from *The Robe* shows how the anamorphic lens compresses the image on film.

## THE NEW PROCESSES

The thrill that started it all. This shot, near the beginning of *This Is Cinerama*, 1952, engulfed the audience and made them feel they were actually on a roller-coaster. To date, none of the other processes has matched the sensation of involvement and participation which Cinerama gives.

*Land of the Pharaohs*, 1955.

*Giant*, 1956. The enlarged screen invited directors to try new forms of pictorial composition.

## TELEVISION VS. THE MOVIES

Hollywood resentment of television simmered down as the major studios took to producing the bulk of television fare on their own back lots and sold their backlogs of old pictures for television viewing. That voracious medium consumed most of these within a few years, but then discovered that, fortunately, they could be shown over and over again. Meanwhile the money from the rentals helped to keep movie production rolling through the crisis years. Gradually, the movies won an insidious victory over their rival.

The revolution was completed in 1966 when *The Bridge on the River Kwai* was sold for two million dollars for a couple of showings and on those evenings pulled seventy million viewers away from their regular television programs. As the prices rose for other important pictures the promise of a television sale began to enter into the planning and financing of new theatrical motion pictures. Color television had come to stay, and, except on rare occasions, few producers would consider making any more pictures in black and white. Far from destroying the movie industry as had been anticipated, television in 1968 supplied one third of its domestic revenue.

Alec Guinness in *The Bridge on the River Kwai,* 1957.

Television, the Enemy. When fifty million Americans deserted
movie theaters for their living rooms, Hollywood took a petty
revenge by making movies featuring scenes that ridiculed the
boob tube. In *Happy Anniversary*, David Niven deliriously
kicked in one set after another.

*Barbarella*, 1968. Barbarella in the love-making tube. Since about 1960 there has been intense competition among female stars—notably Carroll Baker, Raquel Welch and Jane Fonda, seen here—to see who can get nudest, and stay nude longest, for public delectation. Though there are obvious limits to this competition, no lady whose pictures were destined for the American screen has ever quite achieved them. To date, there has always been *something* between some part of them and the camera—be it a love-making tube or, as often in the case of Miss Fonda, her "pretty-pretty" hair.

## THE FALL OF CENSORSHIP

The movies lagged far behind literature and theater in dealing with the changing mores of our times. The chief reason for this time gap was the bind of self-censorship, which had held the motion-picture industry in its grip since 1934 through the enforcement of the Motion Picture Production Code. By the early Sixties, however, censorship, whether voluntary or not, was being challenged on all fronts. An enormous change was about to come over what the movies could show and say.

The distributors of foreign films and independent productions first accustomed American audiences to seeing frank love-making scenes, perversions and more bare flesh than they had ever seen before on the screen, providing competition for the milder efforts of the major companies. Thus challenged where it hurts most—in the pocketbook—the studios insisted on revising the Code and then eventually abandoned it. Even when the new Code went into effect, it did not go far enough, and already motion pictures were going way beyond it and often ignoring it altogether. When the distinguished Italian director Michelangelo Antonioni refused to permit Metro-Goldwyn-Mayer to make the cuts in *Blow-Up* ordered by the Code authorities, that studio released it without a seal of approval, distributing it under the name of one of its subsidiaries, Premier Productions. The use of such subsidiaries was already widespread. "Pictures shall not infer that low forms of sex relationship are the accepted or common thing." Such was the wording of the 1934 Motion Picture Production Code. Prostitution, under the old Code, was never to be explicitly labeled as such. In hundreds of Westerns, audiences learned to accept the polite euphemism of the dance-hall girls. Even as late as the movie version of Truman Capote's *Breakfast at Tiffany's* (1961), in the original of which the heroine is a casual little tramp, Audrey Hepburn was made to interpret the role as a fey

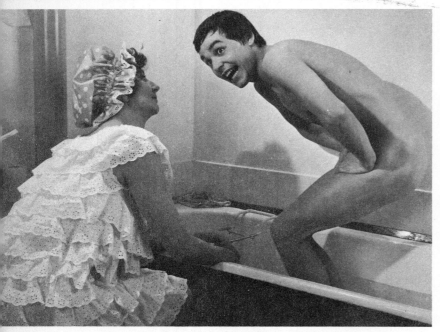

*Here We Go Round the Mulberry Bush*, 1968. Moyra Fraser and Barry Evans. Not to be outdone, males began to enter the nudity competition.

"Be nonchalant," went an advertising admonition of forty years ago. "Light a cigarette." No props for poise were needed by Joey Bishop and friend when surprised by his wife in this scene from *A Guide for the Married Man*, 1967. *In flagrante* isn't what it used to be.

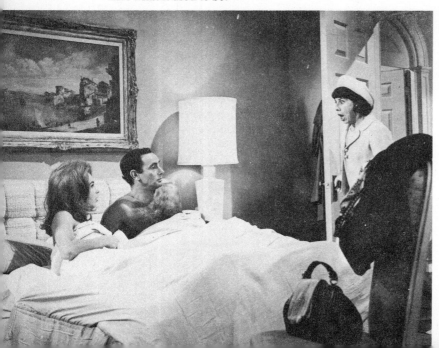

*Irma La Douce*, 1962. There is no doubt about the profession practiced by these young ladies, not even in Jack Lemmon's innocent eyes.

sprite who took large sums of money from men and gave nothing in return. But in 1962 three quarters of *A Walk on the Wild Side* was set in a bordello; in 1963 *Irma La Douce* was labeled by its director Billy Wilder as "the Gettysburg Address of prostitution"; and the filming of Polly Adler's *A House Is Not a Home* in 1964 with its original title intact surely must have made Will Hays, former Film Czar, stand up in his grave, as Sam Goldwyn once phrased it.

By the mid-Sixties, the first shock of titillating scenes had begun to wear off. In 1967 that most lady-like of actresses, Audrey Hepburn, let the word "Bastard!" slip past her elegant lips in *Two for the Road.* In the same year Elaine May, playing the part of a well-brought-up young lady in *Luv,* cheerfully admitted she wished she were a lesbian. All things once forbidden by the Motion Picture Code were being openly discussed or shown on the movie screen. They even became subject for comedy. In *A Guide for the Married Man,* a picture full of flip advice on how to conduct an extramarital affair, there was an hilarious episode in which a nude couple embracing in bed are discovered by the man's wife, whereupon they calmly get up, get dressed, make the bed, all the while pretending that the situation does not exist, until the wife can no longer believe the evidence of her senses. Thoroughly bewildered, she is forced to accept her husband's innocence.

Albert Finney and Audrey Hepburn in *Two for the Road,* 1967.

The new freedom has given us a superabundance of trash and sensationalism. At the same time, however, audiences are now assumed to be prepared for adult subject matter on their motion-picture screens —and, since many of these films are now sold to television, even in their living rooms. It has become possible to present more honestly some of our basic human problems and to reflect with more accuracy how people live today. *Love with the Proper Stranger* (1963) showed its nice young heroine seeking out an illegal abortion as the result of a casual one-night love affair, and the stylish *Two for the Road* gave us a picture of a modern marriage which openly admits that the central core of that institution is what happens in bed, as well as permitting its heroine a brief fling into adultery without undue suffering. Both films presented their once unmentionable topics without provoking either shock or prurience in audiences.

On November 1, 1968, the Motion Picture Association abandoned the old Code system in favor of voluntary classification. A rating administration was established that was authorized to grade all pictures shown in American theaters into four categories as follows: G—suggested for general audiences; GP—for adults and mature young people; R—restricted; persons under 16 not admitted unless accompanied by a parent or guardian; X—those under 16 not admitted. The historic first X certificate was given to *Birds in Peru*, a story of nymphomania. Although somewhat similar classification systems have long existed in other countries, there remain many doubts in industry minds. The American system depends upon exhibitor support, the as yet unclear standards of the classifiers and the voluntary cooperation of all concerned. *Midnight Cowboy* and *I Am Curious (Yellow)* prove an X classification is not fatal. But, one question in particular remains unresolved: will the granting of an X certificate automatically guarantee a large return at the box office for those film-makers who deliberately seek that rating?

Jimmy Stewart, as the defense lawyer in *Anatomy of a Murder*, 1959, holds up the controversial garment that Chicago censors ruled could not be mentioned along with "rape," "semen" or "contraceptive." Director Otto Preminger refused to delete the offending references and won his case in court. Kathryn Grant is in the witness box.

"Sex perversion or any inference of it is forbidden." The Motion Picture Production Code, 1934. In 1956, the revised clause advised that perversion could be shown if "treated with care, discretion and restraint." This is a scene from *The Balcony*, 1963.

Warren Beatty interrupts a love scene between two women, in *Lilith*, 1964.

An enterprising exploitation man took advantage of the popularity of *My Fair Lady* to come up with a catchy title for his grind-house production, *My Bare Lady*. Audrey Hepburn and unknown actress.

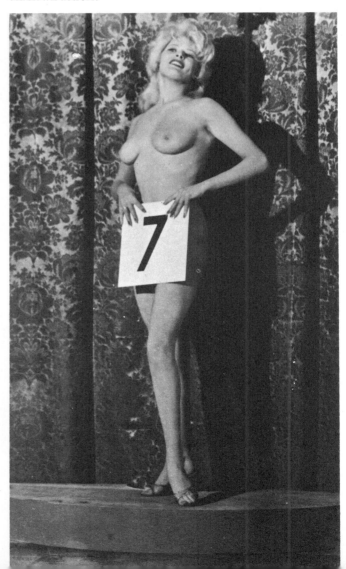

# INDEPENDENCE

## INDEPENDENT PRODUCTION

The old studio system, the Hollywood dream factory that supplied a steady flow of all kinds of pictures to satisfy the movie addiction of millions of Americans, no longer exists. With all its faults and restrictions, with all its pleasures and occasional surprises, the year-in-year-out assembly-line production of movies is gone.

Independent production came largely to replace it for a number of reasons. The competition of television unquestionably had a profound effect on the industry. Other factors were equally important if less well known to the average movie fan. Legal actions of the government ordered major companies to sell their theater circuits and to halt the practice of block-booking. Increasing taxation on personal income led the highest-paid creative figures to become corpora-

tions and enter into production for themselves, financed by the major distributors. Independent productions as well as foreign films were much in demand to fill the product shortage created by the decline of the assembly line.

The old stamping ground of independent souls—United Artists, founded by Douglas Fairbanks, Mary Pickford, Charlie Chaplin and D. W. Griffith—had floundered along somehow for thirty years, never having enough product to provide real competition for the major companies, until in 1950 it was on the verge of bankruptcy. Then, taken over by a new group of dynamic young men, the company was revitalized and took the lead in encouraging independent production, with profit-sharing provisions and a far greater degree of freedom for directors, writers and

Stanley Kramer's *The Defiant Ones*, 1958, was a defiant picture for its day. It attacked race prejudice on a deep emotional level by stressing the Dostoievskian motif of respect achieved through mutual degradation and suffering. The picture took out insurance against its own daring by starring Tony Curtis and Sidney Poitier as two nameless convicts, at the cost of some conviction. But it made money and paved the way for Poitier's popularity and for other race-relations films to come.

Otto Preminger, reputed to be a tyrant to his actors, struggles to get a performance out of the inexperienced teen-ager he had discovered, Jean Seberg, afterward to become the darling of French film-makers as a crop-headed, typical American girl. *Saint Joan,* 1957, was based on a play by George Bernard Shaw, translated into a screenplay by the prestigious Graham Greene, and as such was a genuine experiment in bringing "dangerous" subject matter to the screen—an experiment that failed. The picture was panned by the very critics it was designed to please, and it was a colossal box-office flop. But Miss Seberg rose like a phoenix from its ashes.

*Rachel, Rachel,* 1968. With all the odds seemingly against him, movie star Paul Newman produced and directed his first picture *and* directed his own wife, Joanne Woodward. He succeeded beyond anyone's expectations. Above all, he drew a superb performance from Miss Woodward as a bored and frustrated thirty-five-year-old spinster schoolteacher in a small New England town. Such a chancy project probably would never have been attempted under the old studio system.

performers than Hollywood has countenanced since its earliest days. The tables had turned: to obtain the services of the best-known names, all the majors had to follow in the same direction.

For many years, high-minded idealists believed that independent production was the way to get a greater number of good movies. But when the day of independence finally dawned, the crusaders found that it was not the paradise they had anticipated. Ambitious directors like John Huston, Stanley Kramer and Otto Preminger discovered that, as producer-directors, they not only sat in the seats of their former bosses but also bore their responsibilities to the companies who financed them, to the distributors who released their pictures, and, above all, to that vast world audience whose least common denominator still had to be the crucial factor in their calculations. The nub of their problem was and is that if one of their independent productions lost a lot of money, they ran the risk of never being able to get together

enough capital to make another. In this winner-take-all, loser-lose-all atmosphere, such men were increasingly drawn to expensive and time-consuming productions which often seemed somewhat hollow by comparison with the modest films they made under duress in the assembly-line days but which sometimes gave us our best moviegoing experiences. Of the new conditions of production which thus developed, the time element was the most confounding: important talent was tied up for years in the making of a film that might or might not turn out to be worth it.

When Samuel Goldwyn, who once said, "I don't care whether *The Best Years of Our Lives* makes money as long as everybody in the United States sees it," at last retired at the age of eighty, he gave as his reason that nowadays it takes four years from conception to release to make the type of picture for which he was famous, and he wasn't sure he had all that much time any more.

## HITCHCOCK THE MASTER

By virtue of years of success, the old master of the suspense-thriller could write his own ticket in the Fifties and Sixties. Even in a day when movie patrons are more aware of the director's role than they used to be, few directors can draw a large audience on the strength of their name, as Alfred Hitchcock invariably does. Those who go to see a Hitchcock picture usually do so because it is his, even when, as in the case of *Torn Curtain*, it gets unfavorably reviewed.

As inventive as ever within his own genre, Hitchcock continued in recent years to find new ways to put ordinary people in spectacularly unusual situations and to draw every ounce of fear, guilt and enjoyment from his audience. In keeping with our more violent and shockproof times, however, Hitchcock ventured ever further into the macabre. He said once that *Psycho* had to be made in black and white because he couldn't have gotten away with all that blood in the bathroom if he had used color. After Arthur Penn's *Bonnie and Clyde* in 1967, this is probably no longer true.

*North by Northwest*, 1959. To anyone who hasn't seen the picture, this still might look like a scene from a silent-film comedy, rather a silly one. To the many who have seen it, it is a classic image of terror. But, as with all of Hitchcock, no single image can convey the horror he distills. The impact of this one depends on what went before it—a very short, very quiet sequence on a lonely road, in which we feel with Cary Grant that, though nothing dreadful is in view, something dreadful is about to happen. It does.

The plot of *Vertigo*, 1958, was nearly incomprehensible, but that hardly marred its total effect. For that, Hitchcock relied on the old, basic, universal fear of falling.

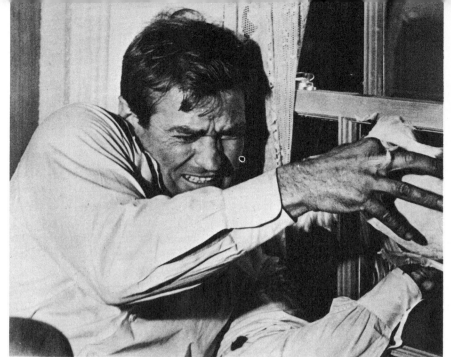

*The Birds,* 1963. To his saga of an avian take-over, Hitchcock was forced by his distributors to add a happy ending. He didn't want to. His original version ended with the refugees from the birds arriving at what they thought would be the haven of San Francisco. Their first sight of the city is the Golden Gate Bridge, every inch of which is lined with roosting birds.

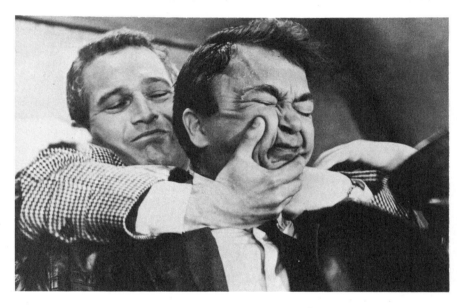

Paul Newman and Wolfgang Kieling in *Torn Curtain,* 1966. This fight, the climax of the picture, unfortunately took place in mid-picture. Even Hitchcock couldn't top murder-by-gas-oven.

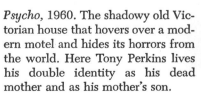

*Psycho,* 1960. The shadowy old Victorian house that hovers over a modern motel and hides its horrors from the world. Here Tony Perkins lives his double identity as his dead mother and as his mother's son.

# INCORPORATED STARS

The nature of our income-tax laws made it profitable for top-echelon performers to incorporate and produce their own vehicles. Instead of wages, they took home stock dividends, pension benefits and corporate profits at a much lower tax rate. At the same time, they claimed, they could at last cast off the shackles of type-casting and give themselves roles worthy of their talents. Some of them might have benefited by recalling Clark Gable's comment when asked if he wanted to produce or direct his own pictures. "It's hard enough for me to act without going into all those monkeyshines. What I want to do is get the money. Let others get the grief."

If a moviegoer can concentrate on credits these days, when they have become a distracting art form in themselves, he may be mystified by the strange names he finds listed there among the producers. Stars seem to find it advisable to hide behind such names as Batjac (John Wayne); Pennebaker (Marlon Brando); Jalem (Jack Lemmon); Byrna Productions and Joel Productions (both Kirk Douglas); or Cooga Mooga (Pat Boone). Some of these companies engage in film production; others are simply the organizations which hire out the services of the actor-owner. They combine in intricate forms such as Mirisch-Llenroc-Batjac, producers of *Cast a Giant Shadow*. It is impossible for anyone outside the industry (and difficult for many inside) to understand just who is making the production decisions. Increasingly, however, once the production and distribution companies have approved script, casting and budget, creative control is in the hands of the executive producer and/or the director, and many actors have assumed one or both of these roles.

Burt Lancaster, originally one of the more successful star-producers, in *The Bird Man of Alcatraz*, 1962.

Marlon Brando was one of those whose acting talents far surpassed their executive abilities. His *One-Eyed Jacks*, 1961, produced and directed for Paramount, was an offbeat Western with a modest budget that flowered into a four-year, five-million-dollar project. Stories circulated to the effect that Brando kept a highly paid crew and set of actors idle all day at the beach waiting for the right light to strike the waves. Brando's name as a star at that time insured a large audience for the picture, but it did not gross enough to cover its exorbitant costs.

Jerry Lewis in *The Nutty Professor*, 1963. He is preparing for his Jekyll-Hyde transformation from meek, myopic little chemistry professor to big bad wolf.

In full make-up, Jerry Lewis stops being actor long enough to take a director's look through the camera.

# JERRY LEWIS

The quadruple threat producer-director-author-star, Jerry Lewis, began his movie career as half of a comedy team with Dean Martin. In 1956, they split up, and Jerry Lewis formed his own production company. He followed the tradition of Charlie Chaplin, Harold Lloyd and Buster Keaton in the kind of comedy he attempted and because he controlled every part of the film-making process. The French intellectuals would also place him with these immortals for what they regard as his remarkable talent. American eggheads have been at a loss to understand this enthusiasm. However, even though Lewis' popularity was greatest abroad, there existed a large, essentially small-town American audience for his movies.

441

*Hercules* breaks out of prison by sheer brute strength and into legend by sheer expenditure of Joe Levine's money and showmanship. The muscle man was played by Steve Reeves, an American actor much in demand for Italian spectacle films.

Sophia Loren expresses the despair of all mankind in Vittorio De Sica's *Two Women*—and considerable joy when she won the Academy Award for the role. Joe Levine is not unhappy about it either.

## THE LAST MOGUL

During the Fifties, while industry executives struck out in new directions to combat falling motion-picture attendance, one man, an unknown small-town theater owner and foreign-film distributor, rose to prominence on an old-fashioned idea—the hard-sell campaign. Joseph Levine bought American distribution rights to a film nobody else wanted, the Italian-made *Hercules,* and promoted it into industry legend. Before he was through, he had grossed in the United States $4,700,000 and proved that old methods still work.

Levine continued to import and distribute and attracted prestige by bringing in some of the most distinguished foreign films of the decade: Vittorio De Sica's *Two Women*, Pietro Germi's *Divorce—Italian Style*, Federico Fellini's *8½*. As he grew more

More kitsch than kultur. Carroll Baker impersonating *Harlow,* 1965, and with George Peppard in *The Carpetbaggers,* 1964, which was one of Joe Levine's biggest moneymakers.

This is the big moment when Dustin Hoffman (in silhouette) breaks up the wedding of Katharine Ross to Brian Avery in *The Graduate,* 1967. A modest venture directed by Mike Nichols with scarcely known actors, the picture hit a responsive chord among the young and not quite so young across the nation and climbed rapidly toward becoming the second biggest box-office attraction of all time.

prosperous, he became a producer, of the new type who signs package deals and arranges financial backing for pictures that bear his name but may actually be produced by someone else. Levine was not at all averse to contributing to the art of the movies as long as his roster of films contained a generous portion of the salable commodities of sex and violence.

Levine became an international operator, keeping companies at work around the world. At the same time, he was a living example of that dying breed who first built the industry, those who came out of a background of poverty, were lacking in formal education and advantages and changed a nickelodeon show into a billion-dollar entertainment business. Levine was still, even in the changing Sixties, the self-made man and the old-fashioned showman.

# A NEW GENERATION OF AMERICAN DIRECTORS

## STANLEY KUBRICK

While startling new talents turned our eyes toward Europe and our established directors marked time, a few new names appeared on the American scene that offered hope we might regain some of our former pre-eminent position in the movie world. There were a handful of directors who questioned and examined our most basic ideas about how to make motion pictures. They explored old genres in a modern spirit and invented a few new ones. Foremost among them was Stanley Kubrick.

Like his French counterparts, Kubrick has a large knowledge and love of his cinema heritage. While the *Cahiers du Cinéma* enthusiasts grew up in the shadows of the Cinémathèque Française screening rooms in Paris, the young Kubrick was spending long hours in the auditorium of the Museum of Modern Art in New York, watching movies made before he was born. The pictures he made were filled with allusions to his favorite movies of an earlier day, just as Godard and Truffaut paid tribute to their masters. Peter Sellers' business with his artificial arm in his role as Dr. Strangelove, for example, found its genesis in Lionel Atwill's performance in *Son of Frankenstein*.

*Paths of Glory*, 1957. The sentinel's arm and rifle tell the story. Kirk Douglas makes his final plea for justice and reason to an impervious and corrupt Adolphe Menjou. This sober yet impassioned film about the unfashionable topic of World War I made people see, with a sudden start, the old war as the first great massacre of the twentieth century and began the vogue for its cinematic reappraisal.

Kirk Douglas in *Spartacus*, 1960. Stanley Kubrick tried his hand at the three-hour spectacle film, two years in the making and at the reputed cost of $12,000,000. He proved it possible to bring a measure of intelligence to the genre without losing any values of epic scale and action for which it has been treasured.

Kubrick, a former still photographer, began making pictures on his own in the Fifties. His first efforts were very cheaply produced, but before long he was successful enough to command industry backing without giving up his choice of subject and full control over his work from the writing to the cutting. Under the old studio system, directors had to turn out a great many more pictures than they do now. Kubrick has gone at it slowly, choosing each new project with care and making only the movies he really wants to make.

It was Kubrick's *Dr. Strangelove; or, How I Learned to Stop Worrying and Love the Bomb*, 1964, following on a group of notable films, that excited the attention of the world at large. This wild, far-out black comedy shook its audiences by making them laugh and then wonder why they were laughing. It turned out that Kubrick gave us a significant evaluation of our times: if we haven't exactly learned to love the bomb, we have learned to live with it.

Kubrick's science-fiction project, *2001: A Space Odyssey*, four years in the making, was the big movie event of 1968. A new kind of movie, it was puzzling and dazzling at the same time. Never were there such extraordinary special effects, nor such an imaginative creation of the outer-space world of the future. Above all, it was lit with the sardonic Kubrick wit, perhaps best expressed in the uncanny sequence in which the more than human computer named Hal was disconnected bit by bit and lost its mental faculties in a horrifying gradual regression. It is the most ambitious effort yet in Kubrick's unfolding purpose to use the screen to tell us something important about what is happening to us all.

*Dr. Strangelove; or, How I Learned to Stop Worrying and Love the Bomb*, 1964. Though George C. Scott is a member of the President's brain trust, met in conclave to decide the world's fate, he seems here but little removed from our simian ancestors.

*2001: A Space Odyssey*, 1968. Keir Dullea, as Mission Commander, is blown into the open air lock of the space ship minus the protection of his space suit.

*Dr. Strangelove.* Another Neanderthal, Slim Pickens, prepares to ride the Bomb of Destiny without an *arrière pensée*. The inscriptions on the bomb are civilization's epitaph.

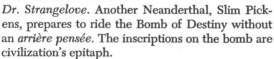

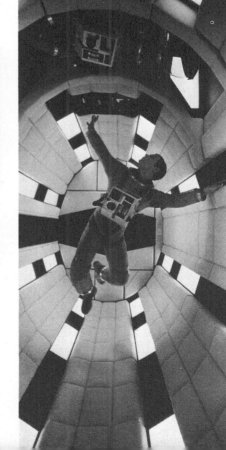

*The Manchurian Candidate,*
1962. The brainwashed Laurence Harvey shoots a soldier
before the unseeing Frank
Sinatra, in a scene cut from the
final version of the film. For
reasons of suspense, this exposition of the treatment that
trained the two Korean war
heroes to become assassins
was dropped.

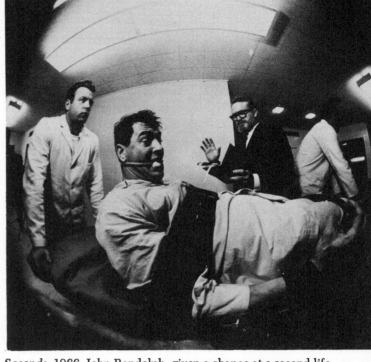

*Seconds,* 1966. John Randolph, given a chance at a second life
and a new identity by a mysterious "organization," emerges
from the special effects devised by James Wong Howe as—
surprise—Rock Hudson.

*Grand Prix,* 1966. In its 175
minutes of thrilling screen
time, this Cinerama production bore an amazing resemblance to a thirty-second television commercial.

# JOHN FRANKENHEIMER

John Frankenheimer came out of the training ground
of television in the mid-Fifties, a place where film-
makers learned to capture audience attention quickly
and boldly. He showed himself an expert technician,
filling his pictures with tension, shock and action, using all the newest kinds of lenses, divided screens,
multiplication of images, jump cuts. Although his
characters and themes seemed to lack something in
the way of emotional involvement, he entertained
with visual surprises. His most admired work to date
is the fantasy *The Manchurian Candidate,* 1962,
about a brainwashed Korean war hero turned into a
deadly weapon for assassination.

## ARTHUR PENN

Arthur Penn, since 1958 making movies intercut with a busy television and theater career, came to the forefront with *Bonnie and Clyde* in 1967. It stirred audiences as they had not been stirred for a long time and excited much critical controversy. The *Newsweek* critic attacked it one week and apologetically reversed himself the next. *The New York Times* critic employed the occasion to launch an all-out attack on violence in the contemporary movie. *Bonnie and Clyde* returned for its subject matter to a dreamlike past, the depression era of the early Thirties and the gangster film it produced; yet it presented an entirely contemporary view of the kind of mindless violence with which the past decade has seemed to be filled. Its makers were concerned about violence; they did not set out to glorify it. Like Kubrick's *Dr. Strangelove, Bonnie and Clyde* is a black comedy that makes its audiences laugh but leaves them deeply disturbed. New-generation directors are not primarily interested, as were their predecessors, in making "happy pictures for happy people."

*Bonnie and Clyde,* 1967. Bank robbery is fun and games.

*Bonnie and Clyde.* Clyde Barrow (Warren Beatty) finds potency in the "shoot out."

Michael J. Pollard, Faye Dunaway and Warren Beatty lead each other on to climaxes of violence in *Bonnie and Clyde.*

# INTERNATIONAL FILM-MAKING

*Doctor Zhivago,* 1965. The snowy steppes and the forests of
Russia were photographed in Finland, near the Arctic Circle,
in the Canadian Rockies, and in Spain.

Some of the international "casts of thousands" used in *Doctor Zhivago*, battling the biting winter cold.

## THE SUN NEVER SETS ON THE AMERICAN CAMERA CREWS

With the end of the war, foreign lands long deprived of Hollywood fare went on a prolonged American movie spree. In a brief time, close to 50 per cent of the major companies' grosses were being earned abroad. But though earned, they could not, with dollars at a premium, be remitted. These blocked funds, however, were available to adventurous picture-makers who quickly discovered that, freed from big studio overheads and union requirements, they could make movies in Italy or Japan more cheaply and just as satisfactorily as in Hollywood. The overseas invasion fitted in nicely with the interests of American stars and directors who could (until hard-hearted legislators changed the law) avoid heavy income-tax liabilities by staying abroad for a year. To the surprise of all concerned, most of these pictures were greeted with delight by New World audiences. As a consequence, out of 288 pictures distributed by the leading companies in 1956, 55 were made in Europe, Africa and Asia. The phenomenal success of *Around the World in 80 Days* and *The Ten Commandments* showed in what direction the trade winds were blowing.

The motives that sent movie-makers abroad in the Fifties were less relevant in the Sixties. Nevertheless, the wanderers did not come home. For one thing, they had discovered the great wide world outside the studio, magnificent locations impossible to duplicate in California. Audiences became less willing to accept rear projection shots, with actors standing in front of a screen image, as the real thing. For another, technicians in many countries had learned the skills that once were available only in Hollywood. Many governments made film-makers welcome by an attractive subsidy program, for which foreigners could qualify if they employed a sufficient number of nationals. Moreover, new and exciting talent was discovered in other countries. Production of television's staple fare largely took over the West Coast studios, and the majority of motion pictures were shot at least in part elsewhere. It seems unlikely that film-making will ever again beat full retreat to the shelter and isolation of Hollywood.

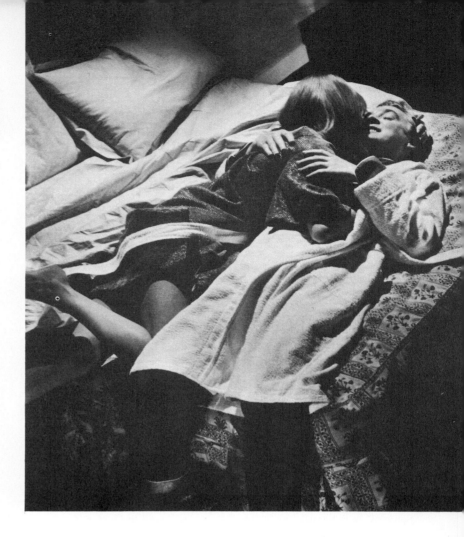

*Fahrenheit 451*, 1966. American money made it possible for Truffaut to make his first movie in color and in a studio, a science-fiction forecast of a totalitarian world where books are destroyed. Oskar Werner makes love to Julie Christie.

# THE INTERNATIONAL FILM

At several times in movie history there were great surges of creative talent in European countries that challenged Hollywood's position as movie capital of the world. In the Twenties, particularly, Hollywood reacted to competition by buying it out, importing the most successful directors and stars. Actresses such as Greta Garbo and Marlene Dietrich and directors such as Ernst Lubitsch took on the color of Hollywood and their films became, for us, American.

In the Sixties, an equally potent foreign wave broke over the American scene: directors such as Michelangelo Antonioni and Federico Fellini in Italy; François Truffaut, Jean-Luc Godard, Alain Resnais in France; Ingmar Bergman in Sweden; and such stars as Jeanne Moreau, Jean-Paul Belmondo, Sophia Loren, Marcello Mastroianni and Monica Vitti. Some of their films were limited to New York art houses. But all across America, in big cities and college communities, foreign films came to be taken for granted as part of the moviegoing scene, at least those that had one or another exploitation possibility, such as the naked Brigitte Bardot in *And God Created Woman*. This time the talents were not imported to California. This time American movies went to the talent.

The result was a hundred hybrids, not quite American, not quite anything else. *Dr. Zhivago*, for instance, was an M-G-M release, financed by an international consortium; produced by Carlo Ponti, an Italian; directed by David Lean, an Englishman; its cast an international melange; shot on location in Spain, Finland and the Canadian Rockies; and shown to date in fifty-four countries. But most people think of *Dr. Zhivago* as a typically American picture—and rightly.

On the other hand, directors such as François Truffaut of France and Michelangelo Antonioni of Italy continued to make films strongly reflecting their personal interests even when they accepted American backing, and produced films in England and America in a language not their own. Their films did not take on that old Hollywood flavor.

*Blow-Up*, 1967. Antonioni's view of modern London showed us a photographer (David Hemming) who cannot relate to life except through the lens of his camera. Here he uses it to "make love" to the model Verushka.

The Beatles, in *A Hard Day's Night*, 1964, might be running away as fast as they can from their Liverpool beginnings.

## Richard Lester

Standing somewhere between the generation of American television graduates and the European experimenters, two directors illustrate the gradual internationalization of the movies—and show, in their careers, how little national origins count any more.

An American by birth and heritage, Richard Lester began his film career in England. His training was in television, primarily commercials, here and in London. He made a celebrated short with Peter Sellers, *The Running, Jumping and Standing Still Film*, and a couple of minor British features, *It's Trad, Dad* and *The Mouse on the Moon*, before being singled out by United Artists to direct a vehicle for the pop-music phenomenon, the Beatles. It was a project turned down by other studios. Lester, instead of giving us the unimaginative showcase we'd had for pop-music singers in the past, created a delirious, joyful style that was as inventive as the Beatles were in their own field. *A Hard Day's Night* was a modest, low-budget production and a fantastic success. It was very influential, although one of these days we may wonder just what was so startling about it. Lester and his imitators have accustomed us to the fast pace, the surprising jump cuts, incongruity in editing, bizarre angles, rapid dislocations, shots that sweep past the action as well as follow it, and all the excess of nervous energy that characterizes the style of the Sixties.

Lester became part of the international school that has its basis in American finance and the Anglo-American market. With more money to spend and the freedom to do what he wanted, he reached for difficult goals. If none of the films Lester made later—*The Knack, Help!, A Funny Thing Happened on the Way to the Forum, How I Won the War, Petulia*—were quite as satisfying as *A Hard Day's Night*, they have shown the marks of a highly original new director. Lester has a tendency to disintegrate whatever property he is working with, be it a novel, play or musical, in order to re-create it in an image of his own. His flashing bits of characterization, his clever tricks and ironies come at an audience so fast that it takes time to catch up with him. Though already "over thirty," he seems to speak for a younger generation.

# Joseph Losey

Joseph Losey first achieved international fame at the age of fifty-four, a time in most men's lives when their careers have already peaked or tobogganed. But the torrents of publicity that followed on the success of *The Servant* (1964) brought to light a complex and variegated professional history to which, for those in the know, his present avant-garde acclaim is an unexpected and rather odd pendant. Born in LaCrosse, Wisconsin, he was a dramatic critic, a stage director in the agit-prop theater of the left-wing Thirties, and a documentary-maker before Dore Schary gave him the opportunity to become what seemed at the time a conventional Hollywood director of violent melodramas with vague liberal overtones. Not the implications of his commercial pictures but his left-wing activities banished him from American studios at the height of the McCarthy hysteria, and for several years he had a lean time of it in exile in England— a political martyr who was also something of a has-been. Since *The Servant* made him a hot property, Losey has used his relative freedom and power to re-explore his lifetime themes and re-exploit his flair for stylization in the service of the new young audience. In *King and Country* (1964), *Modesty Blaise* (1966) and *Accident* (1967) he has underscored a prevalent belief of the Sixties: things are never what they seem.

*The Servant,* 1963. Dirk Bogarde as the servant who insidiously takes over the household of James Fox.

Vivien Merchant and Dirk Bogarde in *Accident*, 1967.

# BLOCKBUSTERS

The industry's former reliance on block-booking was replaced by an abiding faith in the blockbuster. Why, when it is more costly than ever to make movies, did producers insist on making the most expensive kind? One answer is that when a blockbuster hits on target it can make its producers rich beyond the dreams of a Louis B. Mayer. Another is that when competition from television first threatened, it seemed self-evident that the movie screen was better equipped to show spectacle, casts of thousands, acres of sets, miles of panoramic landscape. Today, ironically, the sale to television of just such blockbusters helps to finance new ones, and it seems that the big picture shows up on the small screen after all.

*The Greatest Story Ever Told,* 1965.

*The Bible,* 1966. It had to happen: the Bible on the screen, not in pieces but as a whole. It may have been in the back of Cecil B. De Mille's mind all along, but it took the limitless ambition of Italian producer Dino de Laurentis to set the incredible enterprise in motion. Divine Providence did not look with favor upon his temerity. The distinguished directors he had engaged to direct the various episodes withdrew one by one, leaving only John Huston to command what was left of the original conception. Huston made a saltily effective bravura piece of his acting role of Noah, seen here tending to the elephants in the Ark.

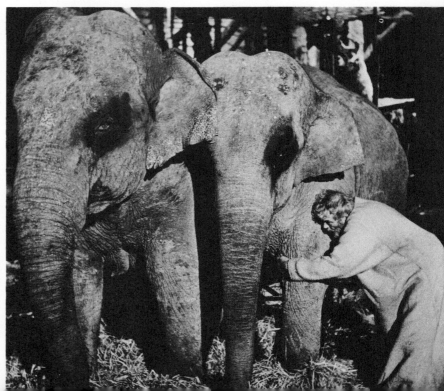

454

*Ben-Hur*, 1959. Though its subject matter was little to his taste, William Wyler accepted the direction of *Ben-Hur* because he knew that the success of such a super-blockbuster would consolidate his commanding position in the industry as a producer-director. Actually, the high spot of the film, the chariot race, was directed by Andrew Marton and Yakima Canutt, the old-time Western star and stuntman.

*El Cid,* 1961. The Cid was the legendary hero of Spain's greatest epic. But Charlton Heston's Cid was largely the hero of Samuel Bronston and the *raison d'être* for the erection of a studio city on the Spanish plains.

*Exodus,* 1960. Paul Newman and David Opatoshu in the prison-break scene. In filming Leon Uris' calculated best seller, Otto Preminger set out to make a modern epic on the actual site of the Biblical ones. The exploits of today's Jews did not earn as much money at the box office as the exploits of their ancestors.

## BIBLICAL AND SECULAR

During the Fifties most of the big money-earners were historical spectacles, with the emphasis on Biblical stories. De Mille was treading a well-worn path to success when he remade *The Ten Commandments,* one of the biggest grossers of all time, and when William Wyler's *Ben-Hur* followed closely behind, the pattern was set. For four successive years the top grosses were earned by *Samson and Delilah, Quo Vadis?, The Greatest Show on Earth* and *The Robe.*

But when a blockbuster misses it can come close to ruining its producers. There was some question for a time whether Twentieth Century-Fox would survive the production of *Cleopatra,* although with its reported five-million-dollar sale to television the company claims that it shows a profit. *The Greatest Story Ever Told* was among the greatest disasters ever told. This beautifully photographed Sunday-school story cost so much to make that it would have had to be fantastically popular in order to pay its production expenses. But a pious Biblical spectacle minus De Mille trimmings of sex and sadism had little box-office appeal. In fact, the Biblical film, so popular in the Fifties, suffered a severe relapse in the Sixties.

*Lawrence of Arabia,* 1962. No more romantic or enigmatic modern hero exists than T. E. Lawrence. But his personal story had to wait to achieve bowdlerized telling until the wide screen needed the sands of Arabia as a new backdrop for tumultuous action.

# THE BLOCKBUSTER
# SUBLIME:
# CLEOPATRA

Elizabeth Taylor, Queen of the Nile, enters Imperial Rome in style.

This 1963 blockbuster almost sank Twentieth Century-Fox. To reach the break-even point, it was said, *Cleopatra* had to bring in over forty million dollars. Fox stockholders are still trembling.

The carefree musical. That's Gene Kelly frolicking amid the sheep in *Brigadoon*, 1954, and Rex Harrison in *Dr. Dolittle*, 1968.

*West Side Story*, 1961. These juvenile delinquents were photographed against a background of their actual milieu, or what seemed to be their milieu, lending a note of documentary realism that accorded oddly with the formalism of the musical. But their dancing restored the whole thing to the realm of make-believe.

*My Fair Lady*, 1964. Rex Harrison as Professor Higgins, Audrey Hepburn as Eliza Dolittle and Wilfrid Hyde-White as Colonel Pickering sing "The Rain in Spain." The whole world danced all night with Julie Andrews when she was Eliza Dolittle on Broadway, but Jack L. Warner refused to waltz with anyone but Audrey Hepburn when the great hit was finally brought to the screen.

*Finian's Rainbow*, 1968.

Franco Nero in *Camelot*, 1968, the Musical Buster that may have marked the downfall of the vogue for multimillion-dollar productions with tunes.

# THE MUSICAL BUSTER

The superspectacular musical replaced the Biblical as the bonanza picture of the early Sixties. A few years earlier the musical, that native American genre, seemed dead. Under current market conditions a multimillion-dollar picture must command a world-wide audience to return a profit. It could not, therefore, so went the reasoning, reflect facets of national life that would not be understood in foreign countries. Nevertheless *West Side Story*, about juvenile gangs in the streets of New York, and *My Fair Lady*, a story built on English class distinctions, did very well indeed throughout the world. Perhaps it was because they shared with other popular musicals a fairy-tale approach to their subjects. The musical form, after all, has always depended strongly on fantasy and artificiality.

Musicals have always been expensive to make. Today the costs are extraordinary. A producer usually begins with an already famous Broadway show and the price paid for this "pre-sold" property is large enough to produce several more modest movies. To guarantee such an investment he must sign up the best known directors, script writers and stars, many of whom, like Richard Burton or Rex Harrison, are likely to be committed years in advance. Jack Warner was unwilling to use Julie Andrews in *My Fair Lady*, despite her creation of the stage role and despite her modest salary, because she was still an unknown quantity at the movie box office. He held out for Audrey Hepburn, which cost him an extra million plus the expenses of a singer to dub in her numbers. After *Mary Poppins* and *The Sound of Music*, of course, Julie Andrews became briefly the hottest star of the day.

In one year *The Sound of Music* jumped to the top of *Variety's* "All-Time Boxoffice Champs," ahead of the long-time leader, *Gone with the Wind*, and it did so to the tune of almost unanimously unfavorable reviews. The time came when the Musical Buster fell as flat on its expensive face as did the Biblical Buster, but meanwhile the mania was responsible for a constant spiraling of the budget. *Camelot* cost a reported eighteen million dollars, *Paint Your Wagon* twenty million.

The curious thing about the success of the Musical Buster is that it did not partake of the new freedom brought about by the fall of censorship. Partial nudity and sadistic violence, usually an essential component of the old-style spectaculars, were not part of the new. The Musical Busters were sentimental, soothing and tuneful. Apparently, in an era of sensation and shock, there is still a large audience that wants to go to the movies to relax and be happy.

## THE SOUND OF MUSIC

The tuneful sound of cash rolling in. . . .

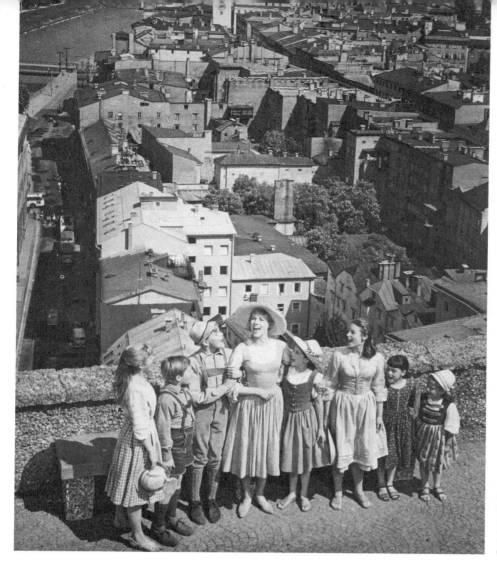

Clean, wholesome Julie Andrews sings her way across the Austrian Alps. *The Sound of Music,* 1965, directed by Robert Wise, was sometimes referred to as "The Sound of Money," representing the sweet melody of more than $135 million.

One of the best achievements of the underground is Kenneth Anger's *Scorpio Rising*, a brilliant tribute to the sinister group who band together in a romantic love of violence and death in motorcycle clubs that make the Marlon Brando gang in *The Wild One* look like a weak tea party.

## THE UNDERGROUND SURFACES

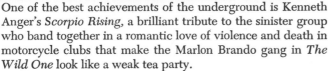

For years there have been American movies made outside the industry, wild experiments that no studio would back and few theaters would exhibit. The most talented of the film-makers would occasionally be absorbed into the system and end up turning out products as commercial as anyone in the industry. Of late, though, the underground film-makers have boiled up in such a ferment of activity that a few of their far-out efforts have begun to seep into theaters across the country. These directors have no interest in joining the establishment; if they have anything in common, it is a desire to put down the establishment.

The best publicized figure of the group is pop-artist Andy Warhol, who turns out his movies as methodically as he used to prepare silk-screen reproductions of comic strips and advertising art. He challenged all known concepts of movie-making by simply turning his camera on the least mobile subjects he could find, or moving his camera, panned and zoomed as erratically and pointlessly as possible. It was his subject matter, however, that made his movies known to the regular theater audience and was responsible for *The Chelsea Girls* and *My Hustler* being shown where no underground film had been seen before. Warhol presents an underworld cast of homosexuals, lesbians, transvestites, sadists and drug addicts who improvise dialogue before the camera as freely as at a private party. He has had an undoubted influence on the technique, or lack of it, of other underground film-makers, and to the watching industry he is a sign of the times, a symbol of how far sensational subjects can be carried after the fall of censorship.

There are hundreds of other film-makers whose work falls outside the scope of this book because it is usually seen by only a small group of interested spectators in private screenings, in college film clubs, at special festivals and in New York's Film-makers' Cinematheque. Too violently individualistic to cohere in schools, about all that they have in common is the difficulty of finding financial support, a desire to expand the horizons of film art and an impatience with the present domination of the movie industry by strictly commercial interests.

A film-maker with one foot in the underground and the other in the professional world is Shirley Clarke, director of *The Connection, The Cool World* and *Jason.* Imbued with a social consciousness that sets her apart from the more nihilistic members of the underground, she tirelessly explores new ways of showing us the under side of society, the ghetto poor, depressed minorities, addicts and misfits, with a respect that is seldom found in commercial cinema.

*Shadows,* 1961. Hugh Hurd, Ben Carruthers and Lelia Goldoni. It was with this film that the underground surfaced. John Cassavetes, an actor, made it as an exercise in direction for himself and as training for its gifted young cast. His budget was less than a shoestring, but, being a professional, Cassavetes was not content to have the film shown in the dank closets which constituted the "underground circuit." He kept working it over until it achieved the theaters. Its success there was small, but its aboveground showings gained it universal respect for its sincerity, insight and conviction. And it showed what *could* be done.

John Cassavetes' *Faces,* 1969.

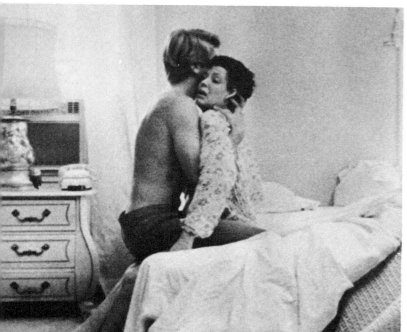

Andy Warhol's *My Hustler.*

*You Only Live Twice*, 1967.

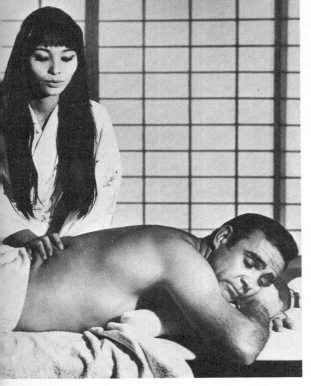

*Goldfinger*, 1964. With Shirley Eaton.

On the evidence, James Bond (Sean Connery) is more often the victim than the aggressor whether the action is sex (this page) or violence (opposite).

*Goldfinger*, 1964.

*From Russia with Love*, 1964.

# NEW GENRES

## SUPER-SPY

The Sixties produced a popular new genre, the Super-Spy. Its super-cool hero is James Bond, Agent 007, associated with the screen personality of Sean Connery, who created the character in a series of five films based on the novels of Ian Fleming. Bond is a connoisseur of all the things money can buy (and he has the money), irresistible to women, equipped with every modern gadget known to science and some that are not, expert in judo and karate. He operates in an international never-never land of spies and counter-spies. The double "0," it was explained to us when *Dr. No* appeared in 1962, means licensed to kill, and Bond kills, as he does everything else, without a trace of emotion. While there have been espionage thrillers before the James Bond series, the real genesis of the new genre might be found in the silent serials, in which the latest scientific gadgets of that day were pitted against mysterious international conspiracies, sinister masked crooks and yellow perils. Like those earlier films, the new type is sheer fantasy, played tongue-in-cheek. However, in keeping with the times, the Super-Spy genre emphasizes sex and violence to a degree never seen before.

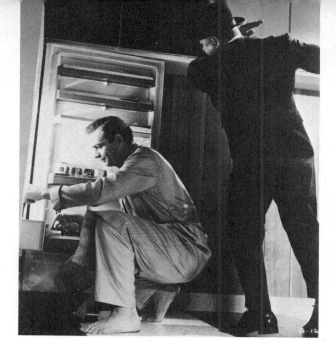

*Goldfinger,* 1964.

*Dr. No,* 1963.

*Dr. No,* 1963.

Ursula Andress in *Dr. No,* 1963.

# THE TEEN-AGE MOVIE

American International Pictures, founded in 1954 by James Nicholson and Samuel Arkoff, refurbished some old genres and invented some new ones. They aimed straight for the teen-age market with low-budget, low-brow movies. They made their mark with the policy of saturation booking, which means placing a picture in hundreds of theaters at once, accompanied by a sensational hard-sell campaign, drawing their audience quickly before word of mouth gets around that the picture does not live up to its promises. Typical of their genius was the title *I Was a Teenage Werewolf*, which earned two million on its own.

At first American International concentrated on science fiction and horror films. Their chief asset was Roger Corman, a prolific director who produced fifty films in ten years, among them a series based on the works of Edgar Allan Poe, featuring the bizarre, the macabre, the sadistic and the silky playing of Vincent Price. Corman's stylish direction and increasingly elaborate set design and costumes lifted his productions a notch above the other equally gory films of the period.

By 1962 the company had begun to have some flops and cast about for more lucrative ideas. They found one in the beach picture, a new genre. This curious type is derived in part from the activities of a small segment of the population living on the Southern California coast. The movies show a group of clean-cut teen-agers who live on the beach, spending their time surfing and dancing to rock music, dressed in the teeniest of bikinis. Aside from showing a lot of bare flesh, their activities are quite innocent. They do not smoke, drink or take pot, and their sexual relationships never go beyond an occasional chaste kiss. They never go home and don't have any visible parents: such grownups as appear are fantasy villains (Vincent Price) or buffoon father-figures that need not be taken seriously (Mickey Rooney, Buster Keaton). Frankie Avalon and Annette Funicello are the ideal hero and heroine in this make-believe world. Such are the movies called *Beach Party*, *Muscle Beach Party*, *Beach Blanket Bingo* and *How to Stuff a Wild Bikini*.

In 1966, American International turned on to the contemporary scene. They originated the cycle cycle, vaguely derived from the cult figure Marlon Brando in *The Wild One* and the glamour of the free-roving motorcycle clubs. The first was *The Wild Angels*, which grossed six million domestically in the year following its release, and follow-ups were soon in production. They noted the era of adolescent demonstrations and made *Riot on Sunset Strip*, the religion of LSD and produced *The Trip*, political interests among teen-agers and brought out *Wild in the Streets*. "Burning issues is what we're after," they announced.

*Bikini Beach*, 1964. What might appear to be a wild orgy is in fact a most innocent and wholesome teen-age exercise, dancing in the fresh sea air.

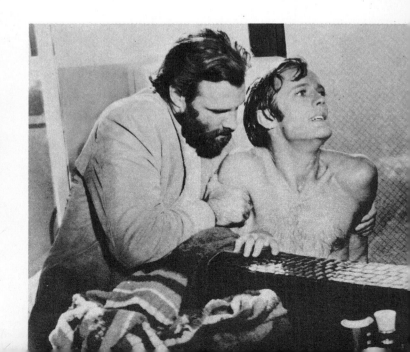

The beginning of a cult. Marlon Brando in *The Wild One*, 1953.

And the living end. American International's *Devil's Angels*, 1967.

◀ *The Trip*, 1967. Bruce Dern is giving tender guidance to the naked Peter Fonda through the ecstasies and terrors of LSD. Peter's visions most often turned out to resemble an old Roger Corman horror movie—unsurprisingly, inasmuch as Corman also directed this one.

The moment of truth in *What Ever Happened to Baby Jane?*, 1962. The dying Joan Crawford tells Bette Davis that it was she, not Bette, who caused the automobile "accident" which crippled Joan physically and Bette mentally.

In *Hush...Hush, Sweet Charlotte*, 1965, Olivia de Havilland was allowed to keep some of her glamour while Bette Davis jettisoned hers more thoroughly than ever.

**Sick, Sick, Sick**

*Psycho*, 1960. Tony Perkins falls apart.

# NEW CATEGORIES OF HORROR

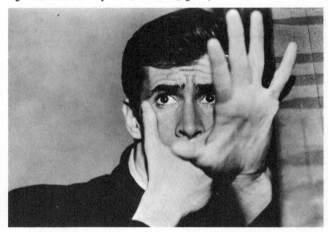

From old legends about werewolves, vampires and inhuman monsters created by careless scientists, the mid-century horror film turned to science fiction, frightening us with invasions from outer space or prehistoric ages. As real science caught up with and surpassed fiction, however, modern man found that the most horrific monster on earth is often himself. The elements of fantasy integral to the new horror film were drawn from the minds of the psychotic and the paranoid.

Perhaps inspired by the success of *Sunset Boulevard*, in which Gloria Swanson and Erich von Stroheim lived in a world of silent-movie memories, out of touch with reality, Bette Davis and Joan Crawford were teamed as former movie stars, Bette mentally and Joan physically crippled, in *What Ever Happened to Baby Jane?* Director Robert Aldrich followed up this great coup with *Hush . . . Hush, Sweet Charlotte*, in which Olivia de Havilland got her chance to become a monster because Joan Crawford, originally scheduled to play with Bette Davis again, became ill. Hammer Films in England added some lesser works to the genre, starring Bette Davis in *The Nanny* and Tallulah Bankhead in *Die! Die! My Darling*. The public enjoyed watching glamorous stars of yesteryear turning into crazy old hags and acting out evil fantasies. It made a joke out of the command to grow old gracefully.

The horror film moved more realistically into the realm of the mentally ill in Alfred Hitchcock's *Psycho*, about a young man with a second identity as his own murderous old mother; in William Wyler's *The Collector*, about an impotent fellow who catches girls as he does butterflies; and in Roman Polanski's *Repulsion*, about the fantasies of a sexually repressed and obsessed young girl. We used to laugh nervously to keep from being too frightened at old horror movies. Now movie-makers are making it harder for us to laugh.

Two science-fiction films from the Fifties. Ben Chapman as the Gill-man in *The Creature from the Black Lagoon*, 1954, from the period of stereoscopic 3-D, when the audience wore special glasses. Grant Williams in one of his smaller stages in *The Incredible Shrinking Man*, 1957. He finally disappeared into the infinite, all as the result of exposure to a cloud of floating gas from some testing of the atom bomb. Both of these films were directed by Jack Arnold.

Mia Farrow discovers that devil worship is alive and flourishing on New York's Central Park West, in *Rosemary's Baby*, 1968, the first American film of Polish director Roman Polanski.

# SCIENCE FICTION

The return to science fiction in 1968 was marked by the unexpectedly cerebral *Planet of the Apes*. Something vaguely familiar—could that be the Statue of Liberty?—in a strange landscape constituted the shock ending. The somebody vaguely familiar under the makeup is Maurice Evans.

The stupendous Western epic was further enlarged by the depth dimensions of Cinerama. Three directors were needed to put together the twelve-million-dollar production of *How the West Was Won*, 1963: John Ford, Henry Hathaway and George Marshall.

Paul Newman and Melvyn Douglas in *Hud*, 1963. This entirely contemporary Western about three generations of ranchers lamented the degeneration of the frontier spirit, echoing the nostalgia felt in countless earlier Westerns.

# THE WESTERN
# IN THE SIXTIES

It seemed for a while that the most enduring American genre, the Western, would be given over entirely to television. In 1948 one quarter of all the films produced by the major companies were horse operas; by 1964 this fraction was reduced to 1/13th. The Western, however, owes a lot of its power to the poetry of action in rugged, widespread landscapes, and this television is poorly equipped to show. The statistics given above are deceptive. Much of what was taken over by the small screen was the program picture, the cheaply made series Western featuring a favorite cowboy star. The quality Western and the epic remained on the wide screen.

Lee Marvin in *Cat Ballou*, 1965, at "The End of the Trail." The Western has produced many self-parodies such as this one, in which Marvin played two roles, one as the menace who wears a silver nose, having lost the original in a gunfight, the other an aged, bleary-eyed, drunken former gunfighter who literally cannot hit the side of a barn.

Certain cheaply made Italian Westerns featuring mindless violence and omitting the moral conflict of the traditional genre were popular not only in Italy but, incredibly, also here. Clint Eastwood, an American living in Italy, became a star through these "spaghetti Westerns" and is seen here in the American *Hang 'Em High*, 1968.

William Holden gets his at the end of *The Wild Bunch*, Sam Peckinpah's bloody and violent Western for 1969. Unlike the "spaghetti Westerns," however, this film had a moral to point in its lengthy stylized gun battles. "It finally makes the spectator feel guilty," said *The New York Times* critic.

After television and after the fall of censorship, Hollywood abandoned its always perfunctory support of virtue in favor of the wholesale pursuit of vice. Perhaps through wishful thinking, the studios decided there was no market for "family" pictures any more. Walt Disney knew better. His *Snow White and the Seven Dwarfs*, in release since 1937, has earned well over $22,000,000.

*The Absent-Minded Professor*, 1961. The Disney family pictures have given a new career and a new personality to Fred MacMurray as the four-square, upstanding, downtrodden, true-blue American paterfamilias—none truer, none bluer. Few remember the MacMurray who starred opposite Carole Lombard and Madeleine Carroll in a long series of sex comedies.

*Mary Poppins*, 1964. The screen debut of Julie Andrews in this vastly successful sugar-plum fantasy identified her to the movie audience as today's most overt and vocal exemplar of goodness, the perhaps unwilling successor to Mary Pickford, Shirley Temple and Janet Gaynor.

## DISNEYLAND

When the American screen went wide open, the Walt Disney studio became almost the sole purveyor of the family picture, the kind of movie that parents might want to attend with their children. Family moviegoing fell off, mostly because television in the home substituted for it, but the scarcity of suitable pictures also made it more difficult. The sweetness and light of the Shirley Temple era and the Andy Hardy pictures had vanished.

Nevertheless the mildly diverting and innocuous Disney films such as *Mary Poppins, The Ugly Dachshund, That Darn Cat, The Absent-Minded Professor, Son of Flubber, Swiss Family Robinson, The Shaggy Dog, The Parent Trap* and *Old Yeller* were remarkably successful, attesting to the fact that a public still exists for this kind of picture. Now, although the studio remains, Walt Disney is no more, and there is more of a vacuum than ever.

Ivan Tors, a few years ago, found that "When my son Steven and I couldn't find a film to go to in all of Los Angeles that day I realized how serious was the vacuum that had to be filled." Tors did try to fill that hole, but the real success of his movies about dolphins *(Flipper)*, friendly wild animals *(Clarence, the Cross-Eyed Lion)* and cowboys *(Africa—Texas Style)* was to serve as pilots for popular television series such as *Flipper, Daktari* and *Cowboy in Africa*. Steven and the other kids were back in front of their television sets.

Nevertheless, the emphatic success of the Disney features, not to mention the fantastic popularity of *The Sound of Music*, seems to guarantee a surprisingly profitable future for movies that entertain without disturbing, that eschew sex and violence, and promote the accepted moral values.

*Pillow Talk*, 1959. Doris Day and Rock Hudson in a split-screen effect that manages to be suggestive at the same time it is undoubtedly quite innocent.

## COMEDIES

Comedies in the Sixties were mostly either frantic efforts to recapture the era of slapstick or black comedies about the ills of contemporary life. Alone, Doris Day kept the romantic comedy afloat well into the period in *Pillow Talk, Lover Come Back, That Touch of Mink*. The wholesome Doris, a modern aggressive girl who still clings to the security of marriage, was chased through chic decorator-styled sets by lascivi-ous worldly men (Cary Grant and Rock Hudson) whom she tricked or cajoled into domesticity, or, having accomplished the latter, maintained her successful business career against her husband's wishes. Then the Doris Day romances began to be undermined by such cynical after-the-wedding guides as *Divorce American Style, Luv* and *A Guide for the Married Man*.

Joe E. Brown in *It's a Mad, Mad, Mad, Mad World*, 1963. This was Stanley Kramer's mad, mad, mad, mad expenditure of Cinerama, countless stars, time and money in a vain attempt to recapture the beautiful insanity of the early days of slapstick.

Peter Sellers and Ursula Andress in *What's New, Pussycat?*, 1965. After the fall of censorship, a revival of the old-fashioned bedroom farce seemed logical.

The old maid and the slob—Jack Lemmon and
Walter Matthau in *The Odd Couple*, 1967. This
stage-derived farce strenuously avoided the implications of homosexuality that nevertheless provided
a titillating undercurrent in the comedy of two refugees from marriage setting up housekeeping together.

Jack Lemmon prepares to move up to the executive
floor in Billy Wilder's savage comedy about the sag-
ging morals of the business world, *The Apartment*,
1960.

Ayllene Gibbons as Ma Joyboy gorges herself in *The Loved
One*, 1965, Tony Richardson's black comedy based on the
Evelyn Waugh satire of the burial customs of the Southern
California natives.

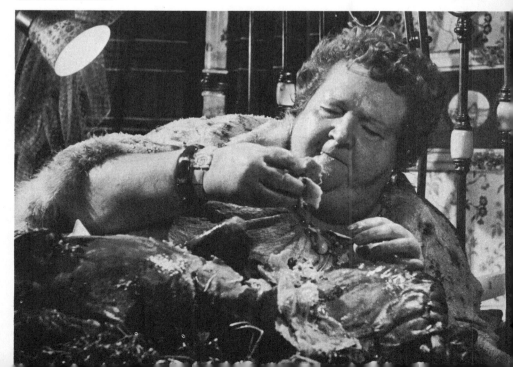

# STARS OF THE SIXTIES

## LIZ AND DICK

The star system, despite stratospheric salaries, is not what it once was, but it is not yet quite dead. We still have star vehicles even though the electric personalities they are supposed to showcase are becoming harder to find. Producers try to make up in quantity what is lacking in quality and stuff stars like raisins into their blockbusters.

In the early Sixties the world's most spectacular couple, Elizabeth Taylor and Richard Burton, could still guarantee an audience for any picture they played in. These two struck echoes of an earlier day when, at the peak of the star system, another couple, Mary Pickford and Douglas Fairbanks, were the Royal Family of the screen. Curiously, when the two stars of the silent movies decided to make their first talking film together, they also chose *The Taming of the Shrew* as an appropriate vehicle. In the Pickford-Fairbanks background there were also former marriages and in their love affair a slight hint of scandal, but in those days it was, at considerable expense, kept quiet, in keeping with the wholesome screen personalities they presented to the world. In spite of the inevitable whispers their romance somehow took on a fairy-tale glow. The Taylor-Burton romance glowed, all right, but with a sulphuric fire. It fleshed out the Sixties image of the free-living sexy woman who fulfills herself in love affairs and the virile pirate-lover who can be tied only by the bonds of passion. Taylor-Burton did their best to give the public what it wanted.

This is the image of Elizabeth Taylor which the American matriarchy carried in its mind when it reacted with screeching indignation to her public liaison with Richard Burton. The fourteen-year-old Liz was entrancing in this scene with Donald Crisp in *National Velvet*, 1945. But time passed, and Miss Taylor grew up. The matriarchs didn't.

By the time the movie audience got to see *Cleopatra*, 1963, it no longer expected to see a couple of characters named Antony and Cleopatra, but just Taylor and Burton in fancy dress.

Among the supporting reasons surmised for Liz's attraction to Burton was the hope that under his tutelage she could become a "real" actress. She certainly was one in *Who's Afraid of Virginia Woolf?*, 1966.

The lovers in *The Comedians*, 1968.

*Reflections in a Golden Eye*, 1967. Being whipped by Elizabeth Taylor might not be as much fun as whipping *her*, but Marlon Brando seems to take it calmly.

As we like it, then and now. Mary Pickford and Douglas Fairbanks in their *Taming of the Shrew*, 1929, and Taylor and Burton in theirs, 1967.

# SIDNEY POITIER

"I'm the only one. I'm the only Negro actor who works with any degree of regularity. I represent ten million people in this country and millions more in Africa; I'm the only one for these people to identify with on the screen, and I'm not going to do anything they can't be proud of. Wait till there are six of us; then one of us can play villains all the time."

This was Sidney Poitier at a press conference. He was the only Negro in America to become a movie star —that is, an acting star and a matinee idol, not a singer or a dancer. The logic of what he said cannot be denied. The changing place of the Negro in American life has only slightly registered in his movie image. The Negro began to be seen more and more often in the theater, in television and in advertising, that last stronghold of the cliché, but very little in movies. A few directors began to use Negroes more freely as extras and in bit parts. There was a subtle bit of casting in that commonplace domestic comedy *Good Neighbor Sam,* when the principals are in judge's chambers, discussing divorce. The judge is heard speaking, the camera slides over briefly to show that he is a Negro, and then retreats. That was a far cry from the days when Negroes were cast only as entertainers and domestics, but of course it was very little. Meanwhile Poitier does bear the burden almost alone.

As for the actual problems of civil rights in this country and the growing anger of militant blacks, these anxieties of contemporary life continued to be ignored (until the very end of the decade) as completely by the commercial cinema as our bitter moral struggle over the war in Vietnam.

Sidney Poitier today.

Sidney Poitier had been around a long time before anyone had the courage to try to realize on his obvious potential as hero and star. It took an unknown independent producer, Ralph Nelson, and an inexpensive film, *Lilies of the Field,* to make the jump. Nelson had the wit to see that the switch could be made by associating Poitier with unassailable Christian charity in the shape of nuns.

*In the Heat of the Night* brushed the abrasive edge of the white-black relationship in the U.S. In this film, Poitier played a Northern black detective who wins the reluctant and then the admiring respect of a typical white Southern police chief. Rod Steiger's playing as the cop was so real that some thought he weakened the conviction of the picture's premise.

Another step in Poitier's rise through the invisible ranks of status. In *To Sir with Love*, 1966, he was the black teacher and eventual savior of some very bad white children.

# STARS
# OF THE SIXTIES

**Female**

The natural woman: sweet, wholesome, ebullient Julie Andrews in *The Sound of Music*, 1965.

The intellectual woman: withdrawn, neurotic, sexy Vanessa Redgrave in *Blow-Up*, 1966.

Jane Fonda captured the look of "The Thirties" for *They Shoot Horses, Don't They?*, 1970.

Barbra Streisand creates her unique category in *Hello, Dolly!*, 1969. One of her lines in her big hit, *Funny Girl*, 1968, was "You think beautiful girls are going to stay in style forever?"

# Male

Steve McQueen in *Nevada Smith*, 1965, represents the Sixties breed of the man of action.

John Wayne, as Rooster Cogburn, the fat old one-eyed belcher and boozer of *True Grit,* 1969, parodies himself as the man of action he long represented. His popularity undimmed by the passing years, he is among the most durable of living male stars.

Dustin Hoffman became an overnight star in *The Graduate,* 1967, and was one of the few quick successes of the Sixties to be able to go on to another role just as popular, though very different—that of Ratso, the slimy little cripple of *Midnight Cowboy,* 1969. In the latter film, seen here, Jon Voight as Joe Buck, the misguided idealist from Texas, made a similar overnight success.

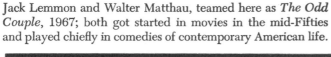

Jack Lemmon and Walter Matthau, teamed here as *The Odd Couple,* 1967; both got started in movies in the mid-Fifties and played chiefly in comedies of contemporary American life.

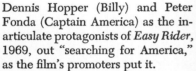

The opening sequence of *Medium Cool*, 1969: the victim of a crash lies moaning on the highway while a television news team matter-of-factly records the event and then, seemingly as an afterthought, puts in a call for an ambulance. Robert Forster plays the cameraman who begins to wonder about the responsibility of the newsman toward the events he records.

Dennis Hopper (Billy) and Peter Fonda (Captain America) as the inarticulate protagonists of *Easy Rider*, 1969, out "searching for America," as the film's promoters put it.

# THE WAY WE LIVE NOW

We have come to a period of change and uncertainty, but the outlines of a new movie landscape "so beautiful, so various, so new" begin to be dimly discernible. The captains and the kings depart but they have been replaced, at least in Hollywood, by no evidence of "an humble and a contrite heart." The ex-talent agents and prematurely sanguine conglomerate executives who occupy, frequently very briefly, the seats of power are presently scrambling to divest themselves of ancient studios and to acquire the freedom to make what pictures they want, where and when they want to.

The question is what kind of pictures they do want. Certain comparatively low-budget films, innocent of stars and traditional production values, beginning with *The Graduate* and continuing with *Midnight*

*Cowboy, Easy Rider, Alice's Restaurant* and *Medium Cool,* are, to the surprise of many, finding greater popularity than the multimillion-dollar extravaganzas such as *Dr. Dolittle, Star!* or *Paint Your Wagon.* The fate of such blockbusters as *Camelot* or *The Battle of Britain* should have convinced even bankers, the least sophisticated of cinematic bird watchers, of the folly of gambling astronomical sums on dated musicals and even more dated war films, when an investment of $350,000 to $3,000,000 can attract larger audiences. Joe Levine, the aging whiz kid of the industry, warns that anyone who invests more than $4,000,000 in a picture should, as Sam Goldwyn is reported to have said of the man who went to the psychoanalyst, have his head examined.

Even more urgent than the need to spend less

At the draft-induction center in *Alice's Restaurant*. Arlo Guthrie is the one wearing a hat and a brooding look.

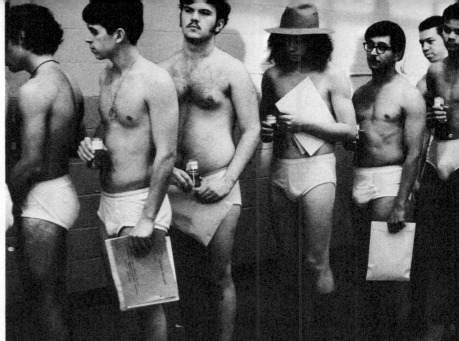

Jon Voight (Joe Buck) trying to get the dying Dustin Hoffman (Ratso) onto a Florida-bound bus in *Midnight Cowboy*, 1969.

Officer Obie of Stockbridge, Massachusetts, gives one of the most amiable performances on record, playing his real-life self in *Alice's Restaurant*, 1969. Here, he looks a bit bewildered at the shenanigans of Arlo Guthrie. William Obanheim, as he is formally known, is said to have remarked: "If I'd known it was going to cause all this commotion, I'd have picked up that garbage myself." ▶

money is the need to spend it more wisely. If the new pictures have any lesson for the industry, it is that audiences can no longer be regarded as wanting nothing but escape in their entertainment. The real strength and vitality of the recent films lies in their ability to engage in our daily lives. Films such as *Easy Rider*, *Alice's Restaurant* and *Medium Cool* forsake conventional structure and plot. They tend to be fragmentary, and, unlike the "well-made film," they shoot abruptly from the middle of one scene to the center of the next, not only without transitions but without beginning or end. In their blurred confusion between reality and make-believe, they reflect a quality of contemporary life and give us back our daily experiences as we receive them on the street and on our television screens. These raw and undigested lumps of reality make free use of our feelings about

events that occur outside the film. In *Alice's Restaurant*, a relaxed and easygoing interpretation of Arlo Guthrie's popular song about bureaucracy, hypocrisy and the draft, we are shown the hospital room where Arlo's father lay helpless for many long years. The real Woody Guthrie had recently died when these scenes were filmed, and an actor plays his part. But Arlo is real, the happening is real, and so is Pete Seeger, come to visit and sing Woody's old songs to him. Similarly, in *Medium Cool*, a more forceful fusion of fictional plot and the real events of our national life, including the assassinations, the protests and the violent 1968 Democratic Convention in Chicago, someone cries to the photographer-director in the midst of filming the battles in the Chicago streets, "It's for real, Haskell!" and that cry is retained on the sound track of the finished film.

# EPILOGUE

It is difficult in the early days of the Seventies to avoid the temptation to predict what movies will be like in the next decade. Yet the authors, with a batting average as picture prophets abysmally low, are determined to resist.

It is true that the low-budget wonders at the very end of the Sixties have in common a denominator fully as important as their cost, absence of stars and free use of nudity, four-letter Anglo-Saxon words and graphic portrayals of copulation, a denominator that may portend a trend. They all concern themselves with the current scene, with the malaise of society, the generation gap, the disillusion of youth with their elders' version of the American dream, the revolution of thought taking place in our midst. To be sure, we've had lots of films critical of society before now, and films in which we've separated ourselves from social problems. In the films of the Fifties, perhaps, we were alienated. In the late Sixties, we became engaged. Whatever real-life nightmares the current films show us, they are not necessarily depressing experiences for the moviegoer. On the contrary, they are often exhilarating, because they involve us in the national life in a very immediate way, rather than providing us with private dreams. The films at the end of the Sixties, probably none of them masterpieces, have a genuine vitality that cannot help but have some influence on the course of American films in the Seventies. What that course may be, or how long that influence may play a part, as promised, the authors will not be so audacious as to forecast.

# INDEX

# ACKNOWLEDGMENTS

WE ALSO wish to thank the following individuals and organizations for help in locating and securing pictorial material and for their permission to include the photographs in this book:

The Academy of Motion Picture Arts and Sciences, John E. Allen, Joseph Aurrichio (RKO), Frederick Bullock (20th Century-Fox), Rodney Bush (20th Century-Fox), Roger Caras, James Card (George Eastman House), Culver Service, Det Danske Filmmuseum, William K. Everson, Filmhistoriska Samlingarna, Nat Gartsman (Warner Brothers), Phillip Gerard (Universal), Bernice Gobel (Columbia), Mrs. Oscar Godbout, Mrs. Judith Greene, Miss Terry Hamill (United Artists), Joseph Homler (M-G-M), Miss Tess Klausner (Paramount), Robert MacGregor (Theatre Arts Books), Mrs. Estelle Nathan (Universal), George Pratt (George Eastman House), Martin Quigley, Jr. (Quigley Publications), Sidney Rechetnik (Warner Brothers), Miss Bea Ross (Republic), Miss Franziska Schacht (New York Public Library), Miss Hortense Schorr (Columbia), Silas Seadler (M-G-M), John Springer (RKO), Al Stern (RKO), Miss Norah Traylen (British Film Institute), Max Youngstein (United Artists). 1957

Allied Artists: *El Cid*, copyright © 1961 Allied Artists Pictures Corp.

American International: *The Trip*, copyright © 1967 American International Pictures; *Devil's Angels*, copyright © 1967 American International Pictures; *Bikini Beach*, copyright © 1964 American International Pictures.

AVCO Embassy: *Harlow*, copyright © 1965 Paramount Pictures Corp., Embassy Pictures Corp. and Prometheus Enterprises, Inc.; *The Graduate*, copyright © 1967 Embassy Pictures Corp.; *Nevada Smith*, copyright © 1965 Paramount Pictures Corp., Embassy Pictures Corp., and Solar Productions, Inc.; *Two Women*, copyright © 1961 Embassy Pictures Corp.

Cinema V: *The Cool World*, copyright © 1964 Cinema V, Ltd.

Columbia Pictures: *Lawrence of Arabia*, copyright © 1962 Columbia Pictures Corporation; *The Wild One*, copyright © 1953 Columbia Pictures Corporation; *Cat Ballou*, copyright © 1965 Columbia Pictures Corporation; *The Taming of the Shrew*, copyright © 1967 Columbia Pictures Corporation; *Anatomy of a Murder*, copyright © 1959 Columbia Pictures Corporation; *Dr. Strangelove; or, How I Learned to Stop Worrying and Love the Bomb*, copyright © 1963 Columbia Pictures Corporation; Sidney Poitier portrait, copyright © 1967 Columbia Pictures Corporation; *Easy Rider*, copyright © 1969 Columbia Pictures, a Division of Columbia Pictures Industries, Inc.

M-G-M: *Ben-Hur*, copyright © 1959 M-G-M; *Blow-Up*, copyright © 1968 M-G-M; *Brigadoon*, copyright © 1954 M-G-M; *Dr. Zhivago*, copyright © 1966 M-G-M; *Grand Prix*, copyright © 1966 M-G-M; *High Society*, copyright © 1956 M-G-M; *How the West Was Won*, copyright © 1963 M-G-M; *National Velvet*, copyright © 1945 M-G-M; *North by Northwest*, copyright © 1959 M-G-M; *The Comedians*, copyright © 1969 M-G-M; *The Loved One*, copyright © 1965 M-G-M; *The Sandpiper*, copyright © 1965 M-G-M; *2001: A Space Odyssey*, copyright © 1968 M-G-M; *Vertigo*, copyright © 1958 M-G-M.

Paramount: *Barbarella*, copyright © 1968 Paramount Pictures Corp., all rights reserved; *Medium Cool*, copyright © 1969 Paramount Pictures Corp. and H & J Pictures Inc., all rights reserved; *Rosemary's Baby*, copyright © 1968 Paramount Pictures Corp. and William Castle Enterprises, Inc., all rights reserved; *The Odd Couple*, copyright © 1967 Paramount Pictures Corp., all rights reserved; *True Grit*, copyright © 1969 Paramount Pictures Corp., Hal B. Wallis and Joseph H. Hazen; *Hud*, copyright © 1962 Paramount Pictures Corp., Salem Productions, Inc. and Dover Productions, Inc.; *The Carpetbaggers*, copyright © Paramount Pictures Corp. and Embassy Pictures Corp.; *Seconds*, copyright © 1965 Paramount Pictures Corp., Joel Productions, Inc. and Gibraltar Productions, Inc.; *The Nutty Professor*, copyright © 1963 Jerry Lewis Enterprises, Inc.; *One-Eyed Jacks* copyright © 1959 Pennebaker, Inc.

Twentieth Century-Fox: *A Guide for the Married Man*, copyright © 1967 Twentieth Century-Fox Film Corporation; *Cleopatra*, copyright © 1963 Twentieth Century-Fox Productions, Inc.; *Dr. Dolittle*, copyright © 1967 Twentieth Century-Fox Film Corporation and Apjac Productions, Inc.; *Hello, Dolly!*, copyright © 1969 Twentieth Century-Fox Film Corporation and Chenault Productions, Inc.; *Hush...Hush, Sweet Charlotte*, copyright © 1964 Associates and Aldrich Company, Inc. and Twentieth Century-Fox Film Corporation; *Planet of the Apes*, copyright © 1967 Apjac Productions, Inc. and Twentieth Century-Fox Film Corporation; *The Seven Year Itch*, copyright © 1955 Charles K. Feldman Group Productions; *The Bible*, copyright © 1966 Dino De Laurentiis Cinematografica, S.p.A.; *The Girl Can't Help It*, copyright © 1956 Twentieth Century-Fox Film Corporation; *The Longest Day*, copyright © 1962 Darryl F. Zanuck Productions, Inc. and Twentieth Century-Fox Film Corporation; *The Sound of Music*, copyright © 1965 Argyl Enterprises, Inc. and Twentieth Century-Fox Film Corporation; *Two for the Road*, copyright © 1966 Stanley Donen Films, Inc. and Twentieth Century-Fox Film Corporation.

United Artists: *Beat the Devil*, copyright © 1953 United Artists Corp.; *The Misfits*, copyright © 1961 United Artists Corp.; *West Side Story*, copyright © 1963 United Artists Corp.; *The Defiant Ones*, copyright © 1958 United Artists Corp.; *The African Queen*, copyright © 1951 United Artists Corp.; *Exodus*, copyright © 1961 United Artists Corp.; *A Hard Day's Night*, copyright © 1964 United Artists Corp.; *The Greatest Story Ever Told*, copyright © 1965 United Artists Corp.; *It's A Mad, Mad, Mad, Mad World*, copyright © 1963 United Artist Corp.; *What's New, Pussycat?*, copyright © 1965 United Artists Corp.; *The Apartment*, copyright © 1960 United Artists Corp.; *Hang 'Em High*, copyright © 1968 United Artists Corp.; *Some Like It Hot*, copyright © 1959 United Artists Corp.; *Happy Anniversary*, copyright © 1959 United Artists Corp.; *Irma La Douce*, copyright © 1963 United Artists Corp.; *Saint Joan*, copyright © 1957 United Artists Corp.; *The Bird Man of Alcatraz*, copyright © 1962 United Artists Corp.; *Paths of Glory*, copyright © 1958 United Artists Corp.; *The Manchurian Candidate*, copyright © 1962 United Artists Corp.; *Midnight Cowboy*, copyright © 1969 United Artists Corp.; *Alice's Restaurant*, copyright © 1969 United Artists Corp.; *Dr. No*, copyright © 1963 United Artists Corp.; *Goldfinger*, copyright © 1964 United Artists Corp.; *From Russia with Love*, copyright © 1964 United Artists Corp.; *You Only Live Twice*, copyright © 1967 United Artists Corp.

Universal Pictures: *Birds in Peru*, copyright © 1968 Universal Pictures France; *Creature from the Black Lagoon*, copyright © 1954 Universal Pictures; *Fahrenheit 451*, copyright © 1966 Vineyard Films; *Pillow Talk*, copyright © 1959 Arwin Productions; *Psycho*, copyright © 1960 Shamley Productions; *Spartacus*, copyright © 1960 Universal Pictures and Bryna Productions; *The Birds*, copyright © 1963 Alfred J. Hitchcock Productions; *The Incredible Shrinking Man*, copyright © 1957 Universal Productions; *Torn Curtain*, copyright © 1966 Universal Pictures.

Walt Disney Productions: *Mary Poppins*, copyright © 1964 Walt Disney Productions; *Snow White and the Seven Dwarfs*, copyright © 1937 Walt Disney Productions; *The Absent-Minded Professor* copyright © 1960 Walt Disney Productions.

The Walter Reade Organization, Inc.; *Faces*, copyright © 1968 The Walter Reade Organization; *The Balcony*, copyright © 1963 The Walter Reade Organization.

Warner Bros.: *Giant*, copyright © 1956 Warner Bros. Pictures, Inc.; *What Ever Happened to Baby Jane?*, copyright © 1962 Warner Bros. Pictures, Inc.; *Camelot*, copyright © 1967 Warner Bros. Pictures, Inc.; *Reflections in a Golden Eye*, copyright © 1967 Warner Bros.-Seven Arts, Inc.; *Land of the Pharaohs*, copyright © 1955 Warner Bros. Pictures, Inc.; *Bonnie and Clyde*, copyright © 1967 Warner Bros. Pictures, Inc.; *My Fair Lady*, copyright © 1964 Warner Bros. Pictures, Inc.; *The Madwoman of Chaillot*, copyright © 1969 Warner Bros.-Seven Arts, Inc.; *Hondo*, copyright © 1953 Warner Bros. Pictures, Inc.; *Rachel, Rachel*, copyright © 1968 Warner Bros.-Seven Arts, Inc.; *The Wild Bunch*, copyright © 1960 Warner Bros.-Seven Arts, Inc.; *Who's Afraid of Virginia Woolf?*, copyright © 1966 Warner Bros. Pictures, Inc.; *Finian's Rainbow*, copyright © 1967 Warner Bros. Pictures, Inc.; *Casablanca*, copyright © 1943 Warner Bros. Pictures, Inc.; *To Have and Have Not*, copyright © 1945 Warner Bros. Pictures, Inc.; *Moby Dick*, copyright © 1956 Warner Bros. Pictures, Inc.; *You Can't Get Away with Murder*, copyright © 1939 Warner Bros. Pictures, Inc.; *The Big Sleep*, copyright © 1946 Warner Bros. Pictures, Inc.